INTERNATIONAL
COMMUNICATION
2nd Edition

INTERNATIONAL COMMUNICATION

2nd Edition

CONTINUITY AND CHANGE

DAYA KISHAN THUSSU

Hodder Arnold

A MEMBER OF THE HODDER HEADLINE GROUP

First published in Great Britain in 2000
Second edition published in 2006 by Hodder Education,
a member of the Hodder Headline Group,
338 Euston Road, London NW1 3BH

www.hoddereducation.com

Distributed in the United States of America by
Oxford University Press Inc.
198 Madison Avenue, New York, NY 10016

British Library Cataloguing in Publication Data
A catalogue record for this book is available from the British Library

Library of Congress Cataloging-in-Publication Data
A catalog record for this book is available from the Library of Congress

ISBN-10 0 340 88892 X
ISBN-13 978 0 340 88892 6

1 2 3 4 5 6 7 8 9 10

Typeset in 10/13pt Adobe Garamond by Dorchester Typesetting Group Ltd, Dorchester, Dorset
Printed and bound in Great Britain by CPI Bath

What do you think about this book? Or any other Hodder
Education title? Please send your comments to the feedback
section on www.hoddereducation.com.

Dedicated to my mother Shrimati Sona Thussu, for her boundless love and care, and to the memory of my father Pandit Shambhu Nath Thussu, who taught me how to be critical.

About the Author

Daya Kishan Thussu is Professor of International Communication at the University of Westminster in London, where he leads a Masters Programme in Global Media. A former Associate Editor of Gemini News Service, a London-based international news agency, he has a PhD in International Relations from Jawaharlal Nehru University, New Delhi. He is the co-author (with Oliver Boyd-Barrett) of *Contra-Flow in Global News* (1992, published in association with UNESCO); editor of *Electronic Empires – Global Media and Local Resistance* (1998, Arnold, London and Oxford University Press, New York); and of *Media on the Move: Global Flow and Contra-Flow* (2006, London and New York: Routledge); co-editor (with Des Freedman) of *War and the Media: Reporting Conflict 24/7* (2003, Sage, London), and (with Katharine Sarikakis) of *The Ideologies of the Internet* (2006, Cresskill NJ: Hampton Press). He is the founder and Managing Editor of the Sage journal *Global Media and Communication*.

Contents

Acknowledgements

The publishers wish to thank the following for permission to use copyright material:

WTO Publications for Tables 3.1 and 3.2 (page 72); Satellite Industry Association for Table 3.3 (page 77); OECD for Tables 3.7, 3.8 and 3.9 (pages 92–94); Haymarket Direct for Tables 4.6 and 4.12 (pages 113 and 125); Screen Digest for Tables 4.8, 4.9 and 5.5 (pages 118, 120 and 155); World Association of Newspapers for Table 4.11 (page 124); ZenithOptimedia for Table 4.14 (page 126); Business Week for Table 5.1 (page 147); European Audiovisual Observatory for Tables 5.9 and 5.11 (pages 159 and 161); IFPI for Table 5.15 (page 174); ITU for Tables 7.1, 7.2, 7.4, 7.10, 7.11, 7.12 and Figure 7.1 (pages 208, 209, 210, 214, 236 and 238); International Intellectual Property Alliance for Table 7.6 (page 225); Internet World Stats for Figure 7.2 and Tables 7.13 and 7.14 (pages 237, 245 and 246).

Every effort has been made to trace and acknowledge ownership of copyright. The publishers will be glad to make suitable arrangements with any copyright holders whom it has not been possible to contact.

Preface to the second edition

Since the first edition of this book was published in 2000, the pace of change in international media and communication has accelerated and many of the emergent trends detected at the turn of the new century have become a reality. The global context within which international communication takes place has also changed profoundly, not least with the attacks on New York and Washington in September 2001 and the resulting open-ended global 'war on terrorism'. Economically, the most significant change has been the steady rise of Asian economies, particularly in China and to a lesser extent in India. The gradual integration of these two Asian giants into the global economy – accelerated by China's membership of the World Trade Organization – has the potential to reorient global economic activity. Technologically, the increasing digitization of media content, as well as the growing importance of online communication, has revolutionized global interactions.

In many ways, technological change is the most important factor in the context of the extensity and intensity of transnational communication. The Internet, for example, has shown extraordinary growth: in 1998, it was accessible to just 3 per cent of the world's population; by 2005 that figure had climbed to 15 per cent. Mobile telephony has also transformed global communication – by 2004 there were more mobile than fixed-line telephones in the world. By 2005 South Korea was leading the world in broadband penetration, while China had emerged as the planet's biggest television market, the world's largest mobile phone user and the top exporter of IT products. These technological and economic changes are affecting the manner in which a growing number of people consume and circulate messages or conduct commerce across national borders.

In parallel with these shifts in global communication patterns, there are also striking continuities: despite a small but significant contraflow, much of media content circulating around the world is still largely emanating from a few selected countries and is owned by even fewer hugely powerful multimedia corporations, mostly based in the United States. These corporations have widened and strengthened their presence worldwide through skilful localization strategies that include producing programmes in local languages and on local themes, as well as 'outsourcing' their work to regional hubs of cultural and creative industries in a digitally linked globe. In the process they seem to have refigured their hegemony, championing and legitimizing the idea of a global free market.

With the globalization of the ideology of neo-liberalism, the General Agreement on Trade in Services (GATS), which includes communication services, has acquired added importance as information and communication technologies have become pervasive. The privatization and deregulation of media and communication industries has continued apace. This has brought a new dynamism to the media sector worldwide, which is particularly pronounced in the global South. The rising international profile of the pan-Arab news network al-Jazeera, the transnationalization of Latin American telenovelas, the globalization of the Indian film industry and the impressive growth of Chinese media are some prominent indicators of this change. However, concerns about the future of public media persist as information becomes a tradable commodity in a market-led communication system dominated by the world's hyperpower.

Mapping and analysing these trends has been a fascinating academic endeavour, facilitated by the availability of instant and truly international information through the Internet – much of it free of charge – from which this edition has benefited hugely. It is gratifying to learn that *International Communication* has already established itself as a key text in the field and has been adopted for courses across the world. In 2004 the book was translated into Mandarin and Korean, thus making it accessible to two major non-English readerships in Asia.

In this revised and thoroughly updated edition, each chapter includes new material, and the final chapter, with its focus on the Internet, has been substantially reworked in the light of recent technological developments. New case studies have been added to reflect key emerging trends in global media and communication and the latest research in the field. These include al-Jazeera; the rise of China; the transnationalization of telenovelas; the Google phenomenon; the trend towards infotainment; and the 'war on terrorism'.

My own academic trajectory has closely followed shifts in international media and its study, having taught specialized courses on global media and communication for over a decade now. In the six years since the first edition of *International Communication*, my research interest in the international dimensions of media, culture and communication has deepened considerably, helped in no small measure by having worked with excellent colleagues and some of the finest students from all over the world at two of Britain's best-known media and communication departments – at Goldsmiths College, University of London and, since 2004, at the University of Westminster. In addition, as founder and managing editor of the Sage journal *Global Media and Communication*, I have also acquired valuable insights into the latest empirical and theoretical work on the subject and continue to have the privilege of interacting with the leading scholars in this rapidly evolving field.

I am very thankful to all the academics who adopted the first edition of this book for their courses and hope that they will find this new edition equally useful. My main ambition has been to provide students and researchers with a comprehensive analysis of the salient developments in international communication under one cover and in an accessible style.

I am also grateful to my editors at Hodder Arnold, Eva Martinez and Matthew Sullivan, for their co-operation and professionalism. I am thankful to Shubo Li, a PhD student at the University of Westminster, for assistance with data collection. As always, my wife Liz has been a tower of strength and support in the updating of this edition and I thank her profusely, and our daughter Shivani and son Rohan, both now in secondary school, for their patience with their overworked professional parents.

Daya Kishan Thussu
London, March 2006

Introduction to the first edition

The world is on the threshold of a new industrial revolution. A revolution which promises to be at least as significant as that which has brought most of the growth of the world's economy in the past two centuries. A revolution which promises to have just as far reaching an impact on a wide variety of aspects of life, and a revolution with global reach. Telecommunications are at the epicentre of this revolution.

(ITU, 1999: 5)

As the new millennium dawned, global television tracked the rise of the sun across the world, with images broadcast live via 300 satellite channels to audiences in each of the world's 24 time zones. At the beginning of the twenty-first century, millions of people can communicate with each other in real time, across national boundaries and time zones, through voice, text and pictures, and, increasingly, a combination of all three. In a digitally linked globe, the flow of data across borders has grown exponentially, boosting international commerce, more and more of which is being conducted through new technologies.

Defined as 'communication that occurs across international borders' (Fortner, 1993: 6), the analysis of international communication has been traditionally concerned with government-to-government information exchanges, in which a few powerful states dictated the communication agenda (Fischer and Merrill, 1976; Frederick, 1992; Fortner, 1993; Hamelink, 1994; Mattelart, 1994; Mowlana, 1996, 1997). Advances in communication and information technologies in the late twentieth century have greatly enhanced the scope of international communication – going beyond government-to-government and including business-to-business and people-to-people interactions at a global level and at speeds unimaginable even a decade ago.

Apart from nation-states, many non-state international actors are increasingly shaping international communication. The growing global importance of international non-governmental bodies – Public Interest Organizations (PINGOs), such as Amnesty International, Greenpeace and the International Olympic Committee; Business Interest Organizations (BINGOs), such as GE, News Corporation and AT&T; and Intergovernmental Organizations (IGOs), such as the European Union, NATO, ASEAN – is indicative of this trend (Hamelink, 1994).

In the contemporary world, international communication 'encompasses political, economic, social, cultural and military concerns' (Fortner, 1993: 1), and, as it becomes more widespread and multilayered, the need to study it has acquired an added urgency. Intellectual and research interest in international aspects of communication, culture and media has grown as a result of the globalization of media and cultural industries. Communication studies itself has broadened to include cultural and media studies, and is increasingly being taught in a comparative and international framework. However, international communication is not yet considered a separate academic discipline, since its concerns overlap with other subject areas (Stevenson, 1992). In some institutions, mainly in universities in the United States, it has been taught within international relations or political science departments, while in Europe and the rest of the world, international communication has yet to find a firm mooring, the proliferation of new courses in global, intercultural and international communication notwithstanding.

The US-based Iranian scholar Hamid Mowlana identifies four key interrelated approaches to international communication: idealistic-humanistic, proselytization, economic and the political (Mowlana, 1997: 6–7). Examples of the first would be the work of British communication scholar Colin Cherry, who has argued that communication can promote global harmony (Cherry, 1978). The economic and strategic implications of international communication have been explored by Armand Mattelart (Mattelart, 1994), while Cees Hamelink has examined politics of world communication (Hamelink, 1994).

The emphasis of this book is on the economic and political dimensions of international communication and their relationship with technological and cultural processes. It aims to provide a critical overview of the profound changes in international media and communication at the threshold of the new millennium, at a time when the political, economic and technological contexts in which media and communication operate are becoming increasingly global. Intercultural communication, which examines the interpersonal contact of peoples of different cultural backgrounds, is outside the remit of this volume, which also does not aim to cover other more personal forms of international communication, such as travel and tourism, educational and cultural exchanges.

From the beginnings of human society, communication has taken place over distance and time – from cave paintings in Australia to the mobile Internet – through contact between different cultures via travel and trade, as well as war and colonialism. Such interactions have resulted in the transporting and implanting of ideas, religious beliefs, languages and economic and political systems, from one part of the world to another, by a variety of means that have evolved over millennia – from the oral, to being mediated by written language, sound or image (Schramm, 1988). The word 'communicate' has its roots in the Latin word *communicare*, 'to share'. International communication, then, is about sharing knowledge, ideas and beliefs among the various peoples of the world, and therefore it can be a contributing factor in resolving global conflict and promoting mutual understanding among nations. However, more often channels of international communication have been used not for such lofty ideals but to promote the economic and political interests of the world's powerful nations, who control the means of global communication.

The expansion of international communication should be seen within the overall context of the growth of capitalism in the nineteenth century. The availability of fast and reliable information was crucial for the expansion of European capital, and, 'in a global system, physical markets have to be replaced by notional markets in which prices and values are assessed through the distribution of regular, reliable information'. Thus the information network 'was both the cause and the result of capitalism' (Smith, 1980: 74). If Britain dominated international communication during the nineteenth and the first half of the twentieth century – primarily through its control of the world's telegraph and cable networks – the United States emerged as an information superpower after the Second World War. In 1944, the US business magazine *Fortune* published an article on 'World Communications', which warned that the future growth of the USA depended on the efficiency of US-owned communications systems, just as Britain's had done in the past: 'Great Britain provides an unparalleled example of what a communications system meant to a great nation standing athwart the globe' (cited in Chanan, 1985: 121).

One key use of international communication has been for public diplomacy, with the aim of influencing the policies of other nations by appeals to its citizens through means of public communication (Fortner, 1993). During the Cold War years, the propaganda of ideological confrontation dominated the use of international communication channels. Ignoring the complexity of media systems, this bipolar view of the world opposed the 'free' US system at the desirable end of a continuum and totalitarian systems at the other, an approach which was 'a strong ideological weapon in the spread of American media enterprises overseas' (Wells, 1996: 2).

With the dismantling of the Soviet Union and the retreat of socialism, as well as the marginalization of the global South in international decision-making processes, the West, led by the USA, emerged as the key agenda-setter in the arena of international communication, as in other forms of global interactions. In the post-Cold War world, so much had changed that, by 2000, a US-led consortium was planning to lease the ailing Russian space station *Mir* as an international space destination and even as a set for Hollywood films (Whittell, 2000).

The move towards the worldwide privatization of former state-run broadcasting and telecommunication networks, championed by such international organizations as the World Trade Organization and the World Bank, has transformed the landscape of international communication. As UNESCO's *World Communication Report* observes:

> The world of communications is gradually changing from an economy of scarcity and government-structured controls to a free economy oriented towards abundant supply and diversity. This change quickens the pace of the elimination of monopolies in the delivery and distribution of information, in both telecommunications and the audiovisual field.
>
> (UNESCO, 1997: 11)

In a market-driven media and communication environment, the public-service role of the mass media has been undermined. Although some national broadcasters continue to receive high audience shares – varying from India's Doordarshan's 80 per cent and the BBC's nearly 35 per cent – in more commercialized television environments such as Brazil, Rede Brasil, the only public-service channel, had an audience of just 4 per cent (UNESCO, 1997). As mass media, especially television, gain more leverage over setting the international agenda (Shaw, 1996), concerns about the growing concentration of media power and its impact on international communication are also increasing.

Although the Internet has received greater attention in recent public debates on international communication, television, being much more widely accessible, is perhaps more influential in setting the global communication agenda. In an era of multi-channel digital broadcasting, the quantity of mainly Western images has multiplied manyfold and with that their power to promote 'virtual wars' or a consumerist way of life. Television images can transcend linguistic barriers and affect national media cultures in a way that other text- or voice-based media cannot. According to the *1999–2000 Satellite Industry Guide*, co-published by the Satellite Industry Association, direct-to-home television was one of the fastest-growing segments, accounting for $20 billion and growing at 30 per cent annually (*Satnews*, 1999).

Though other major economic blocs, such as the European Union and Japan, and some developing countries, notably India, Brazil and China, have gained from opening up the field of global communication, the biggest beneficiary of a liberalized international communication system is the United States, the world's information superpower with the most extensive network of communications satellites, the largest exporter of cultural products and a global leader in electronic commerce.

The USA, and the transnational corporations based there, have a major stake in creating and maintaining an international communication system that favours the free market. It can employ its public diplomacy through extensive control of the world's communication hard and software to promote a vision of a 'borderless' world (for capital but not people). As one commentator put it, the USA dominates

(the) global traffic in information and ideas. American music, American movies, American television, and American software are so dominant, so sought after, and so visible that they are now available literally everywhere on the Earth. They influence the tastes, lives, and aspirations of virtually every nation.

(Rothkopf, 1997: 43)

The 'emerging infosphere – and its potential as a giant organic culture processor, democratic empowerer, universal connector, and ultimate communicator,' is seen as crucial for US public diplomacy (ibid.: 52).

In the post-Soviet world, there appears to be a consensus emerging among US policy-makers that in order to retain US hegemony the preferred option is the deployment of its 'soft power' – its domination of global communication and mediated culture – rather than the force employed by the European empires during the colonial era (Nye, 1990). As Joseph Nye, a former US Assistant Secretary of Defense, and William Owens, a former Vice Chairman of the Joint Chiefs of Staff, argue: 'Information is the new coin of the international realm, and the United States is better positioned than any other country to multiply the potency of its hard and soft power resources through information' (Nye and Owens, 1996: 20).

Promotion of democracy and human rights and a 'free flow of capital' worldwide are the proclaimed aims of US public diplomacy. US foreign policy 'must project an imperial dimension,' counsels a commentator:

> The US role should resemble that of nineteenth-century Great Britain, the global leader of that era. US influence would reflect the appeal of American culture, the strength of the American economy, and the attractiveness of the norms being promoted. Coercion and the use of force would normally be a secondary option.
>
> (Haass, 1999: 41)

However, this rhetoric of democracy, prosperity and human rights sits awkwardly with the unmistakable trend towards corporatization and concentration of global information and communication networks among a few, mainly Western, megacorporations, making them what US media critic Ben Bagdikian has called a 'private ministry of information' (Bagdikian, 1997). Cross-border mergers in the media and telecommunication industries – most notably the merger of America Online with Time Warner, and the $190 billion British Vodafone takeover of German mobile telephone company Mannesmann – in the first few months of the new millennium – have further concentrated media and telecommunication power among a few conglomerates.

Extolling the virtues of such mergers for consumers, *Time* magazine wrote that the AOL-Time Warner deal had the potential for consumers to offer 'whatever they want – books, movies, magazines, music – wherever they want it, whatever way they choose, whether on a TV, a PC, a cell phone or any of the myriad wireless devices that are hurtling toward the marketplace' (Okrent, 2000: 47). However, concerns have also been raised about the adverse effects of such corporatization of international information and entertainment networks on the diversity and plurality of global media cultures, by undermining cultural sovereignty and accentuating the already deep divisions in terms of information resources between and among nations. Crucially, it could also increase the economic and technological dependence of the information-poor South on the information-rich North.

An analysis of the evolution of international communication reveals a dominance and dependency syndrome – the dominance of a few countries by virtue of their control of both the software and hardware of global communication and the dependence of many nations upon them. To understand contemporary international communication one must look at the historical continuities which have given a headstart to some countries and created information poverty among many others. From nineteenth-century imperialism to the 'electronic empires' of the twenty-first century, the big powers have dominated global political, military and economic systems as well as information and communication networks. Though technologies employed for transmission of messages across national borders have changed – from telegraph, telephone, radio, television, to the mobile Internet –

the main actors in international communication have remained the same, despite the emergence of some regional players representing different 'geo-linguistic' groups. The dynamic between continuity and change is then the central theme of this volume.

A recurring issue in the book is the political and economic implications of such supremacy for Southern countries dependent on information and communication channels which remain largely within the control of a few countries and the corporations based there. Admittedly, the South is far from being a homogeneous entity, with varying degrees of media and communication resources, yet the developing countries share a fundamental disadvantage in their inability to influence the global communication agenda, which continues to be set and implemented by the world's most powerful nations.

The book is divided into seven chapters, with a series of case studies to exemplify the main concepts and arguments. Chapter 1 provides a historical context for the study of international communication, examining how communication had an international dimension for centuries before the modern colonial empires emerged. Its role in the expansion of European capitalism across the world is illustrated by a case study of the rise of the British news agency Reuters, whose fortunes paralleled the growth of the British Empire. In the second section, the chapter examines how mass media, especially radio, was used by both blocs during the ideological confrontation of the Cold War. Covert international communication is analysed by focusing on *Radio Free Europe* and *Radio Liberty*, two prime examples of US secret propaganda during the years of East–West ideological battles regularly fought over the airwaves. The third section of the chapter examines the relationship between international communication and development, with a critique of Southern demands for a New World Information and Communication Order (NWICO) which dominated the debate during the 1970s and 1980s and was also affected by the bipolar view of international relations. The case study of India's Satellite Instructional Television Experiment (SITE) programme assesses a pioneering attempt to use television for education and development.

Following on from the historical context, Chapter 2 aims to provide a theoretical overview of competing theories that inform the study of international communication, from Marxist to culturalist and postmodernist analyses of the subject. The chapter introduces a range of theoretical perspectives on international communication over the past century, setting out the arguments of the main theorists and their approaches to its study. The perspectives discussed range from traditional Marxist analysis to dependency theory and neo-Marxism, modernization theory and its critics, theories of globalization and of the information society, as well as cultural studies approaches.

Chapter 3 maps out the expansion of transnational media and telecommunications corporations in the post-Cold War era of free-market capitalism. These are analysed within the macro-economic context of liberalization, deregulation and privatization and the policies of multilateral institutions such as the World Trade Organization (WTO) and the International Telecommunication Union (ITU). The chapter examines the ideological policy shifts in international institutions – from a state-regulated to a market-led environment – along with the convergence of the telecommunications, computers and media industries, lying behind the transnationalization and global expansion of mainly Western media and communication corporations. It then explores the unprecedented growth of the global satellite industry – which provides the hardware for international communication – as a result of the liberalization of the international agreements on satellite broadcasting and telecommunication, focusing on the changing nature of the international satellite consortium, Intelsat, which is in the process of transforming itself from an intergovernmental to a private corporation. In the third section, the chapter discusses why transnational corporations have benefited most from the liberalization and privatization of international communication, taking Rupert Murdoch's News Corporation, the most global of media companies, as a case study.

In Chapter 4 the focus is on the global media market, which has evolved partly as a result of the deregulation and liberalization of the international communication sector in the 1990s, and partly as a consequence of the rapid expansion of new communication technologies, notably satellite and cable. It surveys the key players in the global media and cultural industries: advertising, film, music, publishing, television and news agencies. The chapter includes up-to-date information about the world's most powerful media and communication companies and discusses their strategies in a range of media sectors, demonstrating corporate synergies and the links between production, distribution and marketing of their products in a global marketplace. The chapter addresses questions about the implications of the concentration of ownership of the world's media and cultural industries among a few vertically integrated, global conglomerates. Two case studies – Disney's Entertainment and Sports Network (ESPN), and Cable News Network (CNN), part of AOL-Time Warner, the world's biggest media and entertainment company – contextualize the discussion about the globalization of media markets.

Having established the general pattern of ownership which shows the overwhelming US dominance of the international flow of information and entertainment, Chapter 5 examines the effects of the largely one-way flow of international communication in different socio-cultural contexts, looking particularly at exports of US films and television across the world. The predominance of US media products, especially Hollywood films, is discussed in relation to the European Union and its concerns about the threat to its cultural sovereignty. The chapter then examines questions of homogenization and resistance to the English-language programmes which promote a Western consumerist lifestyle. It explores how mass media interact with and influence consciousness, media cultures and cultural identities, and discusses these within the framework of the debates on media and cultural imperialism. The internationalization of the mainly US-based children's TV channels and Music Television (MTV) are discussed as two examples of how consumerist culture is being promoted through the powerful medium of television. In the final section the chapter examines the process of cultural adaptation, arguing that the homogenization of global cultural products has been counterbalanced by heterogeneous tendencies leading to a hybrid form of global–local interaction. The issue of hybridity – how global genres are adapted to suit national cultural codes – is analysed through the case study of Zee TV, India's biggest private multimedia network.

The focus of Chapter 6 is on contraflow in international media products. Through a series of case studies, the chapter investigates the role of regional actors and the growing reverse flow in media products, which demonstrates how the transnationalization of media organizations has profoundly altered the market in global communications. Such regional players as the pan-Arabic channel Middle East Broadcasting Centre and China's Phoenix television channel, based in Hong Kong, are discussed as powerful regional actors with well-defined geo-lingusitic media and cultural constituencies. The chapter also examines the trend towards the movement of cultural products from the global South to the media-rich North. Brazil's *TV Globo*, one of the world's biggest exporters of television programmes, and India's film industry, the world's largest producer of feature films, are analysed as two prime examples to underline the complexity of international cultural transactions.

The final chapter identifies and analyses some of the key issues in an age of computer-mediated international communication. It examines the impact on contemporary media culture of changes in technology, especially the unprecedented growth of the Internet. Microsoft Corporation, the world's biggest computer software maker, is discussed as a case study of the forces that are leading the new information revolution and also acting as tax inspectors on the new global knowledge industry. The chapter also explores how information and communication technologies such as satellites can be used for both entertainment and surveillance. The liberating and empowering potential of new information and communication technologies is contrasted with the crucial issue of access to them. Examples of alternative communications in an international context are discussed to contextualize the potential of new technologies such as the Internet to empower citizens, while maintaining the refrain that a vast majority of the world's population is excluded from the global information revolution and not benefiting from electronic commerce. It also argues for the need to broaden the analysis of international communication, incorporating a variety of approaches, to provide a framework within which this increasingly complex subject can be analysed.

The book includes maps, diagrams and charts to provide the reader with easily digestible statistical information and references and to combine a clear exposition of both the empirical and the theoretical terrain, with examples from a wide range of international media, including television, film, advertising, news media and publishing. A glossary and a detailed chronology, as well as a comprehensive bibliography, are also appended to make the volume useful for students and researchers alike. Given its international scope and multiperspectival approach, it is hoped that this book will act as a guide to understanding institutions, technologies, production and consumption of global media and communication.

In writing a book of this nature, one accumulates many intellectual and other debts. First and foremost, I am indebted to all the scholars in the field of international communication and other professionals, especially those from trade and business publications, from whose work this volume has benefited enormously. I also want to record my gratitude to the geniuses behind the World Wide Web, giving researchers access to a first-rate international library in one's own home, and on which I have drawn extensively for the book.

Colleagues at Coventry University, where I worked for most of the period this book was in gestation, deserve heartfelt thanks, not least for covering for me while I was on study leave during the autumn of 1999. I also drew sustenance from the generosity of new colleagues at University of North London, whose good-naturedness and understanding were very important in the crucial final weeks of finishing the manuscript. I have been fortunate to work with Lesley Riddle of Arnold, benefiting from her kind support and professionalism, and with Susan Dunsmore, to whose eagle eye for detail in the editing process I am very grateful.

Finally, a special thanks to my wife Elizabeth who was involved in the project from its very inception. I have no hesitation in admitting that any weaknesses of the book are mine, but its strengths reflect her excellent editorial input. Our children – Shivani, 8 and Rohan, 5 – displayed exemplary behaviour and extraordinary patience during the writing of the book, sometimes under trying conditions. As a reward, they have been promised a trip to Disneyland. Having been glued to my computer in a tiny study for the best part of a year, scrolling through hundreds of websites and poring over thousands of pages of reports, books, journals, newspapers and magazines, even I could do with some Disney magic.

chapter one

The historical context of international communication

The study of contemporary international communication can be illuminated by an understanding of the elements of continuity and change in its development. The nexus of economic, military and political power has always depended on efficient systems of communication, from flags, beacon fires and runners, to ships, telegraph wires and now satellites. The evolution of telegraphic communication and empire in the nineteenth century exemplifies these interrelationships, which continued throughout the twentieth century, even after the end of empire. During two world wars and the cold war, the power and significance of new media – radio and then television – for international communication were demonstrated by their use for international propaganda as well as recognition of their potential for socio-economic development.

Communication and empire

Communication has always been critical to the establishment and maintenance of power over distance. From the Persian, Greek and Roman empires to the British, efficient networks of communication were essential for the imposition of imperial authority, as well as for the international trade and commerce on which they were based. Indeed, the extent of empire could be used as an 'indication of the efficiency of communication' (Innis, [1950] 1972: 9). Communications networks and technologies were key to the mechanics of distributed government, military campaigns and trade.

The Greek historian, Diodorus Cronus (fourth century BC) recounts how the Persian king, Darius I (522–486 BC), who extended the Persian Empire from the Danube to the Indus, could send news from the capital to the provinces by means of a line of shouting men positioned on heights. This kind of transmission was 30 times faster than using runners. In *De Bello Gallico*, Julius Caesar (100–44 BC) reports that the Gauls, using the human voice, could call all their warriors to war in just three days. Using fire at night and smoke or mirrors during the day is mentioned in ancient texts, from the Old Testament to Homer.

While many rulers, including the Greek polis, used inscription for public information, writing became a more flexible and efficient means of conveying information over long distances: 'Rome, Persia and the Great Khan of China all utilised writing in systems of information-gathering and dispersal, creating wide-ranging official postal and dispatch systems' (Lewis, 1996: 152). It is said that the *Acta Diurna,* founded by Julius Caesar and one of the forerunners of modern news media, was distributed across most of the Roman Empire: 'as communication became more efficient, the possibility of control from the centre became greater' (Lewis, 1996: 156).

The Indian Emperor Ashoka's edicts, inscribed on rock in the third century BC, are found across South Asia, from Afghanistan to Sri Lanka and writ writers had a prominent place in the royal household. During the Mughal period in Indian history, the *waqi'a-nawis* (newswriters) were employed by the kings to appraise them of progress in the empire. Both horsemen and despatch runners transmitted news and reports. In China, the T'ang dynasty (618–907) created a formal handwritten publication, the *ti pao* or 'official newspaper', which disseminated information to the elite, and in the Ching period (1644–1911) private news bureaus sprang up which composed and circulated official news in the printed form known as the *Ch'ing pao* (Smith, 1979).

In addition to official systems of communication, there have also always been informal networks of travellers and traders. The technologies of international communication and globalization may be contemporary phenomena, but trade and cultural interchanges have existed for more than two millennia between the Graeco-Roman world and Arabia, India and China. Indian merchandise was exported to the Persian Gulf and then overland through Mesopotamia to the Mediterranean coast, and from there onwards to Western Europe. An extensive trans-Asian trade flourished in ancient times, linking China with India and the Arabic lands. Later, the Silk Route through central Asia linked China, India and Persia with Europe. Information and ideas were communicated across continents, as shown by the spread of Buddhism, Christianity and Islam.

The medium of communication developed from the clay tablet of Mesopotamia, the papyrus roll in ancient Egypt and in ancient Greece, to parchment codex in the Roman Empire. By the eighth century, paper introduced from China began to replace parchment in the Islamic world and spread to medieval Europe. Also from China, printing slowly diffused to Europe, aided by the Moors' occupation of Spain, but it was not until the fifteenth century, with the movable type printing press developed by Johann Gutenberg, a goldsmith in Mainz in Germany, that the means of communication were transformed.

By the beginning of the sixteenth century, the printing presses were turning out thousands of copies of books in all the major European languages. For the first time Christianity's Holy Scriptures were available in a language other than Latin, undermining the authority of priests, scribes and political and cultural elites. As a consequence, 'the unified Latin culture of Europe was finally dissolved by the rise of the vernacular languages which was consolidated by the printing press' (Febvre and Martin, 1990: 332). Coupled with vernacular translations of the Bible by John Wycliffe in England and Martin Luther in Germany, the printing revolution helped to lay the basis for the Reformation and the foundations of nation state and of modern capitalism (Tawney, 1937; Eisenstein, 1979).

The new languages, especially Portuguese, Spanish, English and French, became the main vehicle of communication for the European colonial powers in many parts of the world. This transplantation of communication systems around the globe created a new hierarchy of language and culture in the conquered territories (Smith, 1980). The

Portuguese Empire was one of the first to grasp the importance of the medium for colonial consolidation, with the kings of Portugal sending books in the cargoes of ships carrying explorers. They opened printing presses in the territories they occupied – the first in Goa in 1557 and in Macao in 1588. Other European powers also used the new technology and the printed book played an important role in the colonization of Asia.

The Industrial Revolution in Western Europe, founded on the profits of the growing international commerce encouraged by colonization, gave a huge stimulus to the internationalization of communication. Britain's domination of the sea routes of international commerce was to a large extent due to the pre-eminence of its navy and merchant fleet, a result of pioneering work in the mapping out of naval charts by the great eighteenth-century explorers, such as James Cook, enabled also by the determination of longitude based on the Greenwich meridian. Technological advances such the development of the iron ship, the steam engine and the electric telegraph all helped to keep Britain ahead of its rivals.

The growth of international trade and investment required a constant source of reliable data about international trade and economic affairs, while the British Empire required a steady supply of information essential for maintaining political alliances and military security. Waves of emigration as a result of industrialization and empire helped to create a popular demand for news from relatives at home and abroad, and a general climate of international awareness (Smith, 1980).

The postal reform in England in 1840, initiated by the well-known author, Anthony Trollope as Postmaster General, with the adoption of a single-rate, one penny postage stamp (the Penny Black), irrespective of distance, revolutionized postal systems. This was followed by the establishment of the Universal Postal Union in 1875 in Berne, under the Universal Postal Convention of 1874, created to harmonize international postal rates and to recognize the principle of respect for the secrecy of correspondence. With the innovations in transport of railways and steamships, international links were being established that accelerated the growth of European trade and consolidated colonial empires.

The growth of the telegraph

The second half of the nineteenth century saw an expanding system of imperial communications made possible by the electric telegraph. Invented by Samuel Morse in 1837, the telegraph enabled the rapid transmission of information, as well as ensuring secrecy and code protection. The business community was first to make use of this new technology. The speed and reliability of telegraphy were seen to offer opportunities for profit and international expansion (Headrick, 1991; Hugill, 1999). The rapid development of the telegraph was a crucial feature in the unification of the British Empire. With the first commercial telegraph link set up in Britain in 1838, by 1851 a public telegraph service, including a telegraphic money order system, had been introduced. By the end of the century, as a result of the cable connections, the telegraph allowed the Colonial Office and the India Office to communicate directly with the Empire within minutes when, previously, it had taken months for post to come via sea. By providing spot prices for commodities like cotton, the telegraph enabled British merchants, exporting cotton from India or Egypt to England, to beat their competitors easily (Read, 1992).

The new technology also had significant military implications. The overhead telegraph, installed in Algeria in 1842, proved a decisive aid to the French during the occupation and colonization of Algeria (Mattelart, 1994). During the Crimean War (1854–56), the rival imperial powers, Britain and France, trying to prevent Russian westward expansion that threatened overland routes to their colonial territories in Asia, exchanged military intelligence through an underwater cable in the Black Sea laid by the British during the conflict. The Crimean conflict was also notable for the pioneering war reports of Irishman William Howard Russell in *The Times* of London, who was to become the first 'big name' in international journalism.

Similarly, during the Civil War in the United States of America (1861–65), over 24,000 kilometres of cable was laid to send more than 6.5 million telegrams. The American Civil War was not only one of the earliest conflicts to be reported extensively, but also the first example both of co-operative news gathering among the American and European journalists, and of the use of photojournalism.

The first underwater telegraphic cable which linked Britain and France became operational in 1851 and the first transatlantic cable, connecting Britain and the USA, in 1866. Between 1851 and 1868, underwater networks were laid down across the North Atlantic, the Mediterranean, the Indian Ocean and the Persian Gulf. During the 1860s and 1870s, London was linked up by cable to the key areas of the Empire (*see* map, p. 5). The first line between Europe and India via Turkey was opened in 1865. Two other cables to India – one overland across Russia and the other undersea via Alexandria and Aden – were started in 1870. India was linked to Hong Kong in 1871 and to Australia in 1872, and Shanghai and Tokyo were linked by 1873 (Read, 1992). By the 1870s, telegraph lines were operating within most countries in Asia and an international communication network, dominated by Britain, was beginning to emerge. The expansion of cable was marked by the rivalry between the British and French empires, which intensified after 1869, with the opening of the Suez Canal.

The decade from 1870 to 1880 saw the successive inaugurations of communications links between the English coast and the Dutch East Indies (Batavia), the Caribbean network, the line from the British West Indies to Australia and China, the networks in the China and Japanese seas, the cable from Suez to Aden, communication between Aden and British India, the New Zealand cables, communication between the east and south coasts of Africa, and the cable from Hong Kong to Manila (Read, 1992).

In South America, the south transatlantic cable, opened in 1874, linked Lisbon with Recife, Brazil, via the Cape Verde Islands and Madeira. Two years later, a network was established along the coast of Chile. The British cable of 1874 was joined in 1879 by a new French cable across the North Atlantic, with a spur to Brazil, and by a new German cable from Emden to the Azores to Morovia on the African coast, and from there to Recife. By 1881, a network along the Pacific coast from Mexico to Peru was in operation. In the 1880s, France established a series of links along the coast of Indochina and Africa, with networks in Senegal (Desmond, 1978).

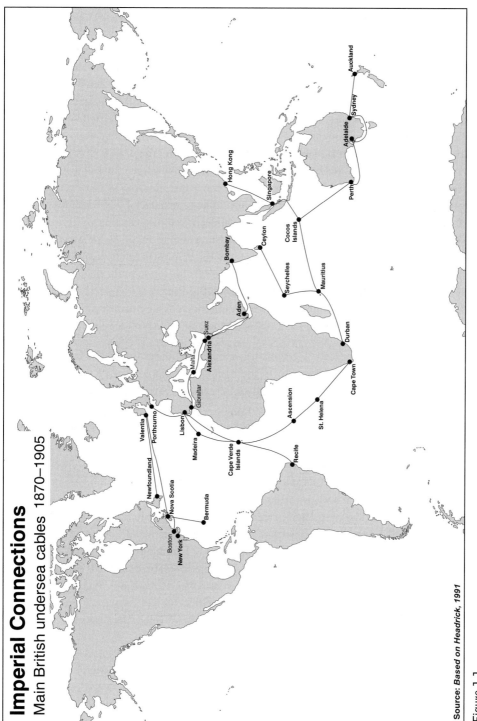

Imperial Connections
Main British undersea cables 1870–1905

Source: *Based on Headrick, 1991*

Figure 1.1

The British-sponsored, Indo-European landline telegraph between India and the Prussian North Sea coast had gone into operation in 1865. The cable had been extended from British shores to Alexandria by 1869, to Bombay in 1870, and other cables had been extended from Madras to Ceylon and from Singapore to Australia and New Zealand by 1873, and also to Hong Kong, Shanghai and the Japanese coast. Connections were made in China in 1896, with a spur of the Great Northern Telegraph Company Danish-owned line across Siberia to Russia and other points in Europe, making possible a Tokyo–Shanghai–St Petersburg–London communications link (Desmond, 1978). Within a quarter of a century, the world's cable networks had more than doubled in length (Hugill, 1999).

Undersea cables required huge capital investment, which was met by colonial authorities and by banks, businessmen and the fast-growing newspaper industry, so that the cable networks were largely in the hands of the private sector. Of the total cable distance of 104,000 miles, not more than 10 per cent was administered by governments. To regulate the growing internationalization of information, the International Telegraph Union was founded in 1865 with 22 members, all European countries apart from Persia, representing 'the first international institution of the modern era and the first organisation for the international regulation of a technical network' (Mattelart, 1994: 9).

According to the International Telegraph Union, the number of telegraphic transmissions in the world shot from 29 million in 1868 to 329 million in 1900 (Mattelart, 1994).

> For the first time in history, colonial metropolis acquired the means to communicate almost instantly with their remotest colonies ... The world was more deeply transformed in the nineteenth century than in any previous millennium, and among the transformations few had results as dazzling as the network of communication and transportation that arose to link Europe with the rest of the world.
>
> (Headrick, 1981: 129–30)

Military operations – such as the Japanese-Russian war of 1904–5, were both assisted and reported by the first trans-Pacific cable, which had been completed in 1902, joint property of the governments of Australia, New Zealand, Britain and Canada. It ran from Vancouver to Sydney and Brisbane, by way of Fanning Island, Suva and Norfolk Island, with a spur from Norfolk Island to Auckland. A connection already existed, established in 1873, linking Tokyo and London, with spurs to Shanghai, Hong Kong, Singapore, Colombo, Calcutta, Bombay and Alexandria, and with cable and telegraphic spurs by way of Singapore and Batavia to Darwin, Sydney and Auckland, where ties were made to the new trans-Pacific cable to Vancouver.

A second trans-Pacific cable was completed in 1903 by US interests, providing a link between San Francisco and Manila, through Honolulu, to Midway Island and Guam, and from there to the Asian mainland and Japan by existing British cables. All of these landing points were controlled by the United States: the Hawaiian Islands had been a US territory since 1900 and Midway was claimed by it in 1867, while Guam and the Philippines had become US colonies as a result of the 1898 Spanish-American War (Desmond, 1978).

Control over cables as well as sea routes was also of enormous strategic importance in an age of imperial rivalry (Kennedy, 1971). The cables were, in the words of Headrick, 'an essential part of the new imperialism' (1981: 163).

The outcomes of the two imperial wars – the Spanish-American War (1898) and the Boer War (1899–1902) – strengthened the European and US positions in the world and led to a rapid expansion in world trade that demanded immediate and vastly improved communications links, as well as more advanced naval capabilities. The new technology of 'wireless' telegraphy (also called radiotelegraphy) promised to meet these needs.

In 1901 Guglielmo Marconi harnessed the new discovery of electromagnetism to make the first wireless transatlantic telegraph transmission, with support from naval armament companies and newspaper groups. The British Empire had a great technological advantage since the Marconi Wireless Telegraph Company of Great Britain dominated global telegraph traffic and had a virtual monopoly on international telegraph exchanges, as it refused to communicate with any system other than its own. The operators of a Marconi apparatus were prohibited from responding to radio signals emanating from a non-Marconi transmitter, a policy that had the effect of blocking the exchange of critically important information relating to the safe passage of ships. However, at the Berlin Conference on Wireless Telegraphy in 1906, the first multilateral agreements on radiotelegraphy were signed and the International Radiotelegraph Union was born. By 1907 Marconi's monopoly was being challenged by other European countries as well as the United States.

As Table 1.1 demonstrates, the Anglo-American domination of international communication hardware was well established by the late nineteenth century, with the two countries owning nearly 75 per cent of the world's cables. Much of the global cabling was done by private companies, with Britain's Eastern Telegraph Company and the US-based Western Union Telegraph Company dominating the cable industry. By 1923, private companies had nearly 75 per cent of the global cabling share, with British firms accounting for nearly 43 per cent, followed by American companies, which owned 23 per cent (Headrick, 1991).

Table 1.1 Cabling the world

	1892		1923	
	length (km)	global share (%)	length (km)	global share (%)
British Empire	163,619	66.3	297,802	50.5
United States	38,986	15.8	142,621	24.2
French Empire	21,859	8.9	64,933	11.0
Denmark	13,201	5.3	15,590	2.6
Others	9206	3.7	68,282	11.7
All cables combined	246,871	100.0	589,228	100.0

Source: Based on data from Headrick, 1991

The dominance of British cable companies, which lasted until the end of the First World War, was based on direct control through ownership and indirect control by means of diplomatic censorship, which Britain exercised over the messages travelling through its cables. Britain had a critical advantage in its control of the copper and gutta-percha markets – the raw materials for the manufacture of cable – since the world rates of these were fixed in London and British mining companies owned copper deposits and mines in Chile, the world's biggest producer (Read, 1992).

Colonial governments supported the cable companies, either scientifically by research on maps and navigation, or financially by subsidies. In 1904, 22 of the 25 companies that managed international networks were affiliates of British firms; Britain deployed 25 ships totalling 70,000 tons, while the six vessels of the French cable-fleet amounted to only 7000 tons. As a result, British supremacy over the undersea networks was overwhelming: in 1910, the Empire controlled about half the world total, or 260,000 kilometres. France, which in contrast to the USA and UK, opted for the state administration of cable, controlled no more than 44,000 kilometres (Headrick, 1991; Mattelart, 1994). The importance of cables as the arteries of an international network of information, of intelligence services and of propaganda can be gauged from the fact that the day after the First World War broke out, the British cut both German transatlantic cables (Hugill, 1999).

After the war, the question of who should control Germany's cables, which had been taken over early in the war, one by the British and another by the French, dominated discussions at the 1919 peace talks at Versailles and reflected the rivalry between the British cable companies and the growing US radio interests for ownership and control of global communications networks. The USA argued that the cables be held jointly under international control or trusteeship and that a world congress be convened to consider international aspects of telegraph, cable and radio communication (Luther, 1988).

US companies challenged Britain's supremacy in the field of international cables and telegraph traffic, which, they claimed, gave unfair advantage to British trade. The American view was that the pre-war cable system had 'been built in order to connect the old world commercial centres with world business' and that now was the time to develop 'a new system with the United States as a centre' (cited in Luther, 1988: 20). Weakened by the war in Europe, British companies began to lose their share of global cable to the Americans, who increased their control on international communication channels by leasing cables from them (Hugill, 1999; Hills, 2002).

Unlike cables, the Americans dominated the new technology of telephones. Following the patenting of the telephone by the Bell Telephone Company, established by the inventor of telephony, Alexander Graham Bell in 1877, telephone production increased in the USA. In 1885, American Telephone and Telegraph (AT&T), later to become the head office of Bell Systems, was founded and for the next 80 years it succeeded in keeping a near-monopoly over US telecommunications networks.

The first international telephone calls were made between Paris and Brussels in 1887. At the end of the nineteenth century, the USA had the largest number of telephones, largely due to the fact that they were manufactured there. International Western Electric, subsidiary of Western Electric, itself owned by AT&T, was the first multinational network of production and sales, setting up branches in most European countries, including Britain, Spain, France and Italy, as well as in Japan, China and Australia (Mattelart, 1994). However, the area covered by telephones was very limited – telephone networks acquired a global dimension only in 1956 when the first telephone cable was laid under the Atlantic.

The era of news agencies

The newspaper industry played a significant role in the development of international telegraph networks, to be able to exploit the rapid increase in demand for news, especially the financial information required to conduct international commerce. The establishment of the news agency was the most important development in the newspaper industry of the nineteenth century, altering the process of news dissemination, nationally and internationally. The increasing demand among business clients for commercial information – on businesses, stocks, currencies, commodities, harvests – ensured that news agencies grew in power and reach (Boyd-Barrett and Rantanen, 1998).

The French Havas Agency (ancestor of AFP) was founded in 1835, the German agency Wolff in 1849 and the British Reuters in 1851. The US agency, Associated Press (AP) was established in 1848, but only the three European agencies began as international ones; not until the turn of the century did an American agency move in this direction. From the start, Reuters made commercial and financial information its speciality, while Havas was to combine information and advertising.

These three European news agencies, Havas, Wolff and Reuters, all of which were subsidized by their respective governments, controlled information markets in Europe and were looking beyond the continent to expand their operations. In 1870 they signed a treaty to divide up the world market between the three of them. The resulting association of agencies (ultimately to include about 30 members), became known variously as the League of Allied Agencies (les Agences Alliées), as the World League of Press Associations, as the National Agencies Alliances, and as the Grand Alliance of Agencies. More commonly, it was referred to simply as the 'Ring Combination' (Desmond, 1978). In the view of some it was a 'cartel', and its influence on world opinion was used by governments to suit their own purposes (Boyd-Barrett, 1980; Mattelart, 1994).

The basic contract, drawn up in 1870, set 'reserved territories' for the three agencies. Each agency made its own separate contracts with national agencies or other subscribers within its own territory. Provision was made for a few 'shared' territories, in which two, sometimes all three agencies had equal rights. In practice, Reuters, whose idea it was, tended to dominate the Ring Combination. Its influence was greatest because its reserved territories were larger or of greater news importance than most others. It also had more staff and stringers throughout the world and so contributed more original news to the pool. British control of cable lines made London itself an unrivalled centre for world news, further enhanced by Britain's wide-ranging commercial, financial and imperial activities (Read, 1992).

In 1890, Wolff, Reuters and Havas signed a new treaty for a further 10 years. Havas emerged stronger than ever – it gained South America as an exclusive territory, and also

Indo-China. Havas yielded its position in Egypt, which became exclusive Reuters territory, but continued to share Belgium and Central America with Reuters. 'The major European agencies were based in imperial capitals. Their expansion outside Europe was intimately associated with the territorial colonialism of the late nineteenth century' (Boyd-Barrett, 1980: 23).

After the First World War, although Wolff ceased to be a world agency, the cartel continued to dominate international news distribution. The first challenge to their monopoly came from AP when it started supplying news to Latin America. With the international news cartel broken by the 1930s, AP and other US agencies, such as United Press (UP), founded in 1907, began to encroach on their terrain. AP began to expand internationally, paralleling political changes in Europe with the weakening of the European empires after the First World War.

Case study

The rise of Reuters

Communication was central to the expansion and consolidation of modern European empires, the largest and the most powerful being the British Empire, which at its height, 1880–1914, dominated a quarter of humanity. The fortunes of Reuters, the most famous international news agency, can be seen to run in parallel with the growth of the British Empire.

The expansion of trade and investment during the nineteenth century had led to a huge growth in the demand for news and contributed to the commercialization of news and information services. Reuters astutely exploited this demand, helped by the new communication technologies, especially the telegraph. For British and other European investors, Reuters telegrams were essential reading for the latest news from various corners of the British Empire and by 1861 these were being published from more than a hundred datelines, including from the major colonies – India, Australia, New Zealand and South Africa.

By the 1870s, Reuters had offices in all the major strategic points of the empire – Calcutta, Bombay and Point de Galle on the southern tip of Sri Lanka, the end of the cable connection with London, from where Reuters supervised its services to South East Asia, China, Japan and Australia. In 1871, Shanghai became the headquarters of the growing Reuters presence in East Asia, and after the beginning of commercial mining of gold in southern Africa in the late nineteenth century, Cape Town became another nodal point in Reuters' global network. By 1914, Reuters news service had three main channels covering the empire: London to Bombay; London to Hong Kong via the Mediterranean to Cairo, Aden, Ceylon and Singapore; and another to

Cape Town, Durban, Mombasa, Zanzibar, the Seychelles and Mauritius (Read, 1992).

The expansion of European capitalism had created a pressing need for improved commercial intelligence and, with the development of communication, the value of world trade itself grew more than 25-fold between 1800 and 1913. This relationship between capital and communication was an aspect of what has been called 'the Reuters Factor', which 'functions like a multiplier that turns an increase in the supply of information into an increase in business' (Chanan, 1985: 113).

Reuters also enjoyed very close relationships with the British foreign and colonial administrations. During the second half of the nineteenth century, the agency increasingly functioned 'as an institution of the British Empire' (Read, 1992: 40). As Britain's most important colony, India played a 'central part in the Reuter empire within the British Empire', constituting a major market for commercial news (Read, 1992: 60). Reuters' revenues from India more than trebled from 1898 (£115,00) to 1918 (£352,00) (ibid.: 83).

Though it claimed to be an independent news agency, Reuters was for the most part the unofficial voice of the Empire, giving prominence to British views. This subservience to imperial authority was most prominent during imperial wars such as the Boer War (1899–1902), during which agency reports supported the British cause and the British troops. In the same way Reuters news from India was mostly related to economic and political developments in the Empire and largely ignored the anticolonial movement.

Defending the Empire came naturally to Reuters: in 1910 Reuters started an imperial news service and a year later the agency made a secret arrangement with the British Government under which it offered to circulate on its wires official speeches to every corner of the Empire, in return for an annual fee of £500 from the Colonial Office. During the First World War, Reuters launched a wartime news service by arrangement with the Foreign Office, which by 1917 was circulating about 1 million words per month throughout the Empire.

Reuters' Managing Director during the war years, George Jones, was also in charge of cable and wireless propaganda for the British Department of Information. Though this service was separate from the main Reuters wire service, whose support for the war was more subtle, it rallied opinion within the Empire and influenced the attitudes of the neutral countries. As one British official wrote in 1917, 'At Reuters the work done is that of an independent news agency of an objective character, with propaganda secretly infused' (quoted in Read, 1992: 127–8).

Though this service was discontinued after the end of the war, Reuters entered into another agreement with the Foreign Office under which the agency would circulate specific messages on its international wires, to be paid for by the government. This agreement remained in force until the Second World War. However, apart from support from the government the major reason for the continued success of Reuters was the fact that it 'sold useful information enabling businesses to trade profitably' (Lawrenson and Barber, 1985: 179).

The wider availability of wireless technology after the First World War enabled Reuters in 1920 to launch a trade service, which became a crucial component of the economic life of the Empire. New technology made it easier to send and receive more international industrial and financial information at a faster speed. As the globe was being connected through transoceanic trade, such information – for example, New York prices for Indian cotton – had a high premium for traders who were depending on the accuracy of Reuters commodity prices and stock market news from around the world.

Reuters' domination of international information was helped by its being a member of the cartel and it remained the world news leader between 1870 and 1914. But the weakening of the British Empire and the ascendancy of the USA forced Reuters to compete with the American news agencies, especially Associated Press, with which it signed, in 1942, a wartime news-sharing agreement, effectively creating a new cartel for news. In the post-war period, Reuters continued to focus on commercial information, realizing that in order to succeed in a free trade environment, it had to work towards integration of commodity, currency, equity and financial markets, 'around the clock and around the world' (Tunstall and Palmer, 1991: 46).

By 2006, what had been started in 1851 by entrepreneur Julius Reuter, using pigeons, had become one of the world's largest providers of financial data via the Internet – 90 per cent of its revenue came from selling business information – besides being the world's largest news and television agency.

The advent of popular media

The expansion of printing presses and the internationalization of news agencies during the nineteenth century were key factors contributing to the growth of a worldwide newspaper industry. In 1838 *The Times of India* was founded, while South East Asia's premier newspaper, *The Straits Times*, was started as a daily newspaper from Singapore in 1858. Advances in printing technology meant that newspapers in non-European languages could also be printed and distributed. By 1870 more than 140 newspapers were being printed in Indian languages; *Al-Ahram*, the newspaper which has defined Arab journalism for more than a century, was established in Cairo in 1875, while in 1890, Japan's most respected newspaper, *Asahi Shimbun* (Morning Sun), was founded. The 1890s in Europe saw a rapid expansion of the popular press – France's *Le Petit Parisien* had a circulation of 1 million in 1890, while in Britain, the *Daily Mail* was launched in 1896 to appeal to a mass readership.

Newspapers were used to articulate the emerging nationalism in many Asian countries. The Chinese nationalist leader Sun Yat Sen founded *Chung-kuo Jih-pao* (Chinese daily paper) in 1899, while in India Mahatma Gandhi used *Young India*, later named *Harijan*, to propagate an anticolonial agenda.

However, it was the USA which had the biggest international impact on media cultures, symbolized by William Randolph Hearst, one of the world's first media moguls. His *New York Journal* introduced the penny press in the USA, while the International News Service, which sold articles, crossword puzzles and comic strips to newspapers, created the world's first syndicate service. It was succeeded in 1915 by the King Feature Syndicate, whose comic strips were used by newspapers all over the world, for most of the twentieth century.

The internationalization of a new mass culture, however, began with the film industry. Following the first screening in Paris and Berlin in 1895, films were being seen a year later from Bombay to Buenos Aires. By the First World War, the European market was dominated by Pathé, founded in 1907 in France, whose distribution bureaux were located in seven European countries, as well as in Turkey, the USA and Brazil. The development of independent studios between 1909 and 1913 led to the growth of the Hollywood film industry, which was to dominate global film production (Mattelart, 1994). In the realm of popular music, the dog and trumpet logo of 'His Master's Voice' (HMV), label of the Gramophone Company, became a global image. Within a few years of the founding of the company, in 1897, its recording engineers were at work in the Balkans, the Middle East, Africa, India, Iran and China. By 1906, 60 per cent of the company's profits were earned from overseas sales (Pandit, 1996: 57). After its merger with the US giant Columbia Gramophone Company in 1931, it formed EMI (Electric and Musical Industries), beginning a process of Anglo-American domination of the international recording industry that lasted throughout the twentieth century and beyond.

By the end of the nineteenth century, US-based advertising companies were already looking beyond the domestic market. J. Walter Thompson, for example, established a 'sales bureau' in London in 1899. The USA, where advertising was given its modern form, was an early convert to the power of advertising, making it the world's most consumerist society. The spending on advertising in the USA increased from $0.45 billion at the start of the century to $212 billion by its end.

In the twentieth century, advertising became increasingly important in international communication. From the 1901 advertisement for the record label His Master's Voice, to De Beers' hugely popular campaign 'A diamond is forever' put out in 1948, advertisers have aimed at international audiences. This trend became even stronger with the growth of radio and television, with Coca-Cola's 1970 'It's the real thing' and Nike's 1988 slogan 'Just do it' being consumed across the world. The American cowboy and masculine trademark of the Marlboro Man, introduced in 1955 and identified with Philip Morris's Marlboro cigarettes, became a worldwide advertising presence, making Marlboro the best-selling cigarette in the world. Though tobacco advertisements were banned on US television in 1971 and since then health groups have fought against promoting smoking through advertisement in the USA and other Western countries, the Marlboro Man was nominated as the icon of the twentieth century by the US trade journal *Advertising Age International.*

Radio and international communication

As with other new technologies, Western countries were the first to grasp the strategic implications of radio communication after the first radio transmissions of the human voice in 1902. Unlike cable, radio equipment was comparatively cheap and could be sold on a mass scale. There was also a growing awareness among American businesses that radio, if properly developed and controlled, might be used to undercut the huge advantages of British-dominated international cable links (Luther, 1988). They realized that, while undersea cables and their landing terminals could be vulnerable, and their location required bilateral negotiations between nations, radio waves could travel anywhere, unrestrained by politics or geography.

At the 1906 international radiotelegraph conference in Berlin, 28 states debated radio equipment standards and procedures to minimize interference. The great naval powers, who were also the major users of radio (Britain, Germany, France, the USA and Russia), had imposed a regime of radio frequency allocation, allowing priority to the country that first notified the International Radiotelegraph Union of its intention to use a specific radio frequency (Mattelart, 1994).

As worldwide radio broadcasting grew, stations that transmitted across national borders had to register their use of a particular wavelength with the international secretariat of the International Radiotelegraph Union, in accordance with an agreement signed in London in 1912. But there was no mechanism for either assigning or withholding slots; it was a system of first come, first served. As a result the companies or states with the necessary capital and technology gained control over the limited spectrum space, to the disadvantage of smaller and less developed countries (Hamelink, 1994).

Two distinct types of national radio broadcasting emerged: in the USA, the Radio Act of 1927 confirmed its status as a commercial enterprise, funded by advertising, while the British Broadcasting Corporation (BBC), founded in 1927, as a non-profit, public broadcasting monopoly, provided a model for several other European and Commonwealth countries (McChesney, 1993).

As the strongest voice in the World Radio Conference in Washington in 1927, private companies helped to write an agreement that allowed them to continue developing their use of the spectrum, without regard to possible signal interference for other countries. By being embodied in an international treaty, these provisions took on the character of 'international law', including the principle of allocating specific wavelengths for particular purposes (Luther, 1988). A major consequence of this conference was to reinforce US and European domination of the international radio spectrum. However, it was the newly formed Soviet Union which became the first nation to exploit this new medium for international broadcasting.

The battle of the airwaves

The strategic significance of international communication grew with the expansion of the new medium of radio. From the outset, its use for propaganda was an integral part of its development, with its power to influence values, beliefs and attitudes (Taylor, 2003). During the First World War, the power of radio was quickly recognized as vital both to the management of public opinion at home and propaganda abroad, directed at allies and enemies alike. As noted by a well-known writer on propaganda: 'During the war period it came to be recognized that the mobilisation of men and means was not sufficient; there must be mobilisation of opinion. Power over opinion, as over life and property, passed into official hands' (Lasswell, 1927: 14).

The Russian communists were one of the earliest political groups to realize the ideological and strategic importance of broadcasting, and the first public broadcast to be recorded in the history of wireless propaganda was by the Council of the People's Commissars of Lenin's historic message on 30 October 1917: 'The All-Russian Congress of Soviets has formed a new Soviet Government. The Government of Kerensky has been overthrown and arrested. Kerensky himself has fled. All official institutions are in the hands of the Soviet Government' (quoted in Hale, 1975: 16).

The Soviet Union was one of the first countries to take advantage of a medium which could reach across continents and national boundaries to an international audience. The world's first short-wave radio broadcasts were sent out from Moscow in 1925. Within five years, the All-Union Radio was regularly broadcasting communist propaganda in German, French, Dutch and English.

By the time the Nazis came to power in Germany in 1933, radio broadcasting had become an extension of international diplomacy. The head of Hitler's Propaganda Ministry, Josef Goebbels, believed in the power of radio broadcasting as a tool of propaganda. 'Real broadcasting is true propaganda. Propaganda means fighting on all battlefields of the spirit, generating, multiplying, destroying, exterminating, building and undoing. Our propaganda is determined by what we call German race, blood and nation' (quoted in Hale, 1975: 2).

In 1935, Nazi Germany turned its attention to disseminating worldwide the racist and anti-Semitic ideology of the Third Reich. The Nazi *Reichsender* broadcasts were targeted at Germans living abroad, as far afield as South America and Australia. These short-wave transmissions were rebroadcast by Argentina, home to many Germans. Later the Nazis expanded their international broadcasting to include several languages, including Afrikaans, Arabic and Hindustani, and by 1945 German radio was broadcasting in more than 50 languages.

In Fascist Italy, under Benito Mussolini, a Ministry of Print and Propaganda was created to promote Fascist ideals and win public opinion for colonial campaigns, such as the invasion of Abyssinia (Ethiopia) in 1935, and support for Francisco Franco's Fascists during the Spanish Civil War (1936–39). Mussolini also distributed radio sets to Arabs, tuned to only one station – *Radio Bari* in southern Italy. This propaganda prompted the British Foreign Office to create a monitoring unit of the BBC to listen in to international broadcasts and later to start an Arabic language service to the region.

The Second World War saw an explosion in international broadcasting as a propaganda tool on both sides. Japanese wartime propaganda included short-wave transmissions from *Nippon Hoso Kyokai* (NHK), the Japan Broadcasting Corporation, to South East and East Asia and also to the west coast of the United States, which had a large Japanese-American population. In addition, NHK also transmitted high-quality propaganda programmes such as *Zero Hour*, aimed at US troops in the Pacific islands (Wood, 1992).

Although the BBC, apart from the Empire Service (the precursor of the BBC World Service), was not controlled directly by the British Government, its claim to independence during the war was 'little more than a self-adulatory part of the British myth' (Curran and Seaton, 1996: 147). John Reith, its first Director General and the spirit behind the BBC, was for a time the Minister of Information in 1940 and resented being referred to as 'Dr Goebbels' opposite number' (Hickman, 1995: 29).

The Empire Service had been established in 1932 with the aim of connecting the scattered parts of the British Empire. Funded by the Foreign Office, it tended to reflect the government's public diplomacy. At the beginning of the Second World War, the BBC was broadcasting in seven foreign languages apart from English – Afrikaans, Arabic, French, German, Italian, Portuguese and Spanish (Walker, 1992: 36). By the end of the war it was broadcasting in 39 languages.

The French General de Gaulle used the BBC's French service, during the war years, to send messages to the Resistance movement in occupied France, and for a time between October 1942 and May 1943, the BBC broadcast a weekly 15-minute newsletter to Russia with the co-operation of the Russian news agency TASS (*Telegrafnoe agentstvo Sovetskogo Soiuza*). It also broadcast *The Shadow of the Swastika*, the first of a series of dramas about the Nazi Party. The BBC helped the US Army to create the American Forces Network, which broadcast recordings of American shows for US forces in Britain, the Middle East and Africa. More importantly, given Britain's proximity to the war theatre, the BBC played a key role in the propaganda offensive and often it was more effective than American propaganda, which, as British media historian Asa Briggs comments, was 'both distant and yet too brash, too unsophisticated and yet too contrived to challenge the propaganda forces already at work on the continent' (1970: 412).

Until the Second World War radio in the USA was known more for its commercial potential as a vehicle for advertisements than a government propaganda tool, but after 1942, the year the Voice of America (VOA) was founded, the US Government made effective use of radio to promote its political interests – a process which reached its high point during the decades of the cold war.

The cold war – from communist propaganda to capitalist persuasion

The victorious allies of the Second World War – the Soviet Union and the West led by the United States – soon fell out as differences emerged about the post-war order in Europe and the rest of the world (Westad, 2005). The clash was, in essence, about two contrasting views of organizing society: the Soviet view, inspired by Marxism-Leninism, and free-market democracy championed by the USA. The defeat of Nazism and the militarism of Japan was accompanied by the US-proclaimed victory of democracy and the creation of the United Nations system. Though the 1947 UN General Assembly Resolution 110 (II) condemned 'all forms of propaganda which are designed or likely to provoke or encourage any threat to the peace, breach of the peace, or act of aggression', both camps indulged in regular propaganda as the battle lines of the cold war were being drawn (quoted in Taylor, 1997).

Soviet broadcast propaganda

In the same year, the Soviet Union revived the Comintern (Communist International) as Cominform (Communist Information Bureau), to organize a worldwide propaganda campaign orchestrated by the Administration of Agitation and Propaganda of the Communist Party Central Committee (AGITPROP). Communist propaganda, a central component of post-war Soviet diplomacy, was aimed primarily at the Eastern bloc and, increasingly, at what came to be known as the Third World.

During the cold war years, TASS remained a major source of news among the media in Eastern bloc countries. The news agency which began as the St Petersburg Telegraph Agency (SPTA) in 1904 underwent a number of name changes before becoming the Telegraph Agency of the Soviet Union (TASS) in 1925. In 1914 it was renamed the Petrograd Telegraph Agency (PTA) and in 1917, the Bolsheviks made the PTA the central news agency; a year later the PTA and the Press Bureau, also under the Council of People's Commissars, were united to form the Russian Telegraph Agency (ROSTA).

Soviet propaganda – in heavy polemical Marxist terms about the ideological clash between communism and imperialism – was couched in the language of the class struggle between the capitalist bourgeoisie and the global proletariat, ideas which fell on receptive ears in countries colonized by European powers.

However, one of the first major propaganda battles the Soviet Union waged was in 1948 against a fellow socialist country – Yugoslavia, where Marshal Tito's efforts to chart a foreign policy independent of dictates from Soviet leader, Joseph Stalin, resulted in a massive propaganda effort to overthrow the leadership in Belgrade. Another test of Soviet propaganda in Eastern Europe came with the crisis in Hungary in 1956, where it had to fight hostile Western propaganda and protect a client regime. Similarly, during the invasion of Czechoslovakia by Warsaw Pact countries under Moscow's orders, Russian broadcasts to Czechoslovakia jumped from 17 hours per week just before the August 1968 invasion to 168 at the height of the crisis, falling back to 84 by September (Hale, 1975: 24).

By the late 1960s, Moscow Radio was the world's largest single international broadcaster – between 1969 and 1972 it broadcast more programme hours than the United States. In addition, it used more languages – 84 – than any other international broadcaster, partly because the Soviet Union itself was a multilingual country. Between 1950 and 1973 external broadcasting from the Soviet Union grew from 533 hours to around 1950 hours per week. This is comparable with the whole of US external broadcasting – the world's largest – including the official Voice of America (VOA), and the clandestine Radio Liberty (RL) and Radio Free Europe (RFE) – at 497 hours per week in 1950 and 2060 in 1973 (Hale, 1975: 174).

Soviet broadcast policies were aimed at countering Western propaganda and promoting

Moscow's line on international affairs among the world's communist parties, which became increasingly important in Soviet thinking after the Sino-Soviet split of 1968. The Sino-Soviet split – more influenced by geostrategic than ideological differences – led to mutual propaganda battles between the communist giants, with Radio Moscow increasing its Chinese language broadcasts from 77 hours a week in 1967 to 200 hours in 1972, while China, which by the early 1970s had become the world's third largest international broadcaster, also increased its broadcasts criticizing Soviet 'revisionism'.

While Soviet broadcasts – known more for their party line than professional journalism – had little impact in the West, in contrast to the popularity of Western broadcasts in the Eastern bloc, they nevertheless set the news agendas in Eastern Europe. The Soviet presence was also evident in the way the news media were organized in many communist countries and among socialist nations of the South.

However, Radio Moscow was no match for Western broadcasters in terms of the power of its transmitters and the availability of broadcasting outlets outside the communist world. Apart from broadcasters in Eastern Europe, Soviet broadcasts had only one other outlet – Radio Habana in Cuba, which was suspended after the ending of the cold war. With their worldwide network of relay stations, the Western powers had a distinct advantage and were able to beam propaganda with little interference (Nelson, 1997). Since there was scant interest among Western populations for Russian international broadcasts, Western governments did not have to worry about jamming them. In contrast, the authorities in Moscow tried to interfere with Western broadcasts, seeing them as a network of 'radio saboteurs' subverting the achievements of socialism.

US broadcast propaganda

Although the Voice of America had been a part of US diplomacy during the Second World War, with the advent of the cold war, propaganda became a crucial component of US foreign broadcasting (Sorensen, 1968; Lisann, 1975; Rawnsley, 1996). The key instruments of US international broadcasting – Voice of America, Radio Liberty and Radio Free Europe, and the American Forces Network – were all state-funded. The VOA was the official mouthpiece of the US Government, the largest single element in the US Information Agency (USIA) and ultimately answerable to the US State Department. Unlike the BBC World Service, it depended on official comment as it only used VOA staff for commentaries, thereby restricting the range of opinions expressed by its programmes and thus straining its credibility as an international broadcaster.

An early indication of the increasing use of radio for propaganda was evident in the way VOA was used to promote US President Harry Truman's 'Campaign for Truth' against communism, following the outbreak in 1950 of the Korean War. The campaign was aimed at legitimizing US involvement in the Korean War, which claimed more than a million lives and became the first test of superpower rivalry in the developing world, a pattern repeated in several other cold war-related conflicts in Africa, Asia and Latin America.

A year later, in 1951, Truman set up a Psychological Strategy Board, responsible to the National Security Council, to advise on international anticommunist propaganda. In 1953, his successor President Dwight Eisenhower appointed a personal adviser on 'psychological warfare'

– resulting in an increased stridency in the anticommunist rhetoric emanating from VOA.

In the United States, propaganda was part of what John Martin, a former researcher for the USIA, called 'facilitative communication' which he defined as 'activity that is designed to keep lines open and to maintain them against the day when they will be needed for propaganda purposes' (Martin, 1976: 263). This included press releases, seminars, conferences and exhibitions, as well as books, films, educational and cultural exchange programmes and scholarships for technical and scientific research (Nincovich, 1981; Manheim, 1994).

VOA operated a global network of relay stations to propagate the ideal of 'the American way of life' to international listeners. The nodal points in this worldwide network linked to the control centre in Washington, included Bangkok for South East Asia; Poro and Tinang in the Philippines for China and South East Asia; Colombo for South Asia; Tangier in Morocco for North Africa; Rhodes in Greece for the Middle East; Selebi-Phikwe in Botswana for southern Africa; Monrovia in Liberia for sub-Saharan Africa; Munich for Eastern Europe and the former Soviet Union; Woofferton in England (leased from the BBC) for the former Soviet Union; Greenville in the USA for Latin America; and Punta Gorda in Belize for Central America (*see* map, p. 20).

The transmitters were chosen for their strategic locations, close to the target zone to ensure a stronger and more stable signal and to overcome possible jamming. In many instances the locations of transmitters remained a secret, as did the broadcasting of subversive and misleading information to confuse the West's cold war adversaries.

Case study

Covert communication – Radio Free Europe and Radio Liberty

Among the explicitly propagandist radio stations that thrived during the cold war were Radio Free Europe (RFE) and Radio Liberty (RL), operating from West Germany. While the Voice of America was the legitimate broadcasting arm of the United States Information Agency, the Munich-based RFE and RL were covert organizations carrying out a propaganda war against communism in Europe. They were part of what is now called 'psychological warfare' in which the 'campaign for truth' became the 'crusade for freedom'.

Free Europe Inc. was established in 1949 as a non-profit-making, private corporation to broadcast news and current affairs programmes to Eastern European countries behind the Iron Curtain. Radio Liberation (the name Radio Liberty was adopted in 1963) was created two years later along the same lines to broadcast to the Soviet Union (Mickelson, 1983).

Both were covertly funded by the US Government, mainly through the Central Intelligence Agency, until 1971, when funding and administrative responsibilities were transferred to a presidentially appointed Board for International

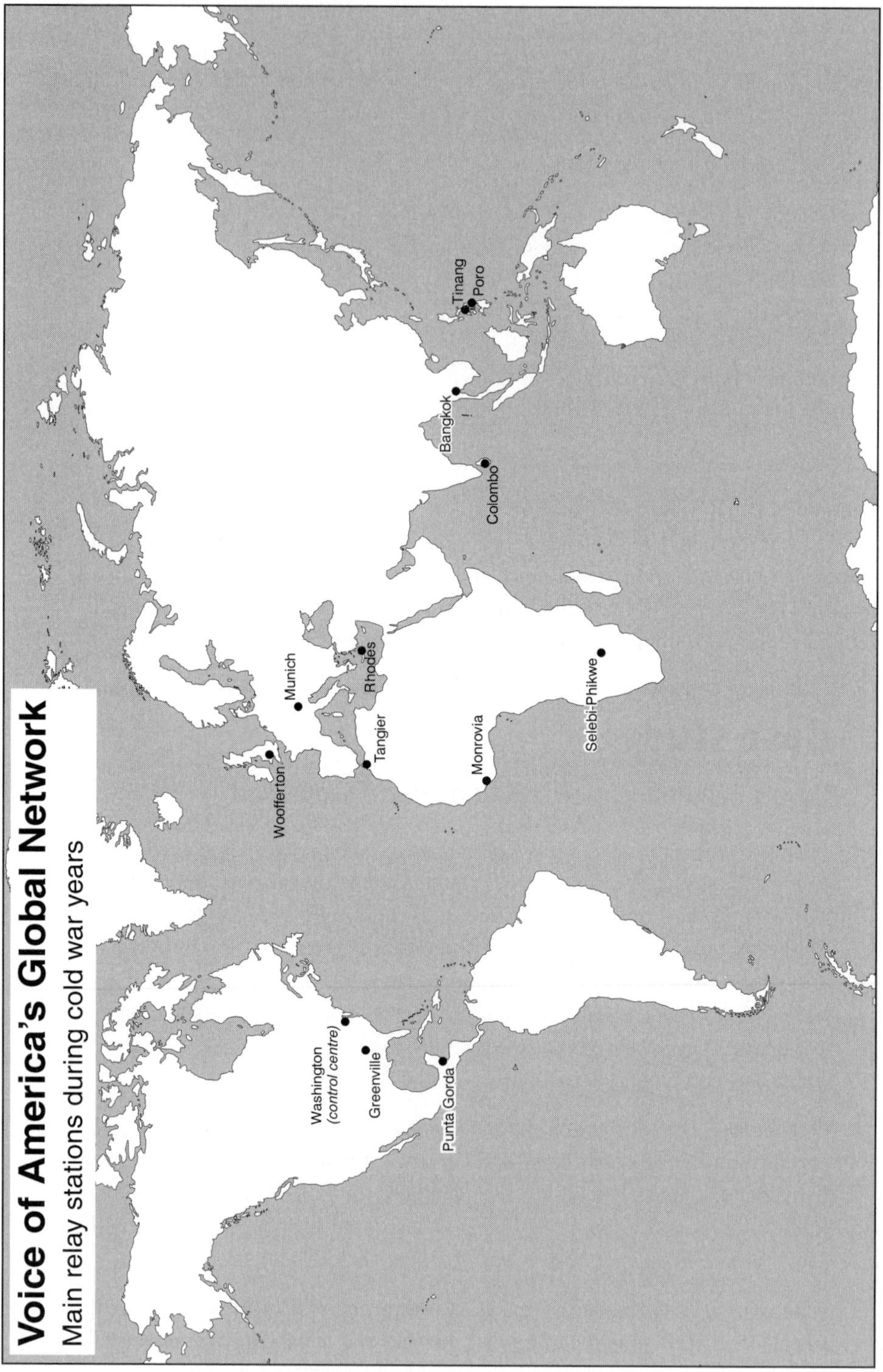

Voice of America's Global Network
Main relay stations during cold war years

Tinang
Poro
Bangkok
Colombo
Munich
Rhodes
Tangier
Monrovia
Selebi-Phikwe
Woofferton
Washington (control centre)
Greenville
Punta Gorda

Figure 1.2

Broadcasting (BIB). The two corporations were merged into RFE/RL in 1975. In 1994, its duties were transferred to the Broadcasting Board of Governors (BBG), which oversaw all non-military US international broadcasting.

Regular broadcasts of RFE began in 1951 and though RL was also established in 1951, it did not begin broadcasting until 1953. Both stations broadcast from studios in Munich: RFE using transmitters in Germany and Portugal for its programmes in Polish, Czech, Slovak, Romanian, Hungarian and Bulgarian; RL from transmitters in Germany, Spain and Taiwan for its programmes in Russian (over half the output) and 17 other languages spoken in the Soviet Union. Fighting communism was the *raison d'être* of these radio stations and therefore programmes were deliberately provocative to the communist governments, broadcasting émigré petitions and extracts from banned books, including works by anti-establishment writers like Alexander Solzhenitsyn and scientists such as Andrei Sakharov.

The often crude and insensitive propaganda broadcasts led to accusations from the Soviet Union of stirring up the 1956 revolt in Hungary. During the crisis, RFE encouraged the Hungarian people to rebel against the communist authorities, even misleading them with promises of the imminent arrival of a 'UN Delegation' – a euphemism for US military intervention – which never materialized, while the Soviet tanks crushed the uprising.

RFE and RL claimed to provide an alternative 'Home Service', intended to challenge the state or party monopoly over the media in the communist countries. The Soviet Union and other members of the Warsaw Pact regularly jammed RFE/RL's signals, denouncing them as a network of 'radio saboteurs', and an integral part of US 'electronic imperialism' (Kashlev, 1984).

Under US President Ronald Reagan's administration US public diplomacy became more strident and radio stations were directed to undertake a 'vigorous advocacy' of American foreign policy (Tuch, 1990). The Polish service of RFE played a key role in its support for Solidarity, the first 'independent' trade union in a communist country. During the industrial unrest of the 1980s, two-thirds of the Polish adult population tuned in and this level of penetration of Western radio was 'a major factor in the Soviets' decision not to intervene militarily in the country as they had in Czechoslovakia in 1968' (Lord, 1998: 62). In 1981, the Munich headquarters of RFE/RL were bombed, allegedly by Soviet secret services (ibid.).

In 1988 Soviet leader Mikhail Gorbachev ended the jamming, allowing RFE/RL signals to reach a broader audience. RFE/RL's contribution to the end of communism in this region is now widely acknowledged (McNamara, 1992; Sosin, 1999). As one broadcaster wrote: 'well before the Iron Curtain rusted – let alone was dismantled – its metal had been perforated by the sounds on the airwaves' (Partos, 1993: 91). Even the Russian President Boris Yeltsin personally intervened to help create an RFE/RL bureau in Moscow after the failed August 1991 coup. After many years in Munich, RFE/RL's headquarters moved to Prague in 1995.

It was only in the 1990s, after the end of the cold war, that these covert organizations came under public scrutiny, especially with the memoirs of George Urban, a former Director of Radio Free Europe (Critchlow, 1995; Urban, 1997). Because of RFE/RL's role in fighting communism, many thought that the radios had fulfilled their mission and might be disbanded. But officials across the region stressed the continuing need for precisely the kind of broadcasts RFE/RL had brought to this region. Nevertheless, RFE/RL did cut back in some areas even as it expanded in others. It closed its Polish Service, while its Czechoslovak Service was substantially reduced and joined with Czech Public Radio to establish a new public affairs radio programme. In 1994, RFE/RL began broadcasts to the former Yugoslavia, and in 1998, it launched its Persian Language Service and Radio Free Iraq. Such out-of-area activities were not new – during the years of the Soviet invasion of Afghanistan, RFE/RL established a bureau in Peshawar in Pakistan for propaganda purposes, and in 1984 a new service, Radio Free Afghanistan, was created within RL, broadcasting in two major languages of Afghanistan – Dari and Pashto (Lord, 1998: 64).

In 2006, RFE/RL was broadcasting for more than 1000 hours a week, in 29 languages to 35 million listeners, to countries stretching from Poland to the Pacific and from the Arctic to the Persian Gulf and 'providing an alternative "home service" to countries where the media are struggling amid chaotic economic conditions to achieve genuine financial and editorial independence' (www.rferl.org). RFE/RL maintains 22 bureaux across the region and has broadcasting links with more than 1000 freelancers and stringers. It uses short-wave broadcasts to reach its listeners, but increasingly it is utilizing AM/FM stations through more than 250 affiliate partners and more than 500 local radio stations in all its broadcast countries. In addition, RFE/RL maintains a multilingual website visited by millions every month.

Apart from Radio Free Europe and Radio Liberty, the United States supported other clandestine radio stations, such as Radio Free Russia, which aimed to use the Christian message to subvert atheistic states. It started operations in 1950 from South Korea and Taiwan as well as from West Germany. Run by the militantly anticommunist Popular Labour Union (NTS), this station also carried religious propaganda in Russian and in the Baltic languages, produced by a parallel organization, Radio Omega.

In addition to political propaganda, religious radio stations also contributed to the ideological battles against 'Godless communism'. One key player was Trans World Radio, which started transmitting the gospel message from Tangier in Morocco in 1954 and has since evolved into one of the world's largest radio networks, broadcasting in 75 languages. By the 1990s, it had an international network of transmitters located in every continent – Monte Carlo and Cyprus for Europe, the former Soviet Union and the Middle East; Swaziland for Africa; Sri Lanka for Asia; Guam for the Pacific region; and Montevideo in Uruguay for Latin America (Wood, 1992: 216).

With the disintegration of the Soviet Union and the collapse of the communist bloc, such propaganda outfits were struggling for a role and the funding for public diplomacy was constantly declining – by 2001 it consisted of less than 4 per cent of the US Government's overall international affairs budget. Despite the growing importance of television in implementing the foreign-policy agenda, the US Congress had reduced the budget for international broadcasting – from $844 million in 1993 to $560 million for 2004. In addition, in 1998 the USIA was merged into the State Department (Hoffman, 2002).

However, the attacks of 11 September 2001 in New York and Washington revived the need for public diplomacy, the main aim of which then became to understand the roots of anti-Americanism, especially among Arab and Muslim countries (Lennon, 2003). During the US invasion of Afghanistan in October 2001, Washington launched the round-the-clock Coalition Information Center, to manage news flow, later upgraded into a permanent Office of Global Communications, to co-ordinate public diplomacy. At the same time, a separate Pentagon Office of Strategic Influence was planned – though later scrapped – to wage secret 'information warfare', including distributing disinformation to foreign journalists.

In 2002, an Arabic-language popular music and news radio station, Radio Sawa ('Radio Together'), aimed at a younger Arab audience, was launched, as well as Radio Farda ('Radio Tomorrow' in Persian), which began transmitting into Iran. In 2004, the Middle East Television Network – Al-Hurra (Arabic for 'The Free One') started broadcasting from Springfield, Virginia, as well as from bureaux in the Middle East, funded to the tune of $102 million by the Broadcasting Board of Governors (BBG), a US federal agency that supervises all non-military international broadcasting.

The BBC

In contrast to US state propaganda, the BBC's External Services prided themselves on presenting a mature, balanced view, winning by argument, rather than hammering home a point, in the best tradition of British understatement. This proclaimed policy of 'balance' gave the BBC more international credibility than any other broadcasting organization in the world. The BBC's dependence on the British Government was evident, since its budget was controlled by the Treasury through grant-in-aid from the Foreign and Colonial Office (now called the Foreign and Commonwealth Office), which could also decide which languages were used for programmes and for how long they were broadcast to each audience. For example, during the Berlin blockade of 1948–49 almost the entire output of the BBC external services was directed to Eastern bloc countries. In addition, the government exerted indirect influence on the BBC since the relay stations and overseas transmitters were negotiated through or owned by the Diplomatic Wireless Service. What distinguished the BBC was its capacity to criticize its own government, however indirectly.

The 'special relationship' that characterized US/UK ties during the cold war years was also in evidence in the realm of international broadcasting. With the establishment of its Russian-language unit in 1946, the BBC World Service played a key part in the cold war through its strategically located global network of relay stations. These included: stations on Ascension Island and in Antigua (where it shared transmitters and relay station with the German radio station Deutsche Welle to cover the Western hemisphere); a multi-frequency broadcasting centre in Cyprus (for the Middle East, Europe and northern Africa); at Masirah, leased from Oman (for the Gulf region); in Seychelles (for east Africa); in Kranji in Singapore (for South East Asia); and in Hong Kong (for east Asia, especially China).

Other Western stations, such as Deutsche Welle and Radio France International (RFI), also contributed to the war of words. RFI, particularly strong in the former colonies of France, had two main relay stations – at Moyabi in Gabon and in Montsinery in French Guiana. In addition, it leased transmitting facilities from commercial Radio Monte Carlo in Cyprus to broadcast to the Middle East. Unlike Britain, France did not play such an important role in the cold war broadcasting battles – RFI was not jammed by the Soviet authorities. Concerned with maintaining its independent foreign policy and with a cultural focus, French international broadcasting concentrated on promoting its culture and commerce in its former colonies in Africa, the Middle East, the Caribbean and parts of the Pacific, not least to boost the export of French broadcasting equipment (Wood, 1992: 199).

Cold war propaganda in the Third World

Another major battle for the hearts and minds of people during the cold war was fought in the Third World, where countries were emerging from centuries of subjugation under European colonial powers. The Soviet Union had recognized that, since the nature of the anticolonial movements in Asia and Africa was largely anti-Western, the political situation was ripe for promoting communism. The West, on the other hand, was interested in continuing to control raw materials and develop potential markets for Western products. Radio was seen as a crucial medium, given the low levels of literacy among most of the population of the developing countries. In addition, the nascent media in the newly independent countries in Asia and Africa were almost always state-controlled and thus less able to compete with foreign media, with their higher credibility and technological superiority.

The Middle East was a particular target for Western broadcasters, given its geostrategic importance as the source of the world's largest supply of oil. It is no coincidence that the Arabic Service, created in 1938, was the first foreign-language section of the BBC's Empire Service, to be followed by the Persian Service in 1940. The French, British and American broadcasters dominated the airwaves in the Arab world, while the Arabic service of Kol Israel (the Voice of Israel) also played a key propaganda role in the Middle East. Western support for the conservative Arab countries and the feudal order they perpetuated was also reflected in the treatment of Arab radical nationalism in Western broadcasting.

The British Government used a Cyprus-based British commercial broadcaster, Sharq-al Adna, to broadcast 'Voice of Britain' anti-Egyptian propaganda, however, 'with little effect'

(Walker, 1992: 75). To counter this, Egyptian President Gamaal Nasser used the radio to promote the idea of pan-Arabism. The Cairo-based 'Voice of the Arabs' was an international service, which in the 1950s and 1960s became the 'pulpit of revolution', notably in the leftist revolution in Iraq in 1958.

Pan-Arab sentiment also helped the Palestinian 'liberation radios' which broadcast regularly and often clandestinely from PLO offices in Cairo, Beirut, Algiers, Baghdad and Tripoli, moving position to avoid Israeli attacks. These radios played an important role in keeping the Palestinian struggle alive. In Algeria, the Voice of Algeria, the radio station of the Front National de Libération (FNL), played an important role in the national war of liberation against the French colonial authorities. In the words of Frantz Fanon, the radio 'created out of nothing, brought the nation to life and endowed every citizen with a new status, *telling him so explicitly*' (Fanon, 1970: 80, italics in the original).

In Asia, in addition to direct broadcasts from the USA, VOA operated from Japan, Thailand (where the Voice of Free Asia was part of VOA) and Sri Lanka. Following the Chinese revolution in 1949, the US priority was to stop the expansion of communism into other parts of Asia. In 1951, the CIA funded the Manila-based Radio Free Asia, notable for its anticommunist stridency. It was later replaced by Radio of Free Asia which continued until 1966 (Taylor, 1997: 43).

During the Vietnam War, US propaganda reached new heights (Chandler, 1981; Hallin, 1986). The Joint US Public Office became the delegated authority for all propaganda activities, the chief aims of which were to undermine the support for communists and to keep the support of the South Vietnamese. These messages were conveyed mainly through dropping leaflets and broadcasting from low-flying aircraft. It is estimated that during the seven years it operated in Vietnam, the USIA, supported by the armed forces, dropped nearly 50 billion leaflets – nearly '1500 for every person in both parts of the country' (Chandler, 1981: 3). Radio played a crucial role in the psychological warfare. The CIA also ran Voice of the Patriotic Militiamen's Front in South Vietnam and two anti-Sukarno operations in Indonesia – Voice of Free Indonesia and Radio Sulawesi.

In Latin America, an area that the USA has traditionally regarded as its sphere of influence, US media propaganda has been intense, especially since the communist revolution in Cuba in 1959 led by Fidel Castro. During the 1962 Cuban missile crisis, President John Kennedy launched a virulent anti-Castro propaganda campaign with his *Alianza para el Progreso* programme, in what was, in the words of the former Director of VOA, George Allen, one of 'the largest concentrations of propaganda effort unleashed against an individual since Stalin tried to purge Tito in 1948' (quoted in Hale, 1975: 101). Unable to dislodge Castro from power and concerned that his success might promote anti-US sentiments in other parts of Latin America, the US Government resorted to using propaganda, notably with the introduction in 1983 of Radio Martí and, later, in 1990, of TV Martí, which Cuba considered a hostile act, violating its sovereignty (Alexandre, 1993).

Given its limited geostrategic importance in international relations, Africa remained a low priority area for cold war propaganda. However, as large areas of the continent were parts of the British Empire, the BBC had been broadcasting to Africa since 1940. In later years, the main broadcasting languages were English, French, Hausa, Portuguese and Swahili.

In the 1970s, VOA broadcast to Africa in English, French and Swahili, primarily to what were known locally as 'wa-benzi' (Mercedes-Benz owners, the African elite). Though Radio Moscow broadcast in several African languages – usually a translation of anti-imperialist material – its effectiveness was limited given the lack of communication infrastructure in many African countries. The Soviet Union invested in transmitters and training courses in Cameroon while the Chinese supported broadcasting in Zambia and Tanzania. Under the socialist government of President Julius Nyerere, Radio Tanzania became the nerve centre of liberation movements in southern Africa and played an important role in the anti-apartheid struggle. However, socialist radio stations were no match for the powerful transmitters of Western broadcasters, such as those for the BBC from Ascension Island and for VOA from Monrovia.

Broadcast propaganda was also used in areas where the cold war was often very hot, such as Angola, where US- and South Africa-backed UNITA (National Union for the Total Independence of Angola) rebels used their own radio station – The Voice of the Resistance of the Black Cockerel – which began broadcasting from South Africa in 1979 and was installed in Angola under the CIA's covert aid programme (Windrich, 1992).

Although developing countries were initially receptive to the Soviet message of freedom from colonialism, in the 1950s and 1960s, the economic power of the West and the dependency on colonial ties, coupled with the increasing influence of modernizing elites, meant that the attraction of communism was waning. As major developing countries, such as India, Indonesia and Egypt, opted for Non-Alignment – a movement founded in 1961 among developing countries which claimed to eschew cold war bloc politics, joining neither a Western nor Eastern alliance – a new perspective on international communication began to emerge. Looking beyond the cold war bipolarity, the Non-Aligned countries demanded that international communication issues be seen in terms of North–South rather than East–West categories.

International communication and development

For nearly half a century, the cold war divided the world into hostile East–West blocs. This had significant implications for the development of Third World countries, most of whom wanted to avoid bloc politics and concentrate on the economic emancipation of their populations. The phrase 'Third World' itself was a product of the cold war, said to have been coined by French economic historian Alfred Sauvy in 1952, when the world was divided between the capitalist First World, led by the United States, and the communist Second World, with its centre in Moscow. The 'Third World' was the mass of countries remaining outside these two blocs (Brandt Commission, 1981; South Commission, 1990).[1] National liberation movements in Asia, Africa and Latin America had altered the political map of the world. The vast territory occupied in 1945 by European colonial powers extended over 36 million sq. km; by 1960, as a result of decolonization, the area under colonial occupation had shrunk to 13 million sq. km. For the newly independent ex-colonial states, international communication opened up opportunities for development.

The Non-Aligned Movement, through the Group of 77, established in 1964, began to demand greater economic justice in such UN forums as UNCTAD, and in 1974, the UN

General Assembly formally approved their demand for the creation of a New International Economic Order (NIEO), a democratic, interdependent economic order, based on equality and sovereignty, including the right to 'pursue progressive social transformation that enables the full participation of the population in the development process' (Hamelink, 1979: 145). While this remained largely an ideal, it provided a new framework to redefine international relations, for the first time after the Second World War, not in terms of East–West categories, but by the North–South divide. At the same time, it was argued that the new economic order had to be linked to a New World Information and Communication Order (NWICO).

The general improvement in superpower relations in the age of détente, as marked by the 1975 Helsinki Conference on Security and Co-operation in Europe (CSCE), encouraged the Non-Aligned countries to demand these changes in global economic and informational systems. The conference recognized the need for 'freer and wider dissemination of information of all kinds' (Nordenstreng, 1986). As Chilean scholar Juan Somavia, writing in the mid-1970s, observed:

> It is becoming increasingly clear that the transnational communications system has developed with the support and at the service of the transnational power structure. It is an integral part of the system which affords the control of that key instrument of contemporary society: information. It is the vehicle for transmitting values and lifestyles to Third World countries which stimulate the type of consumption and the type of society necessary to the transnational system as a whole.
>
> (Somavia, 1976: 16–17)

Apart from highlighting the structural inequalities in international communication, there were also efforts made among many developing countries, often with financial or technical support from the West, to use communication technologies for development. This could take different forms – from promoting literacy and information about health care to spreading consumerism. One area which received particular attention from policy-makers was satellite television, which, given its reach, was considered a powerful medium that could be harnessed for educational purposes and, in the long run, to help change social and cultural attitudes of 'traditional' people and 'modernize' societies.

Case study

Satellite Instructional Television Experiment (SITE)

The use of modern technologies for development purposes was pioneered by the Indian Government when, in 1975, it launched the Satellite Instructional Television Experiment (SITE). The programme, supported by UNESCO, aimed to use satellite technology to assist development by transmitting daily programmes on health, agriculture and education to rural communities.

India's Department of Atomic Energy negotiated a deal with the US National Aeronautics and Space Administration (NASA), which loaned India one of its satellites, Applications Technology Satellite-6 (ATS-6), for a year to make these broadcasts in exchange for sharing the knowledge from the project.

The SITE programmes lasted from 1 August 1975 to 31 July 1976, and the estimated cost to India of the world's largest techno-social experiment was about $6.6 million. The government chose 2400 villages, selected from 20 districts of some of the poorest regions of six contiguous provinces – Orissa and Bihar in the east, Madhya Pradesh in central India, Rajasthan in the west and two southern states, Andhra Pradesh and Karnataka. Most of these villages had little existing communication infrastructure (Agrawal, 1978).

In each village a direct-reception system (DRS) television, a 25-inch, black-and-white set, was installed in a public place for community viewing. Signals were beamed from Ahmedabad and Delhi earth stations to ATS-6, which had a capacity of two audio and one video transmission signals. The use of direct reception systems eliminated the need for costly microwave relay towers. In addition, conventional television sets in 2500 villages and towns received the programmes through terrestrial transmitters.

Members of government institutions, such as the Indian Space Research Organisation (ISRO), teamed up with other experts from the areas of health, education, agriculture and development and the Satellite Television Wing of All India Radio, to produce the daily four-hour programming at three base production units located in Delhi, Cuttack and Hyderabad. The science-education programmes for schools were produced by Space Applications Centre's Ahmedabad and Bombay studios. Several international experts, including Wilbur Schramm, were also involved in the project.

Programmes were broadcast morning and evening in four languages – Hindi, Kannada, Oriya and Telugu. A 30-minute national programme in Hindi (partly live) was broadcast from Delhi for all villages, while the remaining three and a half hours were broadcast in region-specific languages. More than 80 per cent of the reception systems were functioning at any given time in the villages. The availability of visuals and sound generated much interest among the viewers, with a large numbers watching the first programmes, but gradually audience size stabilized to about 100 for the evening broadcast.

Inspired by the dominant paradigm of modernization theories of communication for development (Lerner 1958; Schramm, 1964, see Chapter 2, pp. 42–6) the project aimed to bring about behavioural changes among the rural communities and help them reject traditional social attitudes, which were seen as antithetical to the goals of modernization, but it also reflected current domestic political concerns. Among the primary objectives was to use television for population control – 'family planning' was a major priority for the government of Prime Minister Indira Gandhi.

Modernizing agricultural practices by using high-yielding seeds, pesticides and fertilizers – all part of the ongoing 'Green Revolution' – was another key plank of the programme. Attempts to improve school education, contribute to teacher training and improve health and hygiene were other main objectives of SITE. It is, however, ironical that this innovative project was in operation at a time Gandhi had imposed an Emergency, muzzling the press and arresting opposition leaders.

Of the four hours of programming, one and a half hours were targeted at children aged between 5 and 12 years, to be watched in schools as supplements to the regular school curriculum. The objective was to make learning more interesting through audio-visual teaching tools, hitherto unknown in most villages, and to reduce the drop-out rate, as well as to improve the children's basic skills and instil in them a sense of hygiene (Agrawal, 1978).

Another major objective of the SITE programmes was the development of agriculture, a key sector in a predominantly rural country. The aim was to disseminate relevant information, give demonstrations and provide advice on such matters as improved farming methods, pest control, crops management and poultry and animal husbandry. The programmes were also supposed to provide information about the district-level government organizations responsible for the supply of seeds, fertilizers and agricultural implements. In addition, programmes advised on crop marketing and commodity prices, agricultural credit schemes and had regular reports on weather forecasts. The agricultural programming constituted 30 minutes each day, for each linguistic group.

The third priority area was health care and birth control. Advice was given on nutrition and hygiene, as well as on pregnancy and post-natal care, a vital topic, given that thousands of women died in childbirth in India every year, especially in rural areas.

The programmes were more varied and imaginatively made than the standard fare on Indian television, and many organizations were involved in their preparation. Some programmes used techniques borrowed from traditional folk theatre to make their message accessible to the rural audience, while children's programming used puppets.

Despite such worthy objectives, the results were not very encouraging. A major two-volume report by ISRO evaluating the impact of the programmes recorded only 'modest gains' in the sphere of education, while there was no evidence that the introduction of television in the classrooms had affected drop-out rates. SITE villages showed only a 2–4 per cent higher adoption of birth control, although a year is not long enough to judge any tangible change in traditional attitudes towards 'family planning'. Also, given the community viewing patterns, where gender mixing was unavoidable, women in the age range of 15–24 were discouraged from watching.

There was also little evidence that television viewing had made any significant increase in farmers' knowledge about agricultural practices or a change in attitude towards crop patterns. Anthropological findings, however, indicated that there were subtle social and cultural changes, based on gender, caste and class in the rural setting (Agrawal, 1977).

The advice on crop patterns, the use of pesticides and high-yield seeds was mostly of use to rich farmers with the money to buy new seeds and other agricultural implements. In a country where land distribution is highly skewed in favour of rich farmers, such advice was of little consequence to the poor majority, whose condition could hardly be improved without wider structural changes in the social system. In such desperately poor rural communities, where the majority of inhabitants are landless farmers, school enrolment and drop-out rates, and awareness about health and hygiene, depend primarily on economic factors. Even today, in rural India, many children have to work on the farms, rather than attend school, to supplement their families' meagre incomes.

The government's view was that television would be a key instrument to disseminate development-oriented information and generate public participation and support for social and economic modernization. However, SITE showed that TV played only a limited role in changing behaviour among the audience and instead resulted in indifference towards the medium as well as the message itself. In the absence of relevant and effective complementary support in the lives of the viewers, innovative communication and the use of satellite technology were merely information inputs which in rural India remained little more than a high-sounding idea. Despite its top-down approach to communication and the dissemination of information, the tendency to privilege rural elites and insensitivity to the needs of the rural poor, SITE did create awareness about social problems and brought the experience of audio-visual media to rural communities.

The experiment came to an end when NASA withdrew its satellite, reflecting the dependence of the South on the technology of the North. However, this spurred the Indian government to sanction the development of an indigenous satellite technology, with India becoming one of the first Southern countries to invest heavily in satellite communication. India's first communication satellite, Indian National Satellite (INSAT-1A), was launched in 1982, providing Doordarshan with transponders for networking. The more advanced INSAT satellites increased the capacity to transmit satellite-based programmes for schoolchildren across the country, though their viewership remained very low.

With the gradual commercialization of television in India in the 1980s and 1990s, development-oriented programming became a low priority area, even for state-run broadcasters. For private television companies, both domestic and international, driven by advertising demand, the rural poor are not demographically desirable viewers, and health, education and rural development do not make profitable television. By 2006, India had one of the most sophisticated satellite networks in the developing world, but it was being used more to promote entertainment than to address the development agenda. Yet SITE was one of the more significant examples of using modern technologies for developmental purposes.

The demand for a New World Information and Communication Order

The international information system, the NWICO protagonists argued, reinforced and perpetuated inequality in development, with serious implications for the countries of the South, which were heavily dependent on the North for both software and hardware in the information sector. It was argued by Third World leaders that through their control of major international information channels, the Western media gave an exploitative and distorted view of their countries to the rest of the world.

The existing order, they contended, because of its structural logic, had created a model of dependence, with negative effects on the polity, economy and society of developing countries. Their demands were articulated by Tunisian Information Minister Mustapha Masmoudi, who was later a member of the MacBride Commission. The chief complaints from the long litany of the Third World demands were as follows:

- owing to the socio-technological imbalance there was a one-way flow of information from the 'centre' to the 'periphery,' which created a wide gap between the 'haves' and the 'have nots';
- the information rich were in a position to dictate terms to the information poor, thus creating a structure of dependency with widespread economic, political and social ramifications for the poor societies;
- this vertical flow (as opposed to a desirable horizontal flow of global information) was dominated by the Western-based transnational corporations;

- information was treated by the transnational media as a 'commodity' and subjected to the rules of the market;
- the entire information and communication order was a part of and in turn propped up international inequality that created and sustained mechanisms of neo-colonialism.

(Masmoudi, 1979: 172–3)

Masmoudi argued that there existed a 'flagrant quantitative imbalance between North and South created by the volume of news and information emanating from the developed world and intended for the developing countries and the volume of the flow in the opposite direction'.

He contended that gross inequalities also existed between developed and developing countries in the distribution of the radio-frequency spectrum, as well as in the traffic of television programmes. He saw:

a de facto hegemony and a will to dominate – evident in the marked indifference of the media in the developed countries, particularly in the West, to the problems, concerns and aspirations of the developing countries. Current events in the developing countries are reported to the world via the transnational media; at the same time, these countries are kept 'informed' of what is happening abroad through the same channels.

(ibid)

According to Masmoudi, 'by transmitting to developing countries only news processed by them, that is, news which they have filtered, cut, and distorted, the transnational media impose their own way of seeing the world upon the developing countries' (1979: 172–3).

These structural problems were also echoed by other scholars who viewed the Western-dominated, international information system, with its origins in the international news media network, as geared to Western economic and political interests and projecting their version of reality through these global networks to the rest of the world (Harris, 1981: 357–8).

The demands and proposals for an NWICO emerged from a series of meetings of the Non-Aligned Movement, most notably in Algiers in 1973 and in Tunis in 1976. A landmark was reached with the Mass Media Declaration by the UNESCO General Conference in 1978, which recognized the role the mass media played in development; and in December of that year, the 33rd session of the United Nations General Assembly adopted a resolution on the New World Information and Communication Order (NWICO).

As a result, in 1979 the International Commission for the Study of Communication Problems was set up. The MacBride Commission, as it was popularly known, submitted its final report to UNESCO in 1980, a document which, for the first time, brought information- and communication-related issues on to the global agenda.

The MacBride Commission

The International Commission for the Study of Communication Problems that was established under the chairmanship of Sean MacBride by UNESCO occupies a prominent place in the debate regarding the establishment of an NWICO. The Commission report, commonly known as the MacBride Report, gave intellectual justification for evolving a new global communication order. For this reason the NWICO protagonists considered it to be a seminal document. The Commission was created in 1977 as a direct response to Resolution 100 of the 19th General Session of UNESCO held in Nairobi in 1976. The Commission took two years, after going through 100 working papers especially commissioned for it, to bring out an interim and a final report in 1980.

The Commission had the following 16 members: Sean MacBride, chairman (Ireland), Elie Abel (USA), Hubert Beuve-Mery (France), Elebe Ma Ekonzo (Zaire), Gabriel García Márquez (Colombia), Mochtar Lubis (Indonesia), Mustapha Masmoudi (Tunisia), Betty Zimmerman (Canada), Michio Nagai (Japan), Fred Isaac Akporuaro Omu (Nigeria), Bogdan Osolnik (Yugoslavia), Gamal el Oteifi (Egypt), Johannes Pietar Pronk (Netherlands), Juan Somavia (Chile), Boobli George Verghese (India) and Leonid Zamatin (USSR) (Zamatin was replaced by Sergei Losev during the study).

The Commission was established to study four main aspects of global communication: the current state of world communication; the problems surrounding a free and balanced flow of information and how the needs of the developing countries link with the flow; how, in light of the NIEO, an NWICO could be created; and how the media could become the vehicle for educating public opinion about world problems.

The interim report generated a good deal of controversy as it tended to legitimize the movement towards the establishment of an NWICO. It levelled charges against the Western wire services for their inadequate coverage of the Third World. The 100 background papers that the Commission prepared generated international interest in the NWICO and helped provide insights into the various dimensions of the problems of a global information system. This enriched the debate and raised its standard from mere rhetoric to a more rigorous criticism of international inequity in media relations.

Among its 82 recommendations that covered the entire range of global communication issues, the most innovative were those dealing with democratization of communication (MacBride Report, 1980: 191–233). The Commission agreed that democratization was impeded by undemocratic political systems, bureaucratic administrative systems, technologies controlled or understood only by a few, the exclusion of disadvantaged groups, and illiteracy and semi-literacy. To break through these barriers, the Commission recommended many steps, including:

> participation in media management by representatives of the public and various citizens groups, horizontal communication, counter-information and three forms of alternative communication: radical opposition, community or local media movements and trade unions or other social groups with their particular communication networks.

(MacBride Report, 1980)

Following the UNESCO definition of 'a free flow and a wider and more balanced dissemination of information', the MacBride Report related freedom of the press to freedom of expression, to the rights to communicate and receive information, rights of reply and correction, and the civil political economic-social-cultural rights set forth in the UN's 1966 covenants. The MacBride Report pointed out that the freedom for the 'strong' and the 'haves' had had undesirable consequences for the 'weak' and the 'have nots'. It called for abolition of 'censorship or arbitrary control of information', asking for 'self-censorship by communicators themselves'. The report was critical of the constraints imposed by commercialization, pressures from advertisers and concentration of media ownership. It related the growth of transnational corporations to 'one way flow', 'market dominance' and 'vertical flow'.

It pointed out that some of the strongest transnational corporations, while vociferous for freedom for themselves, were reluctant to open up flows to share scientific and technological information. The Commission charged that under the guise of the free flow of information, some governments and transnational media had 'on occasion tried to undermine internal stability in other countries, violating their sovereignty and disturbed national development'.

The MacBride Report, which was hailed as 'the first international document that provides a really global view on the world's communication problems', received a mixed response. The protagonists of NWICO generally welcomed the report while the West criticized it. The World Press Freedom Committee (WPFC), consisting of journalistic organizations including the International Federation of Journalists, AP, UPI and the American Newspaper Publishers Association (ANPA), was critical of what it considered to be the report's bias against private ownership of media and communication facilities and the 'problems created in a society by advertising' (Singh and Gross, 1981).

Following the submission of the report of the MacBride Commission, at the 21st General Conference Session of UNESCO held in Belgrade in 1980, a resolution for the attainment of an NWICO was passed, thereby formally approving the demand. The resolution proposed:

(i) elimination of the imbalance and inequalities which characterize the present situation;

(ii) elimination of the negative effects of certain monopolists, public or private, and excessive concentrations;

(iii) removal of the internal and external obstacles to a free flow and wider and better balanced dissemination of information and ideas;

(iv) plurality of sources and channels of information;

(v) freedom of the press and information;

(vi) the freedom of journalists and all professionals in the communication media, a freedom inseparable from responsibility;

(vii) the capacity of developing countries to achieve improvement of their own situations, notably by providing their own equipment, by training their personnel, by improving their infrastructures and by making their information and communication media suitable to their needs and aspirations;

(viii)   the sincere will of developed countries to help them attain these objectives;

(ix)   respect for each people's cultural identity and for the rights of each nation to inform the world public about its interests, its aspirations and its social and cultural values;

(x)   respect for the right of all peoples to participate in international exchange of information on the basis of equality, justice and mutual benefit;

(xi)   respect for the right of the public, of ethnic and social groups and of individuals to have access to information sources and to participate actively in the communication process.

(UNESCO, 1980)

Opposition to NWICO

The West, led by the USA, saw in the new order a 'Soviet-inspired' Third World design to control the mass media through state regulation. As a concept it was seen as one fundamentally in conflict with liberal Western values and the principle of the 'free flow of information'. The Western response was also affected by the cold war assumptions which made them place the issues regarding the problems of global news flow in the context of East–West rivalry.

The opponents of NWICO argued that the demand for NWICO was a pretext for Third World dictators to stifle media freedom, to impose censorship and keep away foreign journalists. Such slogans as 'cultural self-determination', 'media imperialism' and 'national sovereignty over a country's communications', they argued, were designed to control channels of communication. The Western news organizations stoutly fought any change in the old information order. They maintained that they were only reporting the reality of life in the Third World – political instability, economic backwardness, human and natural disasters – and that this objective journalism was disapproved of by undemocratic governments in the South.

Many Western observers claimed that UNESCO, the site of those heated debates, was neglecting its true objectives by sponsoring this Third World encroachment on international information and communication. Even the MacBride Commission, which had members from both developed and developing countries, was criticized for providing an intellectual justification for the reform of international communication (Righter, 1978; Jeffrey, 1978; Stevenson, 1988).

The comments of one US observer were typical of this: 'The administration's lack of vigorous opposition to the UNESCO/Soviet/Third World's campaign for the total take-over of all means of communication is an indication that the US is abandoning its traditional values of freedom and opposition to totalitarianism' (Jeffrey, 1978: 67). The Western media viewed the NWICO demands of 'national communication policies', 'national sovereignty over information' and 'democratisation of communications' as 'entailing too interventionist a role for the state and also as likely to result in the exclusion of foreign journalists, with consequent restriction of information flows' (Wells, 1987: 27).

A closer scrutiny of the arguments against NWICO put forward by Western governments and the media reveals that the entire debate was seen only in terms of the threat to the 'freedom of the Press' posed by Third World governments under the new order. As Colleen Roach comments:

> To state that virtually every NWICO-related issue or subject ('social responsibility of the press', 'protection of journalists', 'right to communicate', etc.) was reduced to the slogan of 'government control of the media' is no exaggeration. The reason for this strategy is not merely the US predilection for over-simplification of complex issues, or even the historical commitment to the First Amendment, although these factors are certainly not to be neglected. The emphasis on the 'government control' argument reflects, above all, the need to ensure that the NWICO would not reinforce government-run public sector communications media at the expense of the private sector.
>
> (Roach, 1987: 38)

In the 1970s, when the superpower relations were relatively stable, the New World Information and Communication Order was seen by Southern leaders as an integral part of an ongoing North–South dialogue. Under President Jimmy Carter, for whom defence of human rights was a matter of personal commitment, the US administration appeared to take a favourable view of the problems faced by developing countries. Facing opposition from domestic conservative quarters, which found confusion and contradictions in Carter's human rights campaigns, limited progress was made in this North–South dialogue. However, the Carter administration played an important part in launching UNESCO's International Programme for the Development of Communications (IPDC). The fall of the Shah of Iran in 1979 as a result of anti-Western Islamic revolution, and the Soviet military intervention in Afghanistan in the same year, not only denied Carter a second term in office, but also signified the abandonment of the North–South dialogue and the advent of the new cold war.

NWICO and the new cold war

Riding on a crest of Conservatism which thrived on anti-Soviet rhetoric, President Ronald Reagan redrafted the international agenda, dominated by ideas of a new phase in the cold war. On the world stage, Margaret Thatcher's Conservative government in London became an important partner in this venture. The Reagan administration announced significant restrictions on development aid. 'Trade not Aid' became the catchphrase, and the assistance that was provided was to be primarily bilateral and aimed at promoting developmental projects designed to build up the private sector in developing countries.

With regard to the information debate, which had gained momentum, the Reagan administration followed the same hard-line policies. Reagan's tough line was responsible for cuts in the US allocation for various communication development programmes for the Third World undertaken by the IPDC. Under Reagan's presidency, the attacks on multilateral communication organizations, notably UNESCO, became more strident, culminating in the US withdrawal from the UN body in 1985, followed a year later by Britain. The USA opposed the MacBride Commission Report, arguing that it sought to give control of mass media to Southern governments. It would appear that the US decision was also influenced by business interests, as the memorandum of the State Department made clear: 'the divorce from UNESCO may well foster a greater willingness on the part of the US business and industry interests to support communications development projects' (Harley, 1984: 96).

Despite being the driving force behind IPDC, the USA tried to undermine the programme, demanding a greater freedom for US-based media and telecommunication corporations to explore Southern markets and help build privately owned communication infrastructure as opposed to government telecommunication monopolies (McPhail, 1987; Preston *et al.*, 1989).

The fate of IPDC projects reflected a wider ideological shift under the Reagan-Thatcher era of right-wing governments in the 1980s, from a public service view of media and telecommunication to a privatized and deregulated industry. The 'free flow of information' doctrine, which had defined US policy during the cold war years, received a new fillip with the neo-liberal ideology of the 'free market', expounded by ideologues such as Milton Friedman in the USA and Keith Joseph in Britain.

US communications policy during the Reagan years reflected the goals of US foreign policy. Reagan's self-proclaimed mission of fighting communism, enhanced by the US capacity to exercise control over the world information-communication order and its ability to disseminate a pro-American, anti-Soviet message globally, set the tone for an aggressive public diplomacy. In a sense, Reagan was repeating the 1950s' cold war propaganda effort, when the American media were harnessed, together with the military-industrial complex, to give ideological justification to US foreign policy. Thus, public diplomacy was geared to face the new communist threat and save the 'free world' from the encirclement of the Soviet Union. The International Information Committee (IIC) was established to 'plan, co-ordinate and implement international information activities in support of US policies and interests relative to national security'. Under the IIC, 'Project Truth' was set up, a campaign of an ideological war against the 'evil empire', an effort between the US Information Agency, the Departments of State and Defense and the CIA (Alexandre, 1993: 33).

In order to propagate this message abroad, the Reagan administration strengthened the Voice of America, as well as Radio Free Europe and Radio Liberty. The government started a $1.5 billion VOA modernization programme: additional languages were included and its broadcasting hours were increased. One notable addition was the creation of Radio Martí, the VOA's daily broadcasting service to Cuba (Alexandre, 1993).

International communication at the end of the cold war

If the East–West ideological battle characterized the cold war years of international communication, the fall of the Berlin Wall in 1989 and the break-up of the Soviet Union two years later transformed the landscape of international politics, profoundly influencing global information and communication (Nordenstrang and Schiller, 1993).

Television played an important role during the 1989 revolutions in Eastern Europe, helping to bring the East–West ideological division of Europe to a close. The transition to capitalism was largely peaceful, except in Romania, where at least some of the violence was simulated. The 1989 Timisoara massacre in Romania was ostensibly staged for the world's TV cameras, in what the French sociologist Jean Baudrillard called 'a hijacking of fantasies, affects and the credulity of hundreds of millions of people by means of television' (1994: 69).

The August 1991 coup in Moscow, which led to the break-up of the Soviet Union, was called 'the first true media event in the history of the Soviet Union'. The crisis had been 'profoundly and decisively shaped by the electronic eye that transformed instantly and continuously, elements of a political confrontation into meaningful scripts with their corresponding images, styles, and symbols' (Bonnell and Freidin, 1995: 44). Since the break-up of the Soviet Union, the media in the Eastern bloc countries have gradually been converted to the market (Splichal, 1994; Mickiewicz, 1997).

The end of the cold war, variously celebrated as the dawn of a 'new world order', as 'end of history' (Fukuyama, 1992) and even a 'clash of civilizations' (Huntington, 1993), profoundly changed the contours of international communication. The superpower rivalry had ended and the bipolar world, which had informed debates on international communication for half a century, suddenly had become unipolar, dominated by the remaining superpower, the United States.

Such Russian words as glasnost (openness) and perestroika (restructuring) entered the world's media vocabulary, representing a fundamental change in Moscow's thinking towards the entire gamut of international relations. The globalization of glasnost contributed to a greater openness in international communication, with Western journalists operating freely from behind the former Iron Curtain. The stridency of anti-Western rhetoric was also becoming muted in Moscow, while in the West, doubts were being raised about the relevance of Radio Free Europe and Radio Liberty (Elliot, 1988; Woll, 1989; *Time,* 1988).

This shift also affected debates on international information flows within UNESCO, which in the late 1980s had lost its primacy as the key forum for discussing international communication issues. The focus of debate too had shifted from news and information flows to such areas as global telecommunication and transnational data flows. The Paris-based Organization for Economic Cooperation and Development (OECD) – with its concern about trans-border data flow and the International Telecommunication Union (ITU), through its Maitland Commission Report – and the IPDC were becoming increasingly important international fora (Renaud, 1986). The Maitland Report, which symbolized the change in the traditional role of ITU from being a technical group to a more activist organization, gave higher priority to investment in telecommunication, especially telephones (Ellinghaus and Forrester, 1985).[2]

Another key contributing factor was the availability of new information technologies such as direct broadcasting satellites (DBS), fibre optics and microcomputers. The growing convergence between information and informatics – the combination of computer and telecommunication systems, traditionally dealt with as separate entities – made it essential to re-examine international communication in the light of technological innovations.

As the public ownership of state assets model, represented in its extreme form in the Soviet system, was dismantled, privatization became the new mantra, with the opening up of new markets in Eastern Europe and the former Soviet Union adding urgency to the privatization project. The globalization of communication was made possible with the innovation of new information and communication technologies, increasingly integrated into a privatized global communication infrastructure. The 'time–space compression' that new technologies encouraged made it possible for media and telecommunication corporations to operate in a global market, part of an international neo-liberal capitalist system. As discussed in Chapter 3, the privatization of international communication industries became a major development of the 1990s, accelerated by the liberalization of global trade, under the auspices of the General Agreement on Tariffs and Trade (GATT).

Notes

1. The countries of Asia, Africa and Latin America were also the 'non-industrialized', 'underdeveloped' or 'developing countries'. The term 'the South' gained currency in the 1980s after the Brandt Commission Report which defined 'the South' thus: 'in general terms, and although neither is a uniform or permanent grouping, "North" and "South" are broadly synonymous with "rich" and "poor," "developed" and "developing".' (Brandt Commission Report, 1981, p. 31). This division was later reinforced by the South Commission, adding, 'while countries of the North are, by and large, in control of their destinies, those of the South are very vulnerable to external factors and lacking in functioning sovereignty' (South Commission, 1990: 1).

2. The Independent Commission for World-wide Telecommunication Development, the 17-member commission headed by Sir Donald Maitland of the UK, was established in 1983 by the ITU to recommend ways to stimulate the expansion of global telecommunications. It submitted its report in 1985 (ITU, 1985).

chapter two

Approaches to theorizing international communication

Theories have their own history and reflect the concerns of the time in which they were developed. This chapter examines some that offer ways of approaching the subject of international communication and assesses how useful their explanations are in terms of an understanding of the processes involved. This is by no means a comprehensive account of theories of communication (see Mattelart and Mattelart, 1998; McQuail, 2005), nor does it set out an all-embracing theorization of the subject, but looks at the key theories and their proponents that, together with the preceding chapter on the history of international communication, should help to contextualize the analysis of contemporary global communication systems in subsequent chapters.

It is not surprising that theories of communication began to emerge in parallel with the rapid social and economic changes of the Industrial Revolution in Europe, reflecting the significance of the role of communications in the growth of capitalism and empire, and drawing also on advances in science and the understanding of the natural world. One of the first concepts of communication, developed by the French philosopher Claude Henri de Saint Simon (1760–1825), used the analogy of the living organism, proposing that the development of a system of communication routes (roads, canals and railways) and a credit system (banks) was vital for an industrializing society, and that the circulation of money, for example, was equivalent to that of blood for the human heart (Mattelart and Mattelart, 1998).

The metaphor of the organism was also fundamental for British philosopher, Herbert Spenser (1820–1903), who argued that industrial society was the embodiment of an 'organic society', an increasingly coherent, integrated system, in which functions become more and more specified and parts more interdependent. Communication was seen as a basic component in a system of distribution and regulation. Like the vascular system, the physical network of roads, canals and railways ensured the distribution of nutrition, while the channels of information (the press, telegraph and postal service) functioned as the equivalent of the nervous system, making it possible for the centre to 'propagate its influence' to its outermost parts. 'Dispatches are compared to nervous discharges that communicate movement from an inhabitant of one city to that of another' (Mattelart and Mattelart, 1998: 9). At the same time, contemporary commentators were anxious about the social and cultural impact of the speed and reach of the new means of communication and the rise of a mass society fuelled and sustained by them.

In the twentieth century, theories of international communication evolved into a discrete discipline within the new social sciences and in each era have reflected contemporary concerns about political, economic and technological changes and their impact on society and culture. In the early twentieth century, during and after the First World War, a debate arose about the role of communication in propagating the competitive economic and military objectives of the imperial powers, exemplified in the work of Walter Lippmann on 'public opinion' (1922) and Harold Lasswell on wartime propaganda (1927). Lippmann's concerns were mainly about the manipulation of public opinion by powerful state institutions, while Lasswell, a political scientist, did pioneering work on the systematic analysis of propaganda activities.

After the Second World War, theories of communication multiplied in response to new developments in technology and media, first radio and then television, and the increasingly integrated international economic and political system. Two broad but often interrelated approaches to theorizing communication can be seen: the political-economy approach, which was concerned with the underlying structures of economic and political power relations, and that of cultural studies, which focused more on the role of communication and media in creating and maintaining shared values and meanings (Golding and Murdoch, 1997; Durham and Kellner, 2006).

The political-economy approach has its roots in the critique of capitalism produced by the German philosopher, Karl Marx (1818–83), but it has evolved over the years to incorporate a wide range of critical thinkers. Central to a Marxian interpretation of international communication is the question of power, which ultimately is seen as an instrument of control by the ruling classes. In his seminal text, *German Ideology*, Marx described the relationship between economic, political and cultural power thus:

> The class which has the means of material production has control at the same time over the means of mental production so that, thereby, generally speaking, the ideas of those who lack the means of mental production are subject to it ... Insofar, therefore, as they rule as a class and determine the extent and compass of an epoch, it is self-evident that they ... among other things ... regulate the production and distribution of the ideas of their age: thus their ideas are the ruling ideas of the epoch.

> (cited in Murdoch and Golding, 1977: 12–13)

Much of the critical research on international communication has been an examination of the pattern of ownership and production in the media and communication industries, analysing these within the overall context of social and economic power relations, based on national and transnational class interests. Researchers working within the Marxist tradition are concerned, for example, with the commodification of communication hardware and software and inequalities of access to media technologies.

By the late twentieth century, the growing literature of cultural studies had become increasingly influential in the field of international communication. Social science analyses of mass communication were enriched by concepts from the study of literature and the humanities. Cultural studies, which started in Britain in the 1970s with the study of popular and mass culture and their role in the reproduction of social hegemony and inequality, is now more generally concerned with how media texts work to create meaning (on the basis of analysis of the texts themselves), and how culturally situated individuals work to gather meaning from texts (increasingly based on observation of media consumers). Cultural studies' discovery of polysemic texts (the potential for readers to generate their own meanings) fitted well with a politically conservative era and the reinvigoration of liberal capitalism which accompanied it.

'Free flow of information'

After the Second World War and the establishment of the bipolar world of free market capitalism and state socialism, theories of international communication became part of the new cold war discourse. For the supporters of capitalism, the primary function of international communication was to promote democracy, freedom of expression and markets, while the Marxists argued for greater state regulation on communication and media outlets.

The concept of the 'free flow of information' reflected Western, and specifically US, antipathy to the state regulation and censorship of the media by its communist opponents and its use for propaganda. The 'free flow' doctrine was essentially a part of the liberal, free-market discourse that championed the rights of media proprietors to sell wherever and whatever they wished. As most of the world's media resources and media-related capital, then as now, were concentrated in the West, it was the media proprietors in Western countries, their governments and national business communities that had most to gain.

The concept of 'free flow' therefore served both economic and political purposes. Media organizations of the media-rich countries could hope to dissuade others from erecting trade barriers to their products or from making it difficult to gather news or make programmes on their territories. Their argument drew on premises of democracy, freedom of expression, the media's role as 'public watchdog' and their assumed global relevance. For their compatriot businessmen, 'free flow' assisted them in advertising and marketing their goods and services in foreign markets, through media vehicles whose information and entertainment products championed the Western way of life and its values of capitalism and individualism.

For Western governments, 'free flow' helped to ensure the continuing and unreciprocated influence of Western media on global markets, strengthening the West in its ideological battle with the Soviet Union. The doctrine also contributed to providing, in generally subtle rather than direct ways, vehicles for communication of US government points of view to international audiences (UNESCO, 1982; Mosco, 1996; Mowlana, 1997).

Modernization theory

Complementary to the doctrine of 'free flow' in the post-war years was the view that international communication was the key to the process of modernization and development for the so-called Third World. Modernization theory arose from the notion that international mass communication could be used to spread the message of modernity and transfer the economic and political models of the West to the newly independent countries of the South. Communications research on what came to be known as 'modernization' or 'development theory' was based on the belief that the mass media would help transform traditional societies. This pro-media bias was very influential and received support from international organizations such as UNESCO and from the governments in developing countries.

One of the earliest exponents of this theory was Daniel Lerner, a political science professor at the Massachusetts Institute of Technology, whose classic work in the field, *The Passing of Traditional Society* (1958) – the product of research conducted in the early 1950s in Turkey, Lebanon, Egypt, Syria, Jordan and Iran – examined the degree to which people in the Middle East were exposed to national and international media, especially radio. In this first major comparative survey, Lerner proposed that contact with the media helped the process of transition from a 'traditional' to a 'modernized' state, characterizing the mass media as a 'mobility multiplier', which enables individuals to experience events in far-off places, forcing them to reassess their traditional way of life. Exposure to the media, Lerner argued, made traditional societies less bound by traditions and made them aspire to a new and modern way of life.

The Western path of 'development' was presented as the most effective way to shake off traditional 'backwardness'. According to Lerner:

> [The] Western model of modernisation, exhibits certain components and sequences whose relevance is global. Everywhere, for example, increasing urbanisation has tended to raise literacy; rising literacy has tended to increase media exposure; increasing media exposure has 'gone with' wider economic participation (per capita income) and political participation.
>
> (Lerner, 1958: 46)

Western society, Lerner argued, provided 'the most developed model of societal attributes (power, wealth, skill, rationality)', and 'from the West came the stimuli which undermined traditional society that will operate efficiently in the world today…' (ibid.: 47).

Another key modernization theorist, Wilbur Schramm, whose influential book, *Mass Media and National Development*, was published in 1964 in conjunction with UNESCO, saw the mass media as a 'bridge to a wider world', as the vehicle for transferring new ideas and models from the North to the South and, within the South, from urban to rural areas. Schramm, at the time Director of the Institute for Communication Research at Stanford University, California, noted:

> the task of the mass media of information and the 'new media' of education is to speed and ease the long, slow social transformation required for economic development, and, in particular, to speed and smooth the task of modernising human resources behind the national effort.
>
> (Schramm, 1964: 27)

Schramm endorsed Lerner's view that mass media can raise the aspirations of the peoples in developing countries. The mass media in the South, he wrote, 'face the need to rouse their people from fatalism and a fear of change. They need to encourage both personal and national aspirations. Individuals must come to desire a better life than they have and to be willing to work for it' (ibid. 1964: 130).

The timing of Schramm's book was significant. The UN had proclaimed the 1960s as 'the Decade of Development' and UN agencies and Western governments, led by the USA, were generously funding research, often in conjunction with private companies, through universities and development bureaucracy, notably the newly established United States Agency for International Development (USAID), the United States Information Agency (USIA) and the Peace Corps, to harness the power of the mass media to 'modernize' the newly independent countries of the South.

In the 1970s, modernization theorists started to use the level of media development as an indicator of general societal development. Leading theorists of the 'development as modernization' school, such as Everett Rogers, saw a key role for the mass media in international communication and development (Rogers, 1962; Pye, 1963). Such research benefited from the surveys undertaken by various US-government-funded agencies and educational foundations, especially in Asia and Latin America for what Rogers (1962) called 'disseminating innovations'.

This top-down approach to communications, a one-way flow of information from government or international development agencies via the mass media to Southern peasantry at the bottom, was generally seen as a panacea for the development of the newly independent countries of Asia and Africa. But it was predicated on a definition of development that followed the model of Western industrialization and 'modernization', measured primarily by the rate of economic growth of output or Gross National Product (GNP). It failed to recognize that the creation of wealth on its own was insufficient: the improvement of life for the majority of the populations depended on the equitable distribution of that wealth and its use for the public good. It also failed to ask questions about development for whom and who would gain or lose, ignoring any discussion of the political, social or cultural dimensions of development. In many Southern countries, income disparities in fact increased over the succeeding 30 years – despite a growth in GNP.

Moreover, the mass media were assumed to be a neutral force in the process of development, ignoring how the media are themselves products of social, political, economic and cultural conditions. In many developing countries economic and political power was and remains restricted to a tiny, often unrepresentative elite, and the mass media play a key role in legitimizing the political establishment. Since the media had, and continue to have, close proximity to the ruling elites, they tend to reflect this view of development in the news.

The international communication research inspired by the modernization thesis was very influential, shaping university communication programmes and research centres globally. Though such research provided a huge amount of data on the behaviour, attitudes and values of the people in the South, it tended to work within the positivist tradition of what sociologist Paul Lazarsfeld (1941) had long identified as 'administrative' research, often failing to analyse the political and cultural context of international communication.

However, the outcomes of this type of research in international communication can be useful in analysing the relationship of media growth to economic development, measured in terms of such indicators as sales of communication hardware and gross national product. They are also useful in international promotion of advertising and marketing.

It is important to understand the cold war context in which modernization theory emerged, a time when it was politically expedient for the West to use the notion of modernization to bring the newly independent nations of Asia, the Middle East and Africa into the sphere of capitalism. As Vincent Mosco comments: 'The theory of modernisation meant a reconstruction of the international division of labour amalgamating the non-Western world into the emerging international structural hierarchy' (1996: 121). It is now being accepted that some modernization research was politically motivated. It has been pointed out that Lerner's seminal study was a spin-off from a large and clandestine government-funded audience research project, conducted for the Voice of America by the Bureau of Applied Social Research (Samarajiva,1985).

Despite its enormous influence in the field of international communication, Lerner's research had more to do with the East–West ideological contest of those days of cold war when in the Middle East radical voices were demanding decolonization – Iran had nationalized its oil industry in 1951, leading to the CIA-backed coup, two years later, which removed the democratically elected Prime Minister, Mohammed Musaddiq. Given the prominence of radio propaganda during the 1950s, this research could also be seen as an investigation of radio listening behaviour in a region bordering the Soviet Union. In this context it is interesting to note that Lerner had worked for the Psychological Warfare Division of the US Army during the Second World War.

One major shortcoming of the early modernization theorists was their assumption that the modern and the traditional lifestyles were mutually exclusive, and their dismissive view of the culture of the 'indigent natives' led them to believe in the desirability and inevitability of a shift from the traditional to the modern. The dominant cultural and religious force in the region – Islam – and a sense of collective pan-Islamic identity were seen as 'sentimental sorties into the symbolism of a majestic past'. The elites in the region had to choose between 'Mecca or mechanisation'. The crux of the matter, Lerner argued, was 'not whether, but how one should move from traditional ways toward modern life-styles. The symbols of race and ritual fade into irrelevance when they impede living desires for bread and enlightenment' (Lerner, 1958: 405).

What modernizers such as Lerner failed to comprehend was that the dichotomy of modern versus traditional was not inevitable. Despite all the West's efforts at media modernization, Islamic traditions continue to define the Muslim world, and indeed have become stronger in parts of the Middle East. In addition, these traditional cultures can also deploy modern communication methods to put their case across. In the 1979 Islamic revolution in Iran, for example, radical groups produced printed material and audio cassettes and distributed them through informal networks to promote an anti-Western ideology based on a particular Islamic view of the world (Mohammadi and Sreberny-Mohammadi, 1994). In the twenty-first century, militant Islamists have used satellite television as well as the Internet to propagate their ideology (Burke, 2004).

In Latin America most communication research, often funded by the US Government, was led by proponents of the modernization thesis. However, since the gap between the rich and poor was growing, as elsewhere in the developing world, critics started to question the validity of the developmentalist project and raised questions about what it left out – the relationship between communication, power and knowledge and the ideological role of international organizational and institutional structures. This led to a critique of modernization in Latin America, most notably from Brazil's Paulo Freire, whose *Pedagogy of the Oppressed* (1970/1974) had a major influence on international development discourse, though how far his views were adopted in devising international communication strategies remains an open question.

Southern scholars, especially those from Latin America, argued that the chief beneficiaries of modernization programmes were not the 'traditional' rural poor in the South, but Western media and communication companies, which had expanded into the Third World, ostensibly in the name of modernization and development, but in fact in search of new consumers for their products. They argued that modernization programmes were exacerbating the already deep social and economic inequalities in the developing countries and making them dependent on Western models of communication development.

Partly as a result of the work of Latin American scholars, the proponents of modernization in the West acknowledged that the theory needed reformulation. Despite decades of 'modernization', the vast majority of the people in the South continued to live in poverty, and by the mid-1970s the talk was of the 'passing of the dominant paradigm' (Rogers, 1976). In a revised version of modernization theory, a shift has been detectable from support for the mass media to an almost blind faith in the potential of the new information and communication technologies – in what has been called 'a neo-developmentalist view' (Mosco, 1996: 130). Also noticeable is the acceptance of a greater role for local elites in the modernization process. However, the importance of Western technology remains crucial in the revised version too. According to this view, modernization requires advanced telecommunication and computer infrastructure, preferably through the 'efficient' private corporations, thus integrating the South into a globalized information economy.

Dependency theory

Dependency theory emerged in Latin America in the late 1960s and 1970s, partly as a consequence of the political situation in the continent, with increasing US support for right-wing authoritarian governments, and partly with the realization among the educated elite that the developmentalist approach to international communication had failed to deliver. The establishment, in 1976, in Mexico City of the Instituto Latinoamericano de Estudios (ILET), whose principal research interest was the study of transnational media business, gave an impetus to a critique of the 'modernization' thesis, documenting its negative consequences in the continent. The impact of ILET was also evident in international policy debates about NWICO, particularly through the work of Juan Somavia, a member of the MacBride Commission.

Though grounded in the neo-Marxist political-economy approach (Baran, 1957; Gunder Frank, 1969; Amin 1976), dependency theorists aimed to provide an alternative framework to analyse international communication. Central to dependency theory was the view that transnational corporations (TNCs), most based in the North, exercise control, with the support of their respective governments, over the developing countries by setting the terms for global trade – dominating markets, resources, production and labour. Development for these countries was shaped in a way to strengthen the dominance of the developed nations and to maintain the 'peripheral' nations in a position of dependence – in other words, to make conditions suitable for 'dependent development'. In its most extreme form the outcome of such relationships was 'the development of underdevelopment' (Gunder Frank, 1969).

This neocolonial relationship in which the TNCs controlled both the terms of exchange and the structure of global markets, it was argued, had contributed to the widening and deepening of inequality in the South, while the TNCs had strengthened their control over the world's natural and human resources (Baran, 1957; Mattelart, 1979).

The cultural aspects of dependency theory, examined by scholars interested in the production, distribution and consumption of media and cultural products, were particularly relevant to the study of international communication. The dependency theorists aimed to show the links between discourses of 'modernization' and the policies of transnational media and communication corporations and their backers among Western governments.

Dependency theorists both benefited from, and contributed to, research on cultural aspects of imperialism being undertaken at the time in the USA. The idea of cultural imperialism is most clearly identified with the work of Herbert Schiller, who was based at the University of California (1969–92). Working within the neo-Marxist critical tradition, Schiller analysed the global power structures in the international communication industries and the links between transnational business and the dominant states.

At the heart of Schiller's argument was the analysis of how, in pursuit of commercial interests, huge US-based transnational corporations, often in league with Western (predominantly US) military and political interests, were undermining the cultural autonomy of the countries of the South and creating a dependency on both the hardware and software of communication and media in the developing countries. Schiller defined cultural imperialism as:

> the sum of the processes by which a society is brought into the modern world system and how its dominating stratum is attracted, pressured, forced, and sometimes bribed into shaping social institutions to correspond to, or even to promote, the values and structures of the dominant centre of the system.
>
> (Schiller, 1976: 9)

Schiller argued that the declining European colonial empires – mainly British, French and Dutch – were being replaced by a new emergent American empire, based on US economic, military and informational power. According to Schiller, the US-based TNCs have continued to grow and dominate the global economy. This economic growth has been underpinned with communications know-how, enabling US business and military organizations to take leading roles in the development and control of new, electronically based global communication systems.

Such domination had both military and cultural implications. Schiller's seminal work, *Mass Communications and American Empire* (1969/1992), examined the role of the US government, a major user of communication services, in developing global electronic media systems, initially for military purposes to counter the perceived, and often exaggerated, Soviet security threat. By controlling global satellite communications, the USA had the most effective surveillance system in operation – a crucial element in the cold war years. Such communication hardware could also be used to propagate the US model of commercial broadcasting, dominated by large networks and funded primarily by advertising revenue, as Schiller noted:

> Nothing less than the viability of the American industrial economy itself is involved in the movement toward international commercialisation of broadcasting. The private yet managed economy depends on advertising. Remove the excitation and the manipulation of consumer demand and industrial slowdown threatens.

> (Schiller, 1969: 95)

According to Schiller, dependence on US communications technology and investment, coupled with the new demand for media products, necessitated large-scale imports of US media products, notably television programmes. Since media exports are ultimately dependent on sponsors for advertising, they endeavour not only to advertise Western goods and services, but also promote, albeit indirectly, a capitalist 'American way of life', through mediated consumer lifestyles. The result was an 'electronic invasion', especially in the global South, which threatened to undermine traditional cultures and emphasize consumerism at the expense of community values.

In the revised edition of the book, published in 1992, Schiller argued that US dominance of global communication increased with the end of the cold war and the failure of the UNESCO-supported demands for NWICO. The economic basis of US dominance, however, had changed, with TNCs acquiring an increasingly important role in international relations, transforming US cultural imperialism into 'transnational corporate cultural domination' (Schiller, 1992: 39).

In a review of the US role in international communication during the past half-century, Schiller saw the US state still playing a decisive role in promoting the ever-expanding communication sector, a central pillar of the US economy. In US support for the promotion of electronic-based media and communication hardware and software in the new information age of the twenty-first century, Schiller found 'historical continuities in its quest for systemic power and control' of global communication (1998: 23).

Other prominent works using the 'cultural imperialism' thesis have examined such aspects of US cultural and media dominance as Hollywood's relationship with the European movie market (Guback, 1969); US television exports and influences in Latin America (Wells, 1972); the contribution of Disney comics in promoting capitalist values (Dorfman and Mattelart, 1975) and the role of the advertising industry as an ideological instrument (Ewen, 1976; Mattelart, 1991). Internationally, some of the most significant work has been the UNESCO-supported research on international flow in television programmes (Nordenstreng and Varis, 1974; Varis, 1985).

One prominent aspect of dependency in international communication was identified in the 1970s by Oliver Boyd-Barrett as 'media imperialism', examining information and media inequalities between nations and how these reflect broader issues of dependency, and analysing the hegemonic power of mainly US-dominated international media – notably news agencies, magazines, films, radio and television. Boyd-Barrett defined media imperialism as:

> The process whereby the ownership, structure, distribution or content of the media in any one country are singly or together subject to substantial external pressures from the media interests of any other country or countries, without proportionate reciprocation of influence by the country so affected.
>
> (Boyd-Barrett, 1977: 117)

For its critics, dependency literature was 'notable for an absence of clear definitions of fundamental terms like imperialism and an almost total lack of empirical evidence to support the arguments' (Stevenson, 1988: 38). Others argued that it ignored the question of media form and content as well as the role of the audience. Those involved in a cultural studies approach to the analysis of international communication argued that, like other cultural artefacts, media 'texts' could be polysemic and were amenable to different interpretations by audiences who were not merely passive consumers, but 'active' participants in the process of negotiating meaning (Fiske, 1987). It was also pointed out that the 'totalistic' cultural imperialism thesis did not adequately take on board such issues as how global media texts worked in national contexts, ignoring local patterns of media consumption.

Quantifying the volume of US cultural products distributed around the world was not a sufficient explanation; it was also important to examine its effects. There was also a view that the cultural imperialism thesis assumed a 'hypodermic-needle model' of media effects and ignored the complexities of 'Third World' cultures (Sreberny-Mohammadi, 1991, 1997). It was argued that the Western scholars had a less than deep understanding of Third World cultures, seeing them as homogeneous and not being adequately aware of the regional and intra-national diversities of race, ethnicity, language, gender and class. There have so far been few systematic studies of the cultural and ideological effects of Western media products on audiences in the South, especially from Southern scholars.

Despite its critics (Tomlinson, 1991; Thompson, 1995), the cultural imperialism thesis was very influential in international communication research in the 1970s and 1980s. It was particularly important during the heated NWICO debates in UNESCO and other international fora in the 1970s. However, even a critic such as John Thompson, while rejecting the main thesis, has conceded that such research is 'probably the only systematic and moderately plausible attempt to think about the globalisation of communications and its impact on the modern world' (Thompson, 1995: 173).

Defenders of the thesis found the 1990s' debates criticizing cultural imperialism 'lacking even the most elementary epistemological precaution and sometimes actually bordering on intellectual dishonesty', arguing that the critics of this theory have often 'taken the notion out of context, abstracting it from the concrete historical conditions that produced it: the political struggles and commitments of the 1960s and 1970s' (Mattelart and Mattelart, 1998: 137–8).

With changes in debates on international communication reflecting the rhetoric of privatization and liberalization in the 1990s, theories of media and cultural dependency have become less prominent, though their relevance should not be underestimated (Golding and Harris, 1997; Thussu, 1998a; Hamm and Smandych, 2005; Hackett and Zhao, 2005). Boyd-Barrett has argued that while media imperialism theory in its original formulation did not take into account intra-national media relations, gender and ethnic issues, it is still a useful analytical tool to make sense of what he terms the 'colonisation of communications space' (Boyd-Barrett, 1998: 157).

One of the limits of the cultural and media imperialism approach is that it did not fully take into account the role of the national elites, especially in the developing world. However, though its influence has dwindled, the theory of structural imperialism developed by the Norwegian sociologist Johan Galtung also offers an explanation of the role of international communication in maintaining structures of economic and political power.

Structural imperialism

Galtung argues that the world consists of developed 'centre' states and underdeveloped 'periphery' states. In turn, each centre and periphery state possesses a highly developed 'core' and a less developed 'periphery'. He defines structural imperialism as a 'sophisticated type of dominance relation which cuts across nations basing itself on a bridgehead which the centre of the centre nation establishes in the centre of the periphery nation for the joint benefit of both'. For Galtung, there is a harmony of interest between the core of the centre nation and the centre in the periphery nation; less harmony of interest within the periphery nation than within the centre nation and a disharmony of interest between the periphery of the centre nation and the periphery of the periphery nation (Galtung, 1971: 83).

In other words, there exists in the countries of the South a dominant elite whose interests coincide with the interests of the elite in the developed world. This 'core' not only provides a bridgehead by which the centre nation can maintain its economic and political domination over the periphery nation, but is also supported by the centre in maintaining dominance over its own internal periphery. In terms of values and attitudes, the elite group is closer to other elites in the developed world than to groups in its own country.

Galtung defines five types of imperialism that depend upon the type of exchange between centre and periphery nations: economic, political, military, communication and cultural. The five types form a syndrome of imperialism, and interact, albeit through different channels, to reinforce the dominance relationship of centre over periphery. Communication imperialism is intimately related to cultural imperialism, and news is a combination of cultural and communication exchange (Galtung, 1971: 93).

Periphery–centre relationships are maintained and reinforced by information flows and through the reproduction of economic activities. These create institutional links that serve the interests of the dominant groups, both in the centre and within the periphery. Institutions in the centre of the periphery often mirror those of the developed world and thus recreate and promote the latter's value systems.

According to Galtung, the basic mechanism of structural imperialism revolves around two forms of interaction, 'vertical' and 'feudal'. The 'vertical' interaction principle maintains that relationships are asymmetrical; that the flow of power is from the more developed state to the less developed state, while the benefits of the system flow upwards from the less developed states to the centre states. The 'feudal' interaction principle states that there 'is interaction along the spokes, from the periphery to the centre hub; but not along the rim, from one periphery nation to another' (Galtung, 1971: 89).

Galtung's theory is particularly relevant in understanding global news flow: news flows from the centre and the core to the periphery via transnational news agencies. The effect of this feudal structure is that Southern nations know virtually nothing about events in neighbouring countries that has not been filtered through the lenses of the developed media systems at the centre.

The theory argues that the core's definition of news will be reflected in the news in the peripheral nation. This has been called the 'agenda-setting function' of the international media. Information is transferred to the Southern elite in such a way that primary importance is attached to the same issues the developed world sees as important. The identity of interests between the centre of the centre and the centre of the periphery greatly influences the acceptance of an international agenda.

A striking similarity can be found between Galtung's theory of structural imperialism and Schiller's definition of cultural imperialism. Both maintain that the structure of political and economic domination exercised by the centre over the periphery results in the re-creation of certain aspects of the centre's value system in the periphery.

There is also evidence of a dependency relationship in the field of media and communication research in Southern countries. As British media analyst James Halloran notes:

> Wherever we look in international communication research – exports and imports of textbooks, articles and journals; citations, references and footnotes; employment of experts (even in international agencies); and the funding, planning and execution of research – we are essentially looking at a dependency situation. This is a situation which is characterised by a one-way flow of values, ideas, models, methods and resources from North to South. It may even be more specifically as a flow from the Anglo-Saxon language fraternity to the rest of the world.
>
> (Halloran, 1997: 39)

Dependency theory has enjoyed widespread influence and equally widespread criticism. It was criticized for concentrating on the impact of transnational business and the role of other external forces on social and economic development to the neglect of internal class, gender, ethnic and power relations. Theorists such as Galtung responded by examining the roles of the often unrepresentative elites in the South in maintaining and indeed benefiting from the dependency syndrome. While the globalization of new information and communication technologies and the resultant wiring up of the globe, and the emphasis on cultural hybridization rather than cultural imperialism, have made dependency theories less fashionable, the structural inequalities in international communication continue to render them relevant.

Another concern for scholars working within the political economy approach has been to analyse the close relationship between media and foreign policy. The role of the mass media as an instrument of propaganda for corporate and state power has been an important area of inquiry among critical scholars (Herman and Chomsky, 1988/1994). In their 'propaganda model', US economist Edward Herman and the renowned linguist Noam Chomsky examine, through a range of detailed case studies, how news in mainstream US media systems passes through several 'filters', including the size, ownership and profit orientation of media firms; their heavy reliance on advertising and dependence on business and governmental sources for information; and the overall dominant ideology within which they operate. These elements, write Herman and Chomsky, 'interact with and reinforce one another and set the premises of discourse and interpretation, and the definition of what is newsworthy' (1994: 2).

For Herman and Chomsky, a propaganda approach to media coverage suggests:

a systematic and highly political dichotomisation in news coverage based on serviceability to important domestic power interests. This should be observable in dichotomised choices of story and in the volume and quality of coverage … such dichotomisation in the mass media is massive and systematic: not only are choices for publicity and suppression comprehensible in terms of system advantage, but the modes of handling favoured and inconvenient materials (placement, tone, context, fullness of treatment) differ in ways that serve political interests.

(Herman and Chomsky, 1994: 35)

Despite meticulously researched case studies – ranging from the US media's coverage of the war in Vietnam in the 1960s and 1970s, to its treatment of US involvement in subversive activities in Central America during the 1980s – the propaganda model has received more than its share of criticism, especially in the West. Internationally, however, *Manufacturing Consent*, a title borrowed from a phrase used by Lippmann in a 1922 publication, has had a profound influence. Though criticized for its 'polemical' style, the book remains one of the few systematic and detailed studies of the politics of mass media.

Hegemony

By arguing that the propaganda model succeeds because there is no significant overt coercion from the state, in some ways Herman and Chomsky were following European analyses of the role of ideology and state power in a capitalist society, articulated by, among others, the French Marxist, Louis Althusser, who called the media, 'ideological state apparatus' (1971).

Another major influence on critical theorists, as well as on cultural critics in the study of ideology, is the writing of Italian Marxist Antonio Gramsci (1891–1937). The impact of the ideas of Gramsci, who died in prison under the Fascist regime, has been widespread in critical studies of international communication. However, it was not until the translation into English of his most famous work, *Selections from the Prison Notebooks*, in 1971, that Gramsci's ideas became a major influence in the Anglo-Saxon world.

Gramsci's conception of hegemony is rooted in the notion that the dominant social group in a society has the capacity to exercise intellectual and moral direction over society at large and to build a new system of social alliances to support its aims. Gramsci argued that military force was not necessarily the best instrument to retain power for the ruling classes, but that a more effective way of wielding power was to build consent by ideological control of cultural production and distribution.

According to Gramsci, such a system exists when a dominant social class exerts moral and intellectual leadership over both 'allied' and 'subordinate classes' through its control of such institutions as schools, religious bodies and the mass media. Social and intellectual authority is exercised by the government 'with the consent of the governed': this consent is 'organised' and those consenting are 'educated' to do so, in such a way that its right to govern is rarely challenged (Gramsci, 1971).

One of the most important functions of the state, Gramsci wrote in his *Prison Notebooks*, 'is to raise the great mass of the population to a particular cultural and moral level, a level (or type) which corresponds to the ... interests of the ruling classes'. Schools, courts and a multitude of 'initiatives and activities ... form the apparatus of the political and cultural hegemony of the ruling classes' (Gramsci, 1971: 258–9). This, he argued, was in contrast with a situation in which the dominant class merely rules, that is, coercively imposes its will on subordinate classes. This manufactured consent, however, cannot simply be assumed or guaranteed and has to be renewed, indicating that hegemony is more of a process that has to be reproduced continually, rather than an achieved state of affairs.

In international communication, the notion of hegemony is used widely to explain the political function of the mass media in propagating and maintaining the dominant ideology. This ideology also shapes the process of media and communication production, particularly news and entertainment (Hallin, 1994). Thus it is argued that although the media in the West are notionally free from direct government control, they nevertheless act as agents to legitimize the dominant ideology.

Critical theory

Among the substantial body of research undertaken by the Frankfurt School theorists, the concept of the 'culture industry' – first used by Adorno and Horkheimer in a book entitled *Dialectic of Enlightenment*, written in 1944 and published in 1947 – has received the widest international attention. Identified with the staff of the Institute for Social Research, founded

in 1923 and affiliated with the University of Frankfurt, its key members included Max
Horkheimer (1895–1973), Theodor Adorno (1903–69) and Herbert Marcuse (1898–1979).

Analysing the industrial production of cultural goods – films, radio programmes, music
and magazines, and so on – as a global movement, they identified a trend in capitalist
societies towards producing culture as a commodity (Adorno, 1991). Adorno and
Horkheimer believed that cultural products manifested the same kind of management
practices, technological rationality and organizational schemes as mass-produced industrial
goods such as cars. This 'assembly-line character', they argued, could be observed in 'the
synthetic, planned method of turning out its products (factory-like not only in the studio
but, more or less, in the compilation of cheap biographies, pseudo-documentary novels, and
hit songs)' (Adorno and Horkheimer, 1979 [1947]: 163).

Such industrial production led to standardization, resulting in a mass culture made up of
a series of objects bearing the stamp of the culture industry. This industrially produced and
commodified culture, it was argued, led to a deterioration of the philosophical role of
culture. Instead, this mediated culture contributed to the incorporation of the working
classes into the structures of advanced capitalism and to limiting their horizons to political
and economic goals that could be realized within the capitalist system without challenging
it. The critical theorists argued that the development of the 'culture industry' and its ability
to ideologically inoculate the masses against socialist ideas benefited the ruling classes.

Marrying the psychoanalytical theories of Sigmund Freud with Marxian economic
analysis, the critical theorists borrowed the notion of commodification from Marx, who had
argued that objects are commodified by acquiring an exchange value instead of their
intrinsic value. In their analysis of cultural products, they argued that in a capitalist
economy cultural products are produced and sold in media markets as commodities, and the
consumers buy them not just because of their intrinsic worth but in exchange for
entertainment or to fulfil their psychological needs.

The concentration of ownership of cultural production in a few producers had resulted
in a standardized commercial commodity, contributing to what they called a 'mass culture' –
influenced by the mass media and thriving on the market rules of supply and demand. In
their view, such a process undermined the critical engagement of masses with important
socio-political issues and ensured a politically passive social behaviour and the subordination
of the working classes to the ruling elite.

Marcuse, who migrated to the USA, where he had a huge influence on the labour
movement, argued that technological rationality or instrumental reason had reduced speech
and thought to a single dimension, establishing what he called a 'one-dimensional society'
which had abolished the distance required for critical thought. One of the most incisive
chapters of Marcuse's book, *One Dimensional Man* (1964), discusses 'one-dimensional
language' and frequently refers to media discourse.

In an international context, the idea of 'mass culture' and media and cultural industries
has influenced debates about the flow of information between countries. The issue of the
commodification of culture is present in many analyses of the operation of book publishing,
film and popular music industries. One example of this was the 1982 UNESCO report,
which argued that cultural industries in the world were greatly influenced by the major

media and communication companies and were being continually corporatized. The expansion of mainly Western-based cultural products globally had resulted, it argued, in the gradual 'marginalisation of cultural messages that do not take the form of goods, primarily of values as marketable commodities' (UNESCO, 1982: 10).

This emphasis on ownership and control of the means of cultural production and the argument that it directly shapes the activities of artists has been contested by several writers, arguing that creativity and cultural consumption can be independent of production cycles and that the production process itself is not as organized or rigidly standardized as stated by the Frankfurt School theorists.

The public sphere

A natural heir to the critical theorists, the German sociologist Jürgen Habermas (born 1929) also lamented the standardization, massification and atomization of the public. Habermas developed the concept of the public sphere in one of his earliest books, though it was 27 years before it appeared in English translation as *The Structural Transformation of the Public Sphere: An Inquiry into a Category of Bourgeois Society*, in 1989. He defined the public sphere as

an arena, independent of government (even if in receipt of state funds) and also enjoying autonomy from partisan economic forces, which is dedicated to rational debate (i.e. to debate and discussion which is not 'interests', 'disguised' or 'manipulated') and which is both accessible to entry and open to inspection by the citizenry. It is here, in this public sphere, that public opinion is formed.

(quoted in Holub, 1991: 2–8)

Habermas argued that the 'bourgeois public sphere' emerged in an expanding capitalist society exemplified by eighteenth-century Britain, where entrepreneurs were becoming powerful enough to achieve autonomy from State and Church and increasingly demanding wider and more effective political representation to facilitate expansion of their businesses. In his formulation of a public sphere, Habermas gave prominence to the role of information, as, at this time, a greater freedom of the press was fought for and achieved with parliamentary reform. The wider availability of printing facilities and the resultant reduction in production costs of newspapers stimulated debate contributing to what Habermas calls 'rational-acceptable policies', which, by the mid-nineteenth century, led to the creation of a 'bourgeois public sphere'.

This idealized version of a public space was characterized by greater accessibility of information, a more open debate within the bourgeoisie, a space independent of both business interests and state apparatus. However, as capitalism expanded and attained dominance, the call for reform of the state was replaced by an effort to take it over to further business interests. As commercial interests became prominent in politics and started exerting their influence – for example, by lobbying parliament, funding political parties and cultural institutions – the autonomy of the public sphere was severely reduced.

According to Habermas, the growing power of information management and manipulation through public relations and lobbying firms in the twentieth century has contributed to contemporary debates becoming a 'faked version' of a genuine public sphere (Habermas, 1989: 195). In this 'refeudalization' of the public sphere, public affairs have become occasions for 'displays' of power in the style of medieval feudal courts rather than a space for debate on socio-economic issues.

Habermas also detects refeudalization in the changes within the mass media systems, which have become monopoly capitalist organizations, promoting capitalist interests, and thus affecting their role as disseminators of information for the public sphere. In a market-driven environment, the overriding concern for media corporations is to produce an artefact which will appeal to the widest possible variety of audiences and thus generate maximum advertising revenue. It is essential, therefore, that the product is diluted in content to meet the lowest common denominator – sex, scandal, celebrity lifestyles, action adventure and sensationalism. Despite their negligible informational quality, such media products reinforce the audience's acceptance of 'the soft compulsion of constant consumption training' (Habermas, 1989: 192).

Though the idealized version of the public sphere has been criticized for its very male, Eurocentric and bourgeois limitations, the public sphere provides a useful concept in understanding democratic potential for communication processes (Calhoun, 1992; Dahlgren, 2003 and 2005). In recent years, with the globalization of the media and communication, there has been talk about the evolution of a 'global public sphere' where issues of international significance – environment, human rights, gender and ethnic equality – can be articulated through the mass media, though the validity of such a concept is also contested (Sparks, 1998).

Cultural studies perspectives on international communication

While much of the debate on international communication post-1945 and during the cold war emphasized a structural analysis of its role in political and economic power relationships, there has been a discernible shift in research emphasis during the 1990s, in parallel with the 'depoliticization' of politics, towards the cultural dimensions of communication and media. The cultural analysis of communication also has a well-established theoretical tradition to draw upon, from Gramsci's theory of hegemony to the works of the critical theorists of the Frankfurt School.

One group of scholars who adapted Gramsci's notions of hegemony was based at the Centre for Contemporary Cultural Studies at the University of Birmingham in Britain. Led by the Caribbean-born scholar Stuart Hall, 'the Birmingham School', as it came to be known in the 1970s, did pioneering work on exploring the textual analysis of media, especially television, and ethnographic research. Particularly influential was Hall's model of 'encoding-decoding media discourse', which theorized about how media texts are given 'preferred readings' by producers and how they may be interpreted in different ways – accepting the dominant meaning, negotiating with the encoded message or taking an oppositional view (Hall, 1980).

The model was widely adopted by scholars interested in the study of the ideological role of the mass media. However, the research focus of the Birmingham School was largely British, and more often than not its perceptions of the 'global' were based on the ethnographic studies of migrant populations – their television viewing habits, consumption of music and other leisure activities. The undue emphasis on ethnic and racial identity and 'multiculturalism', tended to limit their research perspectives, exposing them to the danger, for example, of confusing 'British Asian cultural identity' with the diverse cultures and subcultures of the South Asian region, with its multiplicity of languages, ancient religions and ethnicities.

The dominant Western view of the global South is profoundly influenced by Eurocentrism, defined by the Egyptian theorist Samir Amin as constituting 'one dimension of the culture and ideology of the modern capitalist world' (Amin, 1988: vii). Many other scholars from the developing world have argued that contemporary representations of the global South are affected by the way the Orient has been historically constructed in Western thinking, for example, through travel writing (Kabbani, 1986), literature (Said, 1978; 1993) and films (Shohat and Stam, 1994), contributing to the continuing subordination of non-European peoples in the Western imagination. The US-based Palestinian scholar Edward Said explored how dominant culture participated in the expansion and consolidation of nineteenth-century imperialism. Taking the Gramscian view of culture, Said wrote:

> Western cultural forms can be taken out of the autonomous enclosures in which they have been protected, and placed instead in the dynamic global environment created by imperialism, itself revised as an ongoing contest between North and South, metropolis and periphery, white and native.
>
> (Said, 1993: 59)

Though the cultural studies approach professes to give voice to those concerns by addressing such issues as race, ethnicity, gender and sexuality, it has generally given less importance to class-based analysis, despite the fact that championing the 'popular' has been a major achievement of this tradition. The cultural studies approach to communication has become increasingly important in recent years, especially in the USA and Australia, and with its new-found interest in the 'global popular', the trend is towards the internationalization of cultural studies (Abbas and Erni, 2005).

Theories of the information society

Spectacular innovations in information and communication technologies, especially computing and digitization, and their rapid global expansion have led to claims that this is the age of the information society. Breakthroughs in the speed, volume and cost of information processing, storage and transmission have undoubtedly contributed to the power of information technology to shape many aspects of Western and, increasingly, global society. The convergence of telecommunications and computing technologies and the continued reductions in the costs of computing and international telephony have made the case for the existence of the information society even stronger.

According to its proponents, an international information society is being created via the Internet, which will digitally link every home, office and business in a networked society based on what has been termed the 'knowledge economy'. These networks are the information superhighways, providing the infrastructure for a global information society (Negroponte, 1995; Kahin and Nesson, 1997). However, critics have objected to this view of society, arguing that these changes are technologically determined and ignore the social, economic and political dimensions of technological innovation (Webster, 1995, 2004).

The technologically determinist view of communication was promoted by Canadian media theorist Marshall McLuhan (1911–80), one of the first thinkers to analyse the social impact of media technology. Arguing that 'the medium is the message', he maintained that, seen in a historical context, media technology had more social effect on different societies and cultures than media content (McLuhan, 1964). McLuhan, a Professor at the University of Toronto, was working within the tradition of what came to be known as the Toronto School of thought, identified with the research of economic historian Harold Innis ([1950] 1972). McLuhan argued that printing technology, for example, contributed to nationalism, industrialism and universal literacy. Though at the time he was writing, electronic media, especially television, were confined to few Northern nations, McLuhan foresaw the impact of international television, suggesting that new communication and information technologies would help create what he called a 'global village'. The rapid changes in international communications, spurred on by the expansion of direct satellite broadcasting in the 1980s and the Internet in the 1990s, seem to have made the world shrink, generating renewed interest in McLuhan's concept of the 'global village' (McLuhan, 1964).

The term 'information society' originated in Japan (Ito, 1981), but it was the USA where the concept received its most ardent intellectual support. In the USA, even in the early 1960s, the 'economics of information' was being considered as an important area of research activity, as set out in Fritz Machlup's 1962 work, *The Production and Distribution of Knowledge in the United States*, one of the first attempts to analyse information in economic terms. Changes in industrial production and their effect on Western societies informed the work of sociologist Daniel Bell, who became an internationally known exponent of the idea of a 'post-industrial' society – one in which the service industries employ more workers than manufacturing.

In his hugely influential book, *The Coming of Post Industrial Society*, published in 1973, Bell argued that US society had moved from an industrial to a post-industrial society, characterized by the domination of information and information-related industries. Bell contended that not only was more information being used, but a qualitatively different type of information was available. Bell's ideas were keenly adopted by the scholars who wanted to pronounce the arrival of 'the information age'. Another key figure, Alvin Toffler, though more populist than Bell, was very influential in propagating the idea of an information society, calling it the third wave – after the agricultural and industrial eras – of human civilization (Toffler, 1980).

The third wave was characterized by increasing 'interconnectedness', contributing to the 'evolution of a universal interconnected network of audio, video and electronic text communication', which, some argue, will promote intellectual pluralism and personalized control over communication (Neuman, 1991: 21).

In this version of the information society, the democratic potential of new technologies is constantly stressed. However, critics such as Frank Webster emphasize 'historical antecedents', arguing that 'there is no novel, "post-industrial" society: the growth of service occupations and associated developments highlight the continuities of the present with the past' (Webster, 1995: 50). These continuities need to be underlined, especially in the global context, as the transnationalization of media and communication industries has been greatly facilitated by expansion of new international communication networks, for example, among non-governmental organizations and transnational political activists (Frederick, 1992; Tarrow, 2005). The resultant 'time–space compression' is implicated in what has been called, taking up McLuhan's phrase, the phenomenon of 'global villagization' (Harasim, 1994).

With its growing commodification, information has come to occupy a central role as a 'key strategic resource' in the international economy, the distribution, regulation, marketing and management of which are becoming increasingly important. Real-time trading has become a part of contemporary corporate culture, through digital networking, which has made it possible to transmit information on stock markets, patent listings, currency fluctuations, commodity prices, futures, portfolios, at unprecedented speed and volume across the globe.

The growing 'informatization' of the economy is facilitating the integration of national and regional economies and creating a global economy, which continues to be dominated by a few megacorporations, increasingly global in the production, distribution and consumption of their goods and services. The growth of Internet-based trading and e-commerce (electronic commerce) has given a boost to what has been called 'digital' capitalism (Schiller, 1999).

In the analysis of the emerging global information society, the most significant input has come from the Spanish theorist Manuel Castells. In his trilogy *The Information Age*, Castells gives an extensively researched and detailed analysis of the emerging trends in the global condition. The first volume focuses on the new social structures at work in what Castells calls the 'network society'; the second volume examines social and political processes within the context of such a society; while the third volume includes integration and information-based polarization in the international 'informational economy' in which communication becomes both global and customized.

Informational capitalism, Castells argues, is increasingly operating on a global basis, through exchanges between electronic circuits linking up international information systems. This bypasses the power of the state and creates regional and supranational units. In this 'networked' globe, he contends, flows of electronic images are fundamental to social processes and political activity, which has been progressively affected by mediated reality (Castells, 2000a, 2000b, 2004). Though he rejects technological determinism, his ideas are fundamentally shaped by the new technological paradigm.

It has also been claimed that new technologies have contributed to the decline of ideology. For example, a visually based medium such as television has shifted ideology from 'conceptual to iconic symbolism' (Gouldner, 1976). The growing use of computer-mediated communication could further reduce the impact of ideology in daily life, though the empowering potential of the Internet, on the other hand, could create new forms of transnational ideological alliances. However, the possibilities of the Internet creating new communicative space (Poster, 1995) have been opposed with questions about access to the new technologies, within and between nations.

Some critics have been concerned with the growing commodification of personal information, from database marketing to individually targeted personalized advertising and consumer sales (Gandy, 1993). With the growing use of the Internet, companies can exploit commercially valuable data on their users, for example, by so-called cookies (client-side persistent information). Others have raised questions about the use of new technologies for personal and political surveillance (Lyon, 1994). US dominance of global military surveillance and intelligence data gathering through spy satellites and advanced computer networks, for political and, increasingly, trade-related espionage, must also be considered an integral part of the push towards the creation of a global information society. The 'control revolution' (Beniger, 1986), though more pronounced in all modern organizations in 'networked societies', is in the process of going global (*see* Chapter 7, pp. 234–5).

Discourses of globalization

Despite the disputed nature of the utility of globalization as a concept in understanding international communication, there is little doubt that new information and communication technologies have made global interconnectivity a reality (Held *et al.*, 1999; Appadurai, 2001; Held and McGrew, 2003). It has been argued that 'globalisation may be the concept of the 1990s, a key idea by which we understand the transition of human society into the third millennium' (Waters, 1995: 1). The term has also been used more generally to describe contemporary developments in communication and culture. Wallerstein (1974, 1980, 2004) sees globalization as a world system, a theory rejected by others on the grounds that his 'mechanisms of geosystematic integration are exclusively economic' (Waters, 1995: 25); while Robertson argues that 'globalisation analysis and world-systems analysis are rival perspectives' (Robertson, 1992: 15).

In its most liberal interpretation, globalization is seen as fostering international economic integration and as a mechanism for promoting global liberal capitalism. For those who see capitalism as the 'end' of history (Fukuyama, 1992), globalization is to be welcomed for the effect that it has in promoting global markets and liberal democracy. The triumph of democracy is celebrated through increasing emphasis on global governance (UN, 1995), 'cosmopolitan democracy' (Archibugi and Held, 1995) and even 'cosmopolitics' (Cheah and Robbins, 1998). The idea of cosmopolitanism is now being expanded to emphasize social and cultural life (Breckenridge *et al.*, 2002; Beck, 2006). In this view of globalization, the expansion of information and communication technologies, coupled with market-led liberal democracies, are contributing to the creation of what has been called a global civil society (Keane, 2003; Kaldor, 2003), though others have identified tensions between globalization and fragmentation (Clark, 1997).

The economic conception of globalization views it as denoting a qualitative shift from a largely national to a globalized economy, in which national economies continue to predominate within nations, but are often subordinate to transnational processes and transactions (Hirst and Thompson, 1999). The arguments for economic globalization focus on the increasingly internationalized system of manufacture and production, on growing world trade, on the extent of international capital flows and, crucially, on the role of the transnational corporations. Liberal interpretations of globalization see markets playing the key role at the expense of the states. Japanese business strategist Kenichi Ohmae, who has been included in the category of 'extreme globalization theorists', claims that, in the globalized economy the nation state has become irrelevant and market capitalism is producing a 'cross-border civilisation' (Ohmae, 1995).

Both Marxists and world-system theorists stress the importance of the rise of global dominance of a capitalist market economy that is penetrating the entire globe – pan-capitalism is how one commentator described the phenomenon (Tehranian, 1999). With the collapse of communism, the disintegration of the Soviet Union and the Eastern bloc, seen by many as alternative to capitalism, the shift within Western democracies from a public to a private sector capitalism, and the international trend towards liberalization and privatization have contributed to the acceptance of the capitalist market as a global system.

However, questions remain about the extent of globalization. It is argued that many of the indices of globalization are concentrated within the OECD countries, especially between the USA–EU–Japan triad, prompting scholars to talk of 'triadization' rather than the globalization of the world economy. It is beyond dispute, however, that in the post-cold war world, transnational corporations have become extremely powerful actors, dominating the globalized economy. They must compete internationally and will, if necessary, sever the links to the nations where they originally operated, a trend which has been described as a reflection of the 'global footlooseness of corporate capitalism' (Sassen, 1996: 6).

In sociological interpretations of globalization, the notion of culture is of primary importance. British sociologist Anthony Giddens (1990) sees globalization as the spread of modernity, which he defines as the extension of the nation-state system, the world capitalist economy, the world military order and the international division of labour. Waters argues that globalization is 'the direct consequence of the expansion of European culture across the planet via settlement, colonisation and cultural mimesis' (1995: 3–4).

Enthusiasts talk of a new 'global consciousness' as well as physical compression of the world, in which cultures become 'relativized' to each other, not unified or centralized, asserting that globalization involves 'the development of something like a global culture' (Robertson, 1992). Others have been more cautious, arguing that globalizing cultural forces, such as international media and communication networks, produces more complex interactions between different cultures (Appadurai, 1990, 1996). Some have made the case for considering cultural practices as central to the phenomenon of globalization (Tomlinson, 1999).

Global homogenizing forces such as standardized communication networks – both hardware and software, media forms and formats – influence cultural consciousness across the world. However, as the US-based anthropologist Arjun Appadurai argues (1990), these globalizing cultural forces in their encounters with different ideologies and traditions of the world produce 'heterogeneous dialogues'. Appadurai specifies five 'scapes' – ethnoscapes, technoscapes, finanscapes, mediascapes and ideoscapes – to describe the dynamics of contemporary global diversity.

'Ethnoscape' denotes the flow of people – such as tourists, refugees, immigrants, students and professionals – from one part of the globe to another. 'Technoscape' includes the transfer of technology across national borders; while 'finanscape' deals with international flow of investment. 'Mediascape' refers to global media, especially its electronic version – both its hardware and the images that it produces; and 'ideoscape' suggests ideological contours of culture. Appadurai argues that the five 'scapes' influence culture not by their hegemonic interaction, global diffusion and uniform effects, but by their differences, contradictions and counter-tendencies – their 'disjunctures' (Appadurai, 1990).

Some critics see globalization as a new version of Western cultural imperialism, given the concentration of international communication hardware and software power among a few dominant actors in the global arena who want an 'open' international order, created by their own national power and by the power of transnational media and communication corporations (Latouche, 1996; Amin, 1997; Herman and McChesney, 1997). A fear of what the US sociologist George Ritzer called the McDonaldization of society is also expressed by scholars (Ritzer, 1999, 2002). Ritzer says he prefers the term 'Americanization' to globalization, since the latter implies more of a 'multidimensional relationship among many nations' (Ritzer, 1999: 44).

While conceding the pre-eminence of Western media and cultural products in international communication, scholars influenced by post-structuralism dispute whether the global flow of media and cultural products is necessarily a form of domination or even a strictly one-way traffic, arguing that there is a contraflow from the periphery to the centre and between the 'geo-cultural markets', especially in the area of television and films (Sinclair *et al.*, 1996; Thussu, 2006). Ulf Hannerz contests the notion that globalization reinforces cultural movement from the 'centre' (the modern industrial West) to the peripheral 'traditional' world in a largely one-way flow, arguing that centre–periphery interactions are more complex, with cultural flows moving in multiple directions, and thus the outcomes are opposite tendencies, both towards what he calls saturation and maturation, for homogenization and heterogenization (Hannerz, 1997).

Scholars broadly following this line of argument also question the assumptions about the process of homogenization as a result of the diffusion of the Western media and cultural products globally, arguing that the forces of fragmentation and hybridity are equally strong and they affect all societies. Tomlinson argues that 'the effects of globalization are to weaken cultural coherence in all individual nation states, including the economically powerful ones – the imperial powers of a previous era (1991: 175). Others, such as anthropologist Nestor García Canclini ([1989] 1995), see possibilities offered by migration and modernity to broaden cultural territory beyond the nation state. The so-called 'deterritorialization' and the relocation of 'Third World' cultures in the metropolitan centres is considered an enriching experience for the receiving as well as the migratory cultures.

The apparent growth of alternative media and the possibilities opened up by the

Internet are also seen to be a trend towards the disruption of the one-way flow of information. Robertson adopts the concept of 'glocalization', a term whose origins are in the discipline of marketing, to express the global production of the local and the localization of the global, while Nederveen Pieterse (1995) maps out how hegemony is not merely reproduced but 'refigures' in the process of hybridization.

The increased level of transnational information flows, made possible by the new technologies of communication and shifts in the institutional organization – economic, political and legal – on the means of communication, have profoundly affected global media industries. Increasingly, the emphasis is shifting from the traditional approach of considering the role of media in the vertical integration of national societies, to studying information flows which show patterns of transnational horizontal integration of media and communication structures, processes and audiences (Curran and Park, 2000). This has become necessary because of the harmonization of international regulatory and legal frameworks and the globalization of ownership and control in the telecommunication and media sectors – including television, films and online media.

This horizontal communication is facilitating transnational patterns of marketing and political communication, where people are increasingly being addressed across national boundaries on the basis of their purchasing power. Transnational communication is also used by international non-governmental organizations (INGOs) whose politics and actions are being affected by the use of the Internet. The increasingly complex relations between local, national, regional and international production, distribution and consumption of media texts in a global context further complicates the globalization discourse (Thussu, 2006).

Accompanying the dramatic expansion of capitalism and new transnational political organization is a new global culture, emerging as a result of computer and communication technology, a consumer society with a wide range of products and services consumed internationally. Global culture includes the proliferation of media technologies, especially satellite and cable television, that veritably create McLuhan's dream of a global village in which people all over the world watch spectacles like the Gulf War, major sports events, entertainment programmes and advertisements which relentlessly promote free market capitalism.

With the expansion of Internet access, more and more people are entering into the global computer networks that instantaneously circulate ideas, information and images throughout the world, overcoming boundaries of space and time. What kind of international communication this is generating remains a hotly disputed subject, given that culture is an especially complex and contested terrain as 'modern' culture permeates traditional ones and new configurations emerge (Iwabuchi, 2002; Rantanen, 2005; Kraidy, 2005). Some scholars have followed more innovative approaches to understanding globalization in view of the economic rise of Asia (Gunder Frank, 1998; Hobson, 2004). The debates about global culture have been largely ignored by many previous forms of modernization theories that tended towards economic, technological and political determinism. In classical Marxism, culture was sometimes reduced to a crass economic commodity, with scant importance given to local forms of associations – whether based on ethnicity, religion, race or gender. It also did not take on board the issue of cultural diversity, aesthetics and spirituality, being preoccupied with the study of the production and consumption of material culture. For traditional liberalism, the advancement of the modern economy and technology was necessary for creating world markets and consumers.

Both classical Marxists and liberals predicted a borderless world – in the idealized Marxian version the proletariat across the world were to lead international communism that would eliminate nationalism, class exploitation and war, while liberal interpretations saw the market as eroding cultural differences and national and regional particularities, to produce a global consumer culture. Missing from both models has been an understanding of the complexity of the interaction of class with nationalism, religion, race, ethnicity and feminism to produce local political struggles. Despite claims for the end of ideology and history and the 'peace dividend' since the end of the cold war, the world has witnessed a rise in ethnic and religious conflict exacerbated by the events of September 2001 and the subsequent open-ended and global 'war on terrorism' (Hardt and Negri, 2004; Hoge and Rose, 2005).

The intellectual uncertainty that the end of the cold war produced in the West, and the dismantling of the last vestiges of progressive ideology in the former socialist camp, are reflected in an increasing blurring of boundaries between various strands of international communication theory. In this postmodern landscape, there appears to be a fragmentation of theories, with an emphasis on the personal and the local, while macro-level issues affecting international communication are often ignored. Postmodernists argue that developments in transnational capitalism are producing a new global historical configuration of post-Fordism, or postmodernism as a new 'cultural logic' of capitalism (Harvey, 1989; Jameson, 1991). Yet the proliferation of difference and the shift to more local discourses and practices define the contemporary scene, and theory, postmodernists argue, should shift from the level of globalization and its often totalizing macrotheories to focus on the micro, the specific and the heterogeneous. A wide range of theories associated with postculturalism, postmodernism, feminism and multiculturalism and postcolonial studies tend to focus on difference and specificity rather than more global conditions (Lyotard, 1984; Baudrillard, 1994; Bhabha, 1994; Sreberny-Mohammadi, 1994; García Canclini, 1995; Yudice, 2004; Beck, 2006).

A critical international communication theory?

In a postmodern theoretical framework where eclecticism is increasingly replacing essentialism, a critical understanding of the political economy of international communication is essential if one wants to make sense of the expansion, acceleration and consolidation of the US-managed global electronic economy. One significant contemporary theme in international communication research within the critical political economic tradition is the transition from America's post-war hegemony to a world communication order led by transnational businesses and supported by their respective national states, increasingly linked in continental and global structures. The Italian political philosopher Antonio Negri and his American colleague Michael Hardt used the old word 'Empire' to define the new global form of sovereignty (Hardt and Negri, 2000), and what they termed 'the multitude', as 'living alternative that grows within Empire', a type of transnational network of counter-resistance, having the potential to bring global democratisation. The project of multitude, according to Hardt and Negri, 'not only expresses the desire for a world of equality and freedom, not only demands an open and inclusive democratic global society, but also provides the means for achieving it' (Hardt and Negri, 2004: xi).

Critical theorists have focused on international organizations such as the World Trade Organization and the International Telecommunication Union, which have played a crucial role in managing the transition to a market-driven international communication environment. They have analysed transnational corporate and state power, with a particular stress on ownership concentration in media and communication industries worldwide (and the growing trends towards vertical integration), companies controlling production in a specific sector (and horizontal integration) and across sectors, within and outside the media and communication industry (Herman and McChesney, 1997; Tunstall and Machin, 1999; Bagdikian, 2004; McChesney, 1999, 2004). Others have supported movements for greater international information and communication equality, with concerns about incorporating human rights into international communication debates (Hamelink, 1994, 2000; Kaldor, 2003).

Sceptical of the dominant market-based approach, many scholars have defended the public-service view of state-regulated media and telecommunication organizations and advanced public interest concerns before government regulatory and policy bodies, both at national (Garnham, 1990), regional (Collins, 1998; Schiller and Mosco, 2001) and international levels (Mattelart, 1994; Curran and Park, 2000; Hamm and Smandych, 2005). The role of new technologies, especially the Internet, in international communication has also informed the critical research agenda – including conceptualizing the communication diaspora (Karim, 2003; Robins and Aksoy, 2005); the possibilities of resistance and online activism (Castells, 2000b; Curran and Couldry, 2003; Tarrow, 2005; de Jong *et al.*, 2005); and security-related concerns (Hardt and Negri, 2004).

The economic growth of India and the 'peaceful rising' of China – the two ancient civilizations with huge potential to influence the emerging global 'knowledge society' – is likely to affect the way international communication is conceived and conducted (Hobson, 2004). The Chinese version of media marketization – where the state has played a central role in globalization – offers interesting sites for future communication research. The position of religion in international communication is another area which requires urgent attention. A research agenda which aims at internationalizing media, cultural and communication studies has almost become an imperative, given the complexities of global interactions in the age of mobile satellites and digital diasporas (Erni and Chau, 2005). As multi-vocal, multi-directional and multimedia flows, in real time and through digital technologies, become more intensive and extensive, cultural contours of communications will need to be given the prominence they deserve. If the cultural cracks that have emerged in the 'global village' in the wake of 9/11 and its aftermath are not to become chasms, inter-cultural communication will have to be deployed effectively. This would mean working towards an innovative, more inclusive and cosmopolitan research agenda, one that cuts across disciplinary, ethnic, national and religious boundaries to address the emerging 'cartography of global communication' (Thussu, 2006).

chapter three

Creating a global communication infrastructure

In the 1980s and 1990s fundamental ideological changes in the global political arena led to the creation of pro-market international trade regimes which had a huge impact on international communication. The processes of deregulation and privatization in the communications and media industries combined with new digital information and communication technologies to enable a quantum leap in international communication, illustrated most vividly in the satellite industry. The resulting globalization of telecommunications has revolutionized international communication, as the convergence of the telecommunications, computer and media industries has enabled more information to travel more swiftly around a digitally linked globe than ever before in human history.

The new information and communication technologies have helped to create a global communication infrastructure based on regional and global satellite networks, used for telecommunications, broadcasting and, increasingly, electronic commerce. At the same time, there has been a change from state to private control and from a state-centric view of communication to one governed by the rules of the free market, reflecting policy shifts among major powers and multilateral organizations, such as the International Telecommunication Union (ITU).

Analysis of international communication in the past was concerned primarily with government-to-government activities, where a few powerful states dictated the communication agenda, but now an understanding of the world's satellite industry – the hardware of international communication – and its impact on global communication is increasingly important. This liberalization and privatization of international communication has particularly benefited transnational corporations (TNCs), as evidenced through the case study of Rupert Murdoch's News Corporation.

The privatization of telecommunications

For most of the twentieth century, the state was the main provider of national telecommunications infrastructure and equipment and regulator of international traffic. In the 1990s, the state monopolies of Post, Telegraph and Telecommunication (PTT) were forced to give ground to private telecommunication networks, often part of transnational corporations. This shift, which started among some Western countries, has now affected telecommunications globally, with the majority of PTTs privatized or in the process of privatization, which was more advanced in such areas as Internet services: by 2005, only nine per cent of the world's telecoms were state-run for these services (ITU, 2005a).

Since the founding of the International Telegraph Union in 1865, regulation of international telecommunication was the subject of multilateral accord, setting common standards for telecommunications networks across the globe and prices for access to and use of these networks. These conventions were based upon the principles of national monopoly and cross-subsidization, so that national telecom operators such as the British Post Office – which had a monopoly of equipment and services within Britain – could keep the costs affordable for small users by subsidies from international telephony revenues.

In the 1980s, this regulatory framework was criticized as not taking into account technological innovations, such as computing, fibre-optic cables and fax machines. Especially significant was the blurring of the distinction between the transmission of voice and data made possible by these new technologies. As telecommunications traffic increased, so did the demand from transnational corporations for the reduction of tariffs, especially for international services. These companies opposed national monopolies, arguing that a competitive environment would improve services and reduce costs.

In 1984 US President Ronald Reagan announced an 'open skies' policy, breaking the public monopoly and allowing private telecommunications networks to operate in the national telecommunication arena. American Telephone and Telegraph (AT&T), the biggest US telecoms corporation, for example, was split into 22 local companies, which enabled it to enter into new types of business. As a result, the US telecommunication sector was gradually deregulated, liberalized and privatized (Hamelink, 1994).

A year later, Margaret Thatcher's government followed suit in Britain, allowing 51 per cent of British Telecom (the former telecommunications arm of the Post Office) to be privatized, while the Japanese government permitted partial privatization of the national operator, Nippon Telephone and Telegraph (NTT). The privatization of BT and the US/UK demand to reduce the state's role in the telecommunication sector also influenced policy in Europe (Dyson and Humphreys, 1990; Curwen, 1997; European Commission, 1998). Martin Bangermann, European Union Commissioner for Telecommunications, conceded in his report that liberalization was 'absolutely crucial' and that the European Commission had 'got to push organizational restructuring of telecoms operators to prepare for privatization' (quoted in Venturelli, 1998: 134). However, the major European countries proceeded much more slowly in this process, with Germany's Deutsche Telekom, for example, being prepared for sale only in the late 1990s. The general shift from the public-service role of telecommunications to private competition and deregulation had a major impact on international telecommunications policy, shaped by the USA and Europe, which have companies with global ambitions (Braman, 2004).

Free trade in communication products and services

The negotiations of the Uruguay Round of the General Agreement on Tariffs and Trade (GATT, established in 1947 to provide a framework for international trade after the

Second World War) included trade in services for the first time on a par with the traditional commercial and manufacturing sectors. The agenda of this seventh round of GATT talks, which started in 1986 and was the most wide-ranging and ambitious so far, reflected the neo-liberal push towards opening up protected markets. The Final Act of the Uruguay Round, signed in 1994 in Marrakesh, Morocco, for the first time included trade in services, investment and intellectual property rights, in addition to tariff cuts of up to 40 per cent on industrial products, and commitments to remove them further (GATT, 1993).

Their inclusion in the GATT negotiations was the culmination of Western efforts to liberalize the worldwide trade in services (Drake and Nicolaidis, 1992). The USA, leading the West, argued that the world would benefit from the resulting huge expansion in investment and trade. It was estimated that the Uruguay Round, when fully implemented, could boost world income by up to $500 billion, and increase world trade volumes by up to 20 per cent (WTO, 1998).

However, there was tension between the free-marketeers and those who argued for a more regulated system to protect domestic markets and interests. The former wanted to end state intervention in world trade and promote liberalization and privatization (Hemel, 1996). This position was strengthened with the move from GATT to the permanent World Trade Organization (WTO), which came into existence on 1 January 1995, with stricter legal mechanisms for enforcing international trade agreements (Hoekman and Kostecki, 1995).

The WTO was set up with a clear agenda for privatization and liberalization:

> The fundamental cost of protectionism stems from the fact that it provides individual decision makers with wrong incentives, drawing resources into protected sectors rather than sectors where a country has its true comparative advantage. The classical role of trade liberalisation, identified centuries ago, is to remove such hindrances, thereby increasing income and growth.
>
> (WTO, 1998: 38)

As part of this, the WTO also argued that dismantling barriers to the free flow of information was essential for economic growth. It was even implied that it was not possible to have significant trade in goods and services without a free trade in information. The importance of a strong communications infrastructure as a foundation for international commerce and economic development was increasingly emphasized by international organizations (ITU, 1999; World Bank, 1998; UNDP, 1999).

One key outcome of the Uruguay Round was the 1995 General Agreement on Trade in Services (GATS), the first multilateral, legally enforceable agreement covering trade and investment in the services sector and the one with the most potential impact on international communication, though it is also important for other sectors of global trade and investment (Geradin and Luff, 2004). The services sector encompasses financial services (including banking and administration of financial markets), insurance services, business services (including rental leasing of equipment), market research, computer services, advertising and communication services (including telecommunication services – telephone, telegraph, data transmission, radio, TV and news services) (WTO, 1998).

The most significant component of this agreement for international communication was the GATS Annex on Telecommunications. Telecommunications is one of the largest and fastest-growing service sectors and plays a dual role as a communications service, as well as the delivery mechanism for many other services. As a sector of crucial importance to all service exporters for both production and supply, the world market for telecommunications services is expected to triple in the next ten years. Already, by 2004, the overall network-generated revenue had reached $1.3 trillion (UNCTAD, 2005a).

There are interesting similarities between GATS, in particular the Annex, and the 1992 North American Free Trade Agreement (NAFTA) between Canada, the USA and Mexico – the first trade agreement with commitments to reduce barriers to services trade, thus opening up Mexico's services market to US firms (Winseck, 1997). A year after the agreement was signed, Mexico's constitution was amended to allow foreign investment in Mexican media companies (Galperin, 1999).

The Annex encouraged private corporations to invest in privatized telecommunication networks in developing countries and, in turn, Southern governments were encouraged to open up their markets to private telecommunications operators. It also extended the 'free flow of information doctrine' to cover both the content of communication and the infrastructure through which such messages flow.

The GATS Annex set out the rules for trade in telecommunications and dealt with access to and use of public telecommunications transport networks and services. One key guiding principle said that foreign and national suppliers of telecom facilities should be treated equally, thus exposing domestic telecommunications industries to international competition. It obliged countries to ensure that foreign services suppliers had access to public networks and services on an equal basis, both within the national market and across borders.

The rules required free movement of information, including intra-corporate communications and access to databases, with detailed guidance on acceptable conditions for access and use. To ensure transparency, information on charges, technical interfaces, standards, conditions for attaching equipment and registration requirements were to be made publicly available. The Annex also encouraged technical co-operation and the establishment of international standards for global compatibility and interoperability (WTO, 1998).

In essence, the proposed liberal global regime in telecommunication, with fewer restrictions on telecommunication flows and encouragement of investment in infrastructure in the South, aimed to create the conditions to enable transnational corporations to penetrate the 'emerging markets' of Asia and Latin America, where the potential of the services sector was seen to be enormous. According to the WTO, the global trade in services is growing very rapidly (it grew 25 per cent between 1994 and 1997 alone), not least due to advances in information and communications technologies. By 2004, trade in commercial services had exceeded $2.1 trillion (WTO, 1998; World Bank, 1999; WTO, 2005a).

Impact of WTO agreements on international communication

Three major agreements, signed in 1997 under the aegis of the WTO, had a profound impact on global trade, especially in information and communication related areas. In February 1997, 69 WTO countries agreed a wide-ranging liberalization of trade in global telecommunications services. A month later, an agreement was reached to eliminate all import duties on information technology products (which include computers and communications hardware, software and services). Then in December 1997, 102 countries agreed to open up their financial services sector, covering more than 95 per cent of trade in banking, insurance, securities and financial information, to greater foreign competition. Of the three agreements, the most significant for international communication was the GATS Fourth Protocol on Basic Telecommunications Services. The agreement, which came into force in February 1998, obliged the 69 signatories, representing more than 93 per cent of world revenues in telecommunications services, to liberalize telecommunications in their respective countries. All technological means of transmission – cable, radio and satellites – were included in the agreement, although broadcasting of radio and television programmes was excluded. It required the signatories to provide market access and equal treatment to international telecommunication corporations.

Within GATS, the telecommunications sector is divided into two broad categories: basic services (e.g. voice telephone, packet and circuit switched data transmission services, telex, telegraph, facsimile and leased circuits services) and value-added services (including electronic mail, voice mail, online information and database retrieval). During the Uruguay Round, most countries committed themselves to liberalize value-added services, but not basic telecommunications services, so the Fourth Protocol ensured that basic telecommunications were also liberalized (WTO, 1998).

The Ministerial Declaration on Trade in Information Technology Products (Information Technology Agreement), the outcome of the first WTO Ministerial Conference in 1996, ruled that tariffs on information technology products should be abolished by the year 2000. Though the ITA covered six main categories – computers, telecom equipment, semiconductors, semiconductor manufacturing equipment, software and scientific equipment – Northern governments continued to demand the expansion of the agreement to include other information technology products, such as audio, radio, television and video apparatus, telecommunications products and electrical/electronic machines.

The USA, Japan and the EU countries dominate global trade in the information technology sector, though China and South Korea have shown remarkable growth in recent years, doubling their exports of telecommunication equipments between 2000 and 2003 (UNCTAD, 2005a). According to the WTO, the information technology and telecommunication sectors have experienced extraordinary rates of growth in the past three decades. By the late 1990s, world annual sales of personal computers had topped the 50 million mark, exceeding the sales of cars. Since 1996, exports of information and communication goods doubled and have grown at a faster pace than merchandise exports – in 2003, exports of ICT goods exceeded $1.1 trillion, accounting for 15 per cent of world merchandise exports (UNCTAD, 2005a: 24).

Productivity growth in the information technology sector, at almost 5 per cent per year over the 1973–93 period in OECD countries, has been five times as high as overall productivity growth. As a result, by the late 1990s, this sector was accounting for a quarter of economic growth in the USA. By 2004, more than 2 billion telephones and mobile phone connections existed worldwide, many of which were connected to the Internet. Electronic commerce over the Internet, increasingly available through mobile delivery systems, was the latest development in the emergence of an increasingly borderless global economy. It was estimated that by 2005 some 800 million, or nearly 15 per cent of the world's population, were Internet users, though its usage varied significantly between and among nations (UNCTAD, 2005a) (*see* Chapter 7).

The third major WTO agreement was made in December 1997 to open up the financial services sectors, bringing trade in this sector, worth trillions of dollars, under the WTO's multilateral rules. The Agreement on the Liberalization of Financial Services covered more than 95 per cent of world trade in banking, insurance, securities and financial information. As a result of the agreement, banking, securities and insurance services can be conducted across borders, by companies set up in one country supplying services to customers in another. The commitments included improvements in the number of licences available for the establishment of foreign financial institutions and guaranteed levels of foreign equity participation in subsidiaries or affiliates of banks and insurance companies.

These three agreements can be seen as the logical culmination of a process that had its origins in the 1980s debates about what was then called transborder data flow (TDF). The developing world, concerned that such technological innovations as the integrated services digital networks (ISDNs) would make it possible for a huge amount of data to be instantly transferred in or out of countries, wanted to discuss the implications of this for their sovereignty within the UN. However, at US insistence the debate was moved to the OECD, in essence shifting the argument from national sovereignty to one about trade in global information through electronic networks. The 1985 OECD declaration on TDF was unambiguous about the need to dismantle regulations on international movement of data. The TDF, it said, will 'promote access to data and information and related services, and avoid the creation of unjustified barriers to the international exchange of data and information' (OECD, 1985). Since then, even the term 'transborder data flow' has been gradually allowed to fall into disuse, to be replaced by phrases with a more contemporary ring to them, such as 'information trade' (Drake, 1993). With the growing convergence between telecommunication and computer industries, the ability of privatized international telecommunications networks to transmit data across borders unhindered by national regulations became a crucial element in the globalization of financial services, especially banking and insurance, and has contributed substantially to the emerging global electronic economy (*see* Chapter 7).

Why services are important

International trade in commercial services has increased substantially in the past three decades. In 1970, according to the figures from the OECD, the total net trade of OECD countries in the service sector was $2.8 billion, growing to $21.2 billion by 1980 and reaching $30.7 billion by 1991 (OECD, 1993: 26–7). By 2004, according to the WTO, world exports of commercial services had risen to $2.1 trillion. As commercial services have expanded, so has their domination by a few, mostly Western nations, not least by virtue of their financial and technological superiority, though services industries have also benefited such developing countries as India, which has witnessed its exports in commercial services grow nearly sevenfold within a decade – from just over $6 billion in 1994 to nearly $40 billion in 2004 (WTO, 2005b).

Tables 3.1 and 3.2 show that for international trade in commercial services, both infrastructure services (transport and telecommunication) and producer services (banking and insurance), a few rich nations or regions, such as the European Union, the USA and Japan, are predominant, though in the first decade of the twenty-first century, China has shown great potential for growth.

Table 3.1 World exports of commercial services, 1987–2003 ($ billion)

Region	1987	1990	1994	1997	2000	2003
Western Europe	288.1	417.6	495.5	598.1	646	916
Asia	84.2	132.4	221.0	297.8	303	352
North America	99.5	155.1	200.4	259.2	312	330
Latin America	20.4	29.1	41.6	51.3	61	61
Africa	13.4	18.6	22.5	27.7	31	39
World	532.8	788.8	1,036.4	1,311.5	1,435	1,795

Source: WTO, 2005b

Table 3.2 Top 10 exporters of commercial services, 2004

Country/region	Value in $ billion	Global share (%)
EU	427.1	27.8
United States	318.3	20.7
China/Hong Kong	115.7	7.5
Japan	94.9	6.2
Canada	46.8	3.0
South Korea	40.0	2.6
India	39.6	2.6
Switzerland	36.8	2.4
Singapore	36.5	2.4

Source: WTO, 2005b

In 2004, the United States was the largest service exporting country, reflecting the fact that the service sector is the fastest-growing segment of the US economy, and accounting for a fifth of total world services exports. Services exports by the USA have increased steadily over the past two decades – from $77 billion in 1986 to $318 billion in 2004 (WTO, 2005b).

Liberalization of the telecom sector

The opening up of the global market in telecommunication services pitched the International Telecommunication Union against GATT over the regulation of telecommunications. The ethos of the ITU was based historically on the concept of telecommunications as a public utility, with operators having an obligation to provide a universal service. With a policy of co-operation, not competition, the ITU supported restrictions on ownership of and control over telecom operations, in contrast to the neo-liberal telecommunication agenda, which championed privatization and deregulation (Braman, 2004).

Though initially hesitant to accept these changes, the ITU was obliged to play a key part in the shaping of a new, privatized international communications regime in which the standards of universal public service and cross-subsidization were increasingly being replaced with cost-based tariff structures. One area of controversy was the renewed pressure on the ITU from Western governments to reallocate radio and satellite frequencies to commercial operators. Traditionally, the ITU had allocated frequencies on the basis of 'first come, first served'. One result of the expansion of international radio broadcasting during the cold war was that access to the high-frequency end of the radio spectrum for international communication became a contested area between the two cold war blocs. The controversy was fuelled by the defence-related space race, which received new momentum in 1957 with the launch of the world's first satellite, sputnik, by the Soviet Union, which led to a demand for an agreed allocation of space frequencies (Luther, 1988).

Two years later, in 1959, the UN established a committee on the Peaceful Uses of Outer Space, to establish an international regulatory framework with the aim of reducing cold war tensions, which culminated in the Outer Space Treaty in 1967. Article I of this treaty, which forms the basis for international law in the field of space, stated that the exploration and use of outer space 'shall be carried out for the benefit and in the interests of all countries, irrespective of their degree of economic and scientific development, and shall be the province of all mankind'; while its Article II established that outer space 'is not subject to national appropriation by claim of sovereignty, by means of use of occupation, or by any other means' (cited in Hamelink, 1994: 106).

Despite these noble sentiments, the controversy over frequency allocation continued to figure prominently in the ITU's World Administrative Radio Conferences (WARC) in 1959, 1971, 1977 and 1979. By the time of the 1992 WARC conference, held in Torremolinos in Spain, however, the political complexion had changed – superpower space rivalry had ended and the Soviet Union had been dismantled. More importantly, perhaps, in a technologically driven environment, new advances in communications had fundamentally changed the nature of debate. The growing digitization and availability of fibre optics had made it possible for TNCs to transmit globally new communication forms and services, including satellite TV, electronic data and mobile telephony. The mobility and portability of satellite terminals ensured that international communication became much more commodified. Aware of the commercial potential for mobile telephony, the TNCs lobbied at WARC for additional use of the electromagnetic spectrum to effectively offer these new services (Sung, 1992).

In addition, with the fragmentation of the market and the proliferation of operators resulting from the processes of privatization and deregulation, the need to ensure international standards for network compatibility became increasingly obvious. Accordingly, the ITU constitution was amended at the 1998 Plenipotentiary Conference held in Minneapolis, to give greater rights and responsibilities to the ITU's private-sector members. This constitutional change also ensured that private companies would have a larger role in providing advice and making decisions on technical issues. This was a culmination of a process of 'reform', made necessary by the 'changing telecommunications environment', which started at the 1989 Nice Plenipotentiary Conference and was given more concrete shape at the 1992 Geneva conference (MacLean, 1999).

The 1998 conference also agreed a 'Strategic Plan for the Union – 1999–2003', which included proposals to 'improve the structure and functioning of the radio-communication sector, the ITU's biggest and most expensive sector, which was labouring under an increasing regulatory burden'. It also aimed at reviewing international telecommunication regulations, with a view to 'adapting them to the liberalised international environment resulting from the WTO agreements' (MacLean, 1999: 155).

The amendments made to the ITU constitution and conventions opened up the organization to private corporations interested in developing global telecommunications networks and services. ITU members, public and private, were now on an equal footing, with the same rights and obligations. In the area of 'technical recommendation', as one senior ITU official conceded, they 'effectively transfer the power to decide from government to the private sector' (MacLean, 1999: 156).

Under the new international communication regime, the ITU advised countries to dismantle structural regulations preventing cross-ownership among broadcasters, cable operators and telecom companies (ITU, 1999). Since 1990, more than 150 countries had introduced new telecommunication legislation or modified existing regulation, while the percentage of international telephone traffic open to the market had grown exponentially. In essence, the ITU was following the communication agenda set by the world's most powerful nations and the telecommunications corporations based in them. One indication of this was that, following the 1998 OECD Ministerial Conference on electronic commerce, the ITU began to play a leading role among international organizations in the development of electronic commerce, particularly through standardization activities and working with developing countries, where the goal (part of the strategic plan) was to promote global connectivity to the GII (Global Information Infrastructure) and global participation in the GIS (Global Information Society) (US Government, 1995).

The United States saw the creation of a GII as critical for the success of electronic commerce, which required, according to a policy document of the US Government, 'an effective partnership between the private and public sectors, with the private sector in the lead'. Among the governing principles behind the US administration's policy were that the private sector should lead and the government should:

> avoid undue restrictions on electronic commerce; where government involvement is needed, its aims should be to support and enforce a predictable, minimalist, consistent and simple legal environment for commerce; and electronic commerce over the Internet should be facilitated on a global basis.

> (US Government, 1997)

Pekka Tarjanne, the then Secretary General of ITU, welcomed the participation of top telecommunications companies in global policy development. He even suggested that to make the process transparent, the industry itself, rather than the state, should be involved in the process of regulation. The ITU, Tarjanne commented: 'will play an instrumental role in facilitating implementation of the WTO Agreement. This redefined structure and governance of the ITU will fit the landscape of 21st century telecommunications' (Tarjanne, 1999: 63).

The policy of liberalizing the global telecommunication system was greatly influenced by the 1996 Telecommunications Act, which transformed the industry within the USA, facilitating the expansion of private US telecommunications corporations to operate globally. These US-based corporations have in turn played a leading role in pushing the WTO and the ITU to further liberalize global communication. Always a champion of free trade, the United States wants to further reduce the role of its state regulatory mechanisms. The Federal Communications Commission (FCC), for example, saw its role changing from 'an industry regulator to a market facilitator', promoting competition in the international communications market. The aim of the FCC was to refocus to meet what it called 'the challenges of a rapidly progressing global information-age economy and an evolving global communications market'.

> Over the next five years the Commission will pursue an aggressive agenda aimed at increasing competition in communications markets around the world. Increased international competition will benefit American consumers in the form of lower rates for international telecommunications and will open new market opportunities for American companies.

> (FCC, 1999)

Partly as a result of the WTO agreement, more than 100 countries had fully or partially privatized their telecommunications networks. Although the WTO-led liberalization of international communication had transformed global communication, nevertheless demands for further opening up of markets continued. By the end of the 1990s, there were enough indications to show that the US Government had succeeded in building an international communication infrastructure conducive to transnational corporations. The World Radiocommunication Conferences (WRC), in Istanbul in 2000 and in Geneva in 2003, further liberalized global communication infrastructure and moves were afoot towards spectrum harmonization to ensure that satellite systems were able to deliver 3G mobile voice and high-speed broadband services. As Ambassador Janice Obuchowski, Head of the US Delegation, wrote in an official report: 'WRC-2003 was – as most recent radiocommunication conferences have been – a chance for the US to exercise its technological leadership by introducing and expanding the opportunities for new commercial services and applications. All significant US objectives were met. This includes objectives on agenda items with prominent commercial benefits to the US telecommunications and aerospace industries, as well as those agenda items that pertained to key US government systems' (US Government, 2003).

With the increasing privatization of global satellite networks, the satellite industry had the most to benefit from the liberalization of international communication.

Privatizing space – the final frontier

The extraordinary growth of global communications via satellites in the 1990s has been compared to the technological leap forward of cabling the world in the nineteenth century, and, at the dawn of the twenty-first century, satellites were seen as the new 'trade routes in the sky' (Price, 1999). Economic growth and technological progress have fuelled a huge rise in demand for global telecommunications services of all types, resulting in the phenomenal growth of the satellite industry. Satellites are now crucial in providing the cheap, dependable and fast communication services that are essential for international businesses to operate in the global electronic marketplace, especially in such areas as transnational broadcasting and telephony, global banks and airlines, international newspapers and magazine distribution (Parks, 2004).

Ever since the mid-1960s, when geostationary communications satellites first began to provide direct telecommunications links across nations and oceans, they have played a key if unsung role in the development of international communication. Complementing ground-based systems, such as cable and microwave, satellites are able to reach huge areas, unrestrained by geographical terrain. They have enabled the expansion of broadcast and telecommunications services all over the world, from metropolitan cities to the furthest flung islands and remote rural areas. These factors make satellites a lucrative and highly competitive industry in which a few big players operate, given that there are a limited number of orbital slots in the geostationary orbit and multiple satellites covering the same footprint.

To be able to fully exploit space communication services, access to the appropriate radio frequencies and orbital positions is essential. Demand is particularly high for the geostationary (and geosynchronous) orbit (GSO), some 36,000 km above the equator, where satellites move at the same speed as the earth. At this optimal location, communication satellites can cover up to one-third of the Earth's surface. All satellite operators – whether global or regional – have to make use of the 180 available orbital slots (though there are 360 degrees in the orbit, geostationary satellites need at least 2 degrees spacing between each other, halving the number of slots available).

With communication satellites being launched by many countries, for example, India (1983), China (1984) and Mexico (1985), and by regional consortiums, Eutelsat, Arabsat, AsiaSat and Hispasat, the GSO has become very crowded. Though the ITU upholds 'equitable access to the GSO' for all countries, it continues to be dominated by a few nations. In major satellite markets such as Europe, the governments are encouraging private satellite operators. The European Commission's Green Paper on Radio Spectrum Policy, published in 1998, called for 'market-based mechanisms', a euphemism for auctions, to allocate the spectrum in an 'efficient manner' (Oberst, 1999).

More geostationary satellites were launched in the 1990s than ever before. Between 1990 and 1996 – just six years – more satellites were launched than in the past three decades. Since then, as Table 3.3 shows, satellite industry revenue has more than doubled: from $38 billion in 1996 to over $97 billion in 2004. According to a 2004 global survey of satellites by the US-based publication *Via Satellite*, 274 Western-built geostationary commercial communications satellites were in orbit, carrying more than 4000 transponders (components that receive, amplify and retransmit a TV signal) (Mitsis, 2005).

Table 3.3 World satellite industry revenues

Year	Revenue ($ billions)
1996	38.0
1997	49.1
1998	55.0
1999	60.4
2000	73.1
2001	78.6
2002	86.1
2003	91.1
2004	97.2

Source: Satellite Industry Association, 2005

Contributing to this vigorous growth were the international agreements on telecommunications in the late 1990s, especially the WTO's Fourth Protocol, also referred to as the Basic Agreement on Telecommunications Services, which endorsed the US position that the distinction between 'domestic' and 'international' satellite systems was no longer valid in a digitally connected world and that satellite transmissions could cross national borders.

Such has been the change in the global communication industry that even intergovernmental organizations have been driven increasingly by market considerations. This inevitable trend towards the privatization of intergovernmental organizations is demonstrated by the case of Inmarsat (International Marine Satellite). Based in London, Inmarsat was established in 1979 as an internationally owned co-operative of 86 countries to serve the maritime community and is the sole provider of a broad range of global mobile satellite communications for distress and safety communication, as well as communications for commercial applications at sea, in the air and on land.

In 1999, it became the world's first international treaty organization to transform itself into a commercial company. Part of the company's attraction to likely investors was that it would be operating in the fast growing mobile satellite communication industry. With privatization, some of the largest national telecommunication businesses in the world, from among its former member countries, have become the shareholders and backers of the new company which, by 2005, owned a fleet of ten satellites. *Inmarsat-4* satellite, launched in 2005, will enable the creation of the Broadband Global Area Network (BGAN), which will be available to 85 per cent of the earth's landmass (www.inmarsat.com).

Other telecommunications bodies set up along similar lines, such as the Paris-based pan-European intergovernmental organization Eutelsat, the first satellite operator in Europe to broadcast direct-to-home (DTH), was also following the privatization path, euphemistically called the 'restructuring process'. In 2001, its operations and activities were transferred to a private company called Eutelsat SA. The 'transformation' has led to expansion of the company, with six new satellites launched and capacity leased on two others: by 2005, Eutelsat was operating 23 satellites, broadcasting more than 1700 television channels and 860 radio stations to 120 million households in Europe, and Middle East, North Africa, as well as parts of Asia and North America (www.eutelsat.com). In an international context, a more significant change has been the gradual commercialization and privatization of the International Telecommunications Satellite Organization (Intelsat).

Case study

Intelsat

Intelsat was created in 1964 as an intergovernmental treaty organization (in the spirit of the UN) to operate a global satellite system for telecommunications services, offering affordable satellite capacity on a non-discriminatory basis. At the time of its creation commercial satellite communication did not exist and most telecommunications organizations were state-controlled monopolies, operating within a highly regulated environment. As it was the height of the cold war, the Soviet Union and its allies inevitably saw Intelsat as a US instrument to control satellite communication.

Intelsat operated as a commercial co-operative and a wholesaler of satellite communications, providing advanced telecommunications services to its 143 member countries, and indeed to all nations. In 1971, Intelsat endorsed the landmark UN resolution on space communication, made 10 years earlier, that had affirmed that satellite communication should be available to every nation 'as soon as practicable on a global and non-discriminatory basis' (Colino, 1985).

To ensure that the less developed countries could also benefit from satellite technology, Intelsat followed a policy of global price averaging, using revenues from high-traffic routes, such as North America, Europe and Japan, to subsidize the less profitable routes (Gershon, 1990: 249). However, Comsat (the Communications Satellite Corporation, a privately owned corporation with AT&T as its largest stockholder), which represented the USA and therefore the dominant interests within Intelsat, aggressively pushed for commercial applications of satellite television. Contrary to UN resolutions, notes Schiller, the space communications development was affected by decisions 'based on market considerations emphasising capital distributions, volumes of international communications and expectations of profitability' (Schiller, 1969 [1992]: 190).

Although ostensibly a non-profit international co-operative, giving all countries access to the global satellite system, Intelsat has in fact been controlled by a few nations, with eight Western countries accounting for half the controlling shares and the USA holding the largest investment, followed by Britain. The share of investment has ensured that Intelsat, like other international organizations, has reflected the concerns of Western countries. In a technology-driven industry, the countries that control the technology inevitably have greater power to set and implement the policy agenda.

The growth of regional satellite systems, such as Eutelsat and Arabsat, threatened the near monopoly status that Intelsat had enjoyed during the cold war years. In 1989, the decision of the FCC to authorize a private company, Pan American Satellite Inc. (PanAmSat), to provide international carrier services between the USA and Latin America, triggered the process of privatization of satellite-based international communication (Frieden, 1996). As an intergovernmental organization (IGO), Intelsat felt that its statute restricted its commercialization: it could not own or operate its own Earth stations or provide retail services directly to end users in some countries. Most importantly, it also could not set 'market-based pricing for its services'.

Commercialization received a boost with the end of the cold war-related space race, as many Eastern bloc countries, including Russia, joined Intelsat. The International Organization of Space Communications (Intersputnik), which was established in 1971 as a rival to Intelsat to provide satellite communications to socialist countries, began to negotiate with Western satellite companies for joint ventures. By 1999, the politics of space had changed so much that a Russian rocket was used to launch the European satellite, Astra1H, with the world's first commercial Ka-band payload for use over Europe, from the cosmodrome at Baikonur in Kazakhstan.

Reflecting the strides made by satellite communications globally, Intelsat massively expanded its operations in the 1990s. After an agreement with the UN in 1993 to increase satellite services globally, the pace of development was rapid. In Latin America alone, Intelsat's revenues grew from $64 million in 1994 to $130 million in 1997 (Kessler, 1998). In 1997–98, Intelsat launched five new satellites, while the Intelsat IX programme, equipped with Intelsat IX spacecraft, started offering more and enhanced services to operators. In 1998, with revenues exceeding $1 billion for the first time, the organization transferred a quarter of its satellite fleet to a newly created private commercial company, New Skies Satellites, based in the Netherlands, a global system with five satellites. The move was justified by Conny Kullman, the Director General and Chief Executive Officer of Intelsat, in the organization's 1998 annual report:

> The creation of New Skies was a fundamental step toward the full commercialisation of Intelsat, a goal we consider vital to our continued ability to prosper in an increasingly competitive and dynamic marketplace... Competition breeds innovation and technological advancement, which leads to lower prices and better services for customers. The end result is a more vibrant market for all communications companies, and a confirmation that Intelsat's owners are prepared to undertake fundamental change to maximise value to shareholders and customers alike.
>
> (Intelsat, 1999)

In 1999, Intelsat owned and operated a global satellite system of 19 satellites, bringing both public and commercial networks, video and Internet services to over 200 countries and territories around the world. Though more than 60 countries depended entirely on Intelsat for their satellite-based international communications, Intelsat's position was being increasingly threatened by competition from private telecommunications transnationals, both regionally and globally. A 'new Intelsat', a private entity, was set up in 2001. Privatization has opened up the debate about who would have strategic control of the new Intelsat, which still runs the world's largest commercial geostationary satellite network – in 2005 it owned 27 satellites and leased 2 others (www.intelsat.com).

In 1999, the US-based Comsat, the largest individual shareholder in both Intelsat and Inmarsat, merged with Lockheed Martin, one of the world's biggest defence corporations. Comsat was also the largest individual owner in New

Skies. Lockheed Martin became the largest shareholder of the new privatized Intelsat, though it did not retain that position for long as, in 2002, the new Intelsat acquired Comsat World Systems, a subsidiary of Lockheed Martin, and two years later, in 2004, Intelsat bought its share from Lockheed Martin.

By 2005, Intelsat was serving more than 60 US government and military users, as well as NATO entities, with military communication accounting for about 18 per cent of the company's revenue in 2004. At the beginning of 2005, a consortium led by four major US-based private investment groups – Apax Partners, Apollo, Permira and Madison Dearborn Partners – bought Intelsat for $5 billion, in a move towards the further privatization of global communication. In August 2005 it was announced that Intelsat would take over PanAmSat for $3.2 billion. Using a combined fleet of 53 satellites, it will be serving customers in more than 220 countries and territories (www.intelsat.com). The decision reflects synergies between communication and broadcasting interests – PanAmSat has a strong presence in DTH services, while Intelsat has its core strength in telephony and data services.

The privatization of Inmarsat and Intelsat raises important questions about telecommunications access for the world's poorer countries. Intelsat has played a crucial role in bringing satellite technology to the South. The economies of scale coupled with innovations in satellite technology made it possible for Intelsat to progressively cut the rates charged for the use of its services. Under its policy of rate averaging – high-density routes, for example between North America and Western Europe, had lower costs per circuit than low-density routes – much of the developing world came under the latter category. In order to provide services to thin routes, Intelsat charged the same rate for all routes; thus, in effect, the high-density traffic subsidized the others. The new Intelsat is unlikely to continue this practice. Given their economic situation, it would be extremely difficult for poorer countries to afford transponder fees or to acquire other commercial satellite services (Thussu, 2002a). Despite its recent growth, the satellite industry demands very substantial investment and high risk, and only transnational corporations and other large businesses and governments will be able to exploit this communication hardware.

The global satellite industry

Digital technology (with modern satellites experiencing nearly 500-fold capacity increase over 1960s spacecraft), WTO-sponsored deregulation and the rapid privatization of national telecommunications organizations have accelerated the flow of information across national borders. This has resulted in a flourishing global telecommunications industry, led by commercial international satellite and cable communications operators, offering a wider range of services. US companies and a French-led European consortium lead the world market for the manufacture of geostationary satellites. In 2005, the US-based Satellite Industry Association, which represents the leading US commercial satellite corporations, reported that the commercial satellite industry generated $97.2 billion in revenue in 2004, a figure which has more than doubled since 1996, driven primarily by the DTH services, which accounted for $49.5 billion, or about 51 per cent of the entire industry's revenues. As Tables 3.4 and 3.5 show, the industry is dominated by a few, mainly USA-based, corporations, which are leading players in manufacturing satellites and space rocket components as well as ground services and satellite services.

Table 3.4 Global space industry – top five in 2004

Company	Space sales ($ billion)	Total sales
Boeing (USA)	10.3	52.4
Lockheed Martin (USA)	9.6	35.5
Northrop Grumman (USA)	4.5	29.8
EADS (Netherlands)	3.5	3.5
Raytheon (USA)	3.4	20.2

Source: Reprinted with permission from the 1 August 2005 issue of *Space News*

Table 3.5 Top five global satellite operators in 2004

Company	2004 revenue ($ million)	Satellites in orbit
SES Global (Luxembourg)	1560	37
Intelsat (Bermuda-USA)	1040	28
Eutelsat (France)	1037	21
PanAmSat (USA)	827.1	23
JSAT corp. (Japan)	430.7	5

Source: Reprinted with permission from the 1 August 2005 issue of *Space News*

The satellite launch industry (revenues $2.8 billion in 2004) has also witnessed a shift towards commercial rather than government launches: 53 per cent of the total global launches in 2004 were government and 47 per cent were commercial. In 2000, 66 per cent of total global launches were government and 34 per cent were commercial. The three largest US contractors – Hughes Space and Communications, Lockheed Martin and Loral – have between them built more than 70 per cent of the geostationary communications satellites in orbit, while a European satellite consortium led by the French Aerospatiale has built more than 20 per cent of those in orbit. To have a better appreciation of the reach of Western satellite networks, it is useful to examine who the main international and regional satellite players are. Most of the information that follows has been obtained from the websites of the major satellite corporations and the trade press, since little academic work exists on this subject and whatever is available dates very rapidly given the changing nature of the industry.

Hughes Network Systems

Of the world's three biggest satellite manufacturers, Hughes is the most significant, accounting for 40 per cent of the commercial satellite service worldwide. The Hughes conglomerate claims to be 'the most comprehensive vertically-integrated satellite firm in the world'. Among Hughes' main customers is the Luxembourg-based Société Européenne des Satellites (SES), the owner and operator of Astra, Europe's leading DTH satellite system, reaching an audience of 102 million households in Europe. In addition, Hughes is a major supplier for the US defence services, designing and launching the Leasat satellites used by the US government to create a global military communications and surveillance network. Of the 179 satellites built by Hughes since 1963, the first 100 were launched over a period of 17 years, whereas 79 were launched in the 1990s. By 2005, Hughes had become a major player in providing high-speed broadband by satellite, with hubs in the USA, Europe, Brazil, China and India. In 2000, the US defence giant Boeing bought Hughes' satellite operations for $3.75 billion. Boeing, the largest aerospace company in the world, apart from being the world's top manufacturer of commercial and military aircraft, is also one of the biggest producers of defence-related advanced information and communication systems. The deal reinforces close links between civil and military operations among the world's top satellite corporations.

Lockheed Martin Global Telecommunications

The defence industry is also crucial for the satellite manufacturer, Lockheed Martin Global Telecommunications (LMGT), part of the Lockheed Martin corporation, the largest defence contractor in the USA (2004 sales $35.5 billion). In what was termed a space coup, Lockheed Martin formed a joint venture in 1997 with Intersputnik to launch and operate a fleet of advanced communications satellites, creating a global integrated system for communication and broadcasting services. Cash-strapped Intersputnik needed the support of one of the world's best-resourced companies, while Lockheed Martin was interested in Intersputnik's 15 highly valuable GSO slots. By joining forces with the Russians, Lockheed Martin acquired the capacity to transmit video, data and phone services worldwide. Of particular interest were the two Intersputnik slots, registered in Cuba's name, that cover North and South America. In 1998, LMGT established Americom Asia-Pacific, a joint-venture company, owned with GE Americom, to launch and operate a new high-powered Ku-band satellite system. Lockheed Martin was also involved in building a regional mobile personal communications system, including a satellite, ground network and user terminals, for the Asian Cellular Satellite System. For the crucial Chinese market, LMGT has built five satellites, including ChinaStar-1 – to provide voice, data and television distribution services to one of the world's biggest markets. In recent years it has expanded its operations globally and was for three years (2001–4) the main actor within a privatized Intelsat.

Loral Space & Communications

The third key corporation is Loral Space & Communications, one of the world's largest satellite communications companies, which, since 1957, has been awarded contracts to build more than 200 satellites. In 1997, as part of what the company called 'developing the building blocks necessary to create a seamless, global networking capability for the information age', Loral acquired Skynet, then a US provider of transponder capacity, and extended its reach to Latin America with the 75 per cent purchase of Satélites Mexicanos (SatMex). The Orion Network, which was bought in 1998, had licences for orbital slots covering Europe, Latin America and Asia. Loral Skynet's Telstar satellites provided coverage over most of North America, as well as transatlantic coverage through the Orion 1 satellite. In the USA, Loral Skynet had links with EchoStar, the DTH service operating more than 300 channels of digital video and audio programming. Loral Skynet also led the Loral Global Alliance, a worldwide network of satellite capacity on the North American Telstar fleet, the transatlantic Orion 1 satellite and the SatMex fleet for South America, as well as on Europe*Star satellites.

However, one of its recent satellites – Telstar 14 – launched in 2004, could only operate 15 of its 41 transponders, leading to financial difficulties for the company, forcing it to sell some of its North American satellites to Intelsat. Despite this setback, Loral has investments in XTAR, a joint venture with a consortium of Spanish telecommunications companies, including Hispasat, as well as the Spanish Government, which launched its first high-powered satellite, XTAR-EUR in 2005. Loral leases its transponders to provide a platform for the global distribution of television programming, video applications and data service providers. In 2005, among its customers were AT&T, Cable & Wireless, Univision, Telecom Italia and China Central Television.

Regional satellite services

The deregulation and privatization of the global telecommunications market, coupled with the perceived need for a strong communications infrastructure to open up new regions to the global economy, have resulted in fierce competition in regional satellite services. Regional operators in Latin America, the Middle East and Asia are striking alliances to extend their reach and that of their customers beyond their own territories. As a result of the gradual deregulation of broadcasting in Europe, private satellite companies have prospered. Astra (owned by Société Européenne des Satellites – SES) has seen its operations grow significantly since its launch in 1989. By 2005, SES Global had been formed, which owned five satellites and shared 'complementarity' with Americom (which it acquired in 2001) in North America, AsiaSat in Asia and Star One in Latin America. In less than a decade, the market share of satellite reception has risen from virtually zero to more than 26 per cent of TV households in Europe. By 2005, Astra was carrying broadcast (1400 TV and 300 radio channels, both digital and analogue) and broadband services to more than 102 million homes across Europe. SES Global holds a 34 per cent share of AsiaSat, Asia's premier satellite operator, providing broadcast and telecommunications services to 53 countries in the Asia-Pacific region.

In Latin America, PanAmSat, the first private satellite service for the continent, launched in 1988, has made the region important for satellite manufacturers. In 1997, PanAmSat launched three satellites for the Latin American region (PAS-5, PAS-6 and Galaxy 8i) to support the DTH services operated by Sky Latin America and Galaxy Latin America. With the launch in 2003 of Galaxy 13, it entered the era of high-definition-enabled satellite. Though strong in Latin American, PanAmSat also had a significant presence in other parts of the world – Galaxy for North America; PAS-4 (the first commercial satellite for Africa, in operation since 1995, as well as four others); PAS-10 for Asia-Pacific; and PAS-3 and PAS-9 for Europe. By 2004, PanAmSat, now one of the world's leading commercial providers of satellite-based communications services, was operating a global network of 23 geosynchronous satellites. In 2005, PanAmSat was taken over by Intelsat.

In Asia, the most significant development was the launch in 1990 of AsiaSat 1, which not only signalled China's entry into the market for launching commercial satellites, but made available, for the first time, two powerful regional beams, revolutionizing Asian broadcasting and telecommunications services. AsiaSat 1 had 24 transponders and its northern beam covered China, Japan, the Koreas, parts of Russia and Mongolia, while the southern beam stretched from South East Asia to the Middle East. AsiaSat 2, launched in 1995, extended the reach to cover large parts of former Soviet Union and Australia. Between them the two satellites covered 53 countries and two-thirds of the world's population. AsiaSat 3S, launched in 1999, replaced AsiaSat 1, carrying 28 C-band and 16 Ku-band high-powered transponders. AsiaSat 4 was launched in 2003, with 28 C-band and 20 Ku-band transponders, including a broadcast satellite service. In the last 15 years AsiaSat has emerged as the leading regional satellite operator (in 2004, it had 57 transponders), whose telecommunications and broadcast facilities are used by governments, telecommunications services operators, aviation and travel services, financial institutions, news agencies and broadcasters. Without AsiaSat there would not have been a pan-Asian television network like STAR (Satellite Television Asian Region), which in 2005 accounted for a quarter of sales for AsiaSat. Given the growing importance of China within the Asian communication sphere, in 2004, AsiaSat launched a joint venture, Beijing Asia, to provide corporate data networks and services to Chinese companies.

In the Arab world, the regional satellite operator, the Arab Satellite Communications Organization (Arabsat), was established in 1976 by members of the Arab League. DTH services have been available to the Arab countries since the launch of Arabsat 1C in 1992. Other satellites – Arabsat 2A and 2B, whose life span is expected to last until 2012 – have further improved telecommunication services in the region, while the third generation Arabsat (3A) and the Arabsat BSS1, carry Ku-band channels covering the Arab world and Europe. Based in Dirab in Saudi Arabia, and with the Saudi Government as the largest investor, Arabsat also invested in a commercial company – Thuraya Satellite Telecommunications Company, founded in 1997 – to meet the growing telecommunication needs in the region.

Though the geostationary systems continue to grow, they are being brought under the wings of large corporations through mergers, takeovers and regional alliances between major operators. From a commercial perspective, this makes market sense since large systems create economies of scale and boost the argument for further deregulation of satellite communication, especially in the DTH sector, to which several countries have been resistant. Unable to compete with global carriers, many state-run operators have privatized their own satellite systems, as have the intergovernmental satellite operators. The net result of these changes is that the market for satellite services has become increasingly commercial, a trend which is likely to grow, with increasing worldwide use of satellites for Internet and mobile communication and commerce.

Case study

Murdoch's media – 'The eyes of the world are on us'

One major beneficiary of the privatization of the infrastructure of international communication has been News Corporation, the company owned by the Australian-born media tycoon Rupert Murdoch, whose empire straddles the globe. With wide-ranging media interests – from newspapers, film, broadcast, satellite and cable TV, digital TV, television production, to the Internet – News Corporation is a major international player in all aspects of the communications and media market.

Murdoch made skilful use of liberalization of cross-media ownership regulations in Britain and the USA during the 1990s and the entry of private satellite operators into the arena of telecommunications and broadcasting. Risking an enormous amount of money by leasing time on new satellite ventures such as Astra and AsiaSat, he was able to create a truly international media corporation, at the heart of which is satellite television. 'More than any other figure,' writes one observer, 'Murdoch has been the visionary of a global corporate media empire' (McChesney, 1999: 96). The theme for the company's 1999 Annual Report, *Around the World, Around the Clock,* echoed the global nature of News Corporation, 'the only vertically integrated media company on a global scale': 'in the course of 24 hours News Corp. reaches nearly half a billion people in more than 70 countries'.

The range of its media products can best be illustrated by the following extract from the company's 1999 Annual Report:

> Virtually every minute of the day, in every time zone on the planet, people are watching, reading and interacting with our products. We're reaching people from the moment they wake up until they fall asleep. We give them their morning weather and traffic reports through our television outlets around the world. We enlighten and entertain them with such newspapers as *The New York Post* and *The Times* as they

have breakfast, or take the train to work. We update their stock prices and give them the world's biggest news stories every day through such news channels as *FOX* or *Sky News*. When they shop for groceries after work, they use our *SmartSource* coupons to cut their family's food bill. And when they get home in the evening, we're there to entertain them with compelling first-run entertainment on FOX entertainment on FOX or the day's biggest game on our broadcast, satellite and cable networks. Or the best movies from Twentieth Century Fox Film if they want to see a first-run movie. Before going to bed, we give them the latest news, and then they can crawl into bed with one of our best-selling novels from HarperCollins.

It could have added that with the successful 1998 launch of Sky Digital – a multiple-channel subscription service on British Sky Broadcasting (BSkyB), the company has also come to dominate interactive digital television. Murdoch already has considerable clout in Britain, where he owns (apart from BSkyB, which by 2005 claimed to have nearly 9 million subscribers – one-third of UK television households – as well as total revenue of £4 billion), the prestigious *The Times* and *The Sun* (Britain's largest selling popular newspaper, notorious for promoting a journalism based on three Ss: sex, soccer and scandal).

Apart from owning the largest number of English-language daily newspapers around the world, the company also owns Fox Broadcast Network (which in 2005 owned 35 TV stations across the USA), Fox News Channel (and its local affiliates, including scores of sports channels) and *Gemstar-TV Guide International* (a top-selling television magazine), Hollywood giant Twentieth Century Fox, the first pan-Asian network STAR, the newspaper *The Australian* and television channel FOXTEL in Australia, National Geographic Channel International and the publisher HarperCollins (*see* map, p. 88). With worldwide operations, HarperCollins Publishing is a major global presence, with subsidiaries like HarperCollins Europe, HarperCollins Canada and HarperCollins Australia. It also owns Zondervan Publishing House, the world's largest commercial Bible publisher.

Though the USA remains its primary market and since 2004 also News Corporation's headquarters, accounting for 74 per cent of its 2005 revenue, Murdoch has wide-ranging media interests in the world's two biggest consumer markets – India and China. In 2005, Hong Kong-based STAR was operating, either in partnership or alone, over 50 television services in 7 languages to reach more than 300 million viewers across 53 countries. The STAR network spans the world's most populous continent, having a prominent position in India (where News Corporation owns STAR Plus, and partly owned, until 1999, Zee TV, the country's most popular Hindi-language private

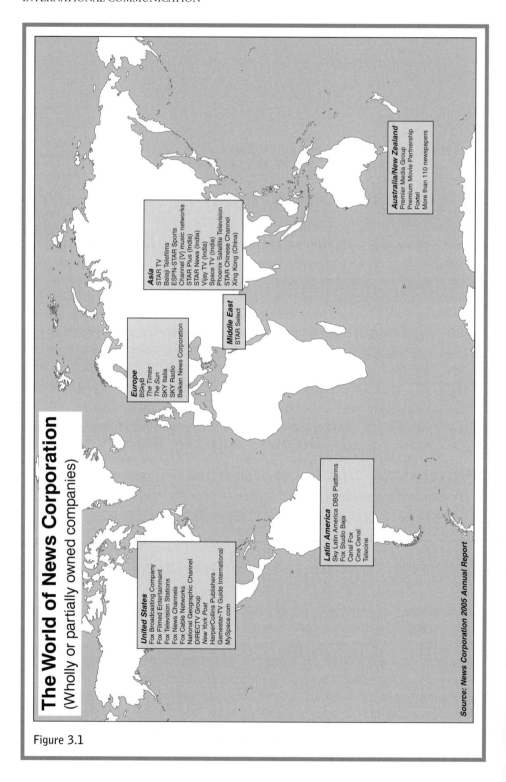

The World of News Corporation
(Wholly or partially owned companies)

United States
Fox Broadcasting Company
Fox Filmed Entertainment
Fox Television Stations
Fox News Channels
Fox Cable Networks
National Geographic Channel
DIRECTV Group
New York Post
HarperCollins Publishers
Gemstar-TV Guide International
MySpace.com

Europe
BSkyB
The Times
The Sun
SKY Italia
SKY Radio
Balkan News Corporation

Asia
STAR TV
Balaji Telefilms
ESPN-STAR Sports
Channel [V] music networks
STAR Plus (India)
STAR News (India)
Vijay TV (India)
Space TV (India)
Phoenix Satellite Television
STAR Chinese Channel
Xing Kong (China)

Middle East
STAR Select

Australia/New Zealand
Premier Media Group
Premium Movie Partnership
Foxtel
More than 110 newspapers

Latin America
Sky Latin America DBS Platforms
Fox Studio Baja
Canal Fox
Cine Canal
Telecine

Source: News Corporation 2005 Annual Report

Figure 3.1

channel) and in China (where it has stakes in Phoenix, the Mandarin-language channel, as well as Xing Kong). As Table 3.6 shows, India is the biggest market for STAR network, which has reach beyond the Asian region, its signals covering a vast swathe of Asia and parts of the former Soviet Union.

Table 3.6 Top five STAR channels in Asia, 2005

Channels	Country	Coverage (millions)
Star Plus	India	50.0
Star Gold	India	38.4
Star News	India	30.0
Star Movies	India	22.4
Xing Kong	China	9.2

Source: *STAR TV*

In the USA, Fox Network is well established, producing such international television hits as *The Simpsons*, competing with three traditional networks – CBS, NBC and ABC. Fox News has redefined broadcast journalism in the USA, changing the way television news is presented and framed. In Latin America, Sky network has agreement with Televisa, the Mexican television giant, and other regional broadcasters for a DTH operation, while among News Corporation's pan-regional Latin American programming channels are Canal Fox, 'the Hollywood channel' – one of the most widely distributed channels in the region – as well as minority shares in Cine Canal and Telecine.

This makes News Corporation one of the world's largest media empires, truly global in its reach and influence. What distinguishes it from its rivals such as Time Warner and Disney Corporation is the fact that it is the only one created, built and dominated by one man – Rupert Murdoch, the 74-year-old Chairman and Chief Executive Officer of News Corporation (Page, 2003).

Murdoch has shown an exemplary knack in dealing with the media and entertainment business. His risk-taking attitude, combined with a deep knowledge of the media industries and an uncanny ability to feel the popular pulse, account for this extraordinary success. He understood, better than any other media baron, the centrality of live sports television, and therefore a crucial element of News Corporation's television strategy was its sports programming and acquiring broadcasting rights to live matches – a major earner for television. In the USA, its involvement in sports is extensive, including live broadcast of the National Football League Super Bowl and baseball's World Series. Fox has affiliations with 25 regional sports networks, which have broadcasting rights to more than 3500 live sporting events, involving most teams in the National Basketball Association, National Hockey League and Major League Baseball, while its FOXTEL has rights to broadcast Australia's National Rugby League. In Latin America its cable-based FOX Sports Network boasts more than 65 million subscribers, while with a Brazilian partner, NetSat, it covers, among others, Brazilian and World Cup soccer and Formula One car racing.

In Britain, News Corporation's key television interests rest with its 37 per cent holding in BSkyB – now Europe's most profitable broadcaster – which made much of its money by buying up the rights to telecast live top football matches and pioneered 'pay-per-view' sports television. In 2005, Sky Sports broadcast more than 25,000 hours of sports on its four channels. It launched Europe's first sports news channel, Sky Sports News, while continuing to broadcast 60 live Premier League games a season and more than 140 other football matches. Since 2006, Sky has also acquired exclusive live telecast rights for cricket test matches. The Global Cricket Corporation (also owned by Murdoch) has marketing and broadcasting rights for the 2007 Cricket World Cup. Having established a base in Britain, Murdoch expanded his business into continental Europe by establishing partnerships in Germany (VOX and TM3) and Italy (Stream). With television operations on four continents, News Corporation's reach into the world's living rooms is unequalled. Television, delivered by broadcast, cable and satellite, remains the fastest-growing part of the company – in 2004, it accounted for 46 per cent of News Corporation's revenue (News Corporation, 2005).

Another key area of importance was Murdoch's use of information technology. To sell its SkyDigital service, Murdoch provided free digital set-top boxes and in less than a year SkyDigital had more than 1 million subscribers, making it the world's most successful launch of a digital platform. Similarly, when television interactive services were introduced with Sky+, the company offered free set-top boxes to new subscribers. News Corporation also owns or has stakes in several information technology companies: NDS, the Israel-based designer and manufacturer of digital broadcasting systems; its US Internet operating subsidiary News America Digital Publishing; and PDN Xinren Information Technology, a joint venture between News Corporation and the *People's Daily*, the mouthpiece of the Chinese Communist Party. Murdoch's business acumen has obviously shown success – News Corporation's revenues have grown steadily. The company's total assets in June 2005 were $54.6 billion.

Parallel to his business acumen is Murdoch's very pragmatic political agenda. Despite being critical of US big business for decades, he took US citizenship in 1984 to meet government regulations on media ownership. He withdrew BBC World Service television from the northern beam of his STAR network in 1992 after the Chinese Government criticized the BBC's coverage of the country. Murdoch's media solidly backed Margaret Thatcher in her efforts to liberalize regulations on cross-media ownership. *The Sun*'s support for Tony Blair was crucial in the 1997 election victory of the British Labour Party. Murdoch was also an ardent supporter of US President George W. Bush and his 'war on terrorism', which most of his media, particularly Fox News, championed relentlessly. This 'Murdochization' of the media has changed the media landscape in the USA and in Britain, and, increasingly, in other countries where Murdoch has been a major player since the 1990s. In essence, this has meant an emphasis on entertainment and infotainment at the expense of the public service role of the media.

News Corporation has used an array of strategies to consolidate its position in Asia – potentially the world's biggest television market. In India, for example, its operations were co-ordinated by Rathikant Basu, a former director general of Doordarshan, India's state television network, and News Corporation Europe was launched in 1998 under Letizia Moratti, the former chairperson of the Italian state broadcasting group, Radiotelevisione Italiana (RAI).

Murdoch's growing political influence as a multimedia mogul, and his extensive control of both information software (programme content) and hardware (digital delivery systems), make him hugely powerful. And since he was one of the first to realize the commercial importance of digital television, investing a great deal of money to get it off the ground, his empire is most likely to dominate the digital globe. With the digitization of content, which News Corporation sees as 'perhaps the most important event in business since the invention of the telephone', it has been able to produce more country-specific television channels and develop many interactive media outlets.

With the growing convergence between digital and interactive television and the Internet, News Corporation's interests are focused on developing advanced electronic programme guides, the portal of the multichannel digital television environment. Its venture capital company, epartners, formed in 1999, was set up to exploit the new opportunities in a digitized and interactive media world.

Murdoch's worldwide presence – with operations in the USA, Europe, Australia, Latin America and Asia – makes him a very significant global media player and News Corporation one of the world's largest media companies, with total 2004 annual revenues of $20.8 billion (News Corporation, 2005). With the acquisition, in 2004, of DirecTV, the largest DTH platform in the USA, investment in DTH operations elsewhere (notably Space TV in India and Sky Italia) and growing engagement with online media by buying Internet-based operations like MySpace.com, as well as the introduction in Britain in 2006 of Sky by broadband and Sky by mobile, Murdoch's influence is likely to continue. As News Corporation's 2005 Annual Report, entitled *The eyes of the world are on us,* notes: '...we have learnt how to integrate our content and distribution assets into a seamless whole that allows us to get the most out of each individual asset – an attribute that further distinguishes us from our peers' (News Corporation, 2005: 5).

The globalization of telecoms

The expansion of global satellite networks is having a significant impact on the international telecommunications industry. Information liberalization and the deregulation which it promotes have led to unprecedented rates of merger activity and corporate consolidation in the information and communications industries. The increasing demand for wireless technologies and mobility is spreading to all aspects of telecommunications and representing a fundamental change that is transforming international communication through the convergence of digital media delivery systems. In addition, mergers and consolidation in these sectors are likely to lead to global dominance by a dozen or so companies of the telecoms market (*see* Table 3.7).

Table 3.7 Top 10 telecoms in 2003

Company	Country where based	Revenue $m
NTT	Japan	91,026
Verizon Communications	USA	67,734
France Telecom	France	52,048
Deutsche Telekom	Germany	50,528
Vodafone	UK	47,962
SBC Communications	USA	42,310
AT&T	USA	36,480
Telecom Italia	Italy	32,983
BT	UK	30,460
Telefónica	Spain	26,739

Source: *OECD Information Technology Outlook: 2004 edition.* © OECD 2004

The main beneficiaries of liberalization during the 1990s were the major telecom operators, which increasingly looked at emerging markets in Asia and Latin America for new subscribers. The opening up of global telecommunications services also benefited the suppliers of telecommunication hardware. The worldwide trade in information and communication products has shown exponential growth as an increasing number of people are deploying these in their everyday life. Though a few, mainly Western, countries, have dominated trade in this sector, with the USA being the biggest exporter, by 2004 China had overtaken the USA to become the world's leading exporter of information and communications technology products, such as mobile phones, laptop computers and digital cameras, exporting $180 billion worth of these products. China's share of total world trade in ICT goods, including both imports and exports, according to data from the OECD, rose to $329 billion in 2004, up from $35 billion in 1996 (OECD, 2004). Other major Asian countries prominent in the IT sector, such as Taiwan, Singapore, South Korea and India, have shown significant growth in the past decade, but more often than not the companies based in these countries are used as 'offshore' units for Western or Japanese TNCs.

The accelerating growth of new digital delivery mechanisms and their rapid globalization has given a boost to telecommunication and related information and communication technologies. According to the OECD, the total revenues of the communications sector, including telecommunication services, broadcasting services and communications equipment, exceeded $1 trillion for the first time in 1998, and as Tables 3.8 and 3.9 show, the top information technology sector – both service and software – is dominated by the Western, more accurately US-based corporations.

Table 3.8 Top 10 information technology services firms

Company	Country where based	Revenue $ billion
EDS	USA	21.7
Tech Data	USA	15.7
Accenture	Bermuda	13.3
CSC	USA	11.3
First Data	USA	8.1
ADP	USA	7.1
CapGemini Ernst & Young	France	6.6
SAIC	USA	5.9
Unisys	USA	5.7
Affiliated Computer Services	USA	3.7

Source: *OECD Information Technology Outlook: 2004 edition*, data for 2003. © OECD 2004

Table 3.9 Top 10 software firms

Company	Country where based	Revenue $ billion
Microsoft	USA	32.1
Oracle	USA	9.4
SAP	Germany	9.0
Softbank	Japan	3.4
Computer Associates	USA	3.1
Electronic Arts	USA	2.5
Peoplesoft	USA	1.9
Intuit	USA	1.6
Veritas Software	USA	1.5
Amdocs	USA	1.4

Source: *OECD Information Technology Outlook: 2004 edition,* data for 2003. © OECD 2004

Implications of a liberalized global communication regime

The global shift from state regulation to market-driven policies are evident in all sectors of international communication. The WTO claims that the expansion of capital through the transnational corporations has contributed to the transfer of skills and capital to the global South, but that it may have contributed also to widening the gap between rich and poor is often ignored. International communication is increasingly being shaped by trade and market standards and less by political considerations – what Cees Hamelink has called 'a noticeable shift from a political to an economic discourse' (1994: 268).

The move to open up world trade by reducing tariff barriers has been applied unevenly: while several developing countries made huge reductions in their tariffs, the developed countries have continued to protect their markets, especially in such sectors as agriculture, stalling the so-called Doha Round (also called Development Round) of WTO.

In addition, giving priority to the service sectors – financial services, insurance, maritime transport, telecommunication – has benefited the North, while the areas where the South might have had an advantage are not given much consideration. One such key resource is labour: while there are specific provisions for free movement of capital associated with GATS, there is no provision for the movement of labour in a 'borderless world'. If anything, immigration laws in the European Union and the USA are being made more stringent.

The major trading blocs have insisted that in a globalized world economy, with growing internationalization of production and consumption, it is important to harmonize domestic laws and regulatory structures affecting trade and investment, and remove any advantage or protection for domestic industries. A global market can only be created, runs the argument, through deregulation and letting the market set the rules of international trade.

Opposition to the process of deregulation and privatization has been undermined by changes in international policy at an institutional level. International organizations, as Schiller noted, 'have either been bypassed, restructured, weakened or neutered' (1996: 123). In 1992, the status of the UN Centre for Transnational Corporations (UNCTC) was fundamentally changed, making it work towards strengthening global market forces as part of the transnational corporation and management division within the UN, which appeared to be positioning itself closer to the operation of international business. As part of his 'quiet revolution' to renew the United Nations for the twenty-first century, the UN Secretary General Kofi Annan built a stronger relationship with the business community. A joint statement issued in 1998 by Annan and the International Chamber of Commerce stressed the UN's role in setting the regulatory framework for the global marketplace in order to facilitate cross-border trade and investment. Increasingly, UN agencies are co-operating with businesses on projects, with mutual benefits. The UN-sponsored World Summits on the Information Society, held in Geneva in 2003 and in Tunis in 2005, also indicated this trend (*see* Chapter 7, pp. 226–7; also December 2005 special issue of the journal *Global Media and Communication*). By 2006, US-induced proposals 'to outsource or off-shore' some of the UN activities, were being mentioned in the business press (Lauria and Nelson, 2006).

Who benefits from liberalization and privatization?

The biggest beneficiaries of the processes of liberalization, deregulation and privatization and the resultant WTO agreements have been the TNCs which dominate global trade. As the primary 'movers and shapers' of the global economy, the TNCs have been defined as having three basic characteristics:

- co-ordination and control of various stages of individual production chains within and between different countries;

- potential ability to take advantage of geographical differences in the distribution of factors of production (e.g. natural resources, capital, labour) and in state policies (e.g. taxes, trade barriers, subsidies, etc.);

- potential geographical flexibility – an ability to switch its resources and operations between locations at an international, or even a global scale.

(Dicken, 1998: 177)

So powerful are the TNCs that the annual sales of the top corporations exceed the GDP of many countries. Their financial power had grown so strong that by 2005 even to join the Fortune 500, the annual list published by the US business magazine *Fortune* of the world's top 500 corporations, the revenue needed was $12.4 billion more than the GDP of Jordan (*Fortune*, 2005: 57). In 2004, Wal-Mart was for the fourth year running the world's largest corporation, with a revenue of nearly $288 billion and profits of $10.3 billion. Not surprisingly, US-based companies – 181 – dominated the list. Total revenue for Fortune Global 500 in 2004 stood at $16,798 billion, while profit was $930 billion, a growth of 27 per cent over 2003. Of the top 10 companies, five were American, four European and one Japanese. US-based companies led in Aerospace and defence, banks, computers, computer services and software and entertainment (*Fortune*, 2005).

Table 3.10 The world's largest corporations in 2004

Name	Revenues ($bn)	Profits ($bn)
Wal-Mart (USA)	287.9	10.3
BP (UK)	285.0	15.4
Exxon Mobil (USA)	270.7	25.3
Shell (UK/Holland)	268.7	18.2
GM (USA)	193.5	2.8
Daimlerchrysler (Germany)	176.7	3.1
Toyota (Japan)	172.6	10.9
Ford (USA)	172.2	3.5
GE (USA)	152.9	16.8
TOTAL (France)	152.6	11.9

Source: *Fortune*, 25 July 2005

According to the 2005 *World Investment Report* from the United Nations Conference on Trade and Development (UNCTAD), the TNCs were rapidly boosting their foreign activities through a variety of non-equity firms (e.g. management contracts, franchising), as well as building technology networks with local enterprises. Most significant, they were also transferring their R&D operations to developing countries (UNCTAD, 2005c). The free-market ideology and the new international trading regime that it produced have encouraged the free flow of capital across a borderless world. Concerns about trans-border data flows and their impact on national sovereignty have been replaced by the race to embrace the global electronic marketplace. According to the *World Investment Report*, in 2004, foreign direct investment flows continued to grow, with the services sector accounting for 63 per cent of the total value of cross-border mergers and acquisitions in 2004, with financial services responsible for one-third of the value. Large TNCs dominate world financial services, not only in terms of total assets, but also in terms of the number of countries in which they operate. Citigroup (USA) tops the list, followed by UBS (Switzerland) and Allianz (Germany). Financial TNCs from France, Germany, Japan, Britain and the USA accounted for 74 per cent of the total assets of the top 50 financial TNCs in 2003 (UNCTAD 2005c).

The information technology revolution has also created a global 'outsourcing' service industry, in which developing countries such as India have excelled: according to the National Association of Software Service Companies (NASSCOM) – the apex body of India's IT industry – the sector has witnessed an annual growth rate of more than 25 per cent, earning $17.2 billion in export revenue for 2005 (NASSCOM, 2006).

However, market-based globalization also has its down side (Stiglitz, 2002; Bardhan *et al.*, 2006). One cumulative effect of a shift from a public to a private agenda is the increase in poverty among the world's poorest, living in the countries on the receiving end of neo-liberal 'reforms', which have yet to deliver for a majority of the world's population.

Table 3.11 Top 10 financial TNCs ranked by assets, 2003

Company	Assets ($bn)	Foreign affiliates	Countries operating in
Citigroup (USA)	1,264	320	77
UBS (Switzerland)	1,221	344	48
Allianz Group (Germany)	1,179	606	48
Mizuho Financial (Japan)	1,115	41	15
Crédit Agricole (France)	1,103	447	41
HSBC Bank (UK)	1,034	573	48
Deutsche Bank (Germany)	1,013	469	40
Mitsubishi (Japan)	995	49	37
BNP Paribas (France)	987	351	48
ING Group (Netherlands)	982	344	34

Source: UNCTAD, *World Investment Report,* 2005

The 2003 *Human Development Report* of the United Nations Development Programme noted that, despite the hype associated with markets generating income and employment, in the 1990s overall average income per head actually declined in 54 countries (UNDP, 2003). Market-based solutions and cuts to the public sector are having a devastating effect on employment, especially in the global South. According to the International Labour Organization, in 2004 half of the world's 1.38 billion workers lived on less than $2 a day; and, despite employment growth among some sectors, especially in Asia, the world's poorest got poorer in sub-Saharan Africa, for example, where the number of workers living on less than $1 a day increased by 28 million between 1994 and 2004, while in Latin America the number of working poor, earning as little as $1 a day, increased by 4.4 million between 1999 and 2003 (ILO, 2005).

chapter four

The global media bazaar

The deregulation and liberalization of the international communication sector in the 1990s was paralleled in the media industries and, in conjunction with the new communication technologies of satellite, cable and digital and mobile delivery mechanisms, created a global marketplace for media products (McAnany and Wilkinson, 1996; McQuail and Siune, 1998; Sinclair, 1999; Page and Crawley, 2001; Geradin and Luff, 2004; Hoskins *et al.*, 2004; Thomas, 2005; Croteau and Hynes, 2006). The fastest-growing use of commercial satellites is for the delivery of media products – information, news and entertainment. As demonstrated by the case study of News Corporation in Chapter 3, it is now imperative for media conglomerates to plan their strategies in a global context, with the ultimate aim of profitable growth through exploiting economies of scope and scale. The convergence of both media and technologies, and the process of vertical integration in the media industries to achieve this aim, have resulted in the concentration of media power in the hands of a few large transnational corporations, undermining media plurality and democratic discourse (McChesney, 1999, 2004; Bagdikan, 2004; Croteau and Hynes, 2005).

Convergence

Before globalization, most media corporations had distinct areas of business: Disney, for example, was primarily concerned with cartoon films and theme-park operations; *Time* was known mainly as a publishing business; Viacom was a TV syndication and cable outfit, and News Corporation was a group which owned a chain of newspapers in Australia. With the privatization of broadcasting across the globe, coupled with new methods of delivering media and communication content – namely, satellite, cable and the Internet – the distinctions between these industries have increasingly dissolved (McPhail, 2006).

With deregulation and the relaxation of cross-media ownership restrictions, especially in the USA and Britain, media companies looked to broaden and deepen their existing interests, and over the last two decades there has been a huge wave of mergers and acquisitions. In 1985 Rupert Murdoch bought Twentieth Century Fox in order to acquire a base in the USA and in 1989 Sony bought Columbia TriStar. In the same year, Time Inc. merged with Warner Communication, forming Time Warner, to which Turner Broadcasting Systems was added in 1995. Disney bought Capital Cities/American Broadcasting Corporation (ABC) in 1995, thereby adding a broadcast network to a traditionally entertainment company. Seagram acquired Universal Studios in 1995 and in 1998 bought music company PolyGram. Viacom bought Blockbuster video distribution and Paramount in 1994 and Bertelsmann purchased Random House in 1998. The $80 billion merger in 1999, of two major US corporations, Viacom and Columbia Broadcasting System (CBS), created at that time the world's largest entertainment and media company in the production, promotion and distribution of entertainment, news, sports and music. However, it was soon to be overtaken by the megamerger of the biggest Internet-based company at the time, America Online (AOL), and Time Warner in the opening weeks of the new millennium, creating then the world's fourth largest corporation, worth an estimated $350 billion.

In the twenty-first century, such trends towards media consolidation are likely to reduce even further the number of corporations controlling both content and delivery internationally. Fewer than 10 corporations, most based in the USA, own most of the world's media industries, with AOL-Time Warner being at the forefront, followed by Walt Disney, Viacom-CBS, Bertelsmann, News Corporation, Telecommunication Inc. (TCI), Sony and the National Broadcasting Corporation (NBC), which entered into partnership with the Paris-based Vivendi Universal in 2003 to create NBC-Universal. All the major television corporations – Disney, Time Warner, News Corporation and Viacom – own multiple broadcast and cable networks and production facilities. With the convergence of the media industries and integration from content origination through to delivery mechanisms, a few conglomerates will control all the major aspects of mass media: newspapers, magazines, books, radio, broadcast television, cable systems and programming, movies, music recordings, video recordings and online services (*see* Table 4.1, pp. 100–3). With the revolution in digital distribution, a whole range of new revenue earning opportunities has surfaced as the media and telecommunications sectors intersect globally. The expanding bandwidth, coupled with the rapid globalization of fixed and mobile networks, as well as the digitization of content and growing use of personal computers worldwide, have considerably helped global media and communication conglomerates to capitalize on emerging markets and experiment with new media products. According to a 2005 report commissioned by NBC-Universal, copyright-based industries were the most important growth drivers in the US economy, contributing nearly 60 per cent of the growth of US exportable products and services – in 2003 the 'core' copyright industries (sometimes also referred to as 'convergence industries', that include software publishers, motion pictures, video, sound recording, advertising, printing, and video and disk rental) contributed $33 billion in export revenues (Siwek, 2005).

Time Warner

The New York-based Time Warner, the world's largest entertainment and information company, has major businesses in movies, publishing, music, cable TV and the Internet. With the acquisition of Turner Broadcasting it gained an international television presence in news and entertainment, from Cable News Network (CNN), the 24-hour global news channel, which claims to be the 'world's most extensively syndicated television news service', (*see* also pp. 135–8) to Turner Network Broadcasting (TNT) and Turner Classic Movies and Cartoon Network, the international children's channel – 'the most widely distributed 24-hour animation network in the world'.

Table 4.1 Media convergence and integration – the top six players

Area of interest	Time Warner	Disney	Sony	Bertelsmann	Viacom	News Corporation
TV channels	**Turner Broadcasting system**, including CNN, TNT, Cartoon Network, and more than 25 international channels **Time Warner Cable** **HBO** **the WB TV** network	**ABC TV Network** ABC Entertainment, ABC Daytime, ABC News, ABC Kids **Cable Networks** ESPN, Disney Channel, ABC Family, Toon Disney, SOAP net, Walt Disney TV Animation, JETIX, E! Networks	**Sony Pictures Television International (SPIT)**, 40 international networks, such as Animax India, AXN Germany	**RTL Group** Television networks and stations, new channels in 2004 include: Plug TV (Belgium), RTL Televizia (Croatia), Traumpartner TV (Germany), M6 (France) Cable Networks	CBS, UPN, Viacom TV Station Groups (40 TV stations in USA) MTV, Nickelodeon, VH1, Comedy Central, Spike TV, CMT, Nick at Nite, TV Land, BET, Showtime, MTV2, Logo, Noggin, the N, mtvU, Sundance Channel	**Fox Broadcasting Co.** (35 stations in USA) **STAR** (11 stations in Asia) Fox News Channel Fox Cable Networks Sky (Europe, Latin America) BskyB (UK) DIRECTV Group (USA)
TV production & distribution	Warner Bros TV	Touchstone Television Buena Vista TV	SPIT	Fremantle Media	Paramount TV CBS Enterprises CBS Entertaining	20th Century Fox TV Fox TV Studios Twentieth TV

Table 4.1 Media convergence and integration – the top six players – *continued*

Area of interest	Time Warner	Disney	Sony	Bertelsmann	Viacom	News Corporation
Film	Warner Bros Entertainment Inc. including Warner Bros Pictures, Warner Independent Pictures, Warner Bros. International cinemas, New Line Cinema Corp.	Walt Disney Studio Walt Disney Pictures, Touchstone Pictures, Hollywood Pictures, Miramax Films, Dimension Films	Sony Picture Entertainment MGM		Paramount Pictures Paramount Home Entertainment	Fox Filmed Entertainment 20th Century Fox Film Co., Fox 2000 Pictures, Canal Fox
Newspapers & magazines	Time Inc. (27 titles, including *Time, People, Fortune*) Time4 Media (17 titles) IPC Media (82 titles) Time Inc. South Pacific (6 titles)	More than 20 magazines, including *Disney Adventures, ESPN The Magazine*		Gruner+Jahr 125 magazines, including *Stern, Brigitte, National Geographic*		*New York Post* 5 newspapers in UK, more than 100 titles in Australia, 5 titles in Pacific area 9 magazines

Table 4.1 Media convergence and integration – the top six players – *continued*

Area of interest	Time Warner	Disney	Sony	Bertelsmann	Viacom	News Corporation
Radio		ABC Radio (71 stations in USA) Radio Disney, ESPN Radio, ABC news radio		RTL Radio	Infinity Broadcasting	Sky Radio
Book publishing	**Warner Bros Book Group** Bulfinch Press Little, Brown and Company Time Warner Audiobooks Warner Books Warner Faith	**Hyperion Books Disney Publishing** Hyperion Books for Children, Disney Press, Disney Editions		**Random House** comprises more than 100 imprints, such as Knopf, Crown (USA), Ebury, Arrow (UK), **DirectGroup** France Loisirs (France), BCA (UK), BMG direct (USA)	Simon & Schuster Group	HarperCollins Publishers
Music & theatre	AOL music	Buena Vista Music Group Buena Vista Theatrical Productions	Sony Music Entertainment (Japan) Inc., Sony BMG Music Entertainment	Sony BMG Music Joint venture; BMG Music Publishing Company	Famous Music	Fox Music
Hardware	TV cable		Electronics products	Arvato Storage Media, Arvato Systems Units		DirecTV

Table 4.1 Media convergence and integration – the top six players – *continued*

Area of interest	Time Warner	Disney	Sony	Bertelsmann	Viacom	News Corporation
Internet & software	America Online Inc. AOL, ICQ, Netscape, Winamp/ Shoutcast, Love.com	Walt Disney Internet Group	Sony Computer Entertainment So.net	Arvato Mobile		MySpace.com
Other		Disney Consumer Produts Disney Hardline, Disney Softlines, Disney Toys, Buena Vista Games, the Baby Einstein Company, Disney Direct Marketing Walt Disney Parks & Resorts	Games Financial Services	Arvato AG is one of the largest internationally networked media services providers Empolis, a content and knowledge management solution company	Viacom Outdoors Paramount Parks	News Outdoor Group Broadsystem Ventures Convey Group Balkan News Corporation National Rugby League (Australia)
2004 Revenue	$42.09 billion	$30.8 billion	$72.73 billion	$17.02 billion	$22.53 billion	$20.8 billion

Source: Based on data from company websites

Time Warner's publishing arm is Time Inc., with its flagship international magazine *Time* and 129 other magazines, including *Fortune, Life, People, Entertainment Weekly* and *Sports Illustrated*. With the acquisition of IPC Media, Britain's largest consumer magazine company (which includes such popular titles as *Homes & Gardens, Marie Claire, NME, TV & Satellite Week*), Time Inc. was by 2006 one of the world's largest magazine publishers. It was also a leading book publisher (Warner Books; Little, Brown) and a direct marketer of books, music, videos and DVDs. The group's other major interest was in filmed entertainment through Warner Brothers, one of the world's best-known film companies, which has evolved into a global entertainment corporation, with businesses ranging from film and television production and product licensing to a broadcast television network. Drawing on its vast library – more than 5700 feature films, 32,000 television programmes and 13,500 animated titles, including 1500 classic cartoons – Warner Brothers products are ubiquitous. On the basis of such international hits as *Harry Potter and the Prisoner of Azkaban* (largest grossing film of 2004); *The Last Samurai* and *Troy*, Warner Brothers became the first studio to cross the $2 billion milestone in overseas box office in one year, leading the industry with $2.2 billion in overseas receipts and $3.4 billion in worldwide box office (Time Warner Annual Report 2004). *The Lord of the Rings* trilogy earned almost $3 billion at the worldwide box office and generated an additional $3 billion in consumer spending on home video and related merchandise.

The group also owns TBS Superstation, which claims to have the largest audience of any cable network in the USA, and Home Box Office (HBO) cable network, with 10 branded channels and more than 34 million US subscribers, and millions more for such internationally successful series as *Sex and the City, The West Wing* and *ER*. Apart from being a supplier of programming, Time Warner is heavily involved in the cable industry, providing digitally compatible cable networks to households in the USA, in second place after TCI, the world's biggest cable operator. After its merger with AOL, Time Warner has become one of the most powerful media and entertainment corporations, with the potential to dominate both 'new' and 'old' forms of media (Hoskins *et al.*, 2004).

Bertelsmann

With annual revenues of more than $17 billion in 2004, the German media giant, Bertelsmann, is not only the world's largest publisher of books and magazines, but also has interests in television, film and radio, in music labels and clubs, and in online services and multimedia, supplying news, entertainment, music and online services in more than 53 countries. Nearly 60 per cent of its business is in Europe, followed by the USA, which accounts for about 35 per cent. Besides owning Random House, one of the world's largest publishing organizations, the company also owns many book clubs in Germany and the USA, and has major publishing interests in France, Spain and Germany.

Founded in 1835, the firm began as a regional publisher of religious books, but expanded its publishing operations in Europe in the 1960s and 1970s, especially through book clubs. Though the corporation has diversified its operations, publishing has remained a key part of its business. In 2006, Bertelsmann was one of the world's largest publishers, with Random House (publishing books in English, German, Spanish, Korean and Japanese) having more than 100 imprints (including Knopf, Bantam and Crown in the US; Century, Ebury and Arrow in Britain; and Siedler, Heyne and Goldmann in Germany). DirectGroup, which co-ordinates book and music clubs in 22 countries, reaching 30 million readers, is a key media trader. Bertelsmann also owns Gruner+Jahr, Europe's leading magazine publisher, producing more than 125 magazines.

The music arm of the corporation, the Bertelsmann Music Group (BMG), produces more than 200 labels, including RCA, Arista and Ariola, along with the world's biggest music club, available in most of Europe, North America, Brazil, Australia, Japan, Singapore and South Africa. Bertelsmann also owns a 50 per cent stake in Sony BMG, enabling it to have access to such global record labels as Columbia Records. Bertelsmann has been a major beneficiary both of the growth of commercial television and radio in Europe and of the privatization of the media in Eastern and Central Europe after the reunification of Germany. In 1997, Bertelsmann's UFA combined with the Luxembourg broadcaster CLT to form CLT-UFA, and by 1999 it was Europe's highest revenue-generating media group. The acquisition of the RTL Group, one of Europe's major television producers, has expanded Bertelsmann's interest in television, which included acquiring, in 2004, M6 in France, Channel 5 in Britain and digital television interests in Croatia and Portugal. Fremantle Media, its production arm responsible for international exports of the 'Idols' format, reflects the importance given to audio-visual media by the company. Bertelsmann has also invested heavily in new technologies through Arvato AG, a major international media services provider, including mobile entertainment via its 250 subsidiaries.

Viacom/CBS

The merger of Viacom and CBS, one of the top TV networks in the USA, announced in 1999, created a huge global media conglomerate. The operations of Viacom, one of the world's largest entertainment companies, span film, TV and publishing and it has been called 'a cradle-to-grave advertising depot', catering to toddlers with children's channels such as Nickelodeon, to youth, by way of MTV, and to the older generation through CBS. The group owns Paramount Pictures, a leading producer and distributor of feature films since 1912, with more than 2500 titles in its library, including such popular films as *The Ten Commandments* and *The Godfather*, and modern blockbusters like *Forrest Gump*, *Deep Impact*, *Star Trek*: *Insurrection* and *Titanic* (the highest-grossing film to date). Paramount also co-produces films with Nickelodeon Movies and MTV Films, utilizing their expertise with children and youth respectively. Paramount Home Entertainment distributes films on video and DVD in more than 45 countries worldwide. With the acquisition in 2005 of DreamWorks, best known for its computer-generated animated feature films (including *Antz* and *Shrek*) and TV programming, Paramount has strengthened its position in Hollywood.

In television, the company has a global presence through such channels as Music Television (MTV), Nickelodeon, VH1, Showtime and The Movie Channel. Its Paramount Television is one of the largest suppliers of television programming for broadcasters worldwide, drawing on a library of 16,000 television episodes. MTV, the most widely distributed network in the world, by 2006 was reaching more than 418 million households in 167 countries, while Nickelodeon, one of the world's largest producers of children's programming, was accessible in 178 million households in over 100 countries.

The group also has interests in publishing through its ownership of Simon & Schuster, which has 34 imprints, including Scribners, Pocket Books, The Free Press and Touchstone, and annually publishes more than 2400 titles, including such international best-selling authors as Dan Brown of *The Da Vinci Code* fame. Building on the success of MTV, in 1995 it launched the MTV Books imprint and children's books under the Nick Jr. imprint. Simon & Schuster is also the world's largest audio publisher, owning Famous Music Publishing, one of the top 10 music publishers in the USA, whose catalogue contains over 125,000 copyrights from more than seven decades of Hollywood films, as well as the music from Paramount's hit television shows, including *Star Trek, The Odd Couple, Cheers* and *Frasier*. The group also has an interest in UCI, an international cinema chain, as well as owning more than 9000 video stores around the world. Viacom's theme parks, which feature characters from its TV programmes, are visited by more than 13 million people each year. The group has a significant Internet presence, including cbs.sportsline.com, mtv.com, vh1.com and Nick.com.

With the addition of CBS, which owns CBS Television Network and its affiliates, and CBS Cable and Infinity Broadcasting Corporation, which operates 163 radio stations, Viacom was set to further consolidate its international media presence, especially in the area of news – in 2006 it owned and operated more than 100 networks. However, on 31 December 2005, Viacom was separated into two publicly traded companies: Viacom Inc. and CBS Corporation (www.viacom.com and www.cbscorporation.com).

The Walt Disney Company

The California-based Walt Disney Company, the world's second largest media corporation after Time Warner, with one of its strongest brands, has interests in four major areas: media networks, studio entertainment, consumer products and parks and resorts. Disney owns ABC, one of the three biggest TV networks in the USA, as well as owning or operating 10 local TV stations and 72 radio stations in the country. The Disney Channel and Toon Disney are two major cable channels in the USA. In addition, Disney owns Entertainment and Sports Network (ESPN) and partly owns, with Hearst and GE, Arts and Entertainment Television (A&E), as well as shares in The History Channel and E! Entertainment channel (the world's largest producer and distributor of entertainment news and lifestyle-related programming, reaching 300 million homes in 120 countries worldwide in 2006).

Disney channels also have an extensive international presence. By 2006, Disney was operating country- or area-specific Disney channels in Britain, Taiwan, India, Australia, Malaysia, France, Italy, Spain and the Middle East. In addition, Disney Channel Worldwide, with 120 million subscribers in more than 70 countries, was operating 24 Disney Channels, eight Playhouse Disney Channels, nine Toon Disney Channels and 18 international Jetix channels, as well as branded blocks of programming distributed to viewers worldwide. In 2006, it also acquired Pixar movie studio, creator of such international animation blockbusters as the *Toy Story* series.

Disney also had minority stakes in television companies in Germany (Tele-München),

France (TV Sport), Spain (Tesauro), the Scandinavian Broadcasting System and Japan Sports Channel. In the area of television production and distribution, the company had a global presence with Buena Vista Television, Touchstone Television, Walt Disney Television and Walt Disney Television Animation, with production facilities in Japan, Australia and Canada. The same was the case in movie production and distribution through Walt Disney Pictures, Touchstone Pictures, Hollywood Pictures, Caravan Pictures, Miramax Films, Buena Vista Home Video, Buena Vista Home Entertainment and Buena Vista International (in 2005, Buena Vista International distributed more than 30,000 hours of programming to 1300 broadcasters across 240 territories). The company established a joint digital cable venture video-on-demand movie service in Britain, FilmFlex, where it already had stakes in GMTV. In addition, Disney had investments in Super RTL and RTL 2 in Germany and HBO services in Central Europe and Latin America. Media networks were the main revenue generators for the company – in 2005, for example, they accounted for just over $13 billion out of the total revenues of nearly $32 billion (www.disney.com).

In international sports broadcasting, ESPN was a dominant presence (*see* pp. 115–18). It owned, among others, half of ESPN STAR in Asia and Net STAR (33 per cent), owners of the Sports Network of Canada. The company also had Professional Sports Franchises through stakes in major US national hockey and baseball teams.

Its publishing arm, Walt Disney Book Publishing, produced Hyperion Books and Miramax Books, and had other subsidiary groups, such as ABC Publishing, Disney Publishing and Fairchild Publishing. The Group also published more than 20 magazines, including *Automotive Industries, Institutional Investor, Disney Magazine, ESPN Magazine, Video Business* and *Top Famille* (a French family magazine).

In the arena of music, Disney owned several recording labels, including Buena Vista Music Group, with its Hollywood Records (popular music and soundtracks for films), Lyric Street Records (country music label), Walt Disney Records and Buena Vista Records.

Another major sphere of operations was its theme parks and resorts – in 2006, the company operated or licensed 11 theme parks on three continents, including: Walt Disney World Resort, Disney's Animal Kingdom and the Magic Kingdom in the USA; Disneyland Paris, Tokyo Disneyland and Disneyland Hong Kong, along with 35 resort hotels, two luxury cruise ships and a wide variety of other entertainment offerings, as well as retailing Disney merchandise, through 660 Disney shops spread across the world. Disney products were also marketed to the interactive gaming community through Buena Vista Games. By 2006, Disney was operating more than 40 websites, while Walt Disney Internet Group was developing content and services for new digital platforms, including a deal with Apple to provide ABC and Disney Channel content on the Apple iPod, as well as such services as Mobile ESPN and Disney Mobile (www.disney.com).

Sony

The Tokyo-based consumer electronics and multimedia entertainment giant, Sony, is the only non-Western global conglomerate: 72 per cent of its 2004 total revenue of $72.7 billion came from overseas sales, with the USA being its biggest market, followed by Europe. Sony is an interesting example of expansion into content creation from a base in hardware and equipment. Since its founding in 1946, the Sony corporation has grown to become a global producer of communication hardware, especially electronics products, which accounted for 67 per cent of sales in 2004. Among its major products are MD systems, CD players, stereos, digital audio tape, recorders/players, DVD-video players, video CD players, digital cameras, broadcast video equipment, videotapes, digital TVs, personal computers, cellular phones, satellite broadcasting reception systems and Internet terminals.

Another area in which Sony had global dominance was the computer games market, accounting for nearly 10 per cent of sales and operating revenue in 2004. Since the sale of the first PlayStation game console in 1994, this sector of Sony has grown extremely rapidly, with sales and revenue showing a more than 200-fold increase in the late 1990s. By developing new genres of software, with advanced computer graphic technology, Sony made video games a major leisure activity among the youth across the globe – by 2006, there were more than 5 million dedicated online gamers living in a virtual world of their own (Castronova, 2005).

Sony's global business interests in music and music publishing – strengthened by its 2004 joint venture with Bertelsmann to create Sony-BMG – were established through a global network of label affiliations. Sony was also a big player in the international entertainment business, producing and distributing films and television programming and syndicating entertainment programming in 67 countries worldwide. Sony owned Columbia TriStar, one of the world's top film and television production companies, which included Columbia Pictures, Screen Gems, Sony Pictures Classics and Columbia TriStar Film Distributors International. Sony's television interests included Columbia TriStar Television, producer of such internationally adapted game shows as *Wheel of Fortune*, Columbia TriStar International Television and Game Show Network.

Sony Pictures Entertainment owned and operated Columbia Pictures Film Production Asia, Columbia Films Producciones Españolas, Columbia Pictures Producciones Mexico and operations in Britain, Brazil and Japan. In 2006, Sony Television International had investments in more than 35 international networks in 100 countries, reaching 240 million viewers worldwide.

Revenues from licensing films and programmes from Columbia's library of more than 3500 films and 40,000 television episodes more than doubled in the past decade. Sony was also involved in local-language film production in Britain, Germany, France and Hong Kong, and television programming in eight languages. Already operating its own international channels, such as Sony Entertainment Television (India), the company was expanding its action channel AXN into East and South Asia, as well as to Latin America and to Spain, and in 2004 started a Japanese animation channel – Animax. Its Game Show Network, jointly owned by the Liberty Media Corporation, had emerged as a 24-hour network devoted exclusively to game shows and game play, available to 54 million homes via analogue, digital and satellite distribution. With its experience in information technology, Sony was well placed to exploit new forms of digital content and distribution. Sony Pictures Mobile, for example, was a main player in mobile entertainment licensing, specializing in branded interactive games and personalization products (www.sony.com).

Other major players

Apart from these top global players, NBC (owned by General Electric) was a major presence in the global media market. By 2006, NBC-Universal was broadcasting approximately 5000 hours of TV programming each year, transmitting to more than 200 affiliated stations across the United States (including 15 Telemundo stations, the fastest-growing Spanish-language network in the USA, which NBC acquired in 2002). Its business channel CNBC had become a major international presence since its launch in 1989, as were its film interests through Universal Studios. The Paris-based Vivendi Group, which owned the Canal+ Group, one of Europe's biggest pay-TV networks, as well as Vivendi Universal Games, a major European producer and distributor of online and computer games, was another major player, especially in Europe along with Britain's Pearson and Italy's Mediaset. Other media conglomerates which had regional rather than global impact included Brazil's Globo group; Zee Network, India's largest multimedia company; and Shanghai Media Group in China. While these 'old' media companies continued to set the global media agenda, by 2006 'new' media corporations, such as Internet giant Google (which a *Time* magazine cover story termed an 'empire'), Microsoft and Yahoo!, were becoming increasingly important in international communication (Ignatius, 2006) (*see* also Chapter 7).

Synergies

As is clear from Table 4.1, a few large conglomerates dominated the global media industries, and the exponential growth in the reach of the media, coupled with diversification of its forms and modes of delivery had made convergence a reality. The media conglomerates can promote their products across virtually all media segments, including broadcast and cable television, radio and online media, mobile telephony and personal digital devices (Vogel, 2004). For example, *The Times* of London can be used to promote Murdoch's television interests in Britain, while TNT films can be advertised on the CNN networks. The exploitation of synergies – the process by which one company subsidiary is used to complement and promote another – by media conglomerates has greatly increased their power over global news, information and entertainment.

Much of the global film and television production and distribution is in the hands of a few Hollywood studios – Paramount Pictures (part of Viacom); Universal Studios (part of NBC-Universal); Warner Brothers (part of Time Warner); Disney; Twentieth Century Fox (part of News Corporation); and Metro-Goldwyn-Meyer (MGM). These companies develop, produce and distribute film and television content, soundtracks, cartoons and interactive products for a global audience. They also generate revenue by charging for the rights to use the characters, titles and other material; and rights from television, films and other sources are licensed to manufacturers and retailers. Typically, a film is first distributed in the theatrical, home DVD and pay-television markets before being made available for worldwide television syndication. Some made-for-TV films are licensed for network exhibition in the United States and simultaneously syndicated overseas. After its showing on a network, a series may be licensed for broadcast on cable. The film soundtrack albums are released by the music publishing arms of the corporations, who also license music from their copyright catalogues for a variety of uses, including recorded music, DVDs, online games, radio, television and films. Concerts and live events are presented at and promoted by the corporation's television channels. Content can also be distributed through mobile communication devices. Corporations such as Disney have their own central synergy departments charged with maximizing company product sales, through cross-selling and cross-promotion strategies involving hundreds of media markets round the world. The model has been compared with a wheel:

> At the hub lies content creation. The spokes that spread out from it are the many different ways of exploiting the resulting brands: the movie studio, the television networks, the music, the publishing, the merchandising, the theme parks, the Internet sites. Looked at this way, the distinction between manufacturing and distribution begins to blur, because the various ways of selling the brand also serve to enhance its value.

> (*The Economist*, 1998: 8)

Despite intense competition among major corporations to control distribution and production to feed satellite and cable channels worldwide, they have many overlapping operations. Media rivals can share content through programming consortia like Latin America Pay TV (News Corp., Universal, Viacom, MGM), HBO Ole and HBO Brasil (Time Warner, Sony, Disney) and HBO Asia (Time Warner, Sony, Universal and Viacom). Likewise, Disney shares programming with TCI in E! Entertainment and News Corp. in ESPN Star Sports in Asia. Sony has aligned itself with Canal Plus, Europe's leading pay-TV company. In movies, Paramount frequently splits costs with studios like Miramax, owned by Disney. Viacom TV stations are major buyers of Sony broadcasting equipment, while Sony Music can be promoted on MTV, owned by Viacom.

Many commentators have expressed fears about the possibility of so much media power being concentrated in so few corporations, claiming that these few, mainly American, conglomerates may act like a cartel in production and distribution of global information and entertainment (Herman and McChesney 1997; Bagdikian, 1983/2004; McChesney, 1999, 2004). Monitoring this trend towards concentration, in his 1983 book, *Media Monopoly*, the US media scholar Ben Bagdikian argued that the US media were dominated by 50 private corporations. By 2004, when the book was republished in its seventh edition, now called *The New Media Monopoly*, the number of corporations controlling most of US media had dropped to just five – Time Warner, Disney, News Corporation, Bertelsmann and Viacom, with NBC as a close sixth.

As Bagdikian, himself a former journalist, writes:

> In 1983, the men and women who headed the 50 mass media corporations that dominated American audiences could have fit comfortably in a modest hotel ballroom. The people heading the 20 dominant newspaper chains probably would form one conversational cluster to complain about newsprint prices; 20 magazine moguls in a different circle denounce postal rates; the broadcast

network people in another corner, not being in the newspaper or magazine business, exchange indignation about government radio and television regulations; the book people compete in outrage over greed of writers' agents; and movie people gossip about sexual achievements of their stars. By 2003, five men controlled all these old media once run by the 50 corporations of 20 years earlier. These five, owners of additional digital corporations, could fit in a generous phone booth. Granted, it would be a tight fit and it would be filled with some tensions'

(Bagdikian, 2004: 27)

In the twenty-first century, it would appear the US-led global media is in the grip of a new communications cartel. The growing involvement of industrial conglomerates in the media business, including such major defence industry players as General Electric (NBC) and Westinghouse (CBS, before it merged with Viacom), also has implications to what is covered by global media and how (Bagdikian, 2004). As one commentator noted:

A market system of control limits free expression by market processes that are highly effective. Dissident ideas are not legally banned, they are simply unable to reach mass audiences, which are monopolised by large profit-seeking corporations that offer programmes supported by advertising, from which dissent is quietly and unobtrusively filtered out.

(Herman, 1999: 18)

Global trade in media products

The global trade in cultural goods (films, television, printed matter, music, computers) almost tripled between 1980 and 1991, from $67 billion to $200 billion (UNESCO, 1998), and has grown at a rapid pace with the liberalization of these sectors across the world. The United States was the leading exporter of cultural products, and the entertainment industry was one of its largest export earners; as Table 4.2 shows, out of the world's top five

Table 4.2 The world's top five entertainers in 2004

Company	Revenues ($ bn)	Profits ($ bn)
Time Warner (USA)	42.8	3.3
Walt Disney (USA)	30.7	2.3
Viacom (USA)	27.0	1.7
Bertelsmann (Germany)	21.1	1.2
News Corporation (USA)	20.8	1.5

Source: *Fortune*, 25 July 2005

entertainment corporations in 2005, four were based in the USA, while the remaining one had substantial US business and corporate connections.

That cultural goods are also becoming services, in the era of GATS, can be seen in the inclusion of the word 'services' in the title of the 2005 UNESCO report on *International Flows of Selected Goods and Services*. The global market value of cultural and creative industries has been estimated at $1.3 trillion and is expanding rapidly. According to the report, between 1994 and 2002, international trade in cultural goods increased from $38 billion to $60 billion (UNESCO, 2005a) and as Tables 4.3 and 4.4 demonstrate, the trade is largely dominated by a few Western nations.

Table 4.3 Exports of selected media products

Region	Books		Newspapers and periodicals		Recorded media	
	Value $million	Global share %	Value $million	Global share %	Value $million	Global share %
Europe	6599	61	3096	70	11,344	61
North America	2317	21	1041	24	3426	19
Asia	1489	14	144	3	3364	18
Latin America and the Caribbean	310	3	78	2	246	1
Africa	35	0.3	6	0.1	20	0.1

Source: UNESCO, 2005a, figures for 2002, rounded to nearest million

Table 4.4 Exports by selected Western nations, $ million

Country	Books	Newspapers and periodicals	Recorded media
USA	1921	880	3069
Britain	1806	745	1640
Germany	1258	711	2281
Spain	686	239	259
France	519	369	741
Italy	510	202	144

Source: UNESCO, 2005a, figures for 2002, rounded to nearest million

Television

As Table 4.5 shows, a significant proportion of the revenue of leading media companies comes from television. Most of the world's entertainment output is transmitted through television, which is becoming increasingly global in its operations, technologies and audiences (Fox, 1997; Smith, 1998; Barker, 1997; Spigel and Olsson, 2004; Chalaby, 2005). One of the most significant factors is the growth in satellite television, which cuts across national and linguistic boundaries, creating new international audiences. According to industry figures, in 2005, some 2.5 billion people across the world watched on average just over three hours of television every day, on more than 3000, mostly private, channels operating in the world. The number of television sets in the world has more than tripled since 1980, with Asia showing the highest growth.

Table 4.5 The sultans of the small screen

Company	2004 total revenue ($ billion)	2004 TV revenue ($ billion)	% of total revenue
Time Warner	42.09	16.83	40
Viacom	22.53	15.08	67
Walt Disney	30.80	12.01	39
News Corp.	20.96	9.22	44

Source: Based on data from company websites

The volume of US trade in cultural products and its capacity to produce and distribute to an international audience ensure that US-based networks are the most prevalent in the global television system (Segrave, 1998; Scott, 2005). In most countries outside the USA, imported programming forms a significant part of the television schedule, making the USA a 'world provider' of television programmes (Dunnett, 1990). Table 4.6 lists the main players in global television, ranked in terms of the number of households where these networks are available.

Table 4.6 Top five global TV networks in 2005

Network	Type	Ownership	No. of households (millions)
MTV Networks	Youth Music	Viacom	418
CNN International	News	Time Warner	260
BBC World	News	BBC	258
Discovery Channel	Documentaries	Discovery Comm.	180
STAR	Entertainment	News Corp.	103

Source: *Campaign*, 2005, issue 22

US entertainment programmes – drama serials, soaps and shows, such as *Star Trek*, *Baywatch*, *Friends*, *ER* and *The X-Files* – are shown on television channels all over the world. In addition, syndication companies also sell 'format rights' for programmes that are more nationally specific, such as game shows. The formats of such US-made shows as *Family Feud* and *Wheel of Fortune* have been adapted for production in many countries (Blumenthal and Goodenough, 1998). Some genres of television, notably animation, music, wildlife documentaries and live sporting events, are relatively easy to sell into different cultural contexts. Wildlife programmes, for example, can translate easily into other languages, since they often do not have a visible presenter and therefore it is cheaper for voice-over track to be laid down.

The US-based Discovery network, making factual programmes about history, science and technology, art, natural history and lifestyle, is the key player in this genre (Fürsich, 2003). From its modest beginnings in 1985, it has grown to become the world's biggest producer of documentaries, though it defines itself as a 'real-world media and entertainment company' reaching 180 million households in more than 160 countries, through its 90 networks. Half-owned by the Ascent Media Group of John Malone, Discovery Networks International (DNI) includes: Discovery Español; Discovery Português; Discovery Europe; Discovery Germany; Discovery India; Discovery Asia; Discovery Southeast Asia; Discovery Australia/New Zealand; Discovery Japan; Discovery Channel Middle East; and Discovery Canada; as well as themed digital channels ranging from travel to lifestyle, and from children's programming to wildlife, history and adventure, available in 35 languages. It also has two joint-venture channels with the BBC – Animal Planet and People+Arts.

Other major global players in this genre are also American. By 2006, National Geographic Television, which had its overseas debut in Britain in 1997, was broadcasting to 151 countries, reaching 230 million households in 27 languages. In the past decade, the History Channel, owned by A&E Television and with a 50–50 joint venture with BSkyB in Britain, has expanded vastly across the globe – from 12 million subscribers in 1995 to 195 million in 2005, growing at an average rate of 32 per cent per year. The Sci-Fi Channel too has viewers around the world. One reason for the international expansion of such channels is that most of their tailoring to local markets is dubbing and subtitling, and the content is portable and generally non-political.

One of the largest sectors of the global television market is adult entertainment TV, which is becoming increasingly personalized and interactive, and was estimated at more than $56 billion annually in 2006. Playboy TV International, which owns and operates Playboy-branded channels, available in North and South America, Australia, Europe and Asia, was the key player. The network has international rights to its huge programmes library and also distributes its content through commercial websites, via mobile platforms, on DVD and to pay-television stations. The other major global player in this area is the Los Angeles-based Private Media Group.

The USA is also a major presence in religious television, which is being increasingly commercialized and globalized. The Family Channel, which has a huge following, was launched in 1977 and became the first 24-hour religious cable network, as the Christian Broadcasting Network (CBN), and was part of Fox Network (1997–2001) before being bought by Disney. By 2006, CBN, a key platform for right-wing evangelist US preacher Pat Robertson, was reaching 200 countries, broadcasting programmes in more than 70 languages. Another major player, the 24-hour Trinity Broadcasting Network, the 'largest worldwide religious network', founded in 1973, was reaching more than 12,460 channels across the world through 47 satellites (www.tbn.org). The Eternal Word Television Network, 'the global Catholic network', which claims to be the world's largest Catholic television network, founded in 1981, was accessible in 2006 to more than 150 million homes in 110 countries on more than 3400 digital channels.

Two major areas of international television are sport and popular music, which reach across national barriers of language and culture, delivering the largest audiences for US networks, ESPN and MTV. MTV, part of the media giant Viacom, is the world's most widely watched television network, which, with its local and regional channels, dominates global youth music, while ESPN is the global leader in sports broadcasting.

Case study

Televising sport globally – ESPN

A major factor in the expansion of satellite and cable television internationally has been television's unique ability to transmit live sports events. As a genre, sports programmes cut across national and cultural boundaries. Sport is a major industry and advertisers are keen to exploit the reach of TV channels dedicated to sport. Live coverage of a prestigious football league match is as much a media event in Cameroon as it is in the Czech Republic. Unlike films, which consumers can rent from video/DVD outlets, the live nature of sports coverage makes it suitable for pay-TV, a fact which media companies are using as an incentive for subscribing. During the 1998 soccer World Cup some games were watched by more than a billion people. The cumulative television audience figure over the 25 match days of the 2002 World Cup reached a total of 28.8 billion worldwide, according to FIFA, which licenses the World Cup broadcasts. No wonder, then, that television rights for this, the most popular sport on the planet, have escalated more than 10 times in the last decade and a half – from $79.3 million in 1990 to more than $1.2 billion in 2006 (FIFA). The cost of global TV rights for the Olympic Games has increased more than tenfold from the Moscow games of 1980 to Athens in 2004. The broadcasting revenues earned by the International Olympic Committee, indicated by Table 4.7, have shown exponential growth in the 1990s and first Olympics of the twenty-first century. Given the escalating cost of broadcasting rights, only broadcasters from the media-rich regions can afford these for major sporting events like the Olympics. US networks have provided up to 75 per cent of total Olympic revenue from TV rights and production costs, with NBC being one of major networks to benefit from this commercialization of sport.

Table 4.7 Olympian broadcasting: summer Olympics

Year	Venue	IOC broadcasting revenue ($ million)
1960	Rome	1.0
1964	Tokyo	1.6
1968	Mexico City	7.5
1972	Munich	17.8
1976	Montreal	32.0
1980	Moscow	101.0
1984	Los Angeles	287.0
1988	Seoul	403.0
1992	Barcelona	636.0
1996	Atlanta	898.2
2000	Sydney	1331.5
2004	Athens	1476.9

Source: International Olympic Committee

One consequence of the soaring cost of rights for sports coverage is the creation of new contests by media giants. In 1998, the Milan-based Media Partners tried to establish a new European Super League football tournament, and in the same year Manchester United, the world's most profitable football club, launched its own channel, MUTV, jointly owned by BSkyB, Granada Media Group and the Club. For a major domestic sporting league such as National Football League (American Football), ESPN signed a $2.2 billion annual fee sports rights agreement with ABC and Fox, for the period 1998–2006.

The increasing commercialization and 'media-ization' of sport are also reflected in commercial sponsorship of the games and teams themselves. The 1996 Olympics in Atlanta, for example, set records by selling more than $1 billion in corporate sponsorship. Merchandising such as baseball caps in the USA and football shirts in Europe, along with corporate public relations and cross-marketing, have become an integral part of televised sports. Apart from selling company products, the trend is towards marketing of sport stars themselves (Bellamy, 1998; Slack, 2004). US basketball player Michael Jordan, England football captain David Beckham and Indian cricketer Sachin Tendulkar have become international advertising icons and therefore effective salesmen.

A symbiotic relationship has evolved between global sport and the international television industry. Given the profit involved, sport networks have to find new and innovative ways to fill their international channels and keep the advertisers happy. ESPN, for example, invested in promoting X Games, started in 1995, featuring the world's top athletes in several sport categories, and expanded around the world.

The Entertainment and Sports Network (ESPN) is the world's leading sports television broadcaster and one of the world's most profitable networks, 80 per cent owned by Disney Corporation, with the remaining 20 per cent owned by the Hearst Corporation. In 2006, its 25 networks reached more than 300 million households in 147 countries around the globe.

ESPN has a share in the pan-European sports network Eurosport, of which it owns 33 per cent, the rest being owned by EBU, TF1 and Canal Plus, reaching 80 million homes in 47 countries in Europe and the Middle East. ESPN's Latin American operation had a viewership of more than 9 million, while with its 50 per cent ownership of Star Sports, part of News Corporation, the ESPN network claims to reach nearly 91 million viewers across Asia. This global television audience is made possible by PanAmSat satellites, which act as its global programme distribution network. ESPN's cable affiliates downlink its customized signals from five PanAmSat satellites, serving the USA and the Atlantic Ocean, Pacific Ocean and Indian Ocean regions.

Apart from its highly popular domestic cable networks in the USA (ESPN, ESPN2, ESPN Classic, ESPNEWS), the network has been steadily increasing its global presence since it launched ESPN International in 1988. In 2006, ESPN International had 25 international networks and syndication, including Sports-i ESPN (Japan), ESPN Asia, ESPN Taiwan, Sky Sports (New Zealand) and ESPN Australia. It owned 50 per cent of ESPN Brazil and one-third of Net STAR, owners of The Sports Network of Canada, and a quarter of Sportsvision of Australia. Syndicated programming from ESPN Radio is broadcast globally, while Hearst Group distributes ESPN Magazine (2006 readership – 11.4 million). ESPN.com is one of the most popular sport websites and Mobile ESPN has an extensive base for content for mobile enthusiasts. In addition, ESPN also has a number of real and online shops. The company has developed global strategies to exploit the explosion of channels on satellite television and the potential of multimillion dollar sponsorship from transnational corporations. ESPN Enterprises has developed such revenue-earning streams as ESPN Videogames, ESPN Music, ESPN Home Entertainment, ESPN Books, ESPN Sports Poll and ESPN Consumer Products. Given that ESPN is the world leader in televising sport, covering 65 sports and airing more than 5100 live and/or original hours of sports programming, it is conceivable that only those sports that are sponsored by big corporations and of interest to the widest possible audience will be encouraged.

Public service to private profit – European broadcasting

The international success of the US-originated commercial model of television has had a profound effect on broadcasting in Western Europe, the world's second richest media market and home to a public-service ethos of broadcasting (Atkinson and Raboy, 1997; Tracey, 1998; Lowe and Per, 2005). The privatization of the European airwaves, a process which started in the late 1980s, had transformed the media landscape by the beginning of the twenty-first century (*see* Table 4.8), epitomized by the entry into the international commercial television arena of the world's most famous public-service broadcaster – the BBC (Steemers, 2004).

Table 4.8 Expansion of TV channels* in Europe

Channel type	1990	1995	2000	2005
Entertainment	14	31	90	170
General	9	23	67	142
Movies	5	13	66	136
Sport	0	21	70	155
News/Business	6	24	65	119
Music	2	14	55	124
Documentary	2	9	65	108
Children	1	8	56	104
Shopping	1	4	20	72
Lifestyle	0	0	4	20
Ethnic	0	4	12	51
Adult	0	3	14	84
Travel	0	3	9	24
Cultural	1	3	14	27
Total	93	242	768	1703

Note: * Cable, satellite and digital terrestrial

Source: Based on data from *Screen Digest*, August 2005

The BBC is Europe's largest exporter of television programmes: in 2005, it registered a total sale of £706 million – up from £135 million in 1998 – and a profit of £52.2 million, with sales of television programmes and formats being at the top (£171 million in 2005). Through its commercial arm, BBC Worldwide, formed in 1994, the BBC has entered into the competitive world media market through a combination of wholly-owned channels and joint ventures. In 2005, the BBC's 19 channels (both wholly-owned and joint-venture) were being watched by 324 million households worldwide, up from 115 million in 1997. Nevertheless exports accounted for only 36 per cent of total programme sales, 12 per cent to the USA and 24 per cent to the rest of the world. Unlike US-based media TNCs, much of the BBC's sales come from within the British market, especially cable and satellite channels – the so-called 'secondary TV market'.

While BBC World, its 24-hour international news service, has yet to make a profit, BBC Prime, its international entertainment channel, has been more successful. Launched in 1992, as a joint venture with the Pearson Group, one of Britain's biggest media corporations, it offers English-language programming, primarily beamed at Europe. The deal with Pearson did not last long, but BBC Prime, now wholly owned by the BBC, continued to be popular among its 21 million subscribers in 100 countries, where its programmes were being subtitled in 12 languages (BBC, 2005b). The BBC's other international channels in 2006 included BBC America (40 million homes in 2005), BBC Food and BBC Japan. Through what it calls 'blue chip partnerships', joint ventures with internationally known commercial companies, the BBC has gradually expanded into the global market. These partnerships are based on mutual benefit: the commercial channels gain by association with the BBC brand, while a cash-strapped BBC can access more resources to produce big-budget programmes. Through its joint venture with Flextech, the BBC had nine channels available on satellite and cable television in Britain: UK TV Gold, Drama, Style, Food, Bright Ideas, Garden, Documentary, People and History. In addition, UK TV was also available in Australia and New Zealand (as a joint venture with Foxtel), while BBC Canada and BBC Kids was a joint venture with Alliance Atlantis.

In 1998, the BBC joined forces with the Discovery Channel to launch a natural history and wildlife channel, Animal Planet, available in 2006 in 227 million homes in 160 countries around the world; while another joint venture, People+Art, was available in more than 14 million homes across Latin America, as well as in Spain and Portugal. In the USA, the BBC also had a deal on sharing programmes and co-production with Boston broadcaster WGBH, on behalf of US public television, and had also co-produced programmes with the A&E network and HBO. Such an approach has allowed the BBC to raise its international profile and brand name and capitalize on its rich library of programmes, selling footage and specialist programmes to broadcasters worldwide, as well as promoting specialized packages, such as in-flight programming, sports programming and programme formats.

The opening up of the audio-visual market, both to pan-European and international operators, has changed the television landscape in Europe, with a 20-fold increase in the number of channels available to European audiences in the past decade and a half – from 93 in 1990 to more than 1700 in 2005, with entertainment channels showing the most robust growth, as shown in Table 4.8. As television channels have mushroomed, public broadcasters are losing audience and increasingly looking to export programmes to sustain themselves. Germany's Deutsche Welle, for example, has been exporting series, documentaries and light entertainment programmes in various languages – by 2006 it had sold more than 23,000 hours of programmes to around 1200 television stations in 106 countries. Private networks, such as Bertelsmann's CLT-UFA, have benefited from the proliferation of channels – and were reaching a pan-European audience through a network of RTL channels in Germany, France, Britain, the Netherlands, Hungary and Poland. Programmes from major French companies, such as Canal Plus International, also had a Europe-wide viewership, as well as in the Francophone regions of North and West Africa. Since 1998, the French-language international channel TV5 – jointly owned by a collection of French, Canadian, Swiss and Belgian public service broadcasters – has collaborated with Canal France International (CFI) to export French programmes. TV5, mostly financed by the French Foreign Ministry, broadcasts 24 hours a day on 5000 cable networks across the world, and is available on 23 satellite platforms which can reach a potential audience of 500 million. Other countries, such as Brazil, Mexico, Egypt, India and China, also export television programmes (*see* Chapter 6).

The international film industry

Though more films are produced in India than in the USA (*see* Table 4.9), global cinema and television screens are dominated by Hollywood: Hollywood films are shown in more than 150 countries, earning billions of dollars annually – in 2005, half of Hollywood's revenue came from overseas markets, up from just 30 per cent in 1980. The US film industry provides the majority of pre-recorded video/DVD, broadcast on millions of television screens around the world – by 2005, Hollywood accounted for 80 per cent of the world's film business (Waterman, 2005). In 1990, world cinema box-office revenue was $11.8 billion; by 1999 it was nearly $17 billion, and, according to the Motion Picture

Table 4.9 The world's top 10 film-producing nations

| Country | Number of films produced | | | |
	1974	1984	1994	2004
India	432	829	754	946
USA	242	366	635	611
Japan	333	333	251	310
China (plus Hong Kong)	146	253	340	276
France	234	161	115	203
Italy	231	103	95	134
Spain	112	75	44	133
UK	88	44	70	132
Germany	80	75	57	121
Russia	–	–	90	120

Source: Based on data from *Screen Digest*, June 2005

Association, by 2004 it had crossed $25 billion (www.mpaa.org).

Internationalization defined Hollywood for much of the twentieth century (Guback, 1969; Jarvie, 1992; Vasey, 1997), a trend which is likely to grow given the proliferation of new ways of delivery of films and film-based programming. Since at least the Second World War, US film corporations have planned their marketing strategies with an international audience in mind, and maximized their revenues by using different types of delivery mechanisms – from movie theatres to television, to home video/DVD, to online and mobile devices (Wasko, 2003; Waterman, 2005). No wonder that many Hollywood films generate more box office receipts internationally than in the USA: the 1998 film *Titanic* grossed more than $1.8 billion in worldwide sales. The USA itself is the world's largest movie market: in 2004, Sony, Warner and Buena Vista all earned revenues of more than $1 billion at the domestic box office.

According to OECD figures, US international trade in films has grown substantially in the past three decades. In 1970, the USA earned $31 million from global rental of films, a figure which was $335 million in 1981, touching $1482 million in 1991 (OECD, 1993). By 2004, according to the Unites States Bureau of Economic Analysis, receipts from film and television rentals had reached $10.4 billion (US Government, 2005). One reason for the presence of US films worldwide is their distribution network. The structural links between producers, distributors and exhibitors of the US film industry, its ties with global banking industries (Aksoy and Robins, 1992) and the extension of such connections to the cable TV industry (Wasko, 2003) all contribute to the pre-eminent position of the USA in the global image market.

International book publishing

In the world of books too, English-language publishing is predominant (see Table 4.10). The global market for English-language books and journals is valued at around $20 billion a year and set to grow, as the demand for English-language books and publications increases worldwide. The USA leads the world's book export market: in 2004, American publishers sold books worldwide worth over $1.7 billion (US Government, 2005). Most of these are popular books by such US publishers as the Reader's Digest Association, which has an international market for its well-known editions of condensed books, books on do-it-yourself, home improvement, cooking, health, gardening and children's books. Another major international presence is that of McGraw-Hill, part of the US-based McGraw-Hill group (2004 revenue, $5.2 billion), publisher of *Business Week*. It is a global publishing and business information services provider, with McGraw-Hill Education being one of the major publishers of Spanish-language material for Latin America (www.mcgraw-hill.com).

With subsidiaries and affiliated companies in Canada, Britain, Australia, New Zealand and South Africa, Random House (part of Bertelsmann), the world's largest English-language trade publisher, includes such publishing groups as Ballantine, Bantam Books (one of the largest mass-market publishers in the USA), Broadway, Crown Publishing, Dell Publishing, Doubleday, Fodor's Travel and Knopf Publishing. Among its main imprints are: Arrow, Bodley Head, Chatto & Windus, Century, Ebury, Heinemann, Hutchinson, Jonathan Cape, Pimlico, Secker & Warburg, Sinclair-Stevenson and Vintage. Bertelsmann also owns Transworld, a major British publisher, with many well-known imprints. Based in the Netherlands, VNU, which owns ACNielsen, the global marketing information operator, active in over 100 countries, is a major player in business-to-business publishing (in 2006, it operated 140 printed publications, 150 trade exhibitions and many websites), as well as being a global leader in measuring the usage of media.

Created in 1998, through the merger of Simon & Schuster and Addison-Wesley Longman (AWL) education businesses, Pearson Education (part of the British-based Pearson Group) is a leading publisher of books in the school, university and professional markets around the world, with group sales for 2004 of $7.1 billion. Pearson, the world's largest book company, also owns the Penguin Group, one of the world's best-known English-language general interest publishers (which includes such well-known brands as Dorling Kindersley, Puffin and Ladybird), with subsidiaries in the USA, Australia, New Zealand, Canada and India. Worldwide, estimates have education publishing as a $100 billion-plus industry. Quoting the British Council estimates that 2 billion people, or one-third of the world's population, will be studying English by 2015, Pearson notes: 'There has never been a better time to be in the business of education' (www.pearson.com). Thomson Learning, formerly known as Thomson International Publishing, is another major international educational publisher, operating in more than 100 countries around the world. Among its publishing arm and imprints are International Thomson Business Press, ITP Asia, ITP Nelson (Canada), ITP Spain/Paraninfo, Nelson ITP (Australia) and Thomas Nelson, UK.

In the field of scientific, professional and business publications, Reed Elsevier – formed after the merger of Reed International and Elsevier NV – is one of the largest in the world, with annual sales of $4.5 billion. Reed Elsevier's principal operations are in North America and Europe and include: Butterworths, LexisNexis, Cahners Publishing Company, Elsevier Business Information, Editions du Juris, Classeur, Reed Business Publishing, Elsevier Science and Reed Educational and Professional Publishing. Elsevier Science is the world's leading publisher of scientific information, with headquarters in The Netherlands and operations throughout the world. The group publishes more than 1200 journals – including *The Lancet*, one of the world's most respected medical journals – in the physical, life, social and medical sciences, and operates an international network of medical communications services. The group's legal division includes the Butterworths group of companies, covering the legal markets in Britain, Australia, Canada, New Zealand, South Africa and South East Asia. LexisNexis is a provider of professional information to the legal, corporate and government markets, mainly in North America; while Reed Educational and Professional Publishing serves the British schools market, as well as the international professional and academic sectors (www.reed-elsevier.com). Another global player in specialized areas such as legal, medical or scientific publishing, is the Amsterdam-based Wolters Kluwer. Other academic publishers with worldwide presence include Taylor & Francis Group (part of Informa business), publishing more than 1000 journals and around 1800 new books each year, and Palgrave Macmillan, Britain's largest independent publisher. Among the university presses, the US Ivy League University presses, such as Yale University Press, had a global reach matched in Britain by Oxford University Press, the world's largest university press and one of its oldest – established in the seventeenth century – which in 2006 had presence in 56 countries.

The reach of these publishing giants is global: via networks of local affiliates, their books and journals are sold in virtually every country in the world. These groups and their imprints publish fiction and non-fiction, both original and reprints, and they appear in all formats – including hardcover, paperback, as well as audio, online, multimedia and other forms for the widest possible international readership.

Table 4.10 Top 10 exporters of books

Country	Value ($ million)	Global share %
USA	1921.4	17.7
UK	1805.7	16.7
Germany	1257.8	11.6
Spain	686.0	6.3
China (plus Hong Kong)	667.5	6.2
France	518.5	4.8
Italy	510.3	4.7
Canada	396.0	3.7
Belgium	362.0	3.3
Singapore	349.9	3.2

Source: UNESCO, 2005a, figures for 2002

The international print media

The US–UK 'duopoly' seems to dominate global newspaper and magazine markets as well. Though seven Japanese and two Chinese newspapers figure among the world's top 10 newspapers in terms of circulation (*see* Table 4.11), they are rarely read outside their countries of origin. In contrast, the Anglo-American press have global reach and influence. Some publications, such as the British weekly news magazine *The Economist*, in fact, sell more copies outside Britain.

One of the most well-known newspapers with an international readership is the Paris-based *International Herald Tribune*, which was jointly owned by the *New York Times* and *The Washington Post*, but was bought in 2003 by the former to effectively make it a slimmed-down overseas version of the *New York Times*. The *IHT* was the world's first newspaper to be distributed by aeroplane in 1928, flying copies to London from Paris 'in time for breakfast', and also the first daily to transmit its pages via satellite from Paris to Hong Kong, in 1980. By 2006 'the world's daily', as it calls itself, was being printed in more than 30 sites across the world and distributed in 180 countries. Though its worldwide circulation had declined from 638,000 in 2000 to 240,500 in 2005, its reach was much wider as it was circulated also as inserts with its partner quality newspapers around the world – these included *Haaretz* (Israel); *Kathimerini* (Greece); *Frankfurter Allgemeine Zeitung* (Germany); *JoongAng Daily* (South Korea); *Asahi Shimbun* (Japan); *Daily Star* (Lebanon); *El País* (Spain); and *Moscow Times* (Russia).

Table 4.11 The world's top 10 newspapers by circulation, 2004

Title	Circulation (million)
Yomiuri Shimbun (Japan)	14.1
Asahi Shimbun (Japan)	12.1
Mainichi Shimbun (Japan)	5.6
Nihon Keizai Shimbun (Japan)	4.6
Chunichi Shimbun (Japan)	4.5
Bild (Germany)	3.9
Sankei Shimbun (Japan)	2.8
Canako Xiaoxi (China)	2.6
People's Daily (China)	2.5
Tokyo Sports (Japan)	2.4

Source: *World Press Trends, the World Association of Newspapers,* 2005

Two American news weeklies – *Newsweek* and *Time* – have shaped global journalism for half a century. In 2006, three editions of *Newsweek* – Atlantic, Asia and Latin America – were distributed in more than 190 countries and had a global circulation of 4 million and a readership of 21 million. With its four regional editions, and circulation of more than 2 million, *Time* reaches nearly 29 million readers globally. The London-based *The Economist* sells more than 80 per cent of its 1 million copies every week overseas, primarily in the USA, which accounts for just over half of its total circulation. The *Guardian Weekly,* one of the world's oldest international newspapers, founded in 1919 and printed in Britain, Canada and Australia, has a small but significant international readership. Apart from carrying reports and analyses from *The Guardian* and *The Observer* (Britain's oldest Sunday newspaper), it also publishes a selection from the *Washington Post* as well as *Le Monde* and *Le Monde Diplomatique,* two of France's most respected newspapers. As Table 4.12 shows, in terms of global circulation 8 of the top 10 publications originate in the USA.

From Table 4.13 it can be seen that US-UK publications lead the field of global business journalism. *Business Week* tops the league, with a global readership of 5.6 million in 120 countries (by 2006 *Business Week* was running Arabic, Indonesian, Chinese and Polish editions). *Fortune,* the world's leading biweekly business magazine, has a global readership of 5 million. The other major publication in this area with a global readership is *Forbes.* The *Wall Street Journal* is the largest circulation daily in the USA and the flagship publication of Dow Jones, the world's leading business publishers. It is read by 5 million affluent Americans and its regional editions make it a major global player. The *Wall Street Journal Europe,* which reaches more than 300,000 business readers in Europe, and the *Wall Street Journal Asia,* the leading pan-regional business newspaper published since 1976 in Hong Kong, with editions in Tokyo and Singapore, have a dedicated readership among the

Table 4.12 The world's top newspapers and magazines, 2005

Publication	Ownership	Global circulation (millions)
Reader's Digest	Reader's Digest Association, USA	23
Cosmopolitan International, USA	Hearst Magazines	9.5
National Geographic	National Geographic Society, USA	8.6
Metro	Modern Times Group, Sweden	6.2
Time	Time Warner, USA	5.2
Playboy	Playboy Enterprise International , USA	4.5
USA Today	Gannett Co., USA	2.5
Wall Street Journal	Dow Jones, USA	2.3
Financial Times	Pearson Group, UK	0.4
International Herald Tribune	New York Times, USA	0.2

Sources: Based on data from *Campaign*, 2005, issue 22

business elite. The newspaper also has a Chinese-language web edition, as well as *Wall Street Journal Americas* in Spanish and Portuguese for the Latin American market. The *Journal*'s nearest competitor, the London-based *Financial Times*, 'the world's most international newspaper, printed in 24 cities with correspondents in 55 countries and readers in over 110', has a circulation of over 453,000 and a global readership in excess of 1 million (www.ft.com).

Table 4.13 The world's top international business newspapers and magazines, 2005

Publication	Ownership	Global circulation
Wall Street Journal	Dow Jones, USA	2,300,000
Business Week	McGraw-Hill, USA	1,450,000
Fortune	Time Warner, USA	1,120,000
Forbes	Forbes, USA	1,061,171
The Economist	Pearson, UK	1,038,522
Financial Times	Pearson, UK	435,000

Source: Based on data from company websites

In the category of general interest magazines, *Reader's Digest* occupies first place, with 48 editions in 19 languages. The family monthly has a global readership of 100 million in 29 countries, and the company which owns *Reader's Digest* had worldwide revenues in 2005 of $2.3 billion, more than 55 per cent of which was generated outside the USA. In the field of lifestyle, travel and health magazines, the New York-based Condé Nast company is a world leader, producing 96 magazines in 18 countries, including such internationally distributed titles as: *Vogue, GQ, Vanity Fair* and *Wired*, with a combined readership in 2005 reaching up to 120 million. *Playboy*, which has a global circulation of more than 4.5 million, was producing 20 international editions in 2006. Bertlesmann-owned Gruner+Jahr, Europe's biggest magazine publisher, producing 125 magazines in 10 countries, was another major player in this field.

International advertising

The global expansion of television and other media could not have been possible without the support of advertisers, central to a commercial broadcasting culture. Global advertising expenditure, according to McCann Worldgroup, one of the world's largest advertising companies, has doubled in the past decade and a half – from $275 billion to an estimated $604 billion in 2006, growing every year in this period except in 2001 (*see* Figure 4.1).

Given the historical importance of advertising in American domestic commercial radio and television, the USA is the world's biggest advertising market, three times bigger than its nearest rival, Japan, in terms of spending on advertising, as Table 4.14 makes clear.

Though print advertising still leads among the top 10 markets, television remains one of

Table 4.14 Top 10 global advertising markets

Country	Advertising spend in 2003 ($ billion)	Predicted advertising spend in 2007 ($ billion)	Change %
USA	149.7	174.3	16.4
Japan	36.3	41.7	15.1
Germany	18.9	18.5	2.5
Britain	16.6	19.7	18.8
France	10.8	11.5	6.8
Italy	8.5	10.6	24.8
China	6.3	12.7	100.3
South Korea	6.5	6.5	0.4
Spain	6.1	7.3	20.1
Canada	5.7	6.7	17.5
Global	345.5	442.1	28.0

Source: ZenithOptimedia

Figure 4.1 Global growth: worldwide advertising 1990–2006

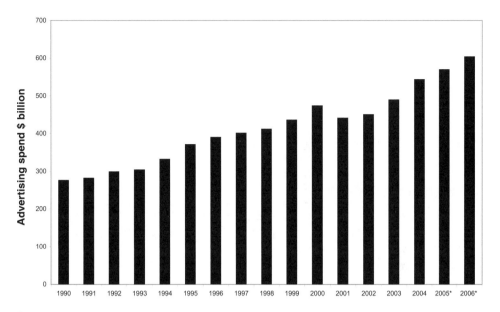

*Estimates
Source: Universal McCann

the fastest-growing advertising media, especially internationally, with the proliferation of television channels across the world and growing acceptance of new digital and mobile delivery mechanisms. Partly because of this experience, US-based advertising agencies also dominate the global advertising industry (*see* Table 4.15).

Table 4.15 The top 10 global marketers by advertising spend

Advertisers	Worldwide advertising spend ($ billion)
Procter & Gamble (USA)	16.1
COI Communications (Britain)	12.1
British Telecom (Britain)	9.6
Ford Motors (USA)	9.5
L'Oréal (France)	7.1
Masterfoods (USA)	6.7
Renault (France)	6.6
Toyota (Japan)	6.5
Vauxhall (Britain)	6.3
Nestlé (Switzerland)	6.3

Source: Based on data from *Marketing*, February, 2003

Table 4.16 Selling globalization: The world's leading advertising conglomerates

Group name	Main companies	Operating in	Sales 2004 $bn
Omnicom Group	BBDO Worldwide DDB Worldwide TBWA Worldwide	100 countries	9.7
WPP Group	Grey Worldwide J. Walter Thompson Ogilvy & Mather Young & Rubicam	100 countries	8.2
Interpublic Group	McCann Worldgroup Low and Partners Foote, Cone & Belding	130 countries	6.3
Publicis	Publicis Worldwide Saatchi & Saatchi Leo Burnett Worldwide	110 countries	5.1

Source: Based on data from company websites

Just four countries dominate the global advertising industry, as Table 4.16 shows, with US-based corporations being the most important. The close links between many top-level advertising and marketing organizations further limit the number of corporations active in global advertising. The Japanese advertising giant Dentsu, one of the oldest advertising agencies in the world, has close business alliances with American and French advertising agencies. Through a network of national subsidies they influence the international advertising industry (Mooij, 1998; Jones, 1999).

The opening up of new markets has ensured that advertising conglomerates can expand their operations without restrictions, installing new networks and facing fewer problems in the repatriation of royalties or profits. Having grown substantially during the 1980s as a result of the deregulation of television, primarily in the USA (Mattelart, 1991), the advertising industry has been transformed into a transnational marketing service for conglomerates. In this role, the advertising industry has gone beyond its traditional business, offering a global package which includes advertising, marketing, promotion, media services, public relations and management consultancy (Dicken, 1998).

The markets might have expanded as a result of globalization, but the key advertising companies have not changed in the past two decades. In 2006, they remain dominated by a handful of largely Western-based advertising/marketing conglomerates (see Table 4.16). Calling itself 'a multidisciplinary global-communications powerhouse', J. Walter Thompson, the world's oldest advertising agency, was by 2006 operating worldwide through its 300 offices in 87 countries, serving over 1200 clients. 'We're big. Very big. And we're everywhere', its website proudly proclaims. It is part of the WPP Group, one of the largest marketing communications networks in the world, which also operates Hill and Knowlton,

Ogilvy Public Relations, Millward Brown and Research International. Even bigger than the WPP group in 2006 was Omnicom Group, which included, among others, DDB Worldwide (operational through 206 offices in 96 countries), BBDO Worldwide, operating in 76 countries, and TBWA Worldwide. More than 54 per cent of its revenue in 2004, however, came from just one country – the USA. Another major player was McCann Worldgroup (part of Interpublic Group), with subsidiaries in 130 countries worldwide, though here, again, more than 55 per cent of revenue in 2004 was generated in the USA.

Across the Atlantic, the Publicis Group, which includes such internationally known advertising companies as the London-based Saatchi and Saatchi – earned more than 40 per cent of its revenue in 2004 in Europe. The big European player in global advertising is Euro RSCG Worldwide (part of Havas, one of the world's largest advertising and communications groups), which claims to be 'global in the truest sense of the word. We're as global as the planet': in 2006 it had 233 offices in 75 countries. Outside the Euro-Atlantic advertising world, the only other major global presence is that of the Japanese advertising company Dentsu, part of the Dentsu Group, although more than 90 per cent of its revenue comes from the Japanese market.

It is often the case that same transnational corporations are the main users of advertising in different regions. As Tables 4.15 and 4.16 demonstrate, the major conglomerates are the advertisers and the advertising agencies are themselves part of major conglomerates, both of which are global in their strategies and approach (Jones, 1999). Some advertisers can also play an important part in television programme production. With its historic role as the originator of the 'soap opera', Procter and Gamble has co-produced programmes, such as *Sabrina: The Teenage Witch* (Blumenthal and Goodenough, 1998). There is, therefore, a community of interest between the advertisers and advertising medium. The trend is towards global branding, as Mooij comments:

> A global brand is one which shares the same strategic principles, positioning and marketing in every market throughout the world, although the marketing mix can vary. It carries the same brand name or logo. Its values are identical in all countries, it has a substantial market share in all countries and comparable brand loyalty. The distribution channels are similar.
>
> (Mooij 1998: 16)

The increasingly international nature of advertising and marketing has led to what is labelled as Globally Integrated Marketing Communications, which ensures a co-ordinated global management of products across country offices and disciplines, essential in contemporary international interactions. In the twenty-first century, the advertising industry is evolving to include advertising and media, public relations, branding, marketing research and corporate communication; used not just by commercial companies, but also by government spin doctors, as well as non-governmental organizations, to brand their versions of truth to an increasingly media-savvy and fragmenting audience.

Global news and information networks

In the realm of international news, US/UK-based media organizations produce and distribute much of the world's news and current affairs output. From international news agencies to global newspapers and radio stations, from providers of television news footage to 24-hour news and documentary channels, the US/UK presence seems to be overwhelming.

News agencies

As collectors and distributors of news to newspapers, magazines and broadcasters globally, news agencies play a central role in setting the international news agenda. It has been argued that news agencies contributed significantly to the globalization and commodification of international information (Boyd-Barrett and Rantanen, 1998). Though traditionally the news agencies sold news reports and still photographs, today they have diversified their operations, for example, by offering video news feeds for broadcasters and online information and financial databases. Most countries in the world have a national news agency – in many cases state-owned or a government monopoly. However, there are only a few transnational news agencies and these continue to be owned by US and British companies. As Table 4.17 shows, two of the world's three biggest news agencies are British or American, with AP leading the trio.

Associated Press

In terms of overall news output, the Associated Press – 'the essential global news network', as it calls itself – is the world's largest news-gathering organization, serving news organizations worldwide with news, photos, graphics, audio and video, claiming that 'more than a billion people every day read, hear or see AP news'. AP operates as a not-for-profit co-operative with its subscribing member organizations, supplying news, photographs, graphics, audio

Table 4.17 The world's top three news agencies

	Associated Press (USA)	Reuters (Britain)	Agence France-Presse (France)
Worldwide bureaux	242	196	140
Countries covered	121	130	165
Languages used	5	19	6
Journalists employed	3700	2300	2000
News output (words per day)	20 million	8 million	4–6 million

Source: Based on data from company websites

and video to an international audience in 121 countries. It also has a digital photo network – supplying 1000 photos a day worldwide to 8500 international subscribers – a 24-hour continuously updated online news service, a television news service (APTN) and AP Network News (largest single radio network in the USA, with 1000 affiliates). Apart from English, AP's service is available in German, Dutch, French and Spanish, while subscribers translate its stories into many more languages. As newspapers, radio and television stations have cut back operations or folded, AP has endeavoured to sell selected, packaged news to non-media organizations, such as governments and corporations.

Reuters

In the world of news, Reuters remains a major actor, supplying news, graphics, news video and news pictures to a global audience (*see* Chapter 1). However, Reuters Holding, the company which owns the news agency, deals in 'the business of information', making its main profit in transmitting real-time financial data and collective investment data to global financial markets. Though it is known as a news agency, it is in fact, in its own words, 'the largest financial information provider in the world'. In 2006, Reuters had 2300 editorial staff working in 196 bureaux in 130 countries. The extent of the reach of Reuters can be gauged by the fact that in 2004 the agency filed more than 2.5 million news items, including 440,000 alerts. In addition, the company provided real-time data on 5.5 million financial records to its clients. By 2006, the company had introduced two new major services: Reuters Trader, a real-time price data and news service for traders, and Reuters Knowledge, corporate information for investment bankers and researchers. 'Know. Now', is Reuters' latest motto (www.reuters.com).

Agence France Presse (AFP)

The third global news agency is the Paris-based Agence France-Presse, with subscribers including businesses, banks and governments, as well as newspapers, radio and TV stations across the world. Though subsidized by the French government, AFP claims to be free from any state intervention in its editorial policy. In fact, Article 2 of AFP's 1957 statute firmly states: 'The Agency shall be independent of all political, economic, philosophical or religious influence'. AFP is particularly strong on coverage of the Middle East and Africa, perhaps reflecting French geo-economic interests. It distributes more than 4 million words daily, as well as 1000 news photos and 50 graphics in English, Spanish, French, German, Arabic, Russian and Portuguese. It has regional centres in Washington, Hong Kong, Nicosia and Montevideo. Facing the competition from the US/UK media, this French agency too has diversified, launching a financial news service, AFX News, based in London, as well as an English-language television service, AFP TV. Despite these changes, AFP remains a French media organization which promotes haute couture, including the launch of AFP Video service, featuring major fashion shows and style trends.

According to UNESCO, the three main news agencies are the source of about 80 per cent of the public's information worldwide and they operate in a commercial environment: though it is a not-for-profit organization, even AP's mission states unambiguously that the agency 'is in the information business'. The dominant position of Western news agencies is based on professional output – a reputation for speed and accuracy in the coverage of international events, though their interpretation may often reflect Western, or more specifically, US editorial priorities.

Other major agencies

United Press International (UPI), 'the world's largest privately owned news service', which was considered one of the 'big four' until the 1980s, is another US-based news agency with international influence, though it has been progressively waning. For most of the 1990s the majority of shares in UPI were owned by Saudi media interests, but in 2000 it was acquired by News World Communications, the company which operates such conservative newspapers as the *Washington Times*. This may have further reduced UPI's international credibility, though it continues to provide news in English, as well as in Arabic and Spanish, to consumers worldwide. Other major Western news agencies with notable international presence include Germany's DPA (Deutsche Presse-Agentur), particularly strong in Eastern Europe, but reaching, in 2006, subscribers in 90 countries and providing news in German, English, Spanish and Arabic; and EFE of Spain, with close links in Latin America.

China's Xinhua news agency, founded in 1931, has expanded steadily since the country began to open its doors for business in 1978 and is increasingly following the route of marketization and privatization. The agency's website has versions in English, Chinese, Japanese, French, Spanish, Russian and Arabic, disseminating mostly positive information about China. TASS, the official Russian news agency, renamed, in 1992, ITAR-TASS (*Informatsionnoe telegrafnoe agentstvo Rossii-Telegrafnoe agentstvo Sovetskogo Soiuza*), had more than 130 bureaux in Russia and other countries, in 2006, mainly among former Soviet republics, distributing on average 40 round-the-clock 'news cycles'. ITAR-TASS, which produced content in six languages, also co-operated with more than 80 foreign news agencies and operated a photo service, the largest of its kind in Russia, and has also entered into joint ventures in operating private and corporate telecommunication networks based on satellite, fibre-optic, microwave, radio and cable lines. The English-language service of Japan's news agency Kyodo, established in 1945, also has an international presence. Drawing on a network of 70 journalists based in 50 overseas locations, the news service reaches news agencies, newspapers, broadcasters and financial information distributors in various parts of the world, as well as such international organizations as the WTO and IMF.

Financial news services

In the globalized free-market world of the twenty-first century, speedy and regular transmission of accurate financial intelligence has become very important for news organizations. The blurring of boundaries between financial news and financial data has contributed to news screens carrying news and financial information side by side or even on a single screen. Reuters, which changed through the 1970s and 1980s, from being merely a news agency to an international electronic data company, is the leading international player in financial news and data. Other global key players in financial journalism are AP-DJ economic news service, formed as a result of AP teaming with Dow Jones, and AFX News, an agency providing real-time news service with a European focus, produced by AFP and the *Financial Times*. However, the most important new player is Bloomberg, which has emerged as a major rival to Reuters' financial market.

Started in 1981 by Mike Bloomberg, a former employee of Salomon Brothers who became the Mayor of New York City in 2001, Bloomberg offers a 24-hour, worldwide, real-time financial information network of news, data and analyses of financial markets and business. By 2006 it was providing financial information to businesses and financial journalists and other users in 126 countries. Its news service, Bloomberg News, available in five languages – English, French, Spanish, German and Japanese – was syndicated in over 250 newspapers around the world. Bloomberg Radio, syndicated through 840 affiliates worldwide, reported market news every hour, while Bloomberg Television – a 24-hour news channel that reports market news – is broadcast throughout the world via its 10 networks, operating in 7 languages, reaching 200 million homes. As it proudly claims: 'Our products drive investment decisions that affect millions of people – and billions of dollars worldwide' (www.bloomberg.com).

Among the dedicated financial news television channels, the most important is CNBC, formed after the merger of NBC and European Business News (EBN) (which is owned by Dow Jones), and its sister channel Asia Business News (ABN). CNBC is almost exclusively devoted to business news from the world markets. Many financial news and information services make revenue from large-scale trading in shares and currencies, and a fluid and insecure financial market can be good news for them since they take commission from weekly currency trading worth billions of dollars. This raises questions about whether their role is promoting and sustaining free-market liberalization of financial markets.

International television news

Two of the world's biggest wire services – AP and Reuters – are also the two top international television news services. These two companies largely control global flow of audio-visual news material, thus influencing global television journalism. In the realm of television news – both raw footage and complete news channels – the US-UK predominance is obvious, as is indicated in Table 4.18.

Reuters Television (formerly Visnews), one of the world's two largest television news agencies, remains a key player in the global trade in news footage, and is used by major news organizations such as CNN and BBC. Reuters also owned 20 per cent of the London-based Independent Television News (ITN). Its rival is Associated Press Television News (APTN), which was launched in 1998 following the acquisition from ABC of TV news agency Worldwide Television News (WTN) by AP, integrating it with the operations of APTV, the London-based video news agency launched by AP in 1994. By 2006 the company had 80 bureaux worldwide. This development indicates further narrowing of international television news sources – just two organizations now supply most of the news footage to broadcasters worldwide. ABC News, part of the Disney empire, had an 80 per cent stake in WTN (formerly UPITN) since 1998, while 10 per cent was owned by the Nine Network Australia and the rest by ITN. Why it sold such a powerful resource – the second largest provider of international television news pictures – is a matter of speculation. One explanation might be that Disney's priorities are in the entertainment business, as news and current affairs, though

Table 4.18 News on television, 2005

Global news channels				
Channel	Viewership	Bureaux	Correspondents	Ownership
BBC World	270 million homes	58	250	BBC
CNN International	165 million homes	26	150	AOL-Time Warner

Global TV news agencies			
Agency	Subscribers	Countries	Ownership
APTN	500	121	Associated Press
Reuters TV	500	80	Reuters Holdings

Source: Based on data from company websites

very influential, can struggle for revenues. By 2006 Reuters Television was providing (apart from its flagship 'World News Service') coverage of financial news, sports, showbiz ('from Hollywood to Bollywood') and ready-to-air packages, as well as 'World News Express', a digital service primarily geared to the needs of webcasting as well as rolling news broadcasters to its subscribers worldwide.

Given their access to global satellite networks, APTN and Reuters Television offer satellite news-gathering deployments around the world. Their feeds are sent with ready scripts to allow immediate broadcasting, and natural sound which can be re-edited with local voice-overs. Through dedicated 24-hour uplinks in Beijing, Hong Kong, Moscow, Jerusalem, New York and Washington, APTN offers individual regional services for Europe, North America, Latin America, Asia-Pacific and the Middle East through its Global Video Wire, a 24/7 operation to cover breaking news.

International news channels

In the category of news channels, the Atlanta-based Cable News Network (CNN) is undoubtedly the world leader. CNN, 'the world's only global, 24-hour news network', best symbolizes globalization of American television journalism, influencing news agendas across the world and indeed shaping international communication.

Case study

CNN – the 'world's news leader'

Started by Ted Turner in 1980 as the world's first 24-hour dedicated television news channel, CNN grew, in just over a decade, to become a premier global news network. From its rather modest origins – CNN was derogatorily referred to by rivals as 'Chicken Noodle Network' – it was able to start an international service within five years of its launch.

One reason for the rapid expansion of CNN was its use of satellite technology. Satellites gave CNN first a national audience in the USA, and CNN was one of the first international broadcasters to take advantage to 'blanket the globe', using a mixture of Intelsat, Intersputnik, PanAmSat and regional satellite signals (Flournoy and Stewart, 1997).

Its move from a national to a global news organization was also due to its aggressive strategy of covering live international news events, through news exchange programmes with more than 100 broadcasting organizations across the world. The resultant *CNN World Report*, started in 1987, was a key factor in its initial acceptance among international broadcasters and its eventual growth (Volkmer, 1999). UNTV, the United Nations television unit, was one of the most prolific contributors to *CNN World Report* – perhaps related to Turner's 1997 announcement of $1 billion gift to the UN – the largest such award the organization had received in its 55-year history.

CNN played an important role in integrating the media systems of the former socialist countries into the Western fold – it was involved, for example, in the 1993 launch of TV 6, the first private television network in Russia; it entered into an agreement with China's CCTV to receive and selectively distribute its programmes, and CNN was one of the first Western news organizations to open a bureau in Cuba. Such moves have won accolades from many, including former US President Jimmy Carter: 'CNN has done more to close the gaps of misunderstanding between the world's people than any enterprise in recent memory' (Carter, in Flournoy and Stewart, 1997: vii).

CNN shot to international fame during the 1991 Gulf War, when its reporters in Baghdad beamed live the US bombing of the Iraqi capital, thus contributing significantly to making it the world's first 'real-time' war, in which television became 'the first and principal source of news for most people, as well as a major source of military and political intelligence for both sides' (Hachten, 1999: 144).

CNN's on-the-spot reporting of global events gave it unparalleled power to mould international public opinion and even contributed to influencing the actions of people involved in the events it was covering. Chinese students protesting against authorities in Beijing's Tiananmen Square in 1989 were aware that the world was watching the unfolding events through CNN – the Chinese government pulled the plug on the CNN transmission before its crackdown on protesting students. Similarly, Boris Yeltsin astutely used the presence of CNN cameras during his very public opposition to the 1991 coup in Moscow, which acted as a catalyst for the break-up of the Soviet Union. Such instances show that networks like CNN can contribute to a new version of TV-inspired public diplomacy, presenting 'opportunities to constantly monitor news events and disseminate timely diplomatic information' (Hoge, 1994: 136). There is little doubt that CNN established the importance of a global round-the-clock TV news network, a concept which 'certainly changed the international news system – especially during times of international crisis and conflict' (Hachten, 1999: 151).

As it gained respectability, CNN also expanded its operations, facilitated by it becoming part of the Time Warner group in 1996. A financial service, CNNfn, was started in 1995 to provide coverage of the stock, bond and commodities markets, and especially breaking stories about business news; a 24-hour sports TV news service, CNN-SI (Sport Illustrated), was added to the CNN platform a year later. By the late 1990s, CNN had regional versions for audiences and advertisers in Europe/the Middle East, Asia-Pacific and Latin America and the United States.

Europe remained one of its key markets, and in 1998, CNNI had become Europe's most watched news channel, reaching 79 million households, broadcasting 24 hours a day to 37 countries, with 4.5 hours a day of programming from its London centre. In 1997, it launched CNN Deutschland, a half-hour daily German-language slot for the German market. In Tokyo, the number of localized transmissions in Japanese through simultaneous translation, on the JCTV cable system, was doubled to 86 hours in 1999 and upgraded in 2003 to CNNJ, a Japan-specific network.

Reflecting that there is a greater need for local news in local languages, and already operating, since 1997, CNN en Español, a Spanish-language channel based in Atlanta for the Latin American market, in 1999, CNN launched CNN Plus in Spain, its first branded local-language version, in collaboration with Sogecable, the cable operator owned by media group Prisa. This was followed by CNN Turk, a Turkic channel started in 1999, and a South Asian version of CNN International in English in 2000; and in 2005 it entered a joint venture with an Indian television company, TV18, to launch a new network, CNN/IBN.

CNN was aiming to expand the localization process in other major non-English markets. CNN has spawned imitators across the world. The existence of global round-the-clock news networks has created a new genre of rolling news, one which is particularly sought after by media personnel and information bureaucracies around the world, especially at the time of an international crisis, such as a military conflict. The so-called 'CNN effect' has generated a debate, notably in the West, about television's perceived powers to shape the foreign policy agenda (Robinson, 2002).

By the end of the 1990s other dedicated round-the-clock global news services – BBC World and CNBC – were in operation. Regionally, too, there were networks such as al-Jazeera, which was labelled the 'Arabic CNN' (see pp. 190–3). In the USA, the three established networks – ABC, NBC and CBS – had to adapt their operations to the 24-hour channel, while Fox network, part of Murdoch's empire, launched a 24-hour news channel. In Britain, apart from Murdoch's Sky News, the BBC was also operating News 24 – a round-the-clock service for the domestic audience, launched in 1997. State broadcasters in both India's Doordarshan and China's CCTV have launched dedicated 24-hour news channels. Among private round-the-clock channels were Murdoch's India-based Star News, the Hindi-language Zee News and Brazil's Globo News, launched in 1996, all available outside their countries of origin. In 2005, Russia launched its own round-the-clock English-language global television channel, Russia Today (RTTV), intended to provide news 'from a Russian perspective'. The French government allocated $41 million in 2005 and $90 million in 2006 to establish a 24-hour international TV news channel, the French International News Channel (CFII), which aims to be the French-language CNN.

Though CNN is watched by a relatively small proportion of viewers, they fall into the category of what CNN calls 'influentials' – government ministers, top bureaucrats, company chief executives, military chiefs, religious and academic elites (Flournoy and Stewart, 1997). Perhaps more importantly, it is constantly being monitored by journalists and news organizations worldwide for any breaking news stories. It is the only network capable of covering international news instantly, given its wide network of correspondents – in 2006 it had 36 international bureaux with 150 correspondents – and its communications resources beam its programmes through a network of 38 satellites to cover the entire globe.

However, it remains an advertisement-based channel, whose output may sometimes lack depth in its desire to catch up with the speed and delivery of stories, and which tends towards infotainment. Larry King, host of one of its most watched chat shows *Larry King Live,* has no hesitation in calling himself an infotainer. As competition grows and more and more national all-news channels appear with the expansion of digital broadcasting, the pressure to be first with the news – TV news is a $3 billion business – is likely to grow. Already there is a discernible tendency among television news channels to sacrifice depth in favour of the widest and quickest reach of live news to an increasingly heterogeneous global audience. In the era of live and instant global communication there is a danger that 'by making the live and the exclusive into primary news-values, accuracy and understanding will be lost' (MacGregor, 1997: 200). For some, the 'CNNization' of television news has become a model for expanding 'American news values around the world' (Papathanassopoulos, 1999: 22).

For many non-Americans, CNN was and remains the voice of the US Government and corporate elite, despite its international presence, its multinational staff (usually US-educated or domiciled) and its claims to be free from US geostrategic and economic interests.

By 2006 CNN was available in more than 186 million television households in 200 countries and territories worldwide. CNN News Group was one of the largest and most profitable news and information companies in the world, available to 2 billion people worldwide. The group's assets included 14 cable and satellite television networks (including CNN Headline News, CNN International, CNN Money, CNN/SI and CNN en Español); two radio networks (CNN Radio and a Spanish version, CNN Radio Noticias); five websites on CNN Interactive (including in Arabic and Japanese); CNN Airport Network; and CNN Newsource, the world's most extensively syndicated news service, with 900 international affiliates. CNN Mobile, launched in 1999, was one of the world's first mobile news and information services. By virtue of the AOL-Time Warner merger of 2000, CNN became part of the world's biggest media and entertainment conglomerate, whose significance in international communications is likely to grow, and its version of world events – more often than not an American one, which might even be delivered in local languages – is likely to define the world view of millions of viewers around the globe.

After CNN, the BBC is the second most important global television news broadcaster. BBC World, its 24-hour global news and information channel, can be seen in more than 270 million homes across 200 countries and territories. Distributed through a global network of broadcasters, satellite packages and cable operators, BBC World offers separate feeds for European, Asian and Latin American viewers, all of which contain regional coverage. It was launched in Europe in 1995 and claims to be Europe's leading news channel, which broadcasts hourly news, as well as current affairs, documentaries, lifestyle and travel features. Although BBC World was planning to regionalize its service in terms of programme scheduling, it will continue to broadcast only in English, with the exception of Japan, where it broadcasts six hours of dubbed programming per night; and since 2001 it has been providing Spanish subtitles for its Latin American viewers.

The news channel can draw on the reputation of BBC World Service Radio. In addition, the UK-based BBC Worldwide Monitoring provides a unique news service based on media reports edited by journalists at BBC Monitoring, part of the BBC World Service. Originally created in 1939, BBC Monitoring has an international reputation for authoritative coverage of political and economic developments in more than 140 countries. Its news is drawn from international and national media sources, and among the users of its material are government offices and embassies, international businesses, investment houses and banks.

Though not as influential as CNN or the BBC, Sky News was the first 24-hour news channel to broadcast to Britain and Europe when it was launched in 1989 (Horsman, 1997). By 2006 it was available to 80 million people across 40 countries (including Israel, South Africa and Australia), though most of its audience was in Europe, and predominantly in Britain. Though originally intended as a British news service, it has increased its international coverage through alliances with other broadcasters, including CBS, ABC and Bloomberg Television. Sky also has an alliance with Reuters, which provides its news gathering. As part of News Corporation, it can also draw on the resources of the Hong Kong-based Star News Asia, and Fox News in the USA.

Euronews, launched in 1993 as a consortium of Europe's public broadcasters, provides 24-hour daily service broadcasting via cable, satellite and digital terrestrial TV to over 155 million viewers in 102 countries. Euronews is the only pan-European news channel to broadcast simultaneously in more than two languages – English, French, German, Spanish, Italian, Portuguese and, since 2001, Russian. It does not have its own network of news bureaux and uses the Eurovision News Exchange, a consortium of public broadcasters, for its programming.

The British presence in the European news market was strengthened in 1997 when ITN (Independent Television News) bought a 49 per cent managing stake in Euronews. However, British involvement in Euronews was short-lived, as ITN withdrew from the news consortium in 2003. Given the linguistic diversity of Europe – the continent has 34 official languages – a multilanguage news network is almost a necessity. In 2006, Euronews operated as a consortium of 16 broadcasters: CT (Czech Republic), CyBC (Cyprus), ENTV (Algeria), ERT (Greece), ERTT (Tunisia), ERTV (Egypt), francetélévisions (France), PBS (Malta), RAI (Italy), RTBF (Belgium), RTE (Ireland), RTP (Portugal), RTR (Russia), RTVE (Spain), RTVSLO (Slovenia), SSR (Switzerland), TMC (Monaco), TVR (Romania) and YLE (Finland).

Global radio

Though radio has given way to television as the main medium of international communication, it still remains an important source of information, especially in the global South. An indication of its importance is the fact that major governments continue to

Table 4.19 Major international radio stations, 2004

Station	Founded	Languages	Weekly listeners	Budget ($ million)
BBC World Service	1931	43	149 million	239
Voice of America	1942	44	100 million	100
Radio France Int.	1975	20	45 million	152
Deutsche Welle	1953	30	28 million	88

Source: Based on data from company websites

support overseas broadcasting (*see* Table 4.19).

In 2006, the BBC World Service was reaching, on average, 149 million listeners a week, directly or through rebroadcasts on local stations. Of these, Africa and the Middle East had the largest share in 2004 – 66 million – followed by Asia, which accounted for about 63 million. Calling itself 'the world's reference point', the BBC World Service is the world's best-known international broadcaster, whose aims include 'promoting the English language and interest' and 'projecting Britain's values' worldwide (BBC, 2005a).

In the post-9/11 period, the BBC World Service has tried to focus on the Arab/Islamic world, and one of its key priorities is to invest in FM distribution, especially in the Arab world. The BBC also has a powerful web presence, with monthly page impressions to its international news site, which includes audio and visual content, reaching 350 million in 2006. The Voice of America was also involved in an Arabic-language popular music and news radio station, *Radio Sawa* ('Radio Together'), launched in 2002 and aimed at a younger Arab audience, as well as *Radio Farda* ('Radio Tomorrow' in Persian), broadcasting to Iran. Through its language services, VOA programming reaches more than 1100 affiliate radio stations; most of these receive programming via one of the 42 satellite circuits that deliver VOA broadcasts worldwide.

In regions of the world where television has not yet penetrated to a great extent, such as Africa, radio remains an important medium. The VOA's Africa Service, formed in 1963, in the wake of the retreat of European colonial powers, produces English broadcasts as well as transmitting its programmes through a network of affiliate radio stations on local private commercial stations. Its French to Africa Service broadcasts to the Francophone African countries, sometimes competing with Radio France International. It also provides VOA-Hausa for Nigeria, Swahili Service for eastern Africa and a Portuguese service for Lusophone regions of Africa.

Given the growing economic importance of China, the Mandarin service of the VOA broadcasts 12 hours a day, to China, Taiwan and to overseas Chinese. The VOA's Korean Service broadcasts to the communist North Korea, with affiliated stations such as Christian Broadcasting System. Since 1994, VOA began distributing its programmes in 19 languages, via the Internet.

Another international radio broadcaster, World Radio Network, formed in 1992, carries live audio newscasts, 24 hours a day, from the world's leading public and international broadcasters. In 2006, it was broadcasting in English, French, German and Russian through a range of delivery mechanisms, including AM, FM and digital satellites. Radio Moscow, which was rechristened The Voice of Russia, after the cold war, broadcasts in 32 foreign languages 77 hours a day. Its 24-hour world service in English is broadcast daily to all continents. Though a latecomer to overseas broadcasting, starting only in 1954, Deutsche Welle (The German Wave) broadcasts in 31 languages and, since 1992, also operates Deutsche Welle TV, a 24-hour daily television service in German, English and Spanish. By 2006 Deutsche Welle was reaching 210 million households via satellite networks and was also available on the Internet at DW-World.de. Its influence in Eastern Europe increased after 1990, with the merger of its operations with Radio Berlin International, the leading broadcaster in the Eastern bloc during the cold war years. Radio France Internationale (RFI was not formally launched until 1975, though its precursor was established in 1931) provides its 24-hours a day service to 250 radio stations, and is particularly strong in Francophone Africa. Since it took over Radio Monte Carlo, a private radio station catering to the Middle East, its audience share has increased to reach a total of 45 million. In 2006, RFI was broadcasting in 19 languages, including Arabic, and had also started an FM service to Africa. Though not as influential as Western radio, China too has an extensive international broadcasting network. The first international service of Chinese radio started in 1941. By 2006, China Radio International was broadcasting 290 hours of news, entertainment and current affairs daily through its 43 language services.

Setting the global news agenda

It is clear from the preceding discussion that the West, led by the United States, dominates the world's entertainment and information networks. It is predominantly Western corporations that are the major global players in most sectors of the media – book publishing, news agencies, international newspapers and magazines, radio and television channels and programmes, music, advertising and films. Apart from showing the validity of the arguments of dependency theorists and the proponents of the NWICO, the evidence presented suggests that Western control and ability to set the agenda of international communication debates have, in fact, increased, despite the proliferation of many non-Western media outlets and growing localization of mainly Western media cultural products.

During the 1970s and 1980s the debates about global cultural flows were mainly concerned with news agencies (see Chapter 1), but with the expansion of television – a medium which transcends language and literacy barriers – the Western way of life, primarily as a consumerist lifestyle, is in the process of being globalized. Though there are more producers of images and information, the global entertainment and information flow between Africa, Latin America and Asia is still mediated, to a large extent, through content provided by Anglo-American news organizations, who share information, visuals and even journalists. It is not unusual to find an ITN report on CNN or CNN visuals on the BBC news. For nearly 40 years, between 1954 and 1993, NBC had an arrangement to share news pictures with the BBC. These exchanges also include magazines and newspapers, given the linguistic, political and cultural affinity between the USA and Britain (Hess, 1996).

A market-led global media system benefits TNCs on whose advertising support the media edifice is ultimately based. As noted in Chapter 3, the TNCs have increasingly taken an active role in promoting a global privatized international network. Corporations have used their media power to placate governments, some have even used it to acquire direct political power. One prominent example was Italian media magnate Silvio Berlusconi, owner of the AC Milan football club, who used his popular appeal and his media empire, crucially satellite channels, to launch his political party, Forza Italia, which vaulted him to Rome as Prime Minister of a right-wing coalition government in 1992, and repeated that performance in 2001, despite charges of corruption against him and his government.

Media organizations are often part of major entertainment conglomerates. Does the corporate nature of the global media industry affect its content? Sometimes, broadcasters themselves exercise self-censorship when dealing with sensitive issues, acting out of deference to their parent company. It is tempting to wonder how people would react if the world's books, visual media and journalism were controlled, for example, by the Chinese. Would they be concerned that such concentration of media power could lead to globalization of a Chinese perspective on world events? However, unlike the media in China, the US media, despite close links with officials, are independent of government control, a fact which adds to their international credibility. At the heart of this credibility is the ability to consistently provide accurate, fast and authoritative news and information to an international audience, something which has been earned over two centuries of journalism – indeed, it has been argued that journalism itself is an Anglo-American invention (Tunstall, 1992; Chalaby, 1996).

Almost from their inception the mass media have operated in a market system. In an age of privatized global communications, is it possible that the Western media are becoming conduits for promoting Western consumerism and a free-market ideology? In the new media landscape, observes one commentator: 'Consumerism, the market, class inequality and individualism tend to be taken as natural and often benevolent, whereas political activity, civic values, and anti-market activities tend to be marginalised or denounced' (McChesney, 1999: 110).

There is a danger that rather than being used by governments for propaganda purposes, as was the case during the cold war years, when anti-communism defined the Western media's ideological orientation, in the era of globalization and increasing corporate control of the channels of international communication, the media may become the mouthpiece of global corporations and their supporters in governments. It has been argued that in Western democracies a symbiotic relationship exists between the media and governments. 'Information is power in the foreign policy sense ... and one may grant the necessity for governments to manipulate it on occasion as they would other instruments of national power', wrote Bernard Cohen in his famous book, *The Press and Foreign Policy* (1963: 279).

If during the heydays of radio, governments could use the airwaves to promote their viewpoint, in the era of round-the-clock global news, they have refined their public diplomacy to the extent that it can be marketed successfully to international publics. This is true as much for the Bush Administration's attempts to 'sell the war' during the 1990–91 Gulf crisis, as for the subsequent military interventions which defined US foreign policy in the 1990s (Seib, 1997). The world's view of US military adventures was, to a very large extent, moulded by the US-supplied images of Operation Just Cause in 1989 in Panama; Operation Provide Comfort (in Northern Iraq, following the Gulf War in 1991); Operation Restore Hope in Somalia in 1992; Operation Uphold Democracy in Haiti in 1994; Operation Joint Endeavor in Bosnia in 1995; Operation Allied Force in Yugoslavia in 1999; Operation Enduring Freedom in Afghanistan in 2001; and Operation Iraqi Freedom in 2003 (Thussu and Freedman, 2003; Allan and Zelizer, 2004).

A study of how television news can influence foreign policy, based on US 'peacekeeping' operations in Iraqi Kurdistan, Somalia, Haiti, Rwanda and Bosnia, argued that the relationship between the government and media is more complex than is sometimes believed.

> The CNN effect is highly conditional. Images and written accounts of the horrors of the post-Cold War world that stream into the offices of government officials do not dictate policy outcomes. Sometimes they suggest policy choices … at other times media reports become an ally for an entire administration, or individual member of it, seeking to pursue new policies.
>
> (Strobel, 1997: 211)

Others have maintained that US media have let the government set the terms of military policy debate in the news and American journalists rarely criticize US military interventions (Mermin, 1999; Western, 2005). In the market-driven media environment there is also a discernible tendency to simplify complex international issues into what may be called easily digestible 'sightbytes', given the proliferation of 24-hour TV and online news culture. In such an environment, the coverage of the South, already 'deplorably infrequent and misleading' may be further reduced (Paterson, 1998: 96). Already, US networks have cut back on their foreign coverage (Utley, 1997). Partly as a result of this and partly as a consequence of depoliticization in many postmodern Western societies, only certain parts of the world – where the West might have geopolitical and economic interests – and particular types of stories, which have wide appeal, are given prominence. So, for example, the ethnic conflict in Sri Lanka barely gets a mention in mainstream media, while when the West decided to bomb Yugoslavia to defend Albanian communities in Kosovo, the coverage was almost wall-to-wall. It is not just a question of the quantity; also crucially important is how issues impinging on Western geopolitical interests are covered by mainstream Western and, by extension, global media, especially television.

The 1999 bombing of Yugoslavia by the North Atlantic Treaty Organization (NATO) was presented by the media as the only course of action to stop 'ethnic cleansing' in its Kosovo province. The media generally omitted to comment on the fact that it was the first incidence of NATO actively interfering in the internal affairs of a sovereign nation, thus rewriting the rules of international law. However, the bombing may have more to do with changing the character of the Western military alliance, from a relic of cold war into a 'humanitarian force' which, with its rapid reaction units, can be deployed anywhere in the world. Already, NATO's remit has been extended to allow it to operate out of area. However, this crucial aspect was rarely discussed in the mainstream media, which focused on the humanitarian aspect of the crisis and how a benevolent West was resolving it (Thussu, 2000a). Despite protestations from Western media organizations, such double standards in reporting are not uncommon and have been well documented in the context of Vietnam (Hallin, 1986), East Timor and Central America (Herman and Chomsky, 1988) and Iraq (Mowlana *et al.*, 1992; Allan and Zelizer, 2004; Aday *et al*, 2005).

However, in recent years the Western news media's credibility has been severely dented, for example by the way they have covered the so-called open-ended and global 'war on terrorism'. As Adam Curtis's series, broadcast on the BBC, has argued, al-Qaida may be little more than an imaginary transnational terrorist network invented to suit geopolitical interests of the US government and 'the politics of fear' that characterizes the new age (BBC, 2004). The 2003 invasion of Iraq was claimed to be part of this wider, pre-emptive war, which was justified as 'regime change' to suit Western geopolitical interests. In such military adventures, under the cloak of humanitarianism, the US government has advanced its geostrategic interests, whether it is in Kosovo (by changing the nature of NATO from a relic of the cold war to a peace-enforcer whose remit now extends to the rugged mountains of Afghanistan, way beyond its traditional North Atlantic territory), in Afghanistan (which has given the US government entry into the energy-rich Central Asian region) or in Iraq (control of the world's second largest oil reserves and capacity to reshape the Middle East (Ali, 2003)).

In the post-cold war, post-9/11 era, communism has been replaced in the media by the threat of 'Islamic terrorism'. The news discourse is also biased in terms of nuclear issues – if a developing country aspires to join the exclusive nuclear club, as Iran has tried to do, the US media, reflecting the US Government's position, tend to argue that such moves would threaten world peace. Exhortations of moral rectitude from the only country which has used nuclear weapons – in Hiroshima and Nagasaki in 1945 – and not balked at dropping chemical weapons in Vietnam, air-fuel explosives in Iraq and bombs tipped with depleted uranium on civilian populations, may not be universally acceptable. Yet, in the absence of a credible alternative media system, the US position – given the reach and influence of the Western media – often becomes the dominant position, whether on nuclear issues, 'war on terrorism', trade policy, human rights or international law.

chapter five

The global and the local in media cultures

The analysis of the explosion in international communication has been preoccupied mainly with the economic dimensions of globalization at the expense of cultural aspects of interactions between and among the world's peoples (Carey, 1988; Tomlinson, 1999; Yudice, 2004; Beck, 2006). Is globalization another term for Americanization? The general pattern of media ownership indicates that the West, led by the USA, dominates the international flow of information and entertainment in all major media sectors. But what is the impact of such one-way flows of global information and entertainment on national and regional media cultures? It has been argued that international communication and media are leading to the homogenization of culture, but the patterns of global/national/local interactions may be more complex. The issue of hybridity – how global genres are adapted to suit national cultural codes – is analysed through the case study of Zee TV, India's biggest private multimedia network.

Globalization of American culture?

As detailed in Chapters 3 and 4, the global communication industries – both hardware and software – are owned by a few transnational corporations, primarily based in the USA. It is US entertainment (films, television programmes, advertising) and information networks (news, documentaries, online information) that have the widest international appeal (Noam, 1996; Segrave, 1998; Marling, 2006). Some argue that such globally transmitted programming will promote a shared media culture, a global village based on the English language and Western lifestyles and values.

The globalization of the privatized, advertisement-driven model of Western commercial television has brought consumer culture to living rooms across the world. As a visual medium, television has a much wider reach than the print media, as millions of people still cannot read or write, even in the twenty-first century. The international dissemination of images transcends linguistic barriers, and global television has 'created a space of its own through a unique merger of entertainment and information technologies' (Schneider and Wallis, 1988: 7). Television is thus central to what Stuart Hall called a 'global mass culture', one dominated 'by the image, imagery, and styles of mass advertising' (Hall, 1991: 27).

This mass culture may be influencing the way people think about their regional or national identities, as they are increasingly exposed to global, which in most part are American, messages. As British cultural commentator Kevin Robins noted, audio-visual geographies are 'becoming detached from the symbolic spaces of national culture, and realigned on the basis of the more "universal" principles of international consumer culture' (1995: 250).

The globalization of consumerism has been variously described as 'Coca-Cola-ization', 'Disneyfication' or 'McDonaldization' (Ritzer, 1993, 2002), creating a credit-card global society modelled on US commercial culture, epitomized by Nike and McDonald's and their promotion by Hollywood or sports celebrities. It has been argued that one reason for the global appeal of US popular culture is its openness and mingling of a multiplicity of cultures, many of which are themselves imports from outside the USA. In their well-known cross-cultural study of the popular American serial *Dallas*, Katz and Liebes proposed three reasons for the worldwide success of US television:

> ... the universality, or primordiality, of some of its themes and formulae, which makes programmes psychologically accessible; the polyvalent or open potential of many of the stories, and thus their value as projective mechanisms and as material for negotiation and play in the families of man; and the sheer availability of American programmes in a marketplace where national producers – however zealous – cannot fill more than a fraction of the hours they feel they must provide.

> (Katz and Liebes, 1990: 5)

Since this study, the demand for programme content has risen exponentially, with the explosion of television channels worldwide, and market logic may be a more powerful explanation of why the US is pre-eminent in global television and popular culture. The fact that *Star Trek* was one of the world's most profitable media franchises, or that *Baywatch* was the most widely syndicated television programme globally, is not necessarily because of their intrinsic entertainment quality or interest, but rather because they were promoted by the huge media conglomerates. Part of this marketing success is also to do with establishing global branding and the internationalization of the advertising industry (Tungate, 2004). According to industry estimates, one-third of the world's wealth can be accounted for by brands and could account for 50 per cent of global wealth within the next 25 years. Table 5.1 shows the leading brand names – in 2005, 8 out of 10 were US-based conglomerates.

Two groups particularly targeted by advertising and branding are children and young people. The Jesuitical principle of catching children at a young and impressionable age, it would appear, has been well learnt by advertisers, as well as media producers. The proliferation of channels by satellite and cable, and the increasing use of mobile devices among young people worldwide, means that they can now target this audience and exploit the synergies between television, telecoms and children's entertainment. With the boundaries between age groups ever blurring, international popular music is another vehicle for producing susceptible proto-consumers via entertainment, as the case of MTV demonstrates.

Table 5.1 The world's top 10 brands in 2005

Brand	Country	Brand value ($ billion)
Coca-Cola	USA	67.5
Microsoft	USA	59.9
IBM	USA	53.4
General Electric	USA	47.0
Intel	USA	35.6
Disney	USA	26.5
Nokia	Finland	26.4
McDonald's	USA	26.0
Toyota	Japan	24.8
Marlboro	USA	21.1

Source: *Business Week*

Children's television – catching them young

Before the liberalization of the media market, the international distribution of children's programming was restricted by the number of TV outlets available and quotas on foreign material in many countries. With the proliferation of television globally, dedicated children's channels have become an integral part of the international television market. According to *Screen Digest*, in just three years, between 1996 and 1999, more than 50 children's channels were launched, with a majority of these being in English (*Screen Digest*, 1999). As their numbers have grown, the channels have increasingly adapted to local languages, though the US domination of this genre has not diminished, despite competition from Japanese animation, such as the global phenomenon of Pokemon (Tobin, 2004).

In 2006, the three major players in global children's television were all US-based – Nickelodeon (part of Viacom-CBS), Cartoon Network (owned by Turner Networks, part of AOL-Time Warner) and the Disney Channel, launched in 1984. The fourth major player, Fox Kids Worldwide, owned by Fox Broadcasting, part of News Corporation, was taken over by Disney in 2001 and rebranded as Jetix. By 2006, Jetix programming was available in 18 languages in 77 countries, reaching 137 million television households, complementing Disney-branded television around the world, including 22 Disney channels.

The global expansion of these companies, often through joint ventures with local channels, has been a major factor in the growth of children's television worldwide. For historical reasons the US television companies are the largest producers of children's programmes, a significant proportion of which is animation. One advantage for children's television channels is that animation translates well in overseas markets, since cartoons require a minimum of cultural interpretation, based as they are on stylized characters. As this type of programming also has a much longer shelf life, these companies, with their large film and programme libraries, are well positioned to supply material to meet the growing worldwide demand (Barrier, 1999). When released in 1937, the Disney classic *Snow White* earned $8.5 million at the box office. Subsequent re-releases have added $300 million, and the *Snow White* video release earned the company more than $500 million in profit.

The United States has been a leading exporter of children's programmes – a series like *Sesame Street* is broadcast in over 115 countries and has 500 internationally licensed products (Morrow, 2005). The USA was the first country to have a specialized children's channel in 1979, when Nickelodeon was launched. By 2006 Nickelodeon reached 137 million households in over 100 countries, with dedicated channels in the USA, Europe, Australia, Asia and Latin America. It also had localized channels in Swedish, Danish, Norwegian, Turkish, Hungarian and Japanese, as well as Spanish and Portuguese for the Latin American market. In 1998, Nickelodeon launched a 24-hour Russian-language channel available in eight countries in the Baltic region and in Central Asia. Nickelodeon can also be seen in the Middle East on the Showtime DTH package; and, since 1999, in Africa on the Multichoice direct-to-home satellite platform; and in India through deals with local media networks.

Having taken over Fox Kids International Networks, Disney has emerged as the most powerful presence in the global children's television market. Disney has a long history of exporting its programming to broadcasters across the world. It launched its first channel in Britain and Taiwan in 1995 and since then has opened channels around the globe: by 2006 Disney channels were reaching more than 120 million subscribers in the USA, Europe, Asia-Pacific and Latin America. Disney Channel Worldwide comprises 24 Disney Channels, 8 Playhouse Disney Channels, 9 Toon Disney Channels (a worldwide cable network) and 18 international Jetix channels, as well as branded blocks of programming distributed to television viewers in more than 70 countries.

In 2006, Cartoon Network, 'the most widely distributed 24-hour animation network in the world', was operating three major divisions: Cartoon Network EMEA (for Europe, the Middle East and Africa); Cartoon Network Latin (for the South American market); and Cartoon Network Asia Pacific.

Most of these organizations also have a children's magazine, and audio and video/DVD units, as well as online shopping and recreation. Nickelodeon, for example, is also a global entertainment brand, with businesses in programming, production, consumer products, online, recreation, publishing and feature films. Nickelodeon Consumer Products has over 100 licensees worldwide, and sells nearly 500 products through mass merchandisers, toy and gift retailers and theme parks.

Children's television has to be seen in its close relationship with the global toy market. It has been argued that TV is central to the expanding demand for new toys – children are most likely to buy the merchandise based on their favourite television characters and the products advertised on the channels they watch with great attention. The US toy industry is among the most successful retail areas involved in licensing. While this is not a new development – between 1933 and 1935, more than 2.5 million watches with the licensed Mickey Mouse character were sold in the USA (Pecora, 1998) – globalization has ensured that these are now global products. Licensed characters offer an easily identifiable toy or storyline, a series of accessories or collectable items, and extra income through royalties. As

Norma Pecora comments: 'No longer are limits of the marketplace defined by national boundaries; rather, the global market is considered foremost in decisions about programme production and distribution, motion picture release, and the marketing of toys and merchandise' (1998: 150). It has been argued that since children's preferences are not well established, they are more vulnerable to the advertising of international brands such as McDonald's, Barbie and Coca-Cola, which are then favoured over indigenous products (McNeal, 1992).

With their powerful marketing resources and huge programme libraries, the commercial children's channels can provide schedules of new services at low cost – which local companies find it hard to compete with. In Britain, for example, Nickelodeon and Cartoon Network had a larger share of the children's audience than other domestic terrestrial channels such as BBC 2 and Channel 4. To compete in the era of multichannel television, the BBC launched two dedicated children's channels in Britain – CBBC and CBeebies. The BBC promotes its children's merchandise internationally as well – *Teletubbies*, for example, was a major international hit and a syndication deal with 40 major city TV stations in China was signed by the BBC in 2005, a year in which TV programme sales, DVD/video sales, merchandising and magazines for children netted £57.7 million for the corporation. The *Tweenies* programme was licensed to 50 countries, and more than 10 million copies of the *Tweenies* magazine have been sold since its launch in 1999. In 2004 BBC Worldwide formed a global publication venture with Penguin to produce children's books (BBC, 2005b).

Case study

MTV Music Television

When this network was born, it forever changed American music and television. Now it's the biggest network in the world.

(MTV)

Since its launch in 1981, as the world's first 24-hour video music network, Music Television (MTV) has emerged as the most visible symbol of the globalization of Western popular music and youth culture (Banks, 1996). With its slogan of 'Think globally, act locally', MTV networks are targeted to suit the musical tastes, lifestyle and sensibilities of 12-24-year-olds throughout the world. By 2006 MTV was reaching – via its 31 international music channels – more than 419 million households in 164 countries, and claiming to be 'the most widely distributed network in the world'. Table 5.2 lists the main elements of MTV's global networks. In 2006, it was broadcasting in 22 languages via 120 locally programmed and operated TV channels, distributed in Asia, Australia, Europe, Latin America, Russia, Africa and the United States, as well as 96 locally operated websites.

Being part of the media giant Viacom-CBS, MTV networks include such brands as Nickelodeon, VH1, Paramount Comedy and VIVA, and diverse media interests, including television syndication, digital media, publishing, home video, radio, recorded music, licensing and merchandising, as well as two feature film divisions, MTV Films and Nickelodeon Movies.

With a presence from Asia to Latin America, from Eastern Europe to North America and Africa (the pan-African MTV base channel, MTV's 100th, was launched in 2005), MTV has also spawned a range of imitations from national popular music television channels, which copy its irreverent style. Though the music charts can be determined locally, there is a predominance of English-language popular or rock music videos on its networks.

Asia was the biggest market for MTV, with more than 132 million households across the continent watching its programmes regularly. MTV in Asia was launched with MTV Mandarin in 1995, reaching via satellite on Apstar 1, Taiwan, Brunei, China, South Korea and Singapore. In the same year MTV Southeast Asia was launched, which can be seen via satellite on Palapa C2 throughout the region, including Brunei, Hong Kong, Indonesia, Malaysia, Papua New Guinea, Philippines, Singapore, South Korea, Thailand and Vietnam. A year later, the English-language MTV India was delivered via satellite on PanAmSat4 to Bangladesh, India, the Middle East, Nepal, Pakistan and Sri Lanka. In the world's most populated continent, MTV's major rival is Channel V, owned by News Corporation.

The second biggest market for MTV was Europe where, in 2006, the network was being distributed via satellite and cable by digital platforms, reaching 117 million homes in 41 countries. In 1996, MTV created four separate services – MTV in Britain and Ireland, MTV Central (Austria, Germany and Switzerland), MTV Europe (35 countries, including Belgium, France, Greece, Israel, Romania) and MTV Southern (Italy). A fifth service, MTV Nordic, was launched in 1998 for the markets of Sweden, Denmark, Norway and Finland. Other additions have included a music and lifestyle channel (Belgium, Holland and the UK); VIVA, a complimentary channel (Austria, Germany, Hungary, Poland and Switzerland); and The Box, an urban music channel (Holland).

MTV's Spanish-language service, MTV Latin America, offers 24-hour programming in 19 countries in Latin America, besides the US Hispanic market, via, among others, PanAmSat 3. With regional headquarters in Buenos Aires and Mexico City, and operating headquarters in Miami, the network's northern feed is distributed to Bolivia, the Caribbean, Central America, Colombia, Ecuador, Mexico, the USA and Venezuela, while the southern feed is distributed to Argentina, Brazil, Chile, Paraguay, Peru and Uruguay.

Table 5.2 MTV's world, 2005

Network	Launch year	Language	Subscribers (million)
MTV	1981	English	88
MTV Network Europe*	1987	English	117
MTV Brasil	1990	Portuguese	18
MTV Latin America	1993	Spanish	13.7
MTV Asia+	1995	English/Mandarin	132.6
MTV2	1996	English	56.9
MTV Germany	1996	German	30.8
MTV Australia	1997	English	1.0
MTV Russia	1998	Russian	27.1
MTV Japan	2000	Japanese	5.4
MTV Canada	2001	English	0.8
MTV Africa	2005	English	–
Global total			**419.4**

* Includes figures for MTV UK, launched 1996, and MTV Nordic, launched 1998
+ Includes 44 million of Mandarin service and 23 million English-language listeners of South East Asian service, launched in 1995; and MTV India, launched in 1996
Source: Viacom, 2005

MTV has also entered into strategic licensing agreements with national companies: MTV Brasil, distributed from São Paulo in collaboration with the Abril Group; MTV Russia, a free-to-air service, available in major Russian cities after a deal with a Russian company; and MTV Australia, the result of an agreement with Optus Vision, are examples of this trend.

As in other transnational media operations, synergies are exploited by MTV, using the brand name to promote a range of Viacom entertainment businesses. The network is used to launch home videos, CD-ROMs, albums, consumer products (from more than 50 international licensees) and books; featuring MTV programming and personalities, as well as online services offering music information and an interactive version of its programmes, MTV2, specializes in interactive television. MTV is often presented as an example of imperatives for localization. As the network itself states: 'MTV tailors its channels to local cultural tastes with a mixture of national, regional and international artists, along with locally produced and globally shared programming' (www.mtv.com).

This makes sense for international advertisers, often record companies, that want to use its global reach and brand name to sell their products. As Banks comments, a service 'targeting youth throughout the world would be much sought after by advertisers seeking to expand their share of the world market for specific consumer goods of interest to youth, including jeans, designer clothes, watches and soft drinks' (1996: 105). Among its main advertisers have been Coca-Cola, which paid $1 million in 1986 to acquire the sole sponsorship rights to the World Music Video Awards, one of the network's most watched television events. Six years in a row – from 1999 to 2005 – MTV has been the world's 'most valuable media brand', according to an Interbrand/*Business Week* survey: 'From music, fashion, lifestyle and sports to attitudes, politics, news and trends, only MTV offers what is consistently fresh, honest and groundbreaking', said the 2005 survey.

For major recording labels and Hollywood companies, the USA is no longer the primary market and the product has to be sold globally. Major Hollywood films and record labels use MTV networks to promote a new film or music video, through commercials and related music videos featuring songs from the soundtrack and clips from the movie playing simultaneously on all of MTV's channels, reaching a global audience. The growing use of broadband has opened up new opportunities to circulate youth music and merchandise. In 2005, MTV launched its first broadband network, MTV Overdrive, which within six months had generated more than 125 million streams of unique MTV content. With 22 dedicated websites, MTV Networks Music, formed in 1999, was, by 2006, the world's leading online music entertainment company, and MTV had broadened its remit and claimed to provide services 'spanning niche brands from pre-school to adulthood, broadcast on air, online and on mobile' (www.mtv.com).

The flow of international television programmes

The global flow of consumerist messages through international television has been seen by some as evidence of a new form of cultural imperialism, especially in the non-Western world (Schiller, 1996). One reason why these messages have become global is largely due to the extensive reach of the US-based media, advertising and telecommunications networks, helping the USA to use its 'soft power' to promote its national interests (Nye, 1990, 2004).

The flow of international television programmes from the West (mainly the USA) to other parts of the world, documented by UNESCO (Nordenstreng and Varis, 1974; Varis, 1985), has become more pronounced in the era of multichannel television; though there is a small but significant televisual contraflow from non-Western world (*see* Chapter 6). Both UNESCO studies confirmed that there is generally a one-way traffic, mainly in entertainment-oriented programming, from the major Western-exporting nations to the rest of the world. Though some peripheral countries (Sinclair *et al.,* 1996) have emerged as exporters of television programmes and films, the USA continues to lead the field in the export of audio-visual products.

In Latin America, for example, a large majority of imports in this sector are from the USA. Even in countries where a strong domestic television industry exists, such as Brazil, Mexico and Argentina, more than 70 per cent of films and television series are imported from the USA (UNESCO, 1998). One key result of the privatization and proliferation of television outlets, and the growing glocalization of US media products, is that American film and television exports have witnessed a nearly a fivefold increase between 1992 and 2004. Receipts for film and television tape rentals, covering 'the right to display, reproduce and distribute US motion pictures and television programming abroad', have shown, according to the US Government's Bureau of Economic Analysis, a steady increase from $2.5 billion in 1992 to $10.4 billion in 2004 (US Government, 2005) (*see* Figure 5.1).

Figure 5.1 Selling Hollywood to the world: US film and TV exports

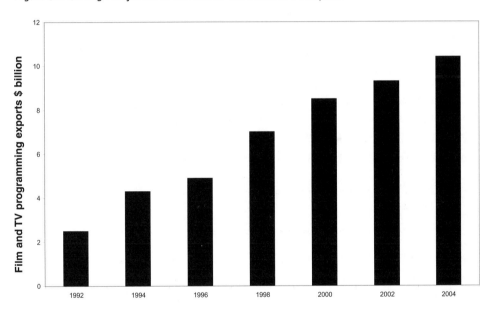

Source: US Government, 2005

In terms of regional distribution, Europe continues to be the largest market for American film and television content: in 2004, the value of exports was $6.7 billion – more than 60 per cent of all US exports in the sector – while the Middle East accounted for merely $114 million (*see* Table 5.3).

Table 5.3 US exports of film and TV programmes by region, 2004

Region	Value of film and TV exports ($ million)
Europe	6787
Asia and Pacific	1835
Latin America	757
Africa	124
Middle East	114
All countries	10,480

Source: US Government, 2005

US media content has visibility across the globe; the disparity between American exports of television programming and films and imports of these products is striking, despite the multicultural rhetoric of US Government and industry. As Table 5.4 demonstrates, in 2004 the US imported TV programmes and films worth $341 million – while exports were worth more than 30 times that at $10,480 million. With its largest trading partner, Europe, US exports ($6787 million) were worth 120 times its imports from the continent ($56 million). This disparity is consistent with recent trends in trade in television. The balance of trade in television programmes between the EU and the USA more than tripled between 1989 and 1993. The trade flows of television programmes for 1995 to 2000 between the EU and the USA shows that EU countries sustained a trade deficit 15 times the total value of their exports to North America (UNESCO, 2005a: 47).

Table 5.4 US exports/imports of film and TV programmes to selected countries, 2004

	Export ($m)	Import ($m)
Britain	1820	34
Germany	970	2
France	914	14
Japan	894	27
Canada	861	29
Netherlands	725	2
Spain	645	1
Italy	560	1
Mexico	284	9
Brazil	197	6
All countries	10,480	341

Source: US Government, 2005

With a fourfold growth in commercial television channels in a decade, the US presence on European television has increased substantially, especially in film-based programming, which is often dubbed into local languages. One reason for this, it has been argued, is that no lingua franca unites European television viewers in front of their screens, and if there is a media 'cultura franca', it is based on American-style popular entertainment forms – soaps, game shows, talk shows, hospital and detective series – but preferably with nationally specific themes and settings (Richardson and Meinhof, 1999: 174–5). With a forecast growth in digital satellite subscribers across the continent, the US programme intake is likely to grow.

If the USA is the media colossus of the world, European television companies are not insignificant. According to the European Audiovisual Observatory, TV company revenues in the European Union rose by €10 billion ($12 billion) between 1999 and 2003, reaching €64.5 billion ($77.6 billion) in 2003, with Britain having the largest share: €17.3 billion or $20.8 billion, followed by Germany (€13.6 billion or $17.1 billion), France (€10.5 billion or $12.6 billion) and Italy (€7,6 billion or $9.1 billion) (European Audiovisual Observatory, 2005). While the US-based companies remain undisputed leaders in selling TV programmes around the world (accounting for more than 70 per cent of all sales), Britain leads the world in the export of television formats: in 2003 Britain sold formats to the value of nearly $1 billion, accounting for 45 per cent of international format sales by hours and 49 per cent by titles (Clarke, 2005).

That the British lead the European television scene is not surprising, given Britain's prominent position within the global creative industries (Hesmondhalgh, 2002). Britain gains substantial earnings from exporting its television programmes: in 2004, it sold programmes worth £863 million ($1513 million) (*see* Table 5.5). According to the British Department of Culture, Media and Sport, the creative industries grew in Britain by an average of 6 per cent annually between 1997 and 2003, and their exports totalled £11.6 billion ($20.3 billion) in 2003 (DCMS, 2005).

Table 5.5 British TV programme sales (£ million)

	2000	2001	2002	2003	2004
Europe	261	248	274	263	271
North America	198	247	332	380	370
Rest of world	208	203	189	170	222
Total	667	697	795	814	863

Source: *Screen Digest,* October 2005

In 2004, France earned over €108 million ($136 million) through exports of television programmes. Among the most popular were the animation series *Totally Spies*, which was sold across the world, including to Cartoon Network in the USA; documentaries such as *Homo Sapiens*, broadcast in countries as diverse as China, Spain, Indonesia, Israel and

Russia; as well as dramas like *Le Père Goriot* (Old Goriot), based on Honoré de Balzac's work – particularly successful in Latin America and Russia.

As television channels have mushroomed, Europe's public broadcasters have increased their export drive. Deutsche Welle, for example, had by 2006 sold more than 23,000 programming hours (including series, documentaries and light entertainment in various languages) to around 1200 television stations in 106 countries. The BBC's television programmes were screened in 100 countries, while in 2005 its exports were worth £61.5 million ($107.8 million) to America; £43.3 million ($75.9 million) for Europe and £22.7 million ($39.8 million) for rest of the world. BBC Worldwide also sold formats for such programmes as *The Weakest Link*, to broadcasters across the globe, while its *Strictly Come Dancing* format was sold as *Dancing with the Stars* and shown in Australia, Holland, Germany, India, South Africa, Russia, Turkey and on ABC America (BBC, 2005b).

In sub-Saharan Africa, the poverty of the region makes it difficult for local television channels to make their own programmes, forcing them to depend technically and financially on international organizations or Western media corporations. Local production is usually limited to television news bulletins, news magazines and a few entertainment programmes. BBC World, Deutsche Welle TV and Canal France International also provide programmes to African broadcasters as free-to-air or in a subsidized form, while commercial broadcasters have started tapping into the African market with such imports as the African version of the internationally successful reality TV show *Big Brother*.

Hollywood hegemony

One key reason for US domination of the global entertainment market is its film industry. Hollywood films are shown in more than 150 countries worldwide and American television programmes are broadcast in over 125 international markets. The Los Angeles-based Motion Picture Association (MPA), sometimes referred to as 'a little State Department', with main branches in Brussels, São Paulo and Singapore, acts 'as leader and advocate for major producers and distributors of entertainment programming for television, cable, home video and future delivery systems not yet imagined' (www.mpaa.org). In 2004, according to MPA, the worldwide box office was worth $25.24 billion, of which the US domestic market accounted for $9.54 billion – 38 per cent of the global total. Even in countries with developed local film-production networks and markets, US films represent a majority of imports, as Table 5.6 shows, and given the global increase in TV channels dedicated to film, it is unlikely that the dependence on US cinema will decrease.

One of the most contested issues in global film exports has been the trade in films between the USA and Europe, one of the world's richest media markets. The audio-visual market in the EU remains overwhelmingly dominated by American productions, while the US market for European films accounted for just about 2 per cent of the US box office in 2004 (*see* Table 5.7). The process of trade deregulation and expansion in the US film and television industry in the 1990s, it is argued, undermined the heavily subsidized European film industry (Nowell-Smith and Ricci, 1998), and the end of the cold war profoundly affected film production in countries of the former Eastern bloc. In the former Soviet Union and among many Eastern European countries, which had a well-developed film industry, globalization has changed the volume and types of films being produced, as major Hollywood studios take control of the new markets.

Table 5.6 US presence in major film-producing countries

Country	Latest data year	Total film imports	US imports (%)
Israel	2003	173	87
India	2003	198	80
Australia	2003	245	73
Mexico	2003	267	64
Spain	2004	461	55
Russia	2004	446	54
Germany	2004	363	37
Italy	2004	349	36
Japan	2004	470	28
France	2004	556	24
Egypt	2003	300	22

Source: European Audiovisual Observatory/national statistics and *Screen Digest*, 2005

Table 5.7 US vs Europe – share of the film market by admissions, 2004

Country/region	US (%)	British (%)	French (%)	German (%)	US-Euro (%)
Europe	59.7	6.1	6.1	4.5	11.7
USA	96	1.5	0.5	0.0	–

Source: Based on data from European Audiovisual Observatory

As Table 5.8 shows, Hollywood has had a major impact on other film-producing countries. Mexico's film industry experienced a dramatic fall in production between 1988 and 1998, possibly affected by the introduction of NAFTA; and in Indonesia the decline was substantial in the last decade. While many countries have witnessed decline, film production has risen in some European countries, often because of joint ventures between European film companies or with the Hollywood giants. In France, for example, 73 out of 203 films produced in 2004 were co-productions with other European and international partners. For Spain, Germany and Britain, this is also a preferred method of dealing with US competition, although in the case of Britain, most joint ventures involve US film companies. In developing countries, many of whom have no film industry of their own, Hollywood films account for a majority of their film imports.

Table 5.8 Hit by Hollywood? Feature film production (selected countries)

Country	1974	1984	1994	2004
France	234	161	115	203 (73)
Germany	80	75	57	121 (27)
Spain	112	75	44	133 (50)
UK	88	44	70	132 (108)
Poland	31	8	20	17
Mexico	44	88	12	21
Brazil	82	90	6	81
Indonesia	8	81	84	15
Hong Kong	147	109	192	64 (30)
Japan	333	333	251	310 (1)
South Korea	141	81	65	82
Thailand	90	134	43	46
Egypt	44	63	57	25
South Africa	34	80	20	–
USA	242	366	635	611 (9)

Figures in brackets indicate co-productions
Source: Based on data from *Screen Digest,* June 2005

The European publics seem to prefer Hollywood glitz and glamour to locally produced cinema. A study on cinema admissions in 34 European countries for 1996–2004, by the European Audiovisual Observatory, found that the cumulative admissions for the top 10 films in this period were all for Hollywood films (*see* Table 5.9). In the same period, the admission for the top five films in Europe (*Bridget Jones's Diary, Notting Hill, The World Is Not Enough, Die Another Day* and *Mr Bean*) were all English-language films, four of which were actually financed by Hollywood companies (European Audiovisual Observatory, 2005).

Worldwide too, it is Hollywood films that have fared best in theatres across the globe – a trend which is well attested (Miller *et al.*, 2005). In 2005, as Table 5.10 shows, the top 10 grossing films were from Hollywood.

The demand for films is likely to grow, given the expansion of film-based channels in new territories such as China, potentially one of the world's largest movie markets. China Central Television has invested in the production of made-for-TV movies to ensure an adequate supply for its dedicated film channel CCTV 6, the second most popular of the national broadcaster channels (launched in 1995). According to the entertainment magazine *Variety*, in China, despite a quota of 20 foreign films per year, Hollywood films have been very successful: *Star Wars: Episode III – Revenge of the Sith* earned $9 million, while *Harry Potter and the Goblet of Fire* took $4.1 million in its opening weekend (McNary, 2005). In India too, Hollywood's presence is likely to grow as Fox's Asia/Pacific Vice President Sunder Kimatrai noted: 'There is a greater awareness of Hollywood films thanks to news channels

Table 5.9 Cumulative admissions for films in Europe: 1996–2004

Film	Country of origin	Year	Admissions (millions)
Titanic	USA	1997	103
Lord of the Rings: The Fellowship	USA/NZ	2001	59
Harry Potter and the Sorcerer's Stone	USA/GB	2001	59
Lord of the Rings: The Two Towers	USA/NZ	2002	54
Lord of the Rings: The Return of the King	USA/NZ/DE	2003	54
Harry Potter and the Chamber of Secrets	USA/GB	2002	52
Star Wars: Episode 1 – The Phantom Menace	USA	1999	45
Finding Nemo	USA	2003	44
Shrek 2	USA	2004	43
Independence Day	USA	1996	42

Source: European Audiovisual Observatory

Table 5.10 Top 10 films worldwide, 2005

Film	Worldwide box-office receipts ($m)
Harry Potter and the Goblet of Fire	850.0*
Star Wars Episode III: Revenge of the Sith	848.5
War of the Worlds	591.4
Madagascar	527.0
The Chronicles of Narnia	473.9*
Charlie and the Chocolate Factory	473.4*
Mr & Mrs Smith	467.3
King Kong	465.5*
Batman Begins	371.9
Hitch	368.1
Total gross top 10	5,437.2

*Still on theatrical release at the end of 2005
Source: Variety

carrying footage of US and UK premieres, local newspapers actually giving additional space to Hollywood news and, lastly, the Internet, which is now cheaper and more accessible to teens' (quoted in McNary, 2005).

In the 1970s Hollywood earned one-third of its revenue overseas; by 2005 more than half of its revenues came from foreign markets. Given the size of Asia and Hollywood's relatively low penetration among the large populations of China and India, the importance of the Asian market cannot be underestimated. Trade liberalization has allowed many more Hollywood movies into Asian cinemas and economic growth has given more people the means to see them. The building of modern multiplexes has dramatically increased the number of venues for film exhibition, while the proliferation of film-only channels and the development of digital distribution technologies have created new markets for film beyond the theatres.

Concerns for cultural diversity

Concerns have been raised about the imbalance in global flows of media products, what one United Nations report has called the 'asymmetries in flows of ideas and goods'. As it notes, 'the unequal economic and political powers of countries, industries and corporations cause some cultures to spread, others to wither' (UNDP, 2004: 90). As Hollywood expands and deepens its presence, national film companies are being threatened. The standardization of programmes on the world's cinema and television screens, 'under the influence of impoverishing, reductive content which trivialises everything', risks the disappearance of cultural and linguistic identities which many societies consider to be a 'basic component of their national sovereignty' (UNESCO, 1997: 17).

Aware that television, like other cultural products, possesses intrinsic qualities which distinguishes it from other commodities, many countries have regulations on maintaining a certain level of local programming on television, though increasingly these are being fought over by global television companies. The domestic content requirements can vary – for example, on the Canadian Broadcasting Corporation (CBC), 60 per cent of entire broadcasting time must be Canadian programmes, while in France, for films and audio-visual programmes, 60 per cent must be European programmes and at least 40 per cent must be original French-language programmes. Despite such measures, American cultural products were more widely in use in France in 2006 than 10 years previously. Empirical research conducted in the late 1990s, examining the origin of films and TV series broadcast on 36 public and commercial channels from six European countries, confirmed that despite support from the European Union to develop a pan-European television industry, US programming dominated the airwaves across Europe (de Bens and de Smaele, 2001).

This is particularly pronounced in the case of films, as indicated by Table 5.11: in 2004, over all, within the EU, nearly 72 per cent of films shown were from Hollywood, 26.5 per cent were European films and just 2.1 per cent of market share belonged to the rest of the world (European Audiovisual Observatory, 2005). For countries with limited or no audio-visual domestic industry the dependence is even more striking: according to UNESCO, more than one-third of the countries in the world do not produce any films at all, while Africa as a whole (constituting 54 countries) has only produced just over 600 films in its history – fewer than India produces every year (UNESCO, 2005a: 47).

Table 5.11 Film market share, selected countries

	Domestic films (%)	USA (%)	Foreign films/Other (%)
India	93	7*	–
USA	83.4	9.8+	6.7
China	55	45*	–
South Korea	54.2	41.2	4.6
France	38.4	47.2	14.4
Japan	37.5	62.5*	–
Germany	23.8	76.2*	–
Italy	20.3	61.9	17.8
Spain	13.4	78.4	8.2
Britain	12.4	83.8	3.8
Russia	12	81	7
Canada	3.5	90.5	6
Australia	1.3	89.9	10.8

*not specified
+European co-production
Source: European Audiovisual Observatory, figures for 2004

At the time of its inception in 1947, GATT recognized the role of audio-visual products in reflecting national cultural values and identities and permitted governments to impose national screen quotas. However, during the Uruguay Round of GATT negotiations in the 1980s, the USA argued that, like other sectors, audio-visual products should follow free-market principles, ending the national import quotas and state subsidies common in Europe. Such quotas were considered by many countries, especially France, as vital to protect the domestic film and television industry from US-style commercialization (Geradin and Luff, 2004). Under the 'cultural exception' (*l'exception culturelle*), public support for cultural industries was ensured and the state promoted and paid for the production and distribution of French cultural products. The French film and television industry, vocally behind this position, protested against the inclusion of audio-visual products in the final text of the GATT, and EU opposition succeeded in excluding audio-visual services from rules of national treatment and market access.

However, these exemptions have since been undermined by the growth of TNC subsidiaries in other countries; for example, if a big US media conglomerate has a subsidiary company based in a country in the European Union, it has to be given the same access to the market as a 'national' company. The EU went on to negotiate these issues within the European context. Through its *Television without Frontiers* directive, adopted in 1989 and amended in 1997, the EU has created a pan-European audio-visual area within which a set of common rules concerning advertising, sports coverage and promotion of European products has been established (Machet, 1999).

It is not surprising that the EU restrictions on market access through quotas were contested by the Americans, as Europe is one of the three richest audio-visual markets, with the USA and Japan. With the rapid development of a wide range of new products and services as a result of digital technology, the audio-visual industry is one of the fastest-growing within the EU. Apart from its economic significance, such dependency can have implications for cultural and linguistic identities. The European Commission considers the audio-visual industry as a 'cultural industry *par excellence*', which has 'major influence on what citizens know, believe and feel and plays a crucial role in the transmission, development and even construction of cultural identities' (EC, 1999: 9).

The EU's position, however, was called into question during negotiations, since Article XIX of the GATS contains a built-in agenda for further liberalization in audio-visual services. In addition, though GATS exempted the broadcasting, film and cable industries, convergence in the industry, with multimedia conglomerates offering video programming, computing and telecom networks over the same technological infrastructure, has blurred the distinction between broadcasting and telecommunications, further strengthening the position of the champions of free trade in the audio-visual sector. It is likely that the lobbyists will continue to pressure the US Government to use its economic and diplomatic muscle to open foreign filmed entertainment markets and push for liberalization of the audio-visual sector in the new round of world trade negotiations (EC, 1999; Geradin and Luff, 2004).

From the European Union to the Islamic world, China and India, concerns have been raised about the impact of media globalization, often equated with Americanization, on national cultures. The Malaysian Prime Minister Mahathir Mohamad's speech at the UN General Assembly in 1996, blaming a handful of Western corporations for destroying 'all our cherished values and diverse cultures', is only one example of such rhetoric (quoted in Berfield, 1996). UNESCO's *World Culture Report* gives many reasons why it is important to preserve cultural diversity, which it sees as a 'manifestation of the creativity of the human spirit', and is required 'by principles of equity, human rights and self determination'; it is needed to 'oppose political and economic dependence and oppression' for 'sustainability', and it is 'aesthetically pleasing to have an array of different cultures', it 'stimulates the mind' and can provide a 'reserve of knowledge and experience' about good and useful ways of organizing society (UNESCO, 1998: 18). Concerns about the impact of the US domination of international communication and media on culture are inextricably linked with the question of language and cultural identity and, in particular, the rise of English as the global language (Crystal, 1997; Graddol, 2006).

Global English

English has emerged in the past 200 years as the lingua franca of global commerce and communication. As was discussed in Chapter 1, the cabling of the world by the British in the nineteenth century gave them an early advantage in promoting their language. British control of global telegraph networks led to English becoming the main language of international trade and services. Until 1923, Britain controlled half of the world's telegraph cables, a position that it lost to the USA as other media forms developed (Headrick, 1991). The US assumption of this pre-eminent position, however, ensured the continuation of English as the key language of global communication, with significant implications for the future of the world's other languages. At the start of the twenty-first century, English tops the hierarchy of international languages, being the main language of multinational interactions and the United Nations system, transnational corporations, international media, including the Internet and scientific and technological publishing. Given the extent of British domination of the globe in the nineteenth and the first half of the twentieth century, the English language acquired the status of being the language of power and prestige, especially in the territories which once formed part of the British Empire (Phillipson, 1992). Even though it is used by the tiny minority of the political and cultural elite, English continues to have a disproportionate influence among many Commonwealth countries, especially in education and literature.

This is particularly noticeable in the field of book publishing, where English-language publishers set the literary agenda globally, which is often detrimental to the interests of writers prolific in other languages. Only those authors who can write in English, or whose works are translated into English, are considered 'international'. Cultural globalization implies a two-way relationship, but more often this is skewed by international power relations, as one Indian novelist observed: 'I have yet to hear that there is any writer in the West who is waiting with trepidation to hear what a critic in India has to say about her/him' (Deshpande, 2000). This is a view shared by many others in India, who argue that languages are 'the real repositories of our thought, sensibility and culture'. Writing in the official journal of India's national academy of letters, *Sahitya Akademy*, one prominent Indian author reflected:

> English, preferably American English, the chief language of the computer and the internet and the accepted vehicle of global communication, if not command, is slowly beginning to replace our languages and make them irrelevant. Encyclopaedias and anthologies of world literature have already begun to be silent on the literatures in India's native languages, taking up for discussion only Indian writing in English: the first death-knell for Indian languages has already been struck.
>
> (Satchidanandan, 1999: 10)

Although such assertions may be contested by those who see the language of the colonial rulers having been adapted, expanded and enriched by Indian literary tradition, with some of the finest writers of contemporary English fiction belonging to the Indian subcontinent, it cannot be ignored that those who are not writing in English are at a disadvantage. Translations, where they exist, are not always of a high standard, a contributing reason for why the world's most frequently translated authors of fiction belong to the works published in the West, as Table 5.12 demonstrates.

Table 5.12 The world's most frequently translated authors

Author	Country	No. of translations
Disney (Walt) Productions	USA	7783
Christie, Agatha	UK	5809
Verne, Jules	France	3756
Lenin, Vladimir	Russia	3481
Blyton, Enid	UK	3300
Cartland, Barbara	UK	3261
Shakespeare, William	UK	3091
Steel, Danielle	USA	2472
Andersen, Hans Christian	Denmark	2387
King, Stephen	USA	2295

Source: UNESCO (www.unesco.org)

Of the 10 most translated authors of fiction in the world (whose books have been translated into 25 or more languages), 7 originally wrote in English, and of 119 works mentioned in UNESCO's *World Culture Report*, only 4 were published in the non-Western world – one each from India, Iran, Columbia and Mexico. The last two were written in a European literary form (novels); the first two – one by Acharya Rajneesh, known more for his 'sex therapy' than spiritualism, and the *Arabian Nights* – are publications which fit Western perceptions of the Orient, conforming to all its exotic features.

Books published in other major languages of the world, especially from the main book-producing nations in the global South – China, South Korea, Brazil, Iran, India and Egypt – do not have an international readership and are rarely given any attention in global media or academic circles. This is as much true of popular fiction as of serious literature. A look at the list of the winners of the Nobel Prize for Literature will show that since its inception in 1902, of the 102 winners of the prize only 11 came from the developing world. Apart from poet-philosopher Rabindra Nath Tagore, who composed poetry in Bengali, and Naguib Mahfouz of Egypt, who writes in Arabic, all the other award winners from the developing world wrote in a European language. Not since Tagore – the first non-European to win a Nobel Prize, in 1913 – has any writer from the Indian subcontinent been considered worthy of the award (though British-based, Trinidad-born, of Indian parentage, Vidiadhar Naipaul was awarded the prize in 2001). Hindi short story writer Premchand, Urdu poets Muhammad Iqbal and Faiz Ahmed

Faiz, and Bengali novelist Sarat Chandra Chatterjee are some of the many other major omissions.

China, where printing was invented, received the honour only in 2000 when Gao Xingjian, the Chinese-born author who lives in France, was awarded the prize. Authors belonging to other ancient cultures, for example, Iraq or Turkey, the cradle of human civilization, do not figure in this coveted list, while many obscure European or American writers have been awarded the prize. Instead, what is in evidence is the literary fashion for 'Third World' literature, which lumps together a rich diversity of literatures from many countries and cultures. As Aijaz Ahmad has argued eloquently, literature from the global South only becomes visible internationally after it has been 'selected, translated, published, reviewed, explicated and allotted a place in the burgeoning archive of "Third World Literature"' – a process controlled by the First World (Ahmad, 1992: 45).

English has been blamed for the loss of indigenous languages in the English-speaking countries – Canada, USA and Australia – and for contributing to undermining national languages in the former British colonies. While English is promoted as a universal language, and widely used on the Internet, this does not reflect the linguistic variety of a world in which, according to UNESCO, 6700 languages are spoken. Of the 34 countries with a rich multilingual tradition (i.e. more than 50 languages in daily use), two-thirds are to be found among the countries of sub-Saharan Africa, South East Asia and the Pacific region, while not a single European nation belongs to this category (UNESCO, 1998). There is also concern that the varieties of spoken English will be affected by the single 'world English'. When the US giant Microsoft launched, in 1999, a new 'global English' *Encarta* dictionary,

Figure 5.2 The world's top 10 languages

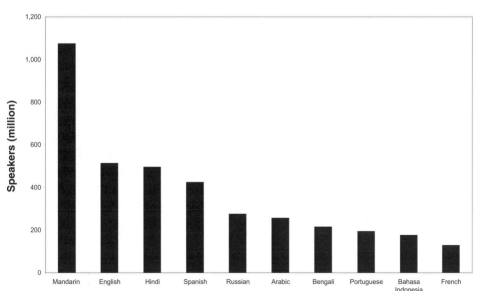

Source: *Ethnologue*

the move was received sceptically even by such traditional guardians of the English language as the publishers of the authoritative *Oxford Dictionary*.

The growth in multichannel television, filled with American programming or its local clones, is likely to extend an American version of the English language to all parts of the world. Will global audiences eventually accept programmes in English and become at least receptively competent in the language? Could communicating in the same language help acquire a collective understanding and even cultural identity? In countries like France, which fear being swamped by US popular culture, attempts have been made to legislate to protect the French language, requiring that public and private companies should not use English expressions in public activities where a French equivalent exists. According to a study published by the British Council, the popularity of the English language is likely to continue, with around 2 billion people learning it by 2016, though other languages such as Mandarin and Spanish may challenge this domination. The global English that emerges may well have an Asian inflection to it (Graddol, 2006).

Regionalization and localization in the media market

Although there is enough evidence of the globalization of Western media products to raise profound concerns for cultures outside the USA, there is also a trend towards the regionalization and localization of media content to suit cultural priorities of audiences, and fears of a homogenized world culture may be premature. Just as market logic leads McDonald's to develop a vegetarian version of the Big Mac in Delhi and the McCarnival in Brazil, so international media organizations are increasingly becoming conscious of the varying tastes of their consumers in different parts of the world in a gradually fragmenting global market. As they now operate in a global market, adapting their products and services to local cultural conditions has become a commercial imperative.

Global media conglomerates tend to make use of local cultural resources in order to promote their products, being influenced not so much by any particular regard for national cultures, but by market forces (Webber, 2003). They realize that people prefer to watch programmes in their own languages; it is also cheaper to dub, for example, Cartoon Network programming into Hindi or a holiday programme into Mandarin, than to produce country-specific television. For broadcasters in the developing world, it makes sense to localize global programming through dubbing or subtitling, as the cost of indigenous production is prohibitive. Even in Europe, regionalization has become a commercial imperative for international broadcasters. Adaptation of US programming is easier in the countries where English is widely used, as in Scandinavia, but in France and Italy subtitled or dubbed programmes are not as popular.

As a result, there is a trend towards publishing regional or local editions of newspapers or magazines; transmitting television channels in local languages and even producing local programming. The strategies adopted to sell these products can have a distinctly local flavour, for example, using national languages to promote cable television programmes through innovative and customized marketing (Moran, 1998). Even BBC channels, initially only available in English, have regionalized their content after attempts to run a BBC Arabic television service and a Hindi-language channel for India in the early 1990s failed. BBC programmes have traditionally done well in countries like Canada – *Antiques Roadshow* was one of the highest-rated shows on CBC, while an Americanized version of the BBC comedy sitcom *The Office* was aired on NBC. Internationally, one of the most successful exports has been the British game show *Who Wants to Be a Millionaire?*, which captured 73 per cent of the market when it was launched in 1998, and has been shown in localized versions in more than 50 countries.

Major US studios are increasingly going for local production facilities in Europe, Asia and Latin America. Columbia TriStar, Warner Brothers and Disney have set up international TV subsidiaries to produce English-language co-productions, to be followed by country-specific programming. Sony contributed to local-language film production in Germany, Hong Kong, France and Britain, and television programming in eight languages. Sony's own branded channels, Sony Entertainment Television (SET), included SET Latin America (Spanish, launched 1995); SET India (Hindi, launched 1995); SET Max (Hindi, launched 2000); as well as AXN (Action adventure channel), launched in India, Japan, Spain, Portugal, Israel and in Latin America and Central Europe; and Animax, Japanese animation channel, launched in 2004. In the same year, Animax India was launched as South Asia's first and only 24-hour-a-day network dedicated to popular animation from Japan (Sony, 2005). Since 2002, SET has operated a joint venture with Discovery to distribute 14 channels – including MTV, NDTV and TEN Sports, under the brand name of 'TheOneAlliance' – to over 50 million homes in India.

Cartoon Network too has indigenised operations in India, producing series on Indian themes, for example on the Hindu religious epics, the *Ramayana* and the *Mahabharat*, as well as a series called *Akbar & Birbal*, drawing on secular historical characters – Birbal was a famously witty and wise figure in the court of Mughal Emperor Akbar (1542–1605) (Barooah-Pisharoty, 2006). In 2004, Disney Channel and Toon Disney launched a local version of their channels in India, where it sees television to be 'a key brand driver to promote other Disney businesses, especially in consumer products, the Internet and mobile communications' (Disney Annual Report, 2005). In 2006, Reuters entered a deal with the *Times of India*, India's largest English-language newspaper, to launch *Times Now*, a television news service following the example of CNN, which, since 2005, had been running a round-the-clock English-language news operation in collaboration with the Indian television software company TV 18, reaching a global South Asian audience.

In China, Disney animation was seen by more than 91 million children in 2005, while 23 Disney-branded programming blocks and Disney Clubs were reaching more than 380 million households. Disney Consumer Products had established more than 1800 'Disney Corners' in Chinese department stores, and Disney Publishing had grown tenfold since *Mickey Mouse Magazine* was launched in China in 1993 (Disney Annual Report, 2005).

Another major presence in Asia is STAR TV, with ESPN-STAR Sports, the result of STAR's agreement with ESPN to provide coverage of pan-Asian and international sport events, becoming Asia's most widely watched channel. STAR TV has aggressively adopted the policy of indigenization, with localized channels including STAR Chinese Channel (for Taiwan), STAR Japan, STAR Plus and STAR News (for India) and VIVA Cinema for the Philippines. The BBC has also expanded into Asia, with the 1998 launch of Animal Planet, its joint venture with Discovery. Global media companies are particularly keen to consolidate their position in the two major markets in Asia – China and India. Increasingly, Asian languages are being used, with Columbia (owned by Sony) making programmes for the vast Chinese and Indian markets. Among the business television channels too Asia is a priority area. By 2006, CNBC Asia, CNBC-TV 18 (India) and Nikkei-CNBC (Japan) were available to more than 34 countries across the Asia-Pacific region. CNBC also had an alliance with China Business Network, a subsidiary of the Shanghai Media Group.

In the Middle East, Western or Westernized TV networks were increasingly localizing their content to go beyond the expatriate constituency in the Gulf region. This 'Arabization' included using subtitles for American programming and moderating intemperate language and depictions of nudity and sex to avoid censorship troubles – in the post-9/11 political environment, such concerns have gained greater significance. However, such US serials as *The Bold and the Beautiful, Dallas* and *Santa Barbara*, which portray the brighter or glamorous side of life, have been popular in the Arab world. In 2005, the Saudi-owned Middle East Broadcasting Centre (MBC) started screening an Arabized version of the popular US cartoon series *The Simpsons*, announced the relaunch of MBC4 to focus on 'programming that will address the needs of the modern Arab woman' and premiered such American programmes as *The Oprah Winfrey Show, Buffy* and reality shows like *Super Nanny*.

Other Westernized networks in the region included the Bahrain-based Orbit, which claims to be 'the world's first fully digital, multi-channel, multi-lingual, pay television service' and, in 2006, was supplying 39 television and 20 radio channels – largely US entertainment in English, as well as Arabic channels – to viewers in 23 countries across the Arab world, as well as 400 free-to-air channels. Showtime, a joint pay-TV venture between Viacom and Kuwait Projects Company, offering 50 channels of predominantly Western entertainment, and Star Select, operating in the Middle East since 1994, distributing its 16 channels, were the other major global players in the region.

In Latin America, traditionally considered as within the 'sphere of influence' of the USA, American networks dominate television, with MTV Latin America in the lead. Since the launch of the 24-hour movie channel TNT Latin America, in 1991, the first pan-regional network in Latin America, available in English, Spanish and Portuguese, US-based television companies have expanded considerably into the Latin market, often using innovative marketing techniques. One of the most popular channels in the region was Canal Fox, a 24-hour pan-regional general entertainment channel, launched in 1993 and available in Spanish, Portuguese and English. Fox's other major regional interests were Fox Kids Network, broadcast in Spanish, Portuguese and English, and Fox Sports Americas, an all-Spanish 24-hour sports network. CNN En Español, CNN's first independently produced 24-hour network in a language other than English, was seen throughout Latin America and among the Hispanic Americans. However, the dream of a single Spanish-speaking marketplace of 300 million, made up of 260 million Latin Americans and 40 million Spaniards, has not materialized. Each country has its own version of the mother tongue, with its own colloquialisms and linguistic and cultural differences. International schemes such as *Ibermedia*, launched in 1997, with Portugal, Spain, Argentina, Brazil, Colombia, Mexico and Venezuela, to fund joint programme productions, have not been very successful. In America's own Hispanic market – 44 million-strong, with a majority under 35 years of age – the two major players were Univisión (owned by a consortium which includes Televisa, the world's largest producer of Spanish-language programming) and Telemundo (owned by NBC since 2002), broadcasting Spanish-language cartoons produced by Nickelodeon.

In Africa, the launch of PanAmSat4 in 1995 heralded the arrival of DTH satellite operators, such as South Africa-based MultiChoice's DStv, in the continent. As a result, the number of commercial satellites covering Africa has increased substantially, though most programming is in the English language. By 2006 MultiChoice had become the key content carrier in anglophone Africa, operating subscription services across the continent, carrying, among others, Discovery, History Channel, National Geographic, Hallmark, BBC, CNN and Cartoon Network. In francophone Africa, TV5 Afrique (part of TV5, the global French-language channel), CFI-TV and Canal Horizons were the most watched pan-African channels, though they had all increased the local content in their programming (Mytton *et al.*, 2005). Though satellite services remain out of the price range of much of Africa's population, the demand for audio-visual content is growing. The opening up of the media as a result of decreasing government control of broadcasting is likely to contribute to the continent's gradual integration with global media culture, from which it is mostly cut off at present. Wherever one looks one can find similar types of programmes being broadcast, although the language and the context may be localized. The globalization of certain television formats may give the impression of homogenization, a kind of McMedia, but, as some scholars have argued, television is simultaneously global and national, shaped by the globalization of media economics and the pull of local and national cultures (Waisbord, 2004).

Regionalization in print journalism

To cater to the needs of regional and national audiences, many global media corporations produce regional editions of their newspapers and magazines, to provide a regional perspective on issues relevant to their respective readerships. In Europe, Asia and Latin America, such publications have a wide circulation. Many of these are produced in English with a regional content focus, while some are also published in other languages.

In the Asia-Pacific region, US-UK-based magazines and newspapers are a significant presence. Although English is used by a small minority of the population in Asia, and the mass market in newspapers and magazines is dominated by Asian languages, pan-Asian newspapers and magazines are only published in English and are owned by major global conglomerates. Though some of the circulation figures are not large, such international publications are read by the small but influential groups of businessmen, financiers and politicians. The regional editions of major US business publications, such as the *Asian Wall*

Street Journal, are essential reading for the Asian business elite.

For many years Asia's leading news magazines were the *Far Eastern Economic Review*, published since 1946 from Hong Kong, and *Asia Week* – the former owned by Dow Jones and the latter part of Time Warner – with significant readerships among affluent groups in Asia (in 2001 *Asia Week* stopped publication). *Fortune* has launched *Fortune Asian* and *Fortune China* editions. In India, both *Time* and *Fortune* magazines have distribution agreements with *India Today*, the country's most widely read publication, with a weekly circulation in 2006 of 1.4 million and a readership of 15 million. BBC Worldwide completed a deal in India in 2005 to acquire 50 per cent of *Filmfare* and *Femina*, two of India's leading magazines. This, according to the BBC, will 'provide a base from which to launch BBC titles in India in the future' (BBC, 2005b). Attracted by the fact that, along with China and Indonesia, India has demonstrated remarkable advertising growth, Anthony O'Reilly, owner of *The Independent* of London, has invested in *Dainik Jagran*, India's largest-selling newspaper, while two other Indian newspapers – *Business Standard* and *Hindustan Times* – have foreign partners, after government policy was liberalized to permit foreign direct investment in print media.

In Latin America, the global players are present in significant numbers, with the *Wall Street Journal Americas* published as a supplement in leading newspapers in nine Spanish-speaking countries in Latin America, and weekly in eight countries, including three Portuguese-language newspapers in Brazil. *Time* also produces a pan-regional newspaper supplement in Latin America in Portuguese and Spanish, called *Time Americas*. *AméricaEconomía*, a Dow Jones publication, was Latin America's leading pan-regional business magazine, published biweekly in Spanish and Portuguese since 1986. *Fortune* also has a Latin American edition, *Fortune Americas*, with a readership of 1.5 million. *Newsweek* has a network of local-language publications – *Nihon Ban*, in Japanese (since 1986), *Hankuk Pan*, in Korean (since 1991) and a Spanish edition (since 1996). In 2000, *Newsweek* in Arabic (*Newsweek Bil Logha Al-Arabia*) and Polish *Newsweek Polska* were launched. While it is arguable whether the international magazines and newspapers promote an Asian or Latin perspective on world issues, it is undoubtedly true that such regional editions have contributed to more coverage of Asia and Latin America, albeit from a business perspective and for the consumption of an English-speaking elite.

Apart from the news publications mentioned above, many international media brands publish local editions of leisure magazines, for example, the three glossy titles published by Hearst Corporation. *Esquire* has 10 editions, including one each for Japan, Britain, South Korea, China and Czech Republic; *Harper's Bazaar* has 16 country-specific editions, including Britain, Australia, Russia, South Korea, Mexico, Czech Republic, Greece and Turkey; while the women's monthly *Good Housekeeping* was published in over a dozen countries, including Japan, Britain, Russia, Mexico and the Philippines. Another women's magazine, *Marie Claire*, was available in 28 countries, including France, Germany, Italy, Japan, Poland, Australia and Brazil; and *Vogue* in a dozen countries, including Russia, South Korea, Japan, Germany, Britain, Australia and Brazil. In 2005, the London-based men's magazine, *Maxim*, launched an Indian edition – its 31st such foray outside Britain. The music magazine *Rolling Stone* had 11 such editions. By 2006, *Playboy* had 20 international editions, in such different countries as Brazil, Japan, Spain and Serbia. As *Time* magazine reported '...local editions of glossies from *Maxim* to *Vogue* are feeding the hunger for gadgets, new duds and fast cars – social ammunition for middle class lifestyles' (Masters, 2006: 49).

A publication like *National Geographic*, which specializes in wildlife, the environment and travel adventure, had a worldwide circulation of more than 9 million in 2006. Given its subject matter, such a magazine translates well for foreign readers, accounting for 20 per cent of its revenue from overseas. Since its international expansion, which started with the launch of a Japanese edition in 1995, the magazine has opted for many regional- and country-specific editions with local partners. Its Latin American edition is published with *Editorial Tele*, while its European editions – German, Spanish, Italian, Greek – are brought out in collaboration with German publisher Gruner+Jahr, part of the Bertelsmann group. By 2006 *National Geographic* was operating 27 local language editions – including in Chinese and Korean. Similarly, the BBC's *Top Gear* magazine had eight internationally licensed editions in 2006 – in Russia, China, the Philippines, Indonesia, the Netherlands, South Korea and Romania, as well as in the Middle East.

Regionalized advertising

Since most of the regional media discussed above are sustained by advertising, it is also important to assess how advertising is being regionalized to cater to national and regional priorities. The localization of advertising and marketing is now received wisdom. As Table 5.13 shows, this strategy is being used in different parts of the world, with a few select agencies operating the regional marketing networks, sometimes through local subsidiaries or by virtue of joint ventures. Regional marketing corporations are increasingly using regional and national languages and different cultural values to sell consumer and other products through the various media (Calder and Malthouse, 2005).

The United States, the country where media advertising had its birth, has already exported its style to various countries, suitably adapted to local tastes and values. In China, the market research sector, non-existent at the beginning of 1990s, has shown extraordinary growth. After China's entry into the World Trade Organization in 2001, it became legal for international advertising agencies to open offices in China without a local partner, allowing a flurry of marketing and advertising activity with corporations such as Motorola wrapping its Beijing headquarters with large outdoor advertisements to boost its profile among Chinese youth. The hosting of the Beijing Olympics, coupled with China's consistently high economic growth, will further interest advertisers, who may be wont to use Chinese celebrities and sell a consumerist lifestyle to the fast-growing urban youth culture in China (Wang, 2005). Martin Sorrell, Chief Executive Officer of WPP, believes that in the longer term, 'growing Americanisation' should 'assure the importance of our industry and its constituent parts, advertising and marketing services' (WPP Annual Report, 2004).

Table 5.13 Top regional marketing networks

Region and agency	Regional gross income ($ million)
Europe	
McCann Erickson Worldwide	856.1
Euro RSCG Worldwide	815.6
Y&R Advertising	755.3
Publicis Worldwide	741.9
BBDO Worldwide	516.3
Asia	
Dentsu	2028.5
Hakuhodo	861.4
Asatsu-DK	354.3
McCann Erickson Worldwide	280.5
J. Walter Thompson	250.8
Latin America	
McCann Erickson Worldwide	307.4
J. Walter Thompson	165.4
Ogilvy & Mather Worldwide	114.5
Euro RSCG Worldwide	110.3
Leo Burnett Worldwide	98.8
The Middle East	
Promoseven (49% McCann Erickson Worldwide)	41.7
Leo Burnett Worldwide	31.8
TMI (part of J. Walter Thompson)	27.3
Impact/BBDO (44% BBDO Worldwide)	25.3
PubliGraphics	24.2

Source: Based on data from *Advertising Age International*, June 2002

Regionalization of pop music

Some genres of international media messages are more global than others. Being less dependent on language and specific cultural traditions, popular music is one such genre, which has arguably helped to create a global youth audience and culture. Western popular music has always drawn on different cultures and traditions, many present within the USA itself, and in the last two decades has appropriated musical forms from around the world, from Mali to Bali, in the fashioning of a 'world music'. The availability of new technologies, such as FM radio, satellite and cable television and the Internet, has facilitated this fusing of musical forms. The flow of rap music and the hip-hop culture in the 1990s, originating from US inner cities to virtually every part of the globe, is an example of this cultural movement (Lull, 1995). This 'world music' has then been packaged and resold back to the world by the recording companies.

As noted in Chapter 4, the global music industry is dominated by a few Western and Japanese conglomerates, which control 80 per cent of the world market. The globalization of such Western television networks as MTV has given a boost to Western popular music. According to the International Federation of Phonographic Industries, the sale of recorded music was worth more than $33 billion in 2004, though this figure is nearly $6 billion lower than 1996, partly because of the growth in online music downloads (IFPI, 2005) (*see* Table 5.14).

Table 5.14 Global music – share of music recording sales by region

Region	1991	1996	2004
Europe	38%	38%	36%
North America	34%	33%	38%
Asia-Pacific	22%	23%	26%
Latin America	2%	6%	3%
Africa/Arab world	0.5%	2%	0.3%
World sales value	$26.5bn	$39.7bn	$33.6bn

Source: Based on data from IFPI

Major music companies, such as the 'big four' – Sony-BMG, Universal Music Group, EMI, Warner Music Group – are taking advantage of this interest. While in most countries in the North, international (generally Anglo-American) music is most popular, in non-Western cultures with a strong indigenous tradition of popular music, such as India and China, the opposite is the case – in China the latter accounted for 92 per cent in 2002 (*see* Table 5.15). Given the preference for local popular music in many countries, media conglomerates are increasingly becoming conscious of the need for localization of their products. To keep up with the growing demand, Warner Music International, with a roster of more than 1000 artists, is increasing its efforts to sign local artists, while MTV has been forced to customize programmes according to local cultural priorities.

In major markets, for example, in China, MTV Mandarin's music list consists of up to 70 per cent music videos from China, Taiwan and Hong Kong, while MTV India's programming consists of only 30 per cent foreign music, the rest being Indian film music. In other parts of the world local VJs are often employed to retain ratings – this is the case in MTV's Portuguese-language network for Brazil and MTV Russia. Likewise the BBC launched *Top of the Pops* in Japan and in Thailand, rehosted in Thai, and BBC Worldwide was working with Universal Music to exploit its huge music and television archive to create DVDs for global distribution. To cater to the upwardly mobile Chinese youth, Channel V has signed a deal with corporate houses to sponsor prime-time lifestyle shows.

Table 5.15 Distribution of popular music – selected countries

Country	International (%)	Domestic (%)
Australia	79	10
South Africa	73	27
Canada	71	23
Germany	49	45
UK	45	49
Russia	39	60
France	36	59
Brazil	30	68
Zimbabwe	19	81
Turkey	16	84
India	10	90
Egypt	5	95
China	5	92

Note: Figures do not add up to 100 per cent as they exclude classical music
Source: IFPI, 2003

Global media – local audience?

As noted, the providers of global media messages are primarily Western, though they employ an array of regional and local strategies to maximize their audiences and advertising revenues. The influence of international communication is often indirect – Western media texts bring with them images of lifestyles, expected social relations and ways of representing the world, which go beyond verbal communication and which survive translation. Most television programmes in India, for example, with their middle-class characters, are aimed at the middle classes with burgeoning aspirations to a 'contemporary' lifestyle and the disposable income to buy the consumer items advertised. There have been concerns that the ideological messages that US-made programmes may promote, such as individualism and hedonism, will damage traditional values, such as respect for elders and the family. The images are also of a very unrepresentative, wealthy urban elite, excluding the vast majority of the population. Speaking to the nation on the eve of the Golden Jubilee of the Indian Republic, the President of India, K. R. Narayanan, reflected:

> ... advertisement-driven consumerism is unleashing frustrations and tensions in our society. The unabashed, vulgar indulgence in conspicuous consumption by the nouveau riche has left the underclass seething in frustration. One half of our society guzzles aerated beverages while the other half has to make do with palmfuls of muddied water.

(quoted in Khare, 2000)

While the presence of imported television products on screens in the South and in Europe is undeniable, the consumption of them is by no means a passive, receptive process. Evidence suggests that there is a 'discount' factor at work with foreign programming and that, where it has been measured, domestic programming tops the ratings (Hoskins and Mirus, 1988). In addition, Western programming is still watched by a relatively small percentage of the population in much of the non-Western world. In many countries in Africa, satellite and cable TV have not yet penetrated vast sections of society, while in other developing countries Western programming is confined to off-prime-time slots.

In many traditional societies, the interaction with mediated Western culture can produce complex results. Martin-Barbero has argued that people 'first filter and reorganise what comes from the hegemonic culture and then integrate and fuse this with what comes from their own historical memory' (1993: 74). This plurality of interpretation of media messages is borne out by the studies of television, the most powerful global medium. International comparative research of family viewing of television (Lull, 1988) and of international news (Jensen, 1998) show that routine viewing in one particular cultural and political context may vary considerably between and within nations. Other forms of differentiation in terms of rural/urban, male/female and class distinctions, also influence media consumption within and between nations. As Lull has argued, 'symbolic messages are polysemic and multisemic and social actors interpret and use the symbolic environment in ways that advance their personal, social, and cultural interests' (1995: 174).

However, it is important to emphasize that though the number of people watching CNN or reading *Time* magazine in developing countries may be tiny, they are often those with power and influence. It could be argued that international communication is promoting a globalized, 'Westernized' elite, which believes in the supremacy of the market and liberal democracy, as defined by the West. The global business channel CNBC notes candidly that 'strong affinity with high net worth individuals and CEOs means our viewers exert both tremendous consumer and commercial influence' (NBC Annual Report, 2004).

The reception and consumption of media in a cross-cultural context pose a complex and contested terrain of academic inquiry, made more difficult with the paucity of many empirical studies. Much more research, especially from a Southern perspective, has to be undertaken to ascertain the impact of Western television on non-Western cultures, and vice versa.

Rather than creating a homogenized culture, globalization of Western culture may be producing 'heterogeneous disjunctures' (Appadurai, 1990). The global–local cultural interaction is leading to a hybrid culture, one, it has been argued, which blurs the boundaries between the modern and the traditional, the high and low culture, and the national and the global culture. Robertson (1992) called such a phenomenon 'glocalization', characterized by cultural fusion as a result of adaptation of Western media genres to suit local languages, styles and cultural conventions, using new communication technologies (Kraidy, 2005). An example of this cultural hybridity can be found in the case of Zee TV, India's first private Hindi-language and most successful satellite channel.

Case study

Zee TV and hybrid television

Launched, in 1992, by the Essel Group of Indian entrepreneur Subhash Chandra, only a year after STAR started beaming through satellite Western programming to India, Zee TV began by offering Hindi-language programmes. Unlike transnational broadcasters, whose largely US-made programmes were watched by the English-fluent urban middle classes, with aspirations to a Western way of life, Zee targeted the mass market, making programmes in a language that the majority of Indians use in their everyday life.

With its pioneering movie-based television entertainment, Zee TV broke new ground in nationally produced entertainment, skilfully adapting and developing local-language derivatives of Western programme formats such as game and chat shows, leisure programming and quizzes. Another case of indigenizing global TV products was its Music Asia channel, an Indian version of Western music channels – MTV and Channel V. By launching the first dedicated music channel, later renamed Zee Music, broadcasting Indian film music mixed with a new genre called Indipop, a pale imitation of Western pop music, Zee became very popular among the youth in India and increasingly among the diasporic audience.

One outcome of the availability of Western television was the mixing of English and Hindi and the evolution of a hybrid media language – Hinglish. Though a form of Hinglish had been in existence in urban north India for decades, it was Zee TV that popularized it. The extensive use of Hinglish on Music Asia contributed immensely to the popularization of Hinglish, particularly among the youth. Zee was also the first network to elevate this new language by using it in the more serious genre of news, which had traditionally been either in pure Hindi or in 'BBC English' (Thussu, 1998b). Such was the impact of this hybridization of languages that most television networks, often aimed at a younger, 'Westernized' urban audience, used Hinglish regularly in their programming.

By using English words, Zee aimed to expand its reach beyond the Hindi-speaking regions of India to cater to regional audiences and the South Asian diaspora, who may be more amenable to a hybrid variety of television. Like other commercial channels, Zee is dependent on advertisers, and is therefore acutely aware that language can influence people in their buying choices, a contributing factor to why it used Hinglish, the language of the urban middle class. The role of television, therefore, has been important in fusing Hindi and English and creating a popular and youthful new lingua franca.

The deployment of an approach of cultural hybridity has been a contributory factor in the expansion of Indian television outside the borders of the country. There is a certain amount of empathy with hybridized languages and culture among the South Asian diaspora. The members of this ethnically, linguistically and religiously diverse group, scattered around the globe, want to keep up cultural links with their countries of origin. Though these groups speak a myriad of languages, most of them at least understand some Hindi, due largely to the popularity of Hindi films. Among the second- and third-generation South Asians who have grown up within other cultures, Hinglish is the language they can relate to relatively easily.

Zee was among the first to recognize the potential of overseas markets for its programming. After STAR TV purchased 50 per cent of Zee TV in 1993, it became Zee's partner in India, facilitating the Zee network's overseas expansion. Zee TV entered the lucrative British market in 1995, when it bought TV Asia, a loss-making channel catering to British Asians. In 1999, it became one of the first channels to go digital in the UK, offering programming in Hindi and other South Asian languages, namely Bengali, Urdu, Gujarati and Punjabi. It was available on the Sky network and by the end of 1990s had become the most popular Asian channel in Britain and continental Europe. Zee also became available to subscribers in Africa after it entered into a joint venture with a South Africa-based platform operator, MultiChoice, in 1996.

By 2006, Zee was claiming to be India's largest vertically integrated media and entertainment company and the 'largest producer and aggregator' of Hindi programming in the world. With more than 30,000 hours of original programming in the library and one of the largest Indian multiple distribution platforms, its programmes could reach 350 million viewers in over 120 countries globally, including the USA, Europe, Africa, the Middle East, South East Asia and Australia (see Table 5.16). Zee had several firsts to its credit: it was the first listed media company in India; the first to launch a Hindi general entertainment channel; a Hindi cinema channel; a 24-hour Hindi news channel; and Dish TV, India's first DTH service; as well as a regional bouquet of channels – Zee Marathi, Zee Punjabi, Zee Bangla and Zee Gujarati.

After STAR started making programmes in Hindi, it became a direct competitor for Zee, creating business rivalry between the two operations of News Corporation in India. In 1999, in an unprecedented action, Zee bought back STAR's 50 per cent share in the company for $300 million, ending years of acrimony and establishing Zee as a major media player in its own right. One early indication of this was Zee's localization strategy, when, in 1999, it unveiled 'Alpha', an umbrella brand for its pay channels in regional languages – Marathi,

Bengali, Punjabi and Gujarati. Having reached more than 61 million homes in the Indian subcontinent, Zee's strategy was then to expand its operations in the lucrative North American market. To cater to the new subscribers the channel is increasingly using English subtitles in its Hindi programmes. Within the diasporic groups themselves, Zee aims to reach language-based niche audiences. In Britain, it already runs Zee Alpha Punjabi channel and has acquired a majority stake in ETC Networks (prominent in music and Punjabi television) and in Padmalaya (catering to the South Indian market and the Tamil diaspora). The diasporic market, especially in Europe and North America, is crucial for the transnationalization of Zee. In 2003, the company launched five new channels for the DTH market – Action Cinema, Classic Cinema, MX, Premiere Cinema and Smile TV – as well as *Trendz*, a fashion channel.

Zee's concern to make programmes in Indian languages may be dictated by market considerations. It recognizes that, despite the influence of the English language in India, the biggest media growth is in regional languages. Though Zee has adapted American TV genres and hybridized them to suit Indian tastes, they have not been the most popular programmes, since they portray a lifestyle with which only a small minority of Indians can identify.

It is no coincidence that the two most popular programmes on Zee TV have a very Indian sound to them. The first one was *Sa Re Ga Ma Pa*, a music programme (launched in early 1990s, but still on air in 2006) where vocalists compete in rounds devoted to classical, folk and film songs before a panel of classical musicians. Another major success has been *Antakshari*, a traditional song-based game, a challenging test of Hindi film music lore, launched in

Table 5.16 The world of Zee, 2005

Region	Launch year	Subscribing households
South Asia	1993	61,000,000
North America and Caribbean	1998	376,000
Southeast Asia and Pacific	2001	224,000
Middle East	1997	172,000
Europe	1995	168,000
Africa	1996	51,000

Source: Zee TV

1993. Both have been extremely popular in India and in South Asia, spawning clones on other channels, and also hosted in the Middle East, Britain, South Africa and the USA; they have helped find new musical talents in India and among the South Asian diaspora.

Taking a cue from its former business partner, Murdoch, Zee has also invested heavily in making sure that the company owns communication hardware as well as programming, though Siticable, India's largest cable company. In 2002, Zee entered a joint venture with AOL-Time Warner, making it 'the largest pay offering network' in India, reaching over 35 million television households.

Its success is reflected in the network's financial gains – Zee's revenues have more than doubled in recent years – from 6.2 billion rupees ($139 million) in 1999 to 13.6 billion rupees ($291 million) in 2005 (Zee Annual Report, 2005). Like other media TNCs, Zee has maximized synergies within its various sectors, benefiting from the fact that it is the largest producer of Hindi-language television programming and has also started to produce and distribute feature films: the 2002 film *Gadar – Ek Prem Katha*, produced and distributed by Zee, was the biggest blockbuster in Indian cinema.

Zee has a major presence across the different programming genres – entertainment, news, cinema and music in Hindi and English and six regional language channels, as well as online services.

Broadcasting live events, syndication services and educational services add to the revenue stream. Given Zee's ownership of cable networks, it is poised to exploit the growing importance of DTH and broadband services. Zee is essentially following the commercial model of television, as its mission statement sets out unambiguously:

> To establish the company as the creator of entertainment and infotainment products and services to feast the viewers and the advertisers. Through these services, we intend to become an integral part of the global market. As a corporation, we will be profitable, productive, creative, trend-setting and financially rugged with care and concern for all stake holders.
>
> (Zee TV, 2005)

By 2006, Zee network was broadcasting in 120 countries, reaching 350 million viewers globally (*see* Table 5.16). Reflecting the growing global ambitions of Zee, in 2004, Subhash Chandra was conferred the 'Global Indian Entertainment Personality of the Year' award by the Federation of Indian Chambers of Commerce and Industry (FICCI), which estimates that the Indian entertainment industry is to grow by an average of 30 per cent every year in the next decade (FICCI, 2004).

chapter six

Contraflow in global media

The globalization of Western media has been a major influence in shaping media cultures internationally. While there are forces for convergence and homogenization, the spread of the US model of professional, commercial television has also brought beneficial changes to some national and regional media industries, leading to a revival of cultural and creative industries. Westernization has parallels with what one commentator has called 'Easternization and South-South flows' (Nederveen Pieterse, 2004: 122). From Japanese animation to Korean and Indian films, from Latin American soap operas to Arabic news, over the last 10 years the media world has witnessed a proliferation of multilingual and multifaceted growth of media content, emanating from regional hubs of creative industries. The availability of digital technology and satellite networks has enabled the development of regional broadcasting, such as the pan-Arabic Middle East Broadcasting Centre (MBC), the pioneering 24/7 news network al-Jazeera or the Mandarin-language Phoenix channel, which caters to a Chinese diaspora. A privatized and deregulated broadcasting and telecommunication environment has enabled an increasing flow of content from the global South to the North, for example, the growing international visibility of telenovelas, while the Indian film industry is an example of a non-Western production centre making its presence felt in a global cultural context.

Viewing the global village

As a result of the developments of the 1990s (*see* Chapter 3), television has come to dominate the media scene in virtually every part of the world, and such icons of global television as CNN and MTV have become ubiquitous. The role of television in the construction of social and cultural identities is now much more complex than in the era of a single national broadcaster and a shared public space that characterized television in most countries in the post-war years. Though national broadcasters continue to be important in most countries, still receiving the highest audience shares, the availability of myriad television channels has complicated the national media discourse. In the multichannel era, a viewer can have simultaneous access to a variety of local, regional, national and international channels, thus being able to engage in different levels of mediated discourse.

In countries where the media systems were tightly regulated by the state apparatus, globalization has brought a fresh and more international perspective: for example, global television has helped to promote media professionalism in Russia (Becker, 2004); and in

China, while still having to operate under a state-controlled media system, journalists feel freer because of the 'marketisation' of media firms, providing them with greater scope for professional practice (Lee, 2003).

Global television has also created the phenomenon of global 'media events' – the live broadcasting of 'historic' events around the world – Olympic Games, Tiananmen Square violence, Operation Desert Storm, natural or human disasters (Dayan and Katz, 1992). The worldwide coverage of the televised trial of US sportsman O. J. Simpson in 1995, the death and funeral of Princess Diana in 1997, the millennium celebrations in 1999, the terrorist attacks in New York and Washington in 2001, the US invasion of Iraq in 2003 and the Asian tsunami of 2004, can be added to the list of such shared global media experiences.

Transnational corporations, governments and non-governmental organizations, as well as militant groups, have harnessed the power of television as well as the Internet to put across their case. The role of 'spin' in contemporary politics in the Western world is now well documented (Corner and Pels, 2003; Franklin, 2004; Brader, 2005). In other parts of the world too, the use of television for political purposes is on the increase (Sussman and Galizio, 2003). Television images of emotionally charged funerals of soldiers, broadcast on Indian news channels during the 1999 border conflict with Pakistan, were exploited by media and the Indian government to boost public morale (Thussu, 2002b). In Venezuela, President Hugo Chávez used television to have his own three-hour face-to-face show, with live phone-ins from the audience, which attracted more than 11 million viewers in a country of just 23 million. Chávez has also been the spirit behind *Telesur*, the first pan-Latin American news network, launched in 2005 on a not-for-profit basis and aiming to be 'anti-hegemonic'. Other groups, such as radical Islamists, have made use of managing and manipulating the visual image to further their political or cultural causes (Burke, 2004; Hill, 2006). Lebanon's Hizbullah runs the satellite channel *al-Manar*, while Med-TV, set up in 1995 in London by Kurdish exiles, and closed down in 1999 under pressure from the Turkish government, was a key player for the Kurdish diaspora. Visual media can have tremendous power to influence political and social attitudes. As Reeves and Nass observe: 'Media can evoke emotional responses, demand attention, threaten us, influence memories, and change ideas of what is natural. Media are full participants in our social and natural world' (1996: 251).

The globalization of such a powerful visual medium has tended to increase Western cultural influence, but other models do exist, argued a UNESCO *World Culture Report*, based on 'different cultural institutional and historical backgrounds and such alternatives are likely to multiply in the era of globalization, in spite of appearances, which may paradoxically witness greater diversity than uniformity' (UNESCO, 1998: 23). As Chapter 5 noted, the US-led Western media conglomerates have used an array of strategies, including regionalization and localization of their content, to extend their reach beyond the elites in the world and to create the 'global popular'. The proliferation of satellite and cable television channels, made possible with digital technology and growing availability of communication satellites, has undoubtedly made the global cultural landscape much more complex.

While its well-publicized commercial agenda has been criticized, the globalization of Western or Western-inspired television also has benefits. It has contributed to the creation of jobs in media and cultural industries, for example. As localization becomes part of the business strategy of media transnationals, more jobs are created in these industries in many developing countries to make programmes that take account of the cultural context. At the beginning of the 1990s there was no television industry worth the name in India, which until 1991 had just one state-controlled channel, little more than a mouthpiece of the government and notoriously monotonous. By 2006 there were more than 300 channels, some joint ventures with international operators. This expansion demanded new programme content – from news to game and chat shows, from soap operas to documentaries – which has been provided by a burgeoning television industry.

It has also been argued that the extension of Western media, and with it 'modernity', across the globe has a liberatory potential that can contribute to strengthening liberal democratic culture (Elster, 1997; Jenkins and Thorburn, 2003) and promoting gender equality and freedom from the 'national strait-jacket' (Kapur, 1997). There is little doubt that digital technologies have made it possible to beam a range of specialized channels across the world, some in local or national languages, which are giving more choice to consumers and opening up their window on the world. This is particularly the case in many developing countries, where the media, especially broadcasting, had been under state control, and where often unrepresentative and sometimes unelected governments could use the airwaves to control their populations, severely restricting plurality of opinions and possibilities of open discussion.

The Western style of professional television journalism, essentially based on independence from government control, has influenced programme-making in many countries. Examples of the adoption of this kind of journalism include the current-affairs programmes such as *We the People* on NDTV in India, and critical investigative programmes such as *Jiaodian Fangtan* (Focal Report) on China's CCTV, which, in the words of one Chinese scholar, has 'proved that television can play a role in being the people's and not just the Party's mouthpiece' (Zhao, 1999: 303). In Turkey, the privatization of television has challenged the monopoly of the state-run national broadcaster Turkish Radio and Television Authority (TRT), and brought 'openness and plurality' to the airwaves (Catalbas, 2000: 144). There is also more evidence of liberalism in the press. After the advent of 'multi-partyism' in Africa, there has been a rapid increase in the number of privately run small newspapers and magazines. As state after state moves towards democracy, this trend is likely to grow.

In other areas of the media too, examples can be given of how globalization has improved the quality of media products. Expansion of Western publishing houses in the global South has had a positive impact. For example, after NAFTA, US publishing giants such as McGraw-Hill and Prentice Hall entered the Mexican publishing market, opening up new avenues for Mexican writers as they become popular in the USA, with many more being translated into English. The English translation of the Mexican author Laura Esquivel's novel *Coma agua para chocolate*, sold more than a million copies in the USA, as well as 200,000 copies in the Spanish market in the USA, leading to what one Mexican scholar called, surely with hyperbole, the 'Latinization of the United States' (UNESCO, 1998: 164). Similarly, since the launch of Penguin India, in the early 1990s, many books on

Indian politics, economics and culture, including a series of translations of Indian classics, have been produced to international publishing standards and are also available for a wider global market, given the vast marketing network of Penguin. In more recent years, Penguin has also started publishing books in Hindi and Malayalam.

Discontents of cultural globalization

Despite such welcome developments, the growing Western cultural presence has also produced discontent in some countries, especially in the Islamic world. The extreme manifestation of this was the terrorist attacks in New York and Washington on 11 September 2001, which on the one hand resulted in a backlash in the West against militant Islam, and on the other stoked the fire of anti-Western, or more specifically anti-American, sentiment. This has been characterized as a clash of civilizations (Huntington, 1993) and a 'clash of fundamentalisms' (Ali, 2001). This was prefigured in the 1979 Islamic revolution that overthrew the Shah of Iran, which was spurred not so much by modernization as by opposition to what Iranian intellectuals called 'westoxication', the adoption and flaunting of superficial consumerist attributes of fads and commodities, originating in the USA. Though Iran may be an extreme case of an anti-Western cultural backlash, degrees of xenophobic reaction emerging in response to such superficial elements of a Western way of life, often mediated through television, can be found in many other non-Western cultures – the ideological revival of *Hindutva* (Hinduness) in India is a case in point (Rajagopal, 2001).

Countries such as China, Singapore, Saudi Arabia and Iran have tried to restrict the reception of Western satellite television by introducing licensing regimes. Iran banned Western television on the grounds that it was culturally inappropriate in an Islamic nation, primarily because of the sexual content and orientation of Western television programmes, films and advertising. In other traditional societies like India, worries have been expressed about the representation of women in the media, especially advertising (Joseph and Sharma, 1994).

There is also a feeling that in the McWorld, culture is being commodified to the extent that it impacts on the religious sensibilities of various communities (Barber, 1995). In Asia, Western culture, based on individualism and mediated primarily through television, is seen as undermining traditional Asian values, revolving around the family and the community (Goonasekera, 1997; Goonasekera *et al.*, 2003; Thomas, 2005). In China, the release of Disney's 1998 animation film *Mulan* was delayed by the government, unhappy with the portrayal of aspects of Chinese culture in the film. Despite its theme and supposed cultural sensitivity, *Mulan* did not do very well in China. Partly as a reaction to perceived Westernization of their cultures and partly as a reaction to the alleged distortion in representations of non-Western cultures in the global media, many countries have experienced a cultural revival, often influenced by religious groups and encouraged by political establishments, acting as a barrier to the flow of Western media products.

In India, for example, the phenomenal success of two television serials based on the Hindu epics *Ramayan* and *Mahabharat*, telecast in 1988, have arguably contributed to the rise of a Hinduized version of Indian identity, undermining the secular basis of Indian society (Mitra, 1993; Rajagopal, 2001). Eleven years after they were broadcast on India's official television network *Doordarshan*, repeats of both *Mahabharat* and *Ramayan* were being shown on Zee TV and Sony TV, respectively, still managing very high ratings. The exceptional popularity of such programmes has led to the production of many more religious serials. At their height in 1997, nearly a dozen 'mythologicals', as they were called, were being shown on television, representing an alliance between what an observer aptly called 'godland and adland' (Jain, 1997).

In China, the revival of the traditional *Beijing opera* and the screening of classics on television have contributed to a renewed interest in the country's history and culture, after half a century of its denigration under Maoist ideology. Episodes of the TV series *Outlaws of the Marsh*, screened on CCTV in 1998, drew 900 million viewers. Other leading Chinese classic novels, including *Journey to the West*, *A Dream of the Red Mansions* and *Romance of the Three Kingdoms*, have been adapted for TV.

In the Muslim world, where a majority of the populations perceive Islam as a civilization rather than a culture, Western liberalism has its most robust resistance. This is reflected not merely in the political discourse characterized by anti-Western rhetoric, but also in the symbolism of interactions with Western cultural artefacts. In 1996, Iran released Sara, who wore Islamic dress – its answer to the glamorous US doll Barbie, which has iconic status among young girls across the world. The Bosnian Muslims also had their own doll, called Amina, while the Arabs had one called Leila.

These examples show that fears of a global harmonization of culture, due to the globalization of Western television forms and formats, may not be entirely justified. Although Western domination of the global media and communication industry remains strong, the cultural interactions between Western media products and non-Western societies are deeply complex. There is little doubt about the existence of American cultural products worldwide, though how these are used and interpreted by various cultures remains largely unexplored, given the limited number of concrete case studies which systematically examine these issues.

Often the discussion has focused on the media consumption of the ruling elites in developing countries, ignoring the majority of populations for whom Western products – be that Hollywood films, pop music or computer-related leisure activities – are inaccessible and, even if available, are not easy to relate to. Not surprisingly, people prefer entertainment in their own language, catering to their own cultural priorities – one key reason why most imported programmes rarely make it to prime-time slots in the world's television schedules. Audiences can critically negotiate with an imported programme – something more than many have given them credit for.

The tendency to lump together the 'third world' as one homogenized Other in many Western discourses – unfortunately within both the critical and liberal traditions – is partly responsible for such an omission. Obvious unfamiliarity or limited and often distorted understanding of history, traditions, languages and cultures of many developing countries leads to such undifferentiated views of the 'majority world'. One only has to look at the popularity of the Indian film industry, discussed below, in South Asia, or the telenovelas in Latin America to discount notions of passive viewers in the developing world. Some critical scholars seem to have given far too much credit to the media's capacity to shape a nation's cultural agenda. To give just one example – despite 200 years of British colonial subjugation, the vast majority of Indians practice their own religion, speak their own languages and pursue their traditional culture. It is therefore unlikely that a CNN or an MTV will achieve what the British Empire failed to do. This is not to argue that US-led media are not influential, but to submit that the interaction is much more complex and there are aspects of Western media and culture which have been easily adapted and assimilated by non-Western cultures.

However, anti-Western and, more accurately, anti-American sentiments are partly related to the broader geopolitical and cultural changes in the international environment in the post-cold war era, when a radicalized Islam is supposed to have replaced communism as the pre-eminent transnational threat to Western interests, exemplified by shadowy networks such as al-Qaida, with their alleged links to 'rogue' states. In this imagining of transnational politics, influenced by the discourse of the 'clash of civilizations' and strengthened by the events of 11 September 2001, militant Islam has characteristics that are inimical to a modern, secular, and rational market-democracy. The surveillance of Muslim citizens of Europe and the USA; the French government's ban on wearing Islamic headscarves in state schools; and the publication in September 2005 of offensive cartoons of the Prophet Muhammad in a Danish newspaper and their republication in the French newspaper *France Soir*, as well as newspapers around Europe, leading to wide-scale protests and scores of deaths in many Arab and Islamic countries, are some indicative examples of the cultural clash between the West and the Islamic countries.

Global counterflow of television

A more nuanced understanding of the complex process of international cultural flow will show that the traffic is not just one-way – from North to South – even though it is overly weighted in favour of the former. Evidence shows that new trans-border television networks, as well as online communication communities, are appearing, some from the periphery to the metropolitan centres of global media and communication industries (Hartley, 2005; Thussu, 2006). There is growing trade too in cultural goods given the increasing volume and velocity of multidirectional media flows that emanate from such Southern urban cultural centres as Cairo, Hong Kong and Mumbai (Curtin, 2003).

Such non-Western countries as China, Japan, South Korea, Brazil and India have become increasingly important in the circulation of cultural products, as indicated by Table 6.1. Japanese animation, film, publishing and music business was worth $140 billion in 2003, with animation, including manga (comics), anime (animation), films, videos and merchandising products bringing in $26 billion, according to the Digital Content Association of Japan (JETRO, 2005). South Korea has emerged as a major exporter of entertainment – film, television soap operas, popular music and online games – with television dramas such as *Jewel in the Palace* being extremely popular in China, prompting commentators to speak of a Korean wave (the '*Hallyu*') sweeping across East and South East Asia (Shim, 2006).

Table 6.1 Export of cultural goods by selected non-Western countries, $ million

Countries	Books	Newspapers and periodicals	Recorded media
China*	668	40	510
Japan	108	34	371
Russia	240	15	59
Mexico	120	33	146
South Korea	72	4	175
India	43	13	191
Brazil	12	11	11
Turkey	8	2	13
South Africa	19	2	8
Egypt	6	1	0.3

* Includes Hong Kong and Macao
Source: UNESCO, 2005a, figures for 2002, rounded to nearest million

The deregulation of broadcasting, which has been a catalyst for the extension of private television networks, has also made it possible for private satellite broadcasters to aim beyond the borders of the country where the network is based. Traditionally, state broadcasters have seen their roles confined to the borders of the nation state. Apart from major powers, whose broadcasting had an international dimension, most countries have had to make programmes for a domestic audience. This was particularly the case in the South. In contrast, the private channels, primarily interested in markets and advertising revenues, had a more liberal media agenda. This basic difference between state-centric and market-oriented broadcasting has been a key factor in the expansion of many Southern broadcasters into the lucrative Northern markets, aiming to reach diasporic communities. Being part of global conglomerates, such as Phoenix and Zee until 1999, has given them the technical and managerial support to operate as a global channel. The extension of satellite footprints and the growth of DTH broadcasting have enabled networks such as Zee to operate in an increasingly global communication environment. Such groups represent Southern media organizations which are becoming visible across the globe, and feeding into and developing what has been referred to as the emergent 'diasporic public spheres' (Appadurai, 1996).

Cultures of diaspora

One reason for the proliferation of such transnational channels is the physical movement of people – what Appadurai has called 'ethnoscape' – from one geographical location to another, carrying with them aspects of their culture. Cultures have always been affected by external influences as a result of trade, proselytization and migration, from the expansion of Christianity and Islam to colonialism and decolonization. In the twenty-first century there are significant populations of South Asians in Britain, North Africans in France, Turks in Germany and Latin Americans in the United States. Over 20 million people were forced to leave their countries of origin in the 1990s as a result of conflicts or poverty. The bulk of migration has taken place within the countries of the South: more than 70 per cent of the population of the United Arab Emirates, for example, consists of foreign workers, a majority of them coming from the Indian subcontinent. This has made the oil-rich Gulf region a key target for media organizations based in India, with television channels, video and audio tape companies and film distribution networks vying with each other to provide cultural goods to what remains a rich market. In addition, there is an increasing internationalization of a professional workforce, employed by the transnational corporations, international non-governmental organizations and multilateral bureaucracies. As a result, with a few exceptions, most nations of the twenty-first century have sizeable minorities and many countries are multilingual.

Table 6.2 Where migrants live

Region	Number of migrants (million)	Share of region's population (%)
Europe*	56.1	7.7
Asia	49.9	1.4
North America	40.8	12.9
Africa	16.3	2
Latin America	5.9	1.1
Australia	5.8	18.7

Note: * Including European part of former USSR
Source: UN Global Commission on International Migration 2005, figures for 2000

Table 6.3 Hosting migrants – the world's top five countries

Country	Number of migrants (million)	Share of world's migrants (%)
USA	35	20
Russia	13.3	7.6
Germany	7.3	4.2
Ukraine	6.9	4.0
India	6.3	3.6

Source: UN Global Commission on International Migration 2005, figures for 2000

Although migrants have learnt to live with their host cultures and the majority communities too have largely accepted their presence, they are still seen, at least culturally, as 'different'. For many developing countries, however, migration brings tangible gains: remittances from migrant communities were almost triple the value of Official Development Assistance – in 2004, transfers of remittances were worth about $150 billion, with double that amount being transferred informally (UN, 2005). The Southern presence in the metropolitan centres of the world, brought about by a process of what has been called 'deterritorialization', which García Canclini has described as 'the loss of the "natural" relation of culture to geographical and social territories' (1995: 229), has received most attention. The issue of identity is central to migrant lifestyle, living as they often do 'between cultures' (Bhabha, 1994). The conflict between the dual identity of the host country and the aspiration to be part of the culture of the country of origin, sometimes an imaginary 'homeland', makes them susceptible to accepting cultural hybridity (Anderson, 1991). The nature of cultural mixing, as Martin Barbero has argued, can lead to a hybridization of cultures. Iranian cable television in Los Angeles, for example, has had to tread a careful line between providing programmes which retain a traditional Islamic way of life with those which display the local consumerist lifestyle in the USA (Naficy, 1993).

According to a report of the UN Global Commission on International Migration, there were nearly 200 million migrants in 2005, up from 82 million in 1970, counting only those who have lived outside their country for more than one year. This figure included 9.2 million refugees. More than 60 per cent of all migrants lived in the developed world – from 1980 to 2000, the number of migrants living in the developed world increased from 48 million to 110 million. As a result of globalization of jobs and commerce, populations around the world have experienced a great deal of mobility, confirmed by the fact that, in 1970, migrants comprised 10 per cent of the population in 48 countries, while by 2000, in 70 countries, 1 in 10 residents was a migrant. Although migration is often discussed in the context of the Western world, the phenomenon is global – from 1975 to 2001, for example the number of foreign workers in Japan increased from 750,000 to 1.8 million (UN, 2005).

In the past, diasporic communities have used different types of media to keep in touch with their culture – from letters, books, newspapers and magazines, to audio tapes and videos and DVDs of films. Satellite television opens up possibilities for transnational broadcasters to cater to specific geo-linguistic groups (Karim, 2003; Chalaby, 2005). For example, the Chinese minority in Malaysia can receive programming from China, and Algerians in France can watch Algerian and other Arabic channels. The demand for such channels also reflects the lack of provision for minority communities by mainstream media and national broadcasters.

New communication technologies have made it possible for broadcasters from many developing countries to export their media products successfully. Turkey's TRT launched TRT-INT in 1990 to transmit programmes via Eutelsat to Turkish-speaking populations in Western Europe, mainly aimed at the 2 million-strong Turkish population in Germany. Two years later, in 1992, it launched a trans-border broadcasting channel, TRT AVRASYA TV (renamed TRT Turk), aimed at the Turkic-speaking populations in Central Asia, who share language, religion and cultural affinities with Turkey and whose cultural sovereignty was undermined by decades of domination by Soviet communism.

Such expansion has been possible because of availability of satellite platforms. In Britain, South Asian channels, including Zee, Sony, Star and B4U, were available on Sky's digital network, while in the USA, such platforms as Echostar DISH system and DirecTV provided a range of programmes for various diasporic groups. It is a popular fallacy that the growing availability of such channels has contributed to a greater awareness of cultural differences in the world's metropolitan centres and a trend towards multiculturalism. These channels are not watched by the members of the host majority, however, even though some advertisers have found them a useful means to target a niche audience, leading to the further fragmentation of the audience and ghettoization of minorities.

Globalization of geo-linguistic television

With the acceleration of movement of populations around the world, primarily as a result of economic activities, major geo-cultural markets, based on languages such as English, Spanish, Mandarin, Hindi, Arabic and French, are becoming increasingly prominent in transnational communication. Networks aiming at a specific demographic/linguistic population segments in various countries represent attempts at creating supranational public spaces, based on cultural and linguistic affinities. Networks such as Zee (Hindi), Middle East Broadcasting Centre (MBC) (Arabic), and Phoenix (Mandarin) represent distinct geo-linguistic categories, although their influence and reach may be wider than just among the speakers of the particular language group towards which they are primarily targeted.

Among the regional geo-linguistic areas, the growth of pan-Arabic television is one of the most interesting media developments of the late 1990s, affecting the 280 million people living in the Arab world (Sakr, 2001). By 2006 more than 150 channels were accessible in the Arab world, as a special report in *The Economist* noted: 'With 150 channels to choose from, Arabs are arguing, comparing and questioning as never before' (*The Economist*, 2005). Media has traditionally been under the direct control of the state in many Arab countries and the growing popularity of international television has raised questions about the suitability of some programming in what remains one of the world's most conservative areas, with strict regulations, especially about the depiction of women on television or in the cinema. Partly as a reaction to the availability of Western television in the region, pan-Arabic channels such as MBC have become an established part of the Arab broadcasting scene. A key objective of these channels is to broadcast Arabic-language programmes to Arab nationals living in Europe and North America – more than 5 million Arabs live in Europe and another 2 million in North America. This well-established and wealthy diaspora has created a lucrative market for Arab broadcasters.

Intra-Arab communication was first established by the international Arabic newspapers, written with datelines across the Arab world, edited in London and printed in major world capitals, using satellite communications. The newspapers, such as *al-Sharq al-Awsat* (started in London in 1978) and *al-Hayat* (originally a Beirut newspaper, which was resurrected in London in 1988), cover issues of importance to Arab readers. In 2006, *al-Hayat* was being printed in London, Frankfurt, Cairo, Bahrain, Beirut and New York, with a combined circulation of 170,000.

Prior to the availability of satellite television, regional broadcasting was largely about exchange of government propaganda between Arab state-regulated broadcasters through such organizations as the Arab States Broadcasting Union. In the 1990s, with the rise of a privatized Arab satellite broadcast television, a new type of pan-Arabic television emerged, challenging state broadcasting monopolies. The success of round-the-clock news such as CNN after the 1991 Gulf War made the Arabs look for a new market of broadcasting, influenced by American journalistic and production values.

The launch of a new generation of satellites helped broadcasting. Arabsat, a consortium comprising the members of the Arab League, launched its first communications satellite in 1985. In the 1990s, the development of new satellite technology, especially the new Ku-band, set aside specifically for direct-to-home broadcasting, allowed more traffic on satellites, making them cheaper to run. The expansion of Arabsat has ensured that pan-regional satellite television can prosper in the region, given the linguistic, religious and cultural affinities among Arab countries. Increasingly, Arab citizens who live in the global North are also being linked to this shared experience. The Saudi-owned MBC has emerged as the key free-to-air pan-Arabic television entertainment network, its position strengthening after it took over, in 2001, Lebanon's popular entertainment channel Future International, also available to Arab audiences in the USA through the Echostar Dish system.

Operating since 1991, and for many years based in London (it has moved its headquarters to Dubai), by 2006, MBC was one of the most widely viewed channels in the Arab world, claiming an audience of 130 million viewers. Its main rivals in the region include the Lebanese Broadcasting Corporation and the Cairo-based Arab Radio and Television (ART). By providing news and entertainment to the Arab world and among the Arabic diaspora, channels like MBC could help shape a new kind of Arab identity – one based on a regional or geo-linguistic rather than national identity. As the wealthiest market and the dominant owner of satellite television in the region, Saudi Arabia has a major role in the Arab media. However, the Saudi position has been undermined by the growing popularity of such networks as al-Jazeera (Sakr, 2001; Lynch, 2006).

Case study

Al-Jazeera – the 'island' that became a global news phenomenon

The Qatar-based al-Jazeera ('island' in Arabic), which since its launch in 1996 has redefined journalism in the Arab world, is a prominent example of contraflow in global media products. By 2006 this pan-Arabic 24/7 news network was claiming to reach 50 million viewers across the world, undermining the Anglo-American domination of news and current affairs in one of the world's most geopolitically sensitive areas. If the live broadcast of the 1991 US military action against Iraq contributed to making CNN a global presence, the 'war on terrorism' has catapulted al-Jazeera into an international broadcaster whose logo can be seen on television screens around the world. In the region, satellite networks have led to what one commentator has called 'the structural transformation of the Arab public sphere' (Lynch, 2006). It was al-Jazeera that broadcast the video tape of Osama bin Laden, the self-styled leader of al-Qaida, in the wake of 9/11; and when the American forces started bombing Afghanistan in October 2001, it was the only television network on the ground to provide live coverage (Sakr, 2001; El-Nawawy and Iskandar, 2002). However, unlike CNN, Fox News or BBC World, its cameras were less restrained in focusing on images of devastation and suffering that bombing inevitably entails. Among its detractors are the autocratic Arab governments, which find its professional output a threat to their conventional ways of controlling information.

By the time the USA invaded Iraq in March 2003, al-Jazeera had already evolved into a serious and even alternative network – and not just in the Arab world. Its English-language website, launched at the time of *Operation Iraqi Freedom*, became a popular source for journalists, activists and others interested in the nuances of that conflict. By inviting Western as well as Israeli experts into its studio-based debates, al-Jazeera helped broaden the terms and scope of the Arab media discourse, in the process also earning the displeasure of Islamic fundamentalists, as well as left-wing opinion in the region. It may have ruffled feathers among the Arab political elites, but for millions of Arab citizens its news bulletins and such programmes as *al-Itijah al-Mua'akis* (Counter-trend) have a dedicated and enthusiastic pan-Arabic audience.

One reason the network has reached such acceptance is the professionalism of its output – the core of its multinational staff had had the experience of working for transnational broadcasters such as the BBC, which pioneered the idea of pan-Arabic television news by launching *BBC Arabic* in 1994, in conjunction with the Saudi-owned Orbit. The service was abandoned in April 1996 when the BBC in the UK aired stories that Saudis found objectionable, including a report on its flagship current affairs programme *Panorama*, which explored the issue of capital punishment in the Kingdom. The BBC's loss was the Arab world's gain. However, the financial stablity of al-Jazeera has remained not very sound, as advertisers have tended to keep away from such a controversial network. At the time of its launch, the Emir of Qatar, Hamad bin Khalifa al-Thani, provided $140 million and the network was supposed to be self-sufficient in five years, which, by 2006, had not materialized.

Al-Jazeera has had more than its share of controversies (Zayani, 2005; Lynch, 2006): it has been called the 'terrorist network' and 'the voice of bin-Laden'. Whatever its shortfalls, the channel has given satellite television news a new lease of life and transformed a previously parochial Arab media. The network has earned the wrath of the US government: its Kabul office was bombed and during *Operation Iraqi Freedom* its bureau in Baghdad was hit by a missile from a US warplane, killing correspondent Tareq Ayoub, while its Madrid correspondent was imprisoned on charges of having links with al-Qaida. Despite being demonized as the channel of Osama bin Laden by airing his taped messages for the wider world, it has provided an alternative source of information emanating from a news-rich arena.

Al-Jazeera has faced stiff competition in the regional news market from rival networks, including Abu Dhabi TV. The biggest challenge has come from MBC-owned *al-Arabiya*, which, since its launch in 2003, has been operating a 24-hour news network based in Dubai, claiming to epitomize 'Arab modernism' – a code for its pro-Western orientation. It claimed to be 'rational but not rigid, informative and daring without being controversial'. To counter its critics that it was politically biased – for example, in its coverage of the Palestinian Intifada, referring to the suicide bombers as shaheeds (martyrs) – in 2004 al-Jazeera published a Code of Ethics, which included the aim to: 'Treat our audiences with due respect and address every issue or story with due attention to present a clear, factual and accurate picture while giving full consideration to the feelings of victims of crime, war, persecution and disaster, their relatives and our viewers, and to individual privacy and public decorum'.

Recognizing that English-language channels only interest a very small, though influential, segment of society, in 2005 the BBC announced a free-to-air round-the-clock television news service, specifically for the Arab region, the first directly government-funded international television service to be launched by the BBC. The announcement coincided with the launch of the English-language version of al-Jazeera channel in 2006, the same year in which al-Jazeera news became 'accessible anytime anywhere through SMS'. With its largely British staff, the English language al-Jazeera International was poised to make its presence felt globally, though it was not clear who was the intended audience. One target could be the Muslim minorities scattered across the world (Alterman, 2005). However, given its language, the network's potential viewership is not confined to Islamic populations. As one recent study of al-Jazeera concluded: 'The information age is upon us and in the decades ahead we can expect only more al-Jazeeras, adding to an ever greater torrent of information, as regional ideas spread around the world and become global' (Miles, 2005: 426).

China's 'peaceful rising' and global communication

One of the most significant developments in the arena of international communication during the first decade of the twenty-first century has been the rise of China as a major economic power. As the world's largest country in terms of population, and one of its oldest continuing civilizations, China has a significant cultural role in the era of globalization. Parallel to its economic liberalization, China has used an array of strategies to ensure that its viewpoint is visible in the global media-sphere. Within two years of the establishment of China's only national English-language newspaper, *China Daily*, in 1981, a North American edition was launched in New York, followed in 1992 with *Reports from China*. This 'Voice of China' or 'Window to China', as it is sometimes called, by 2005 had a global circulation of more than 200,000, one-third of which was among its mostly business-oriented readers in more than 100 countries. The online edition of the newspaper, launched in 1996, had an average daily traffic of more than 5 million. The *People's Daily*, the authoritative Chinese newspaper which was founded in 1948, had a circulation of 3 million in 2005 and a major presence on the web – the online English-language edition was launched in 1998. In addition to English, the online edition also had Chinese, Japanese, French, Spanish, Russian and Arabic versions. Similarly, the official Chinese news agency Xinhua's English-language website had versions in these languages, disseminating mostly positive information about China and news about the world at large.

The expansion of CCTV-9, the English language network of the China Central Television, reflects the recognition by the Beijing authorities of the importance of the English language as the key to success for global commerce and communication and their strategy to bring Chinese public diplomacy to a global audience. An English-language channel was launched domestically in 1986, and in 1993 English-language programmes were carried on the Mandarin-language international channel CCTV-4. It was only in 2000 the CCTV-9 was launched as a global English channel, with news and current affairs at its core; by 2006 it was covering the globe via six satellites, and claimed 2.3 million subscribers outside China.

However, it is private television networks which have shown greatest mobility as far as Chinese media flows are concerned. The Hong Kong-based Mandarin-language, Phoenix Chinese Channel, a general entertainment channel offering news, sports, music, drama, movies and variety shows, part of Rupert Murdoch's News Corporation, is one such example which has benefited from the gradual opening up of China, traditionally a closed society and for half a century a communist country. As its mission statement from the 2004 Annual Report says: Phoenix 'brings the world closer to China and China closer to the world' (2005: 6). In the decade since it hit the airwaves in 1996, Phoenix has emerged as a key example of a geo-linguistic television news and entertainment network, which has made its presence felt among Chinese-speaking communities around the world (more than 35 million Chinese people live outside China). Claiming to blend traditional Chinese culture with the Westernized ethos of Hong Kong, which until 1997 was a British colony, Phoenix has attracted TV personnel from Hong Kong, Taiwan, mainland China and from among the Chinese diaspora. More importantly, it has been able to attract multinational companies to advertise on the channel. By 2006 Phoenix claimed to have audiences in Asia-Pacific, Europe, North America and North Africa, covering more than 90 countries with its five channels: Phoenix Chinese, Phoenix Movies, Phoenix InfoNews, Phoenix Chinese News and Entertainment (aimed at audiences in Europe) and Phoenix North America Chinese.

Phoenix sees itself as 'the window to the world for the Chinese global community' and says it 'seeks to promote a free flow of information and entertainment within the Greater China region' (www.phoenixtv.com). Phoenix InfoNews, launched in 2001, provides what it terms 'quality news coverage of current events with impartial and objective analysis for viewers in the global Chinese community.' It broadcasts to audiences in China and 50 other countries in Asia-Pacific via AsiaSat3, and in 2004, it began broadcasting in the USA via Echostar, as well as in Malaysia and Singapore. InfoNews was launched on 3G mobile telephones in Hong Kong in 2005. Given its mix of entertainment and infotainment, Phoenix has a transnational visibility, and can be accessed in South East Asia, Australasia, Europe and the USA. But its largest audience is in mainland China, where it reaches over 42 million households, which equates to more than 140 million viewers.

Television played an important role in China in legitimizing and popularizing its policy of economic liberalization, introduced in the late 1970s after the death of Mao Tse Tung, the leader of the 1949 communist revolution. The gradual glasnost detectable in Chinese news and current affairs programmes can also be attributed to economic liberalization. Since China is increasingly keen to integrate with global financial and information markets, the accent of news and information programmes is on economic and trade issues. The change of attitude is also discernible in the way authorities deal with the foreign media. Though still in control of information channels, the Communist Party has given up its rhetoric of the 1980s, which saw the West as a source of 'spiritual pollution' and 'bourgeois liberalization'. Instead, the party now happily embraces what it calls market socialism and promotes bohemian consumerism and individualism (Zhao, 1999; Hockx and Strauss, 2006).

For their part, transnational media corporations have to tread a careful line in dealing with what is still a one-party state. Especially sensitive are news and current affairs issues, for example, the Chinese definition of human rights may differ considerably from that of the US Government. Such sensitivities were behind STAR TV's summary removal in 1994 of the BBC from its northern beam covering China, after the Chinese Government complained of the BBC's coverage of human rights issues in the country. After that, News Corporation undertook measures to placate the Chinese Government, including setting up, in 1995, an information technology joint venture with the *People's Daily*; publishing (under HarperCollins imprint) the English translation of a biography of the Chinese leader Deng Xiaoping; and showing on Phoenix, in 1997, a series of 12 one-hour episodes on the life of Deng, made by CCTV. In 1998, Murdoch cancelled a HarperCollins contract to publish the memoirs of Chris Patten, the controversial last governor of Hong Kong. News Corporation was the first major international media company to open an office in Beijing in 1999, the year when, for the first time on the Chinese mainland, *Channel [V] Chinese Music Awards* were held in Shanghai. More recently, in 2006, Google ignored concerns about censorship to operate a Chinese-language search engine, following the example of another Internet giant, Yahoo!, which has been doing business in China for over a decade.

Though Hong Kong – home to such trans-Asian networks as STAR TV and Channel V (both part of Murdoch's media empire), as well as TVB, the largest Chinese programme producer in the world – has a separate administrative structure, a growing tendency towards co-operation with the mainland in circulation of cultural products is in evidence. Hong Kong's films and television industry has preferential access to the huge Chinese mainland market under the China/Hong Kong Closer Economic Partnership Agreement (CEPA), aimed to remove restrictions on the number of Hong Kong films released in the mainland. Films such as *Crouching Tiger Hidden Dragon* (2000), *Hero* (2003) and *The House of Flying Daggers* (2004) have put China on the global entertainment map. In a more popular category, the marshal arts 'action cinema' has global fans, while Chinese actors like Jacki Chan, Maggie Cheung Man-yuk, John Woo, Michelle Yeoh and Gong Li are internationally recognized (Morris *et al*, 2006).

As a regional Chinese television channel, backed by one of the world's biggest media conglomerates and sympathetic to the government in China, Phoenix is an important vehicle for international advertisers – in 2004, more than 90 per cent of Phoenix's revenue (which exceeded 1 billion HK dollars), came from advertising – though its capacity to raise critical issues and fight censorship – overt and covert – remained limited. Apart from their economic value as champions of consumerism, such channels can also create a greater sense of cultural solidarity among the Chinese-speaking peoples in the region. Liu Changle, the CEO of Phoenix and owner of Today's Asia, the company which owns Phoenix with Murdoch (the two own 75 per cent of the company), described Phoenix as a TV broadcaster that is different from mainland channels, different from Hong Kong channels, and also different from those in Taiwan. Phoenix claims to seek to transcend the various components of the Greater China and offer 'Chinese viewers a media service that is global in outlook and independent of local political attachments' (www.phoenixtv.com). Particularly significant will be its role in narrowing political differences between China and Taiwan, which Beijing refuses to recognize as a separate nation. Phoenix could contribute towards closer cultural ties among people of Chinese descent, one based on cultural and linguistic affinity rather than nationality.

Media exports from the South to the North

Apart from the regional broadcasters discussed above, which are likely to become more important in the coming years, there are also international players from the global South, whose presence is increasingly being felt in international cultural communication. In the evolution of channels like MBC, al-Jazeera and Phoenix, global, regional and national experiences interplay and produce something that is unique, the impact of which on media globalization is yet to be adequately assessed. The following case studies offer two main examples of this contraflow of cultural products from the South – Latin American telenovelas and the Indian film industry.

Case study

The transnationalization of telenovelas

The international acceptance of a genre like the soap opera is in itself an interesting story. This globally popular genre has evolved from its origins in French and English serial novels – through serializations in magazines and newspapers, to their adoption by US radio and television and then adaptation as a genre at a global level (Allen, 1995). One key example of cultural exports from the South to the North is the Latin American soap opera, the telenovela, which has become increasingly global in its reach (Large and Kenny, 2004; Martinez, 2005; Rosser, 2005). The transnationalization of telenovelas has been made possible through such televisual factories as Televisa in Mexico, Venevisión in Venezuela and Globo TV in Brazil, the leading producers of telenovelas, and their global distribution deals with such groups as Dori Media Group. The Brazilian media giant TV Globo and Mexico's Televisa (the world's largest producer of Spanish-language programming, which, in 2004, earned $175 million from programming exports, largely from telenovelas) are the two primary exporters of this popular genre of television across the globe (Rosser, 2005). By 2005 the telenovela – Latin America's major cultural export – had developed into a $2 billion industry, of which $1.6 billion was earned within the region and $341 million outside, being broadcast in 50 languages and dialects and reaching 100 countries (Martinez, 2005). The appeal of the genre lies in the melodramatic and often simplistic narrative, which can be understood and enjoyed by audiences in a wide variety of cultural contexts (Sinclair, 1999).

Though US-generated programmes, films and cartoons are widely shown on Latin American television channels, prime time is dominated by telenovelas (Fox, 1997). TV Globo, which made telenovela into an export product, is part of Rede Globo, one of the world's largest multimedia conglomerates, which owns Brazil's leading newspaper *O Globo* (founded 1925); Globosat satellite; the Globo radio system (inaugurated in 1944); a publishing firm; a music company; and a telecommunications firm (Mattelart and Mattelart, 1990). Launched in 1965 in collaboration with the US-based Time-Life group, TV Globo was instrumental in building a national network, based on the commercial television culture of the USA. With US financial, managerial and technological help, Globo was able to bring television to the masses in Brazil: though Time-Life withdrew in 1968, the US model continued to be the guiding principle for TV Globo. In the early years, the telenovelas were sponsored by transnational corporations such as Procter and Gamble, Colgate-Palmolive and Unilever. Gradually, however, production was taken over by Globo. This was made possible partly because of massive support from the Brazilian government.

TV Globo was aligned with the successive authoritarian governments following the 1964 military coup. The right-wing military dictatorships, which dominated Brazilian politics until 1985, used this powerful medium to legitimize their rule and shape public opinion. In return, the Globo group received special treatment from the Generals, who besides investing heavily in Brazil's telecommunications infrastructure – including national satellite networks – gave TV Globo most of government advertising. The launch of Brazil's first telecommunications satellite, Brazilsat, in 1985, facilitated the further expansion of TV Globo. Such government support not only enabled the commercialization of television, but also helped to create a sense of Brazilian national identity (Mattelart and Mattelart, 1990). As a result of the close ties with the military regime, the Globo group was allowed to have a virtual monopoly on media in Brazil, restricting alternative viewpoints to emerge in a country deeply divided in social and economic terms (Mader, 1993). TV Globo entered the international market in 1975, with exports of telenovelas to Portugal. *Gabriela*, a telenovela based on an adaptation of a best-selling novel, telecast daily in Portugal, was a major hit, leading to the charge of 'reverse colonization' (Lopez, 1995). In subsequent years, Brazilian telenovelas became extremely popular in Portugal and their style was adapted for domestic production. To reach a bigger audience in Latin America, TV Globo started dubbing its programmes in Spanish, the most widely spoken language in Latin America and also one of the fastest-growing languages in the USA.

One of TV Globo's biggest international successes was the historical romance *Escrava Isaura* (Isaura the Slave Girl), which was a great hit in Italy, France, the former Soviet Union and, particularly, in China, where 450 million viewers watched the series. The Chinese translation of the book on which it was based sold 300,000 copies (Oliveira, 1993).

Globo expanded its operations globally as television channels proliferated in the wake of the satellite revolution: in 1995 it established a consortium of DTH broadcasters with, among others, News Corporation and Televisa, to provide a range of programming to the continent. Since 1993, Globo has exported television formats even to well-established broadcasters such as the BBC, whose game show *Do the Right Thing* was adapted and licensed from TV Globo and based on the Brazilian format *Voce Decide* (You Decide), which has been adapted in 37 countries as diverse as China and Angola (Moran, 1998). In 1977, Globo was making an annual profit of $1 million from the export of telenovelas; in 2004 profits had reached $20 million. By

2006, TV Globo was producing hundreds of telenovelas and miniseries and exporting its programmes to more than 130 countries worldwide, annually selling around 26,000 hours of programmes in the international market – from Latin America to Southern and Eastern Europe, to Asia, Africa and the Arab world. Some of its most successful exports have included *Terra Nostra* (Our Land – broadcasting rights sold to 84 countries), *Escrava Isaura* (Isaura the Slave Girl – sold to 79 countries), *Laços de Família* (Family Ties – sold to 66 countries) (www.redeglobo.com.br). Telenovelas are edited to make them intelligible, with fewer specific Brazilian references, and many are dubbed in different languages, especially in Spanish for other Latin American countries, still the biggest market for such a genre.

The international success of TV Globo is based primarily on its commercial nature. In the advertising-driven media environment, with few regulations on what can be advertised, TV Globo has consistently used its programmes to promote consumer products, 'merchandising' being integrated into the narrative, either by actors directly advertising a product or through product placement, when the consumer items appear in the programme (Tufte, 2000). Apart from such crass commercialism, TV Globo also claims to use what it calls 'social merchandising', weaving public information – such as awareness of gender rights and birth control – into the plots. International organizations such as UNICEF have acknowledged the importance of such methods in reducing the infant mortality rate in Brazil.

It is debatable to what extent TV Globo reflects the realities of Brazilian life. Is it a localized version of US television, a 'creolization' of US commercial culture? Such a form of programming, common in much of Latin American television, it has been argued, could be seen as legitimizing free-market capitalism, substituting the government's hegemony with private initiative, which is also projected as the key link between national and international culture (Martin-Barbero, 1993). One key example of the contraflow is the growing export of telenovelas to the relatively affluent Latino population in the United States, which constitutes more than 13 per cent of the US population – 'the richest Hispanics in the world'. The availability and popularity of Latin American telenovelas in the USA has also been labelled 'reverse media imperialism' (Rogers and Antola, 1985). Such US-based networks as Univision ('reaching 98 per cent of US Hispanic Households') have imported telenovelas from Mexico, Brazil, Colombia, and Venezuela: in 2004 alone, it paid $105 million in licensing fees to Televisa (Martinez, 2005). As Bielby and Harrington have argued, this reverse flow has also influenced soap operas in the USA, leading to 'genre transformation', especially in the daytime soaps (Beilby and Harrington, 2005). Venezuelan scholar Daniel Mato has suggested that telenovelas help in the construction of a transnational 'hispanic' identity (Mato, 2005).

The success of telenovelas outside the geo-linguistic market of Spanish-Portuguese consumers shows the complexity of media consumption patterns. Such novelas as *The Rich Also Cry* were very successful in the 1990s in Russia, where Channel One Russia has signed a deal with Globo TV. Sony developed its first telenovela in 2003 – *Poor Anastasia* for Russian network CTC – while Germany's RTL2 broadcast Televisa's *Salome.* The telenovelas have also been popular in, among others, Romania and Bosnia (Martinez, 2005). This expansion into Central and Eastern Europe represents the trend towards transnationalization. The genre has become internationally popular, including in Germany, with the advent of domestically produced telenovelas, such as *Bianca: Road to Happiness,* produced by Grundy UFA and shown in 2004 on the public channel ZDF. In India, Sony successfully adapted the popular Colombian telenovela, *Betty la Fea,* into Hindi as *Jassi Jaissi Koi Nahin,* becoming one of the most popular programmes on Indian television (Large and Kenny, 2004). Encouraged by such successes, Globo was planning, in 2006, to launch an Indonesian telenovela channel, Televiva.

The transnationalization of telenovelas is a reality of global television, as one commentator noted:

> 'In all, about two billion people around the world watch telenovelas. For better or worse, these programmes have attained a prominent place in the global marketplace of culture, and their success illuminates one of the back channels of globalization. For those who despair that Hollywood or the American television industry dominates and defines globalization, the telenovela phenomenon suggests that there is still room for the unexpected.
>
> (Martinez, 2005)

However, it is important to remember that, unlike US media giants, TV Globo's primary market is among the Latin countries, and none of its telenovelas has had an international impact comparable with US soaps such as *Dallas* or the cult following of *Friends* or *Sex and the City.* The challenge that organizations such as Globo pose to the traditional dominance of the USA in the world audio-visual trade is, as one observer notes, 'more conceptual than real: that is, it has more to do with our theoretical common wisdom about that dominance than with the actual degree of commercial threat' (Sinclair, 1996: 51). Indeed, it can be argued that television channels such as TV Globo are instrumental in legitimizing consumerist values and are more often than not complementary rather than oppositional to the US-based media transnationals.

Case study

The other Hollywood – the Indian film industry

India is among the few non-Western countries to have made their presence felt in the global cultural market. Particularly significant, though largely ignored in mainstream international scholarship and journalistic writing on films, popular music and television, is India's $3.5 billion Hindi film industry based in Mumbai (formerly Bombay), the commercial hub of India. In terms of production and viewership it is the world's largest film industry: every year a billion more people buy tickets for Indian movies than for Hollywood films. In addition to productions from 'Bollywood', there are strong regional centres making films in India's other main languages, notably Tamil, Bangla, Telugu and Malayalam. More films are made in India each year than in Hollywood (*see* Chapter 4, Table 4.9), but their influence is largely confined to the Indian subcontinent and among the South Asian diaspora, though in recent years many 'crossover' films have changed this situation (Desai, 2004; Kaur and Sinha, 2005).

Within months of the invention of the motion picture by the Lumière brothers in France in 1895, films were being shown in Bombay and film production in India started soon afterwards, in 1897. In 1913, Govind Dhundiraj Phalke, better known as Dadasaheb Phalke (the father of the Indian film industry, in whose honour India's highest award for films is named), launched the first full-length feature film, *Raja Harishchandra*, based on the life of a mythological king of ancient India. In the silent era (1913–31), more than 1200 films were made in India (Rajadhyaksha and Willemen, 1999). In 1931, India entered the sound era and the first sound film – talkie – was Ardeshir Irani's *Alam Ara.* By the end of that year, 28 full-length feature films in three languages were released – of which 23 were in Hindi, 4 in Bangla and 1 in Tamil. Since then, the growth of feature films has been remarkable – from 84 in 1932 to 173 in 1942, to 233 in 1952, to 315 in 1962 (Rajadhyaksha and Willemen, 1999). Hindi films dominated these productions, but there were other major regional film industries, notably Tamil, Bangla, Telugu and Malyalam. In 1999, India boasted of being home to the largest film industry in the world, producing the highest number of films of any country. Given the size of India's 1 billion population and the place that cinema has among people's leisure activities, cutting across regional, class, gender and generational divisions, it remains the most popular form of entertainment (Mishra, 2002; Pendakur, 2003; Kaur and Sinha, 2005). Every day more than 14 million Indians see a movie – not only in urban and suburban areas, but also in rural parts of the country, often in makeshift cinema houses.

The unprecedented expansion of television in the 1990s and early 2000s was a boost for the movie industry, as many dedicated film-based pay channels have emerged. In addition, advancements in technology and the availability of satellite and cable television have ensured that Indian films are regularly shown outside India, dominating the cinema of South Asia and defining popular culture in the Indian subcontinent and among the South Asian diaspora. Hindi films are shown in more than 70 countries and are popular in the Arab world, in central and South East Asia and among many African countries. However, in terms of earning revenue from film exports, India is no match for the USA – India's share in the global film industry, valued in 2004 at $200 billion, was less than 0.2 per cent. One reason for the popularity of Indian films among other developing countries is their melodramatic narrative style, often a storyline which emphasizes dichotomies between the poor-pure-and-just vs rich-urban-and-unjust, enlivened with song and dance sequences. Films have also contributed to the burgeoning popular music industry, and a mainstream Indian film is unlikely to succeed without prominent musical support. Although most of the films are social and family-oriented dramas, Indian film-makers have also experimented with other major genres of cinema, such as historical, mythological, comic, supernatural and 'Western'.

Even before India became an independent nation, films from India were being exported to South East Asian and African nations (Barnouw and Krishnaswamy, 1980). In fact, within a year of the launch of sound movies, the Motion Picture Society of India (which in 1951 became the Film Federation of India) was established and a Hindi film weekly *Cinema Sansar* (Cinema World) had been launched.

The formative years of Indian cinema were profoundly influenced by the anticolonial movement (Kaul, 1998). A progressive message of communal harmony and national integration was fostered through films – extremely important in a country of very low literacy. Of particular significance was the contribution of the Indian People's Theatre Association (IPTA), whose 1946 film, *Dharti Ke Lal* (Children of the Earth), directed by prominent progressive writer Khwaja Ahmad Abbas, was the first film to receive widespread distribution in the Soviet Union, while the 1957 feature *Perdesi* (Foreigner) was the first Indo-Soviet co-production.

By the 1950s the mainstream Indian cinema was producing internationally known films which have since acquired the status of classics. Prominent among these were Raj Kapoor's 1955 sentimental and moral tale with progressive overtones, *Shri 420* (Mr 420), which became immensely popular in the Soviet Union; Guru Dutt's 1957 film *Pyaasa* (The Thirsty One), a tense melodrama, and the prominent director's 1959 autobiographical work *Kaagaz Ke Phool* (Paper Flowers), India's first cinemascope film, known for its brilliant camerawork. Mahboob Khan's 1957 national epic *Mother India* was a landmark commercial success, which acquired the status of an Indian *Gone with the Wind*. The first partly coloured movie, K. Asif's 1960 epic *Mughal-e-Azam*, based on the legend of princely romance during the reign of Mughal Emperor Akbar, is often considered India's most accomplished historical film.

There has been a progressive tradition within film-making, addressing such issues as exploitation based on class, caste or gender. Three prominent examples of this trend are Bimal Roy's 1953 realist drama *Do Bhiga Zameen* (Two Bhiga of Land) about land reform; Shambhu Mitra's 1957 film *Jagte Raho* (Stay Awake), which won the Grand Prix at Karlovy Vary Film Festival that year, and *Garam Hawa* (Hot Winds), directed by M. S. Sathyu, a powerful 1973 film about communal issues in the wake of India's partition.

However, it was not the star-studded movies, but a low-budget film in a regional language – Bangla – which put India on the international cinema map. Satyajit Ray's debut film *Pather Panchali* (Song of the Little Road), released in 1955, won international critical acclaim and continued to run for more than seven months in New York, setting a new record for foreign films released in the USA.

The film is part of the Apu trilogy, based on the works of noted Bengali novelist Bibhuthibhushan Bandhopadhyaya – the other two films in the trilogy were *Aparajito* (The Unvanquished), 1956, and *Apur Sansar* (The World of Apu), released in 1959. Ray's only non-Bengali feature was the 1977 film *Shatranj Ke Khiladi* (The Chess Players), based on a story by eminent Hindi writer Premchand. Ray was more than just an outstanding film-maker – he excelled in other creative areas too, being an author and painter, and editing and illustrating the children's magazine *Sandesh* (Message) (Robinson, 1989). He was presented with the *Legion d'honneur* by the French President François Mitterrand in 1990 and, in 1992, just a few weeks before his death, was awarded an Oscar for lifetime achievement in film.

Ray's influence was profound, inspiring a new generation of film-makers, contributing to a trend of 'parallel' cinema, which started with the 1969 film *Bhuvan Shome*, directed by noted Bengali film-maker Mrinal Sen, and followed by two other releases in the same year – Basu Chaterjee's *Sara Akash* (The Whole Sky) and *Uski Roti* (Our Daily Bread), directed by Mani Kaul. Other prominent films in this genre were the 1972 film *Maya Darpan* (Mirror of Illusion), directed by Kumar Shahani, *Ankur* (The Seedling), directed in 1973 by Shyam Benegal, and the critically acclaimed 1980 film *Aakrosh* (Cry of the Wounded) by Govind Nihalani.

Among the regional films this trend was to be seen in such films as Pattabhi Rama Reddy's 1970 Kannada feature *Samskara* (Funeral Rites) and in *Shantata! Court Chalu Aahe* (Silence! The Court is in Session), the 1971 political film directed by noted Marathi playwright Vijay Tendulkar. Internationally acclaimed regional film-makers include Ritwik Ghatak, the Bengali genius, best known for his 1960 film *Meghe Dhaka Tara* (The Cloudcapped Star), and Adoor Gopalakrishnan from the southern state of Kerala, best known for his 1977 film *Kodiyettam* (The Ascent).

Though critically acclaimed nationally and internationally and funded by state organizations such as the Film Finance Corporation (renamed the National Film Development Corporation in 1980), the so-called 'parallel cinema' has hardly made a dent in popular choice in films, which continues to revolve around musical films with an undemanding script and, increasingly, foreign locales. Most Indian and indeed foreign viewers of Indian films are more comfortable watching a fast-paced action movie, such as the 1975 megahit *Sholay* (Embers), a massively popular adventure film directed by Ramesh Sippy, or a musical family drama *Hum Aapke Hain Koun* (Who am I to you), directed in 1994 by Sooraj Barjatya. The globalization of Indian television has ensured that more and more Indian films are being watched by a varied international audience. This has made it imperative for producers to invest in subtitling to widen the reach of Indian films. The changing global broadcasting environment and the availability of digital television and online delivery systems means that Indian films will be available to new audiences. In 1999, B4U or Bollywood for You, Britain's round-the-clock digital television channel for Hindi movies, 'the first South Asian digital channel in the northern hemisphere', was launched. Indian film-makers are aiming to reach the coveted Northern markets, privileging scripts which interest the diasporic audience – by 2004 exports accounted for nearly 30 per cent of the industry earnings (FICCI, 2004; UNESCO, 2005a).

In 1995, *Dilwale Dulhaniya Le Jayenge* (The Brave Heart Will Take the Bride), starring Shah Rukh Khan, was the first major film to focus on an Indian family, based in Britain – the film had a 10-year uninterrupted run in a Mumbai cinema until 2005. Director Karan Johar's 1998 love story *Kuch Kuch Hota Hai* (Something is Happening), his 2001 family drama *Kabhi Khushi Kabhi Gham* (Sometimes Happiness, Sometimes Sorrow) and 2003 love triangle *Kal Ho Na Ho* (If Tomorrow Comes) – the first mainstream Indian film set entirely in the West – did extremely well in the overseas market. These successes have ensured that Indian films are being seen as a serious export earner. In 1999, the Indian Government passed a law exempting export earnings from films from tax. Subhash Ghai's love story *Taal* (The Beat) and Barjatya's 1999 musical, extolling the virtues of extended family *Hum Saath Saath Hain* (We Stand United), had the distinction of being the first Indian films to make it to the top 20 slot in the US film trade magazine *Variety*'s box office chart. One result of such interest is that diasporic film-makers such as Mira Nair (director of *Monsoon Wedding)* and the British-based Gurvinder Chaddha (director of *Bend It Like Beckham* and the 2003 film *Bride and Prejudice*, which earned more than $25 million worldwide) have acted as a bridge between Western and Indian popular cinema.

Indian film exports witnessed a 20-fold increase in the period 1989–99. Plans for joint ventures between Indian film producers and Hollywood giants received a boost with the decision of the Indian Government, announced in 2000, to allow foreign companies to invest in the Indian film industry. PricewaterhouseCoopers valued the entertainment and media sector in India at $7 billion in 2004 and it was expected to grow at about 14 per cent in the next five years, to reach over $10 billion by 2009 (FICCI, 2004). The globalization of Indian films can also be witnessed in the growing trend of non-Indian actors appearing in Indian films. Recent examples include British actress Antonia Bernath in the 2005 film *Kisna – the Warrior Poet*, shot simultaneously in Hindi and English, with the English print shortened by an hour to accommodate Western audiences. Another British actor, Toby Stephens, previously cast in the 2001 commercially and critically acclaimed *Lagaan* (Land Tax), played a key role in the 2005 historical film *Mangal Pandey: The Rising,* set in the colonial period, while British actress Alice Patten starred in the 2006 hit *Rang De Basanti.*

Though this may make Indian films more visible in the global market, there is a danger that they might lose their cultural distinctiveness. By 2005, however, such neologisms as 'Bollyworld' were being used – referring to an Indian cinema 'at once located in the nation, but also out of the nation in its provenance, orientation and outreach' (Kaur and Sinha, 2005: 16). The Indian Government and the corporate world see Indian popular culture as part of India's 'soft' power. During the 2006 World Economic Forum in Davos in Switzerland, iPods loaded with Indian popular and classical music, as well as CDs about the country's economic prowess, were distributed to delegates to the annual meeting of the world's most powerful corporations, to raise India's profile in the global community' in a $3 million public-private promotional campaign called 'India Everywhere', which included shows by film choreographer Shamak Davar (Kripalani, 2006).

As a UNESCO report noted:

> Indian film production is progressively catering to foreign audiences. Although small by comparison with American productions, the revenues generated by Indian movies abroad have registered a ten-fold expansion in the last 10 years. For the estimated $990 million earned by the Indian film sector in 2004, revenues from overseas have already reached $220 million. Today the value of Indian cultural and creative industries is estimated at $4.3 billion. This sector is growing at an annual rate close to 30 per cent and analysts forecast that exports may continue to grow by 50 per cent in the coming years. An important factor in this impressive performance is that Indian companies are succeeding in bringing international audiences to the cinemas, in addition to the traditional diaspora communities of the USA, the United Kingdom and the Middle East. This strategy includes expansion to non-traditional countries, both industrialised and emerging, such as Japan and China.
>
> (UNESCO, 2005a: 44)

These examples of a counterflow of cultural products in no way show that the Western media domination has diminished. There is a temptation, even a valorization, of seeing such a flow having the potential to develop counter-hegemonic channels at a global level. Indeed, as seen in the case of Zee in Chapter 5 and Phoenix in this chapter, both channels were modelled on transnational corporations and Phoenix is still part of a top media conglomerate. Their output too is relatively small and their global impact restricted to the diasporic communities, their primary target market. They are all market-driven private organizations for whom the most important consideration is to make a profit. Therefore, the emergence of regional players contributing to a 'decentred' cultural imperialism is not likely to have a significant impact on the Western hegemony of global media cultures.

Nevertheless, there does exist a blurring of boundaries, mixing of genres, languages and a contraflow of cultural products from the peripheries to the centres. The process of what has been called 'transculturation, hybridity and indigenisation' (Lull, 1995: 153) has sometimes made scholars enthuse about the possibilities of developing parallel cultural discourses. In the first decade of the twenty-first century, though the West continues to set the international cultural agenda, non-Western cultures are more visible than ever before. The international interest in Chinese and Korean cinema, the globalization of Afro-Caribbean style of music, and the growing popularity of Karaoke (Mitsui and Hosokawa, 1998) point to this trend. Japanese computer games, manga and anime are a major influence among the youth in the West. By 2006, the Japanese puzzle sudoku had become all the rage among newspaper readers in the Western world, with companies vying with each other to produce an electronic version of the number game for mobile telephones and hand-held devices.

In an age of globalization, an Indian film-maker Shekhar Kapur can direct Elizabeth, a quintessentially English feature film, while a Taiwanese-born director, Ang Lee, can make such 'Western' films as Jane Austen's *Sense and Sensibility* and Oscar-winning 'gay cowboy' movie *Brokeback Mountain*. Indian film musician A. R. Rahman composed a popular musical, *Bombay Dreams*, for audiences in Britain and the USA, as well as music for Chinese films. Hollywood hits such as The Matrix borrow filmic conventions from Tokyo and Hong Kong. West African beats mingle with Arabic tunes, which are adapted in Indian film songs – Brazilian soap operas are watched by Ghanaians; Tai Chi is becoming a popular activity with many Westerners – all these are indications of what has been called the postmodern sensibility. Such categories as 'world music', 'world cinema' and 'global culture' are routinely mentioned in media and academic discourses. Yet the desire to experience the new is balanced by that to protect cultural sovereignty. As Mahatma Gandhi, voted the Man of the Millennium in a BBC online poll, once remarked:

> I do not want my house to be walled in on all sides and my windows to be stuffed. I want the culture of all the lands to be blown about my house as freely as possible. But I refuse to be blown off my feet by any.

(cited in UNESCO, 1995)

chapter seven

International communication in the Internet age

Communication technologies were crucial in the establishment of European domination of the world during the era of colonial empires. The new technologies of the nineteenth century 'shattered traditional trade, technology, and political relationships, and in their place they laid the foundations for a new global civilisation based on Western technology' (Headrick, 1981: 177). If trains and ships facilitated the movement of manufactured products from one part of the world to another, fibre optics, satellites and the Internet have enabled the trade of information instantly across the globe. From telegraph to telephone, radio to television, computers and now the mobile Internet, international communication has been shaped by technological innovation. The convergence of telecommunication and computing and the ability to move all forms of data via the Internet revolutionized international information exchange (Castells, 2000a, 2000b, 2004). At the same time, information processing has become far cheaper and faster, bringing about what *Business Week* called 'the Internet age' (*Business Week*, 1999).

The digitization of images, text and sounds has increased exponentially the speed and volume of data transmission compared with analogue systems. The introduction of digital communication was closely linked to the availability of new fibre-optic cable for telephones and television, but even the constraint of laying cables has been removed with wireless transmission via satellite. Combined with the continually increasing growth in computing capacity and concomitant reduction in costs, the convergence of computing and communication technologies has opened up potential for unprecedented global interconnectedness through the Internet (UNDP, 2001, 2005a).

The dawn of the Internet age

The origins of the Internet (short for Inter-network) lie in the US Department of Defense's Advanced Research Projects Agency Network (APRANET), created in 1969 as a communication network linking top defence and civilian branches of the US administration in case of a Soviet nuclear attack. In 1983, APRANET was divided into military and civilian sections, with the latter giving rise to the Internet. For the next decade this operated as a network among US universities and research foundations The explosion in the use of the Internet took off with the establishment of the World Wide Web (WWW) in 1989, which began as a network of servers using a set of common interface protocols, developed by a British computer specialist, Tim Berners-Lee, of CERN in Geneva. Any individual using these protocols could set up their own 'home page' on the web. Each page or website is given a unique address or URL (universal resource locator) and Hypertext Transfer Protocol (HTTP) allows the standardized transfer of text, audio and video files, while the use of Hypertext Markup Language (HTML) enables links to be made from one document to another anywhere on the web (Hafner and Lyons, 1996; Berners-Lee and Fischetti, 1999).

In the history of communication, it took nearly 40 years for radio to reach an audience of 50 million, and 15 years for television to reach the same number of viewers – but it took the WWW just over three years to reach its first 50 million users (Naughton, 1999). The uptake of the Internet has been extraordinary: in 1995 it had just 20 million users – by 2000 it had 400 million; in 1993 there were just 400 websites in the world – by 2000 there were 200 million. This was made possible by the revolution in communication technologies – data transfer costing $150,000 in the 1970s was just 12 cents in 1999, while the speed of microprocessors has doubled every 18 months (UNDP, 2001). By 2006, the Internet, 'the fastest-growing tool of communication', was a global medium; from just 3 per cent of the world's population in 1995, by 2005 it was reaching more than 15 per cent, nearly a billion people, although 90 per cent of these lived in the industrialized countries. This breaks down as: North America, 30 per cent; Europe, 30 per cent; and Asia-Pacific, 30 per cent; with Sweden having the highest penetration rate (74 per cent). Other countries with high access rates included Hong Kong (71 per cent), Denmark (69 per cent) and the United States (69 per cent) (OECD, 2005; UNESCO, 2005b). The growing usage of broadband for enhanced capacity, speed and quality of data transmission follows a similar pattern of unequal distribution, as indicated by Table 7.1.

Table 7.1 Regional differences in Internet and broadband use

	Internet subscribers (millions)	Broadband subscribers (millions)	% of total subscribers	subscribers per 1000 inhabitants
Africa	5.8	0.1	2	0.17
Americas	97	47	49	57.29
Asia	157	60	40	19.16
Europe	114	40	36	51.34
Oceania	6.8	1.6	24	62.94
World	381	150	40	27.56

Source: ITU, figures for 2004. Reproduced with the kind permission of ITU

The mobile, wireless world

The convergence of the Internet and mobile telephony enabled by satellite communication amounts to a new telecommunications revolution. There was increasing realization that, despite the continuing expansion of telephone companies and cable TV providers to connect users to higher-speed lines, it would be cheaper for consumers to receive entertainment and information by satellite. Satellite communication also offers the widest possible customer base, given that even in heavily wired Western Europe and North America an estimated 30 per cent of customers are far from major population centres. The satellites in low, medium and geostationary orbits provide universal voice data, multimedia and 'Internet in the sky' services across the planet. For businesses, one key technological development (the arrival in 1999 of Wireless Application Protocol (WAP)) has enabled mobile telephones to offer Internet access and high-speed wireless 'value-added' services, contributing to the exponential growth of mobile telephony. While fixed telephone networks took more than 130 years to reach 1 billion subscribers, it took only 15 years for the mobile industry to rise from just 11 million subscribers in 1990 to 2 billion by 2005, a year when the number of mobile phones exceeded fixed lines in the world (ITU, 2005a). Table 7.2 and Figure 7.1 demonstrate the patterns of growth of mobile telephony.

Table 7.2 Mobile phone communication

Region	Subscribers (millions)	% of population	% of total phone subscribers
Asia	708	19	57
Europe	572	71	64
Americas	370	43	56
Africa	76	9	75
Oceania	20	63	59
World	1,752	28	59

Source: ITU, 2005, figures for 2004. Reproduced with the kind permission of ITU

Third-generation mobile systems have enabled Internet access at high speeds, and with the huge demand for mobile access to voice and broadband data services, this is creating a new industry. The world's leading manufacturers and operators of mobile telephones – Ericsson, Motorola, NTT DoCoMo, Vodafone and Nokia – are entering into alliances with network equipment companies to build a wireless Internet. In the new wireless world, the electronic organizer, personal computer and mobile phone are combined into one portable gadget connected to the Internet via satellite, enabling users to buy or sell shares, book tickets, shop online, listen to music, watch a video, receive the latest news or play online games. With broadband new services have been developed, such as high-speed Internet, e-commerce, entertainment and interactive services. In 2005, only 10 per cent of mobile

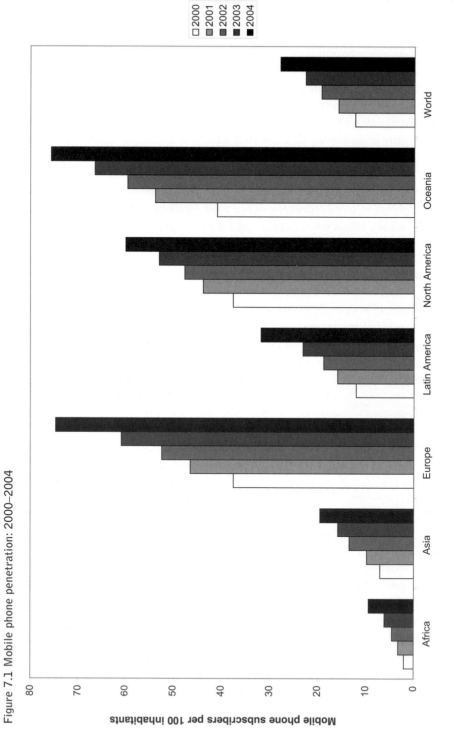

Figure 7.1 Mobile phone penetration: 2000–2004

Source: ITU, 2005

phones were capable of playing music; according to industry estimates, this will increase to 50 per cent by 2008.

The convergence of mobile technologies and broadband has opened up new revenue streams for selling music, games, gambling, adult content, video and personalization services to consumers worldwide. Mobile entertainment, according to industry estimates, is likely to generate revenues of more than $42 billion by 2010. As more mobile handsets become capable of playing video, TV brands are migrating to what has been called the 'fourth screen' – after cinema, TV and PC. Fox was the first network to recognize the potential for this smaller screen when, in 2005, it launched *24: Conspiracy 'mobisodes'* – a 24-part series of one-minute episodes linked to the hit drama shown on Fox, Sky and other Murdoch networks (Sandin, 2005). The success of Apple's iPod has triggered the creation of a new term for broadcasting – the podcast, a term coined by a *Guardian* journalist and rapidly taken up by mainstream broadcasters such as the BBC, which, in 2006, was podcasting a range of its radio programmes.

With interactive digital television, consumers can dial up the programme of their choice, or a film they have missed in the cinema, and pay for what they watch, or, if watching a live sporting event, viewers are able to pause and get instant replay at any time. Electronic programme guides select and inform viewers about programmes in which they might be interested. Tapeless VCRs, where images are 'streamed' to the computer, can also be set to record the user's favourite programmes or programmes on particular subjects, even without the user's knowledge. Although it offers viewers greater choice and freedom to use television in a more active way, such technology can also make consumers vulnerable to exploitation by direct marketing and advertising, as well as having implications for security and privacy. Another, quicker and cheaper technology for delivering multimedia information is the Data Broadcasting Network (DBN), which allows data services to use the existing infrastructure of DTH satellite broadcasters to distribute electronic content directly to personal computers. It uses a DBS broadcasters' extra satellite transponder space to broadcast content into the home via the consumer's satellite dish. With the satellite's footprint, many subscribers can be reached from just one transmission, making data broadcasting cheaper than upgrading the public telephone networks to be able to provide the high bandwidth required for multimedia services. This also opens up possibilities for DTH operators of new revenue streams. At the heart of the technological push to provide seamless communications is the potential use of the Internet as a global marketplace.

Harmonizing global technical standards

The unprecedented growth in the volume of international communication and the conduct of business through the Internet has made it imperative for transnational corporations to demand the harmonization of standards of equipment and frequencies so that telecommunication and broadcasting equipment can be used across national borders. They are taking a lead role in setting worldwide standards in new communication technologies, since the standardization of equipment and frequencies is an essential basis for servicing a global market. The USA, in co-operation with the ITU (which defines global telecommunication standards) and the Geneva-based International Organization for

Standardization (ISO), created a global communication system to include mobile telephony. In the early 1980s, the EU decided to impose a common standard within its borders – the Global System for Mobile Communications (GSM), which has become the standard of choice in most countries. The Nordic region, home to some of the world's leading mobile networks, was among the first to establish a cellular standard (the Nordic Mobile Telephone system, NMT), creating a market for regional equipment manufacturers. Even though NMT never became the dominant standard globally, it provided Nokia with experience in producing mobile phones. Japan has also developed its own standard – Personal Digital Cellular (PDC).

In mobile telephony, as in other communication arenas, such as the Internet, the US Government promoted the private sector development of technical standards, set up and guided by 'the requirements and processes of the marketplace', and opposed efforts by governments to impose standards or to use standards for electronic commerce as non-tariff trade barriers (FCC, 1999). In 1997, the Steering Committee of Global Standards Conference, comprising TNCs as well as governments, endorsed private sector leadership in standards development. Mobile or cellular networks evolved from 'first-generation' analogue networks to 'second-generation' digital systems, which for a period operated as a mix of analogue and digital systems, with different networks often co-existing in the same country. The ITU did not issue technical recommendations for first- or second-generation mobile systems. However, the unprecedented growth of mobile networks forced the ITU to create a global standard for 'third-generation' wireless, thus eliminating existing incompatibility between rival standards. Third-generation networks used a much higher frequency, producing a quantum leap in the capacity available and making it possible to download data at high speeds and quality, preparing the way for services such as interactive games. The ITU's International Mobile Telecommunications-2000 initiative brought together different types of networks – cellular, cordless, wireless and satellite systems – and thus enabled the possibility of seamless global roaming in which users can communicate across borders, using the same telephone number and handset.

It is in the interests of the countries and corporations that dominate global trade to ensure that electronic commerce operates in a free-market environment. Within the WTO, the USA argued that new regulations should not be imposed upon online service providers that might hinder e-commerce. Under US pressure the WTO's Ministerial Conference adopted a declaration in 1998 committing members to refrain from imposing customs duties on electronic transmissions. The USA demanded a more inclusive Information Technology Agreement II, to further liberalize global trade in information technologies. Its policy was unambiguous: 'enforce existing agreements and secure new agreements to make electronic commerce 'a seamless global marketplace' to ensure 'a free flow of commerce' (US Government, 1999).

The Internet and a 'free flow of commerce'

Technological developments, combined with the liberalization in trade and telecommunications, have acted as catalysts for e-commerce. This has been made possible largely because of the opening up of global markets in telecommunications services and information technology products that are 'the building blocks for electronic commerce' as a result of the WTO agreements discussed in Chapter 3. Trade on the Internet has taken hold very quickly (*see* Table 7.3). The Internet has dramatically lowered transaction costs and facilitated online transnational retail and direct marketing. The 'e-corporations' operating in a 'net-centric world' break businesses free of their geographic moorings.

Table 7.3 E-commerce in the USA (billion $)

	2000	2003
Manufacturing e-commerce		
E-commerce	756	843
Total manufacturing	4208	3980
Wholesale trade e-commerce		
E-commerce	241	387
Total wholesale trade	2742	2946
Retail e-commerce		
E-commerce	28	56
Total retail	3059	3275
Selected services e-commerce		
E-commerce	37	50
Total selected services	4647	5077

Source: UNCTAD, 2005a

Though, as Table 7.3 shows, most e-trading is between businesses, it is also having a profound effect on the retail market – online business is undermining offline transactions. Increasingly, global trade in computer software, entertainment products, information services and financial services is taking place using the Internet. In the USA, the world's largest market for e-commerce, a majority of Americans now shop online, with computer software, airline tickets and books being among the main products bought (UNCTAD, 2005a). The so-called 'webonomics' favours the world's rich countries. In 2004, three portals – AOL, MSN and Yahoo! – accounted for more than one-third of the time consumers spent online, while the three along with Google accounted for 52 per cent of US online advertising spending. As monetary transactions via the Internet become more secure and new services are offered, e-commerce is likely to gain more converts: in 2004, the worldwide commercial backbone services and the broader network services industry sales were estimated to be $1.3 trillion, and among the 300 operators that provided such services, the predominance of US-based companies was clear, in spite of the growing decentralization of the Internet, as Table 7.4 shows (UNCTAD, 2005a).

Table 7.4 Top 10 companies on the Net

Company*	Unique visitors (millions)
Microsoft (MSN)	107.4
Yahoo!	97.4
Time Warner (AOL)	96.9
Google	77.3
US Government	53.8
eBay	53.4
InterActiveCorp.	40.9
Amazon	38.6
RealNetworks	32.9
Walt Disney Internet Group	32.3

Note: * Parent companies owning multiple domains or URLs
Source: ITU, figures for 2005. Reproduced with the kind permission of ITU

One of the biggest potential growth areas for e-commerce is Asia, which in 1998 had just over 14 million people online, and an estimated 364 million by 2006, accounting for 36 per cent of the world's Internet users. With its economy growing steadily for the last two decades and its gradual integration with the global economy, particularly since joining the WTO in 2001, China was emerging as a major market for e-commerce and a formidable economic power. Recognizing this, US corporations began to make deals with Chinese companies – Yahoo! launched a Chinese site in 1998, while News Corporation was involved in developing two websites, ChinaByte and CSeek. In 1999, the most popular Chinese-language portal, Sina, was backed by Goldman Sachs, Sohu by Intel and Dow Jones, while China.com was supported by AOL; Google launched a China-specific search engine in 2006.

Case study

The 'Googlization' of global communication

If Microsoft dominated global electronic communication for much of the 1990s and continues to be the world leader in the computer software industry in the twenty-first century, Google has changed the way information is accessed, processed and used around the world. And if Bill Gates, the world's richest individual and founder of Microsoft, has the status of an international icon, Larry Page and Sergey Brin, the two research students from Stanford University who set up Google, have within a very short span of time acquired global fame (Vise and Malseed, 2005; Battelle, 2005; Lanchester, 2006).

Derived from the mathematical term 'Googol' (1 followed by 100 zeros), Google is the world's largest and fastest Internet search engine, making more than 100 million searches every day and covering 8 billion web pages. It was founded in 1998, became a public company in 2004 and by 2006 was the world's fastest-growing corporation, with a market capitalization of $129 billion. With the digital revolution has come information overload and the problem of finding what you want on the net, creating the need for search engines. Its consumer-friendly service has made Google the leader of online search engines (Battelle, 2005). Though the company prides itself on providing free services, as its mission states: 'organizing the world's information and making it universally accessible and useful' – these are paid for by advertising. The 'sponsored links' which appear on the results page are paid for by people who bid for specific words or combinations of words (Vise and Malseed, 2005; Battelle, 2005).

Given the range of services that Google provides – from email to shopping, from academic resources to news, music and television programming – it has become the first port of call for many seeking online information (see Table 7.5). So pervasive is its influence that the word 'google' has become a verb in its own right.

The unprecedented popularity of Google among the users of the Internet has raised alarm bells among established businesses, as well as governments. Concerns have been raised, for example, about its high-resolution satellite imagery, including detailed maps of sensitive locations, which could be used by hostile groups nationally and internationally. Media and telecom companies are also worried about losing audiences to Google News, which draws from more than 4500 news sources, or to Google Talk, which can make transnational telephony as cheap as the cost of local calls. Publishers could also lose huge revenues if Google Book Search were to realize its promise of making 'the full text of all the world's books searchable by anyone'. In 2006, Google was digitizing millions of books from the libraries of the world's three leading universities: Michigan, Stanford and Oxford, as well as providing access to the out-of-copyright volumes.

There are also concerns about privacy: Google's Desktop Search tool searches for information on users' own computers and every search is logged on Google's database and stored indefinitely. The company also installs a cookie on the computer of everyone who uses it, which helps log that user's searches, and since every computer has a unique IP address, visits to websites can be traced back to the computer making them. In addition, Google's superfast email service, Gmail, which has shown as robust a growth as Hotmail, can be scanned as well as used for advertisements (Lanchester, 2006).

Table 7.5 Google search and services

Froogle	'Smart shopping' search service
Gmail	E-mail service
Google Base	Classified advertisements
Google Book Search	Full text of books
Google.com	General search engine
Google Data	Data service
Google Earth	Satellite maps and imagery
Google Groups	Create or search discussion groups
Google Images	Pictures, 2 billion images
Google Maps	Country and street maps
Google Mobile	Mobile devices
Google News	Global news from 4,500 sources
Google Scholar	Academic articles
Google Talk	Internet telephony
Google Video Beta	TV service
Music Search	Online music
Translation	Translation service
Toolbar	Searching information on users' own PCs

Source: Google.com

Google has many country- and language-specific search engines, but when, in early 2006, it started a Chinese version, it came in for strong criticism that it had agreed to censorship by the Chinese authorities in order to operate in potentially the world's largest market. In fact, Google had been involved in China since 2005, when it acquired part of Baidu, China's biggest search engine.

Google has revolutionized the manner in which people can access and process information. The turbo speed with which this can be done is astounding – within seconds one can find information on any topic or event. However, some might argue that such speed may also contribute to intellectual laziness and plagiarism, and that a generation is growing up with a tendency to skim the surface of an issue rather than make an effort to go deeper into it.

Nevertheless the search engine has enabled a quantum shift in the volume and quality of information that can be procured – from around the world and at speeds unimaginable even at the beginning of the twenty-first century, and free of charge as long as one has access to the Internet. As digital connectivity increases and the Internet becomes multi-vocal, the 'Googlization' of communication is likely to become global.

Media online

The Internet has emerged as the fastest-growing part of the media sector. With the reducing cost of computers and telephone networks, more and more people are connecting to the Internet for their media needs – whether for information or entertainment. E-retailers such as online bookseller Amazon or e-Bay have customers across the globe. With the convergence between the Internet and television, media corporations are developing strategies that operate across multiple platforms. The merger of America Online and Time Warner to create an Internet-based media giant is indicative of the commercial potential of this new medium. Signed in 2000, the deal marked the coming of age of the Internet, bringing together television, film, radio, publishing and computing. In this marriage of the old and the new media, AOL provided its Internet subscriber service via Time Warner's huge cable network, while the media giant used AOL's customer base to gain new consumers for its media products.

Founded in 1985, America Online has become one of the world's biggest Internet companies, whose stock value increased from $5 billion in 1996 to $164 billion at the beginning of the twenty-first century. One of America's largest Internet service providers (ISP), AOL also owned another well-known ISP, CompuServe, as well as Netscape, then the most widely used browser among 'net-izens' worldwide. Its informal style helped to make AOL famous, promoting online 'chat rooms' for people looking for romance. It gave the world the message 'You've got mail!', later the title of a successful Hollywood film about a love story blossoming in virtual space. With the number of Internet users rising rapidly, all the major media corporations see the potential of using the new medium to exploit synergies between their print, broadcast and online operations in a multimedia environment, which is increasingly interactive. BBC Online and CNN.com, both credible news portals, encourage interactivity, enabling audiences to join live debates.

Within a year of the development of the WWW, most major newspapers in the USA had started a web edition and all the major broadcasters had a presence on the Internet. In the initial years these were seen more as a supplement to the main newspaper or magazine rather than entities in their own right, though apart from the *Wall Street Journal* no newspaper on the web was making a profit. In Britain, *The Guardian* was one of the pioneers of online news, with its Guardian Unlimited, which by 2006 had more than

11 million readers, in contrast to the circulation of its print edition of around 400,000. A web presence has become an integral part of media organizations, seen as a new media platform rather than an extension of existing media, not only in the media-rich North, but increasingly across the world (Ahlers, 2006). There was also a trend among transnational media to localize by translating content into major languages – for example, CNN has dedicated websites in Arabic, Japanese, Korean and Turkish.

Media organizations have regular email-alerting services, distributing customized news and information straight to the consumer – without charge. With mobile telephones linked to the Internet, news has become instant and personalized. Now the news comes to subscribers rather than the other way round. With WAP, phones were able to offer direct access to the Internet, triggering fears that the newsroom would become redundant. CNN, which gave the world the concept of *Headline News*, launched in 1981 in the USA to update viewers on news every 30 minutes, took the lead again by providing a personalized service through its alliance with Nokia to offer news that was specifically designed for phones. Since 1999, CNN has also been running MyCNN, a personalized news service. Other Internet content providers too were tailoring their products for phone users. Though there has been a proliferation of media outlets, paralleled with a fragmentation of audience, much of online news content was still on the websites of old news media, dominated by a few brand names. A survey in the USA found that for three years running – 2003–2005 – Yahoo News, CNN, MSNBC and AOL News were the four major news sites (Project for Excellence in Journalism, 2006).

In this media environment, the boundaries between advertising and programming are constantly blurring. The growth of cable and satellite television has already made the task of selling products less cumbersome and the development of interactive television and online retailing means that advertisers will no longer have to conduct expensive and time-consuming market research, but will have access to relevant information about individuals' leisure and consumption habits. In the age of narrowcasting, the consumers are self-selected on such specialist channels as MTV, ESPN or CNN, and their purchasing patterns and predilections can be relatively easy to monitor for advertisers.

The international media survive on advertising. Programme production on television would be prohibitive if it were dependent on subscribers only, while newspapers and magazines would have to double their cover price if they were not supported by advertising. However, advertising on the Internet can be more complex (Hollis, 2005). Surfers may just ignore the advertisers' logos on the margins of the screen, unlike TV, where advertisement breaks in the middle of movies or TV programmes are the norm. Despite accounting for a small proportion of global advertising, the growing commercialization of the Internet and its increasing use among consumers are likely to make it a sought-after advertising medium: according to a study by PricewaterhouseCoopers, in 2004 advertisers in the USA spent $9.6 billion on Internet advertising. With the availability of digital technology, online advertising has become very sophisticated, using high-quality streaming audio and video and animation, the so-called 'rich media' experience.

Advertisers recognize that, increasingly, a large portion of the revenue for online media companies comes directly from the consumers, through satellite and cable TV subscriptions, buying DVDs or downloading music or movies via broadband access, rather than from advertising or sponsorship. The new online media environment offers the possibilities of avoiding pervasiveness of advertising, through such devices as pop-up blockers. For television, such technology as TiVo and DVRs has given viewers capability to skip advertisements, and, as the convergence between television and the Internet becomes more acceptable, this trend is likely to grow: in 2004, Yahoo! and Google had already launched video search engines, while distributing video content remained a key part of the media strategies of the three major portals – Yahoo!, MSN and AOL. In such an environment, advertisers are using innovative approaches to sell products, including producing 'advermovies, advergames and other forms of advertainment', so that consumers download the advertisements or copy and forward their URLs for wider circulation (Bruner, 2005).

Given the nature of the Internet, online advertising can be used by corporations to record not only every transaction, but also which advertisement the consumer clicks on and how long they stay on it. Apart from making one-to-one marketing possible, this type of information has security and privacy implications, since it can also be misused by corporations or governments. By being able to monitor and record patterns of Internet use, governments can control citizens' political activities, while businesses can have access to private information – about bank accounts, insurance details and spending habits of consumers, which can be traded for marketing purposes.

Case study

The globalization of infotainment and edutainment

The growing commercialism of mass media, especially of television, as a result of privatization, deregulation and the opening up of new markets, has changed the ecology of broadcasting. The shift from public-service to ratings-conscious television, broadcasting to a heterogeneous global audience and dependent on corporate advertising, has implications for news agendas and editorial priorities (Franklin, 1997; Gitlin, 2002).

The perceived dilution of news and information as a result of a global market-driven journalism has become a concern for media theorists in relation to its impact on the public sphere. In the 1970s, years before the media globalization and commercialism of airwaves, the US media critic Neil Postman argued that public discourse was assuming the form of entertainment (Postman, 1985). In the era of real-time global communication, it is possible that the speed and quantity of news is undermining its quality, accuracy and context. In Europe, home to public-service broadcasting, many have called for strengthening the public-service ethos of journalism.

According to a UNESCO definition:

> Public Service Broadcasting (PSB) is broadcasting made, financed and controlled by the public, for the public. It is neither commercial nor state-owned, free from political interference and pressure from commercial forces. Through PSB, citizens are informed, educated and also entertained. When guaranteed with pluralism, programming diversity, editorial independence, appropriate funding, accountability and transparency, public service broadcasting can serve as a cornerstone of democracy
>
> (UNESCO, 2006a)

In Britain, for example, the BBC has been partly financed through the licence fee paid by the British public, so that, at least in theory, programme-makers do not have to chase ratings, and make quality programmes, which 'inform, educate and entertain', in that order. The proliferation of all-news channels has also impacted on European news networks, where there is a tendency to move away from a public-service news agenda – privileging information and education over the entertainment value of news – to a more market-led, 'tabloid', version of news, with its emphasis on consumer journalism, sports and entertainment.

However, contemporary journalism, especially on TV, has to operate in a fiercely competitive, commercial and increasingly fragmented news market, which in order to attract consumers is adopting the form of 'infotainment'. This can be seen as part of a general tendency in television, described by French sociologist Pierre Bourdieu as 'demagogic simplification' (Bourdieu, 1998).

Emerging during the late 1980s, the term 'infotainment' has become a buzzword – a neologism that refers to an explicit genre-mix of 'information' and 'entertainment' in news and current affairs programming. The phenomenon, particularly prominent in television news, also describes a kind of news where style triumphs over substance, the mode of presentation becoming more important than the content. Infotainment appears to be the answer to attracting the 'me' generation of media users, prone to channel-hopping and zapping, as well as more inclined towards online and mobile news. Influenced by a postmodernist MTV-style visual aesthetics, as well as SMS language, this generation is used to visual acceleration and has little patience for complex narrative structures of news bulletins.

Infotainment as a genre makes use of visual forms that first emerged in the production of TV commercials and music videos, styles that are now influencing news presentation, including fast-paced visual action in a postmodern studio, computer-animated logos, eye-catching visuals and rhetorical headlines from an often glamorous anchor person. Such styles of presentation, with their origins in the ratings-driven commercial television news culture of the USA, are becoming increasingly global, as news channels attempt to reach more viewers and keep their target audiences from switching channels or abandoning news networks altogether.

While this mode of communication may seem more inclusive and potentially liberatory, the implications for the transmission of the public information necessary for democratic discourse are grave (Sparks and Tulloch, 2000). In this age of ever shorter sound- and sightbites, the question arises as to whether this 'turbo news' can allow a critical assessment and reflection of the content presented, or whether information overload erodes the potential for anything other than a superficial response.

In the era of multimedia journalism, reporters have to work under the tremendous pressure of 'deadlines every minute,' leaving them little time to investigate a story, research and reflect on a 'live' event before it is transmitted. Their editors want to make the story as timely and dramatic as possible. In wartime reporting, when a great deal of disinformation/misinformation is in circulation, the journalist's task of sifting truth from half-truths and rumours becomes even more complicated (Thussu and Freedman, 2003).

One result of the proliferation of news outlets is a growing competition for audience and, crucially, advertising revenue, at a time when interest in news is generally declining. In the USA, audiences for network television peak-time news bulletins declined substantially, from 90 per cent of the television audience in the 1960s to 30 per cent in 2000, partly as a result of many, especially younger, viewers opting for online news sources (Project for Excellence in Journalism, 2006). In Britain, the audience for current affairs programming fell by nearly 32 per cent between 1994 and 2001 (Hargreaves and Thomas, 2002).

News gathering, particularly foreign news, is an expensive operation, requiring high levels of investment, and, consequently, media executives are under constant pressure to deliver demographically desirable audiences for news and current affairs programming to contribute to profits, or at least avoid losses. In the USA, one major recent development has been the acquiring of key news networks by conglomerates whose primary interest is in the entertainment business: Viacom-Paramount owns CBS; ABC is part of the Disney empire; CNN is a key component of AOL-Time Warner and Fox Network is owned by News Corporation. This shift in ownership is reflected in the type of stories that often get prominence on television news – stories about celebrities from the world of entertainment, for example, thus strengthening corporate synergies (Bennett, 2003).

Another indication of the growing popularity of infotainment is the global expansion of non-fiction television, of such hybrid genres as docusoaps and 'reality TV', which combine, often skilfully, the factual approach of documentary narrative with the entertainment values of television drama, thus blurring the boundaries between fact and fiction (Fürsich, 2003; Mathjis *et el*, 2004; Hill, 2005). Though these new genres of television may be making more audiences interested in television news, this seems to be happening at the expense of serious factual programming, which they often replace, with the danger of further eroding the level of public understanding of global affairs. A report from the Third World and Environment Broadcasting Project, a consortium of UK-based non-governmental organizations, noted that 'increasingly prominent within factual international programming are genres that reveal little about the realities of life for non-British people living outside this country: travel programmes; series following British adventurers; documentaries about 'Brits abroad' and reality game-shows in 'exotic' locations' (Barnett and Dover, 2004).

The situation is worse in the USA, with a much longer history of commercialism, where news has further reduced its already small window on the world. A Pew survey showed 'powerful evidence that broad interest in international news is most inhibited by the public's lack of background information in this area' (Pew Center, 2002). Critics argue that media are privileging softer stories over hard-nosed analysis and that this contributes to an erosion of the public sphere in a Habermasian sense, where the consumer is unable to differentiate between public information and corporate propaganda.

In a media-saturated world, education too has been commodified and globalized, as the Internet through satellite offers a new market for educational services internationally. As this technology expands and becomes more affordable, distance learning has potential as a global industry. Multimedia universities may be the answer to providing education to students across the globe, and already many universities are offering their courses through the Internet. The world's major distance-learning institutions, such as Britain's Open University, Chinese Television University and India's Indira Gandhi National Open University, are developing into significant players in global online education. However, there is a danger that in a commercialized system, when education becomes a service industry under GATS, open to the market forces, the university may lose its traditional role (Bok, 2003). It is also possible that public education might be undermined by transnational private educational enterprises, which may be more interested in 'edutainment', and use the media power of global giants like Microsoft and Disney to project their courses around the world. And these may be delivered through digital mechanisms: by 2006, McGraw-Hill was already producing, through Cisco Systems Global Learning Network, course-specific articles and websites for personal digital assistants (PDAs) in English, Spanish and Portuguese.

However, making education entertaining without sacrificing quality can have tangible benefits, such as the US children's programme *Sesame Street,* broadcast around the world. An increasing number of prime-time BBC documentaries are now made in conjunction with the Open University, and are positioned as the first stage in a 'learning journey', which hopes to engage viewers with the subject and encourage them to take follow-up academic courses. It has been suggested that media can be harnessed successfully to educate in an entertaining manner through the so-called entertainment-education paradigm, defined as 'the process of purposely designing and implementing a media message to both entertain and educate, in order to increase audience members' knowledge about an educational issue, create favourable attitudes, shift social norms and change overt behaviour' (Singhal and Rogers, 2004: 5).

Distance learning can revolutionize education, especially in the developing world – the world has witnessed a gradual improvement in literacy levels. According to UNESCO, the global literacy rate increased from 56 per cent in 1950 to 70 per cent in 1980, 75 per cent in 1990 and 82 per cent in 2000, and is expected to reach 86 per cent by 2015. Despite wars, conflict and human and natural disasters, the world has shown an extraordinary growth in literacy: in the middle of the nineteenth century only about 10 per cent of the world's adults could read or write; by 2000, more than 80 per cent had minimal reading and writing skills. This despite the fact that the global population has increased from about 1.2 billion in 1850 to over 6.4 billion in 2005 (UNESCO, 2006b). However, worldwide more than 771 million adults were still illiterate in 2000 and therefore the potential of mass media for education remains hugely under-explored – a fact exacerbated by the lack of information and technological infrastructure in the global South.

Digital copyright and regulation

A significant proportion of e-commerce, such as music, video or publishing, involves the sale and licensing of intellectual property. To promote this trade, sellers must feel sure that their intellectual property will not be stolen and buyers must know that they are obtaining authentic products. International agreements to establish effective copyright, patent and trademark protection are therefore necessary to prevent piracy and fraud. While technology, such as encryption, can help combat piracy, a legal framework is necessary to protect intellectual property, and to provide effective recourse when piracy occurs.

For TNCs it is critical that the legal framework for electronic commerce is governed by principles valid across international borders. Protection of copyrighted works – including motion pictures, computer software and sound recordings – disseminated via the Internet, performances and sound recordings in the digital environment have brought the issue of intellectual property to the fore. New formats for storing music, from MP3 to Apple's iPod, make it very easy to share, over the Internet, recordings that can be played on PCs as well as mobile devices. Listeners downloaded billions of songs from websites free of charge, threatening the $38 billion-a-year recording industry. Now corporations are encouraging consumers to pay for downloads by providing attractive and affordable products: in 2006, Universal Pictures blockbuster *King Kong* became the first movie available to download, while Murdoch's Sky network in Britain launched an online version of its movie channel, allowing consumers to download up to 200 films. Digital technologies make the tracking of copyright infringements more difficult as any intellectual property encoded as a digital data stream can be copied perfectly via the Internet. Digital technology has also threatened traditional methods of distribution, when text messages, images, audio and video can all be distributed electronically. This issue is not completely new: in the 1960s, publishers tried to restrict photocopies, the recording industry fought hard to stop development of magnetic cassette recorders and film-makers tried to stop the spread of low-cost video cassette recorders.

International treaties for the protection of copyrights, notably the Berne Convention for the Protection of Literary and Artistic Works, provide nations with a means of protecting copyrighted works under their own laws. In 1996, the World Intellectual Property Organization (WIPO), a UN specialized agency, which promotes the protection of intellectual property rights, updated the Berne Convention and provided new protection for performers and producers of sound recordings by adopting two new treaties – the WIPO Copyright Treaty and the WIPO Performances and Phonograms Treaty (commonly referred to as the 'Internet Treaties'). Both treaties – which entered into force in 2002 – include provisions relating to technological protection and copyright management information and facilitate the commercial applications of online digital communications.

The USA has consistently pressured countries to implement the WTO's Agreement on Trade-Related Aspects of Intellectual Property (TRIPS), which came into force in 1996, and to join the two WIPO treaties. It has demanded that all countries establish laws and regulations that provide protection for copyrighted works, and that these are implemented and enforced. Another significant effect on electronic commerce is the issue of legal protection for databases.

One major lobbying group demanding stringent regulations to protect intellectual property is the International Intellectual Property Alliance (IIPA). It was formed in 1984 to represent US copyright-based industries – films, videos, recordings, music, business software, interactive entertainment software, books and journals. The IIPA consists of the American Film Marketing Association; the Association of American Publishers; the Business Software Alliance; the Interactive Digital Software Association; the Motion Picture Association of America; the National Music Publishers' Association and the Recording Industry Association of America. According to a 2005 report, *Copyright Industries in the U.S. Economy*, prepared for the IIPA, the estimate for trade losses in 2005 due to piracy, based on preliminary data, was $15.8 billion (*see* Table 7.6) with global losses estimated at $30–35 billion.

Table 7.6 Losses due to copyright piracy

Product	Amount ($ million)
Business software	8,028
Records and music	2,563
Motion pictures	1,976
Entertainment software	2,653
Books	607
Total	**15,827**

Source: IIPA press release, 13 February 2006

The significance of intellectual property in the US economy can be gauged from the fact that the intellectual property income of the USA jumped from $1.1 billion in 1970 to $4.8 billion in 1983 and $13.8 billion in 1991 (OECD, 1993). In 1997, in the USA, the copyright industries accounted for $348.4 billion, or 4.3 per cent of the GDP. The foreign sales and exports of the copyright industries were $66.85 billion. Between 1977 and 1997 their share of GDP grew more than twice as fast as the remainder of the economy, while employment in these industries more than doubled, to 3.8 million. By 2002, the total copyright industries amounted to 12 per cent of the US economy, or $1254 trillion in GDP (IIPA, 2004).

Organizations such as the IIPA were instrumental in including TRIPS in the Uruguay Round of GATT and most developing countries were obliged to be in full compliance with TRIPS requirements by 2000. The extension of this international intellectual property regime has raised concerns among many developing countries, which see these as new taxes on knowledge, aimed to benefit the TNCs – according to the UN, industrialized Northern countries hold more than 90 per cent of all patents worldwide. This can block access to new technologies' innovation and knowledge diffusion and restrict the competitive power of developing countries (Bettig, 1996; UNESCO, 2005b).

Another major area for concern is the possibility of conflict between Internet domain names, which function as a source identifier on the Internet, and trademark rights, if the same or similar trademarks for similar goods or services are registered in different countries. As Tables 7.7 and 7.8 demonstrate, the disparity between the top 10 and lowest 10 countries in terms of numbers of hosts is striking: more than 25 million for Japan as against just 1 for Sudan. The United States, with total domain name hosts of under 2.5 million in 2006, does not figure in the top 10 countries, as many US-based corporations may be registered under .net and .com domains. As the use of domain names as source identifiers has increased, the courts have attributed intellectual property rights to them.

The US Government played a crucial role in the privatization of the Internet domain name system (DNS), when, in 1998, in alliance with TNCs, it set up the Internet Corporation for Assigned Names and Numbers (ICANN) to manage the system (Hamelink, 2000). Under a 1999 agreement signed with the US Government, ICANN can accredit domain name registrars from around the world to provide competitive registration services for the .com, .net and .org domains (nearly 395 million such domain names were operating in 2006, *see* Table 7.9).

The question of Internet governance dominated the deliberations of UN World Summit on the Information Society (WSIS). A 40-member Working Group on Internet Governance

Table 7.7 Domain name distribution – top 10 countries

Country	Domain name	Total number of hosts
Japan	jp	25,044,349
Netherlands	nl	14,976,121
Italy	it	11,279,864
Germany	de	10,013,373
France	fr	7,018,115
Britain	uk	6,655,412
Australia	au	6,129,033
Brazil	br	5,143,234
Canada	ca	4,008,534
Poland	pl	3,978,760

Source: Internet Software Consortium (http: //www.isc.org/), figures for January 2006

Table 7.8 Domain name distribution – lowest 10 countries

Country	Domain name	Total number of hosts
Republic of Congo	cg	1
Sudan	sd	1
Sierra Leone	sl	1
Somalia	so	1
Liberia	lr	3
Haiti	ht	5
Chad	td	5
Comoros	km	5
Cape Verde	cv	8
Bhutan	bv	8

Source: Internet Software Consortium (http: //www.isc.org/), figures for January 2006

Table 7.9 Distribution of top-level domain names by host count

	Domain	Hosts
net	Networks	174,654,486
com	Commercial	116,041,415
edu	Educational	10,054,012
mil	US Military	2,172,422
org	Organizations	1,641,550
Total		394,991,609

Source: Internet Software Consortium (http: //www.isc.org/), figures for January 2006

(WGIG), comprising governments, corporations and NGOs, was set up by the United Nations after the first phase of WSIS, held in Geneva in 2003. It defined Internet governance as 'the development and application by governments, the private sector and civil society, in their respective roles, of shared principles, norms, rules, decision-making procedures, and programmes that shape the evolution and use of the Internet' (WSIS, 2005).

One controversial issue was the 'unilateral control' by the US Government of the Internet backbone, including domain names through ICANN; another was the uneven distribution of costs that Internet service providers (ISPs) based in developing countries had to pay to access the international circuits. Apart from Internet domain names and addresses, Internet governance also includes such public policy issues as online security and stability, data protection and privacy rights and multilingualism on the Internet, as well as access to the use of the Internet. At the second phase of WSIS, held in Tunis in 2005, many countries, including China, demanded an international treaty organization, while France called for an intergovernmental body, comprising a few elite nations, to govern the Internet. However, the USA succeeded in retaining control, although an Internet Governance Forum (IGF) was established, but it had no involvement in the day-to-day running and technical operation of the Internet.

The Internet and political communication

Once hailed as a democratizing and even subversive communication tool, the commercialization of the Internet is perceived by some as betraying the initial promise of its potential to create a 'global public sphere' and an alternative forum. In its early days, the Internet was seen as a mass medium whose fundamental principles were based on access to free information and a decentralized information network. For many the Internet had opened up possibilities of digital dialogues across the world (Negroponte, 1995; Cairncross, 1997) and given freedom of speech its biggest boost since the US Constitution got its first amendment (Naughton, 1999). Unlike traditional communication, which followed a top-down, one-to-many model, online communication was seen as a many-to-many dialogue and thus inherently more democratic.

However, the Internet has also provided a platform for extremist organizations – from supremacist groups electronically transmitting Nazi merchandising and hate propaganda, to militant Islamic cells which do not hesitate in showing videos of beheadings on their websites (Burke, 2004). Others, such as radical Palestinian groups, operate anti-Zionist websites, while the Tamil Tigers have carried their battle with the Sri Lankan Government into cyberspace through such sites as Eelam.com (Downing, 2001; Atton, 2004). The world's 'first informational guerrilla movement' was the Zapatista National Liberation Army, which fought for self-rule in Mexico's Chiapas state. Subcommandante Marcos, the leader of the uprising in 1994, became an international hero, largely through the movement's use of the Internet to promote their cause (Castells, 2000b).

Internationally, the most significant political role that the Internet has played is in promoting links between community groups, non-governmental organizations and political activists from different parts of the world (Rodriguez, 2004; Cammaerts and Audenhove, 2005; Taylor, 2005). One major success of such activism was the use of the Internet to mobilize international support against the Multilateral Agreement on Investment (MAI). The MAI, which was being discussed within the OECD, if approved, would give extraordinary powers to TNCs, especially with regard to freedom to move capital from one country to another. Through a concerted international effort, which included flooding the relevant ministries of the OECD governments, major TNCs and other intergovernmental organizations with emails, the activists were able to stop the agreement going ahead (Kobrin, 1998). The Internet also played a major role in organizing and publicizing the very public opposition to growing corporate control of global trade, leading to the scuppering of the WTO's ministerial meeting in Seattle in 1999. At subsequent high-profile meetings of the World Bank, the IMF and the WTO, as well as annual summits of G8, the 'anti-globalization movements' have used the Internet to mobilize global public opinion (Lid, 2003; Jordan and Taylor, 2004). The World Social Forum, a configuration of diverse civil society groups which has been meeting annually since 2001, prefers to use the phrase 'alter-globalization' rather than anti-globalization, thus avoiding its negative connotations and promoting a globalization which respects democracy, human rights and economic equity. Its slogan – 'Another world is possible' – has been a rallying cry for activists across the planet (Leite, 2005).

The Internet has influenced the mass media in a substantial way: not only has it provided a new platform for media organizations to reach consumers, but it has also changed the timeframe of news production and distribution. In an era of real-time news, journalists are under increasing pressure to provide up-to-the-minute information, while ordinary citizens can access the world's top news organizations – news agencies, 24-hour news channels, once available only to journalists – without being mediated by editorial control of news organizations. This can be particularly problematic at a time of conflict when news may be censored. During the 1999 NATO bombing of Yugoslavia the Internet was widely used by computer-hacking 'cyboteurs' on both sides. The independent Serbian radio station B-92 used its website to provide information about the war, free of Yugoslav

Government control, and the Voice of America website became very active during the first days of bombing. Such organizations as Iraq Body Count (www.iraqbodycount.org), a US-based ongoing project – the 'world's only independent and comprehensive public database of media-reported civilian deaths in Iraq' – has been used since the 2003 US invasion of Iraq as a credible source by journalists around the world. Online media sources have also been integral to the global opposition to the so-called 'war on terrorism'.

The Internet has also greatly influenced the speed with which news is disseminated, making it more difficult for governments or corporations to suppress information. One example of this was the 1998 revelation about US President Bill Clinton's affair with a White House intern Monica Lewinsky on *The Drudge Report*, which catapulted US journalist Matt Drudge into the global spotlight. Within hours of the story breaking on the Internet, millions of Americans had knowledge of what turned out to be the one of the biggest sexual scandals in US political history, leading to the impeachment of the President. The story had become so widespread that the mainstream media had little option but to cover it. The Internet was instrumental in the publication in late 1998 of the report by the President's Prosecutor Kenneth Starr, which was made available first on the Internet, and thus to 55 million people, even before its official release. So pressured were the media to cover it live that networks like CNN had a correspondent reading it straight from text scrolling on the screen. This was an early example of how the Internet had the potential to loosen, if not abandon, editorial control over media content. In India, the website *Tehalka.com* ('sensation' in Hindi) almost cost the government of Prime Minster Atal Bihari Vajpayee, when in 2001, in an undercover operation, the New Delhi-based news portal exposed the corruption involved in defence deals.

It is undoubtedly the case that the Internet has been an extraordinary source of information for journalists, from government documents, to TNC annual reports, to NGO viewpoints – all are available to journalists with computer and telephone access. This has meant that they can research a story in greater detail, and given the global nature of the Internet, they can also include 'other' perspectives. Most major media organizations now regularly provide background information on contemporary issues through their web pages. The new medium has also contributed to journalists becoming connected to each other, reading about other countries through websites or watching their television channels. This can happen both in a regional and an international context.

A blogosphere beckons

The growing importance of online media is attested by media monitoring groups. A Project for Excellence in Journalism report notes

> ... a seismic transformation in what and how people learn about the world around them. Power is moving away from journalists as gatekeepers over what the public knows. Citizens are assuming a more active role as assemblers, editors and even creators of their own news. Audiences are moving from old media such as television or newsprint to new media online.

> (Project for Excellence in Journalism, 2006)

In the new digital media world consumers can create their own content and distribute it to a potentially global audience. While most of this content barely rises above the mundane and the banal, there has also been extraordinary growth in political communication through the so-called blogs (short for weblogs or diaries) (Blumenthal, 2005). One early success of this phenomenon was the so-called Baghdad blogger, who filed from the Iraqi capital as the US bombs fell around him in 2003 and has since acquired something of a minor celebrity status among observers of the US invasion and the subsequent chaos in Iraq. In an interesting case of media mutation, the blogger, Salam Pax, was given a regular column in *The Guardian* and a video diary was broadcast on the BBC. A collection of his weblogs has also been published in book form. Blogs were an integral part of the 2004 presidential campaign in the USA, especially effectively used by the presidential candidate Howard Dean, whose Blog for America served as a nerve centre for the campaign, reflecting a new level of civic engagement in the political process (Kerbel and Bloom, 2005).

So big had they become that by 2005 some blogs had a larger audience share than well-established news sites. For example, the US-based Blogspot, a blog hosting service and part of the Google-owned Blogger.com, received a larger audience of unique users across its million-plus blogs collectively than NYTimes.com (Bruner, 2005). By 2006 such terms as moblog – a blog maintained via a mobile phone, usually containing both text and pictures – and Vlog – video blog, used to display various forms of video images, also known as a vog – had become popular.

In many countries the growing use of the Internet and its potential power to provide alternative viewpoints and exchange of information beyond national borders have generated anxiety (Downing, 2001; Atton, 2004). In the digital era, some have argued, filtering software and protocols may in fact make censorship easier. Governments do not have to confiscate printing presses producing subversive propaganda from underground bunkers, they can simply route all Internet traffic through electronic gateways, which they can control. A country such as Saudi Arabia, which has state-controlled media, did not give its citizens online access until it had effectively tinkered with the code of the Net to filter out all 'objectionable' material, while Iran programmed the chat rooms of its online network so that only two people could speak to one another at a time (Shapiro, 1999). Singapore and China require Internet service providers to filter 'objectionable' material – mainly sexual or political content. China has blocked access to some Western websites, and security and defence issues have been a key concern for Chinese authorities, especially after the information about China's first unmanned spacecraft was revealed on a Chinese website two days before its launch in November 1999. Since then the government has devised new measures to control online activities and monitor bulletin boards, chat rooms and newsgroups. However, the authorities have not always been successful – during the 2003 outbreak of SARS in parts of China, texting had become so common among the Chinese popluation within and outside the mainland that, despite initial denials by the authorities, the world came to know about the health crisis.

Unlike in the West, privacy laws in many developing countries are non-existent or not applied rigorously, making it easier for authoritarian governments to monitor email traffic. The generally small number of approved Internet providers in any individual country can help monitor and control Internet access, making it difficult for Internet activity to escape government purview. Issues concerning financial security have also come to the fore with electronic commerce. It has been argued that economic intelligence on global trade can be manipulated through faulty analysis or misinterpretation of commercial data. Referring to the foreign-exchange crisis in Thailand, Mexico and Brazil in the late 1990s, one US observer commented, 'much of the sea of information on which modern markets float is polluted with misinformation' (Rothkopf, 1999: 95).

Case study

The global 'war on terrorism'

In the post-9/11 era, the US-led 'war on terrorism' has tended to dominate foreign news around the world. The open-ended nature of the conflict and its global reach, coupled with the US doctrine of 'pre-emptive strikes', has led to concerns about a deteriorating international security environment. Almost impervious to the growing unease among educated opinion internationally about US unilateralism, US-dominated international media have generally presented the 'war on terrorism' in an 'Us vs Them' binary, and in highly moralistic language (Lewis, 2005).

A myth is being created that in the post-cold war era, a radicalized Islam has replaced communism as the pre-eminent transnational threat to Western interests, exemplified by shadowy networks such as al-Qaida, with their alleged links with 'rogue' states. In this version of international politics, influenced by the discourse of the 'clash of civilizations', and strengthened by the events of 11 September 2001, militant Islam has characteristics that are inimical to a modern, secular and rational market democracy. Such terrorism, it is also argued, can only be reciprocated by force, as the militants seem to be unwilling or incapable of taking part in reasoned debate and discussion (Lewis, 2005).

Moreover, this view of Islamic militancy is undifferentiated: Lebanon's Hizbullah, Palestinian Hamas, Indonesia's Jemaah Islamiyah, Abu Sayyaf group in the Philippines, Hizbul-Mojaheddin in Kashmir, Abu Mousab al-Zarqawi's supporters in Iraq and Chechen rebels are all presented as part of a seamless, transnational terror network. The fear that weapons of mass destruction may fall into the hands of such networks is at the heart of the US security agenda. The US-led global and open-ended war on terrorism is portrayed by the media as part of a strategy to make the world a safer place. The corollary of this narrative is that the West, led by the United States, the world's only hyperpower, is committed to bringing democracy and protecting human rights around the world, even if it requires 'pre-emptive strikes' or 'regime change'. These assertions have been presented in the media in a moralistic tone for international consumption mainly through 24/7 news networks.

In the media discourse on Islam, a tendency is evident to present the world's 1 billion Muslims as potential terrorists. Often the distinction between 'political Islam' and 'Islamic fundamentalism' is collapsed in media coverage. There is a long history of the US Government harnessing and cultivating radical Islamic groups fighting 'communism' in Afghanistan during the 1980s (Mamdani, 2004). Profoundly influenced by cold war thinking, it was normal to see the Afghan Mujaheddin routinely labelled in Western media reports as 'freedom fighters'. These fighters for freedom have now become enemies of freedom. Al-Qaida, claimed to be led by Saudi fugitive Osama bin Laden, himself a creation of the CIA, may have more to do with 'the politics of fear' of the US Government to justify the 'war on terrorism' than any tangible global organization, as Adam Curtis's series *The Power of Nightmares*, broadcast on the BBC, has argued (BBC, 2004).

Western involvement in the Islamic world has a long and complex history, steeped in medieval crusades and modern colonial conquests, as Rashid Khalidi has shown (Khalidi, 2004). In more recent years, Western support for the creation of Israel and its suppression of Palestinian aspirations has contributed to anti-Western sentiment. Despite the fact that sections of Islamic militant groups – whether in Palestine, Chechnya or Kashmir – have used terrorist activities as an extreme manifestation of political protest, and some 'Islamist' groups have descended into extortion rackets and criminal syndicates, as evident in occupied Iraq, the vast majority of Muslims have nothing to do with terrorism.

However, the 'war on terrorism' may have in fact brought Islamic militancy to hitherto secular Iraq. The powers of Iraqi dictator Saddam Hussein were exaggerated to such an extent in the media coverage that he was seen not only as a major threat to the Middle East region, but also to the world at large. The allegation that this avowedly secular Arab leader had links with Islamic terror groups placed him on a different scale of danger in the post-9/11 world. Another key concern in media coverage of the 'war on terrorism' is about the possibilities of Islamic terrorist groups gaining access to nuclear bombs. In the post-Soviet era, this discourse has been provided with respectability by numerous high-powered reports, academic articles and conferences, although there has been no evidence of any non-state actors acquiring nuclear weapons.

The argument that Iraq was in possession of nuclear weapons and had the capacity to deploy them within 45 minutes was presented in the media as a compelling reason for invading that country. A great deal of scepticism about these claims was expressed by many, including such senior international bureaucrats as Hans Blix, head of the UN Monitoring, Verification, and Inspection Commission (Blix, 2004). Yet most media gave a short shrift to any dissenters and continued representing these threats as real. However, as the subsequent events showed, this claim was without any basis whatsoever. Since the 'liberation' of Iraq, the focus of nuclear and other weapons of mass destruction turned to neighbouring Iran and its nuclear weapons programme. News coverage became full of alarming reports about the 'nuclear threat' posed by Iran.

Such interventions are often framed in the media in terms of a US mission to spread democracy, freedom and human rights in the world. A series of US military actions after the cold war, from regime change in Panama in 1989 to the installation of a new regime in Iraq in 2004, have been almost invariably framed in a discourse of humanitarianism and high moral rectitude. This is reflected also in the way the operations were named by the Pentagon: from *Operation Just Cause*, to depose President Manuel Noriega of Panama, to *Operation Iraqi Freedom*, launched in 2003 to 'liberate' Iraq from the dictatorship of Saddam Hussein. Other examples of such moralistic nomenclature include: *Operation Provide Comfort* – intervention in Iraqi Kurdistan in 1991; *Operation Restore Hope* – the 1992 invasion of Somalia; the 1994 *Operation Uphold Democracy*, undertaken ostensibly to restore to power Haiti's democratically elected President Jean-Bertrand Aristide; and *Operation Enduring Freedom* – the 2001 invasion of Afghanistan.

With the support of a largely compliant media, including such propaganda networks as *al-Hurra* (Arabic for 'The Free One'), the US Government has arguably succeeded in transforming its myths about the 'war on terrorism' into reality. In the process, it has almost unilaterally redrawn the rules of international military intervention to further its own geostrategic and economic interests (Thussu, 2005). The unilateralist ideology propounded by the so-called neoconservatives (neocons) is increasingly shaping US foreign policy. Former Central Intelligence Agency director James Woolsey, member of the Project for the New American Century, described the invasion of Iraq as the onset of the 'Fourth World War' (the third being the cold war), indicating that this is likely to continue for years, if not decades, to come. It may even spread to other parts of the world, just as the cold war was globalized.

However, such unilateralism is generating anti-US sentiment. A major international survey – part of Pew Center's Global Attitudes Project – noted that

> ... anti-Americanism is deeper and broader now than at any time in
> modern history. It is most acute in the Muslim world, but it spans the

globe – from Europe to Asia, from South America to Africa. And while much of the animus is aimed directly at President Bush and his policies, especially the war in Iraq, this new global hardening of attitudes amounts to something larger than a thumbs down on the current occupant of the White House.

(Pew Center, 2005)

Almost impervious to such anti-American sentiments, the US Government is determined to continue this 'long war' on terror, victory in which 'depends on information, perception, and how and what we communicate'. As a report from the US Defense Department notes:

The War on Terrorism – a war of long duration – differs from the kind of conflict for which the Department traditionally prepared. Our focus is increasingly on the search for small cells of terrorists and on building the capacity of our partners. However, we must also retain the capability to conduct sustained conventional combat operations and to protect the homeland. *We must prevail now while we prepare for the future.*

(US Government, 2006: page A-7, italics in original)

Global electronic surveillance

The struggle over control of international information has been a main tenet of international communication. As was noted in Chapter 1, the international means of communication – cables and radio – have always had important strategic functions in war. More than 70 per cent of satellites launched during the cold war years were used for defence purposes – both superpowers used satellites to spy on each other's nuclear capabilities. In the post-cold war era there is a growing realization by the US military that information and communication technologies are an important element in their arsenal. In recent 'humanitarian crises', increasingly, a 'central role is being given to Psychological Operations (PSYOPS)' (Taylor, 1997: 148).

Electronic warfare would also be a key element in a cyberwar (Taylor, 2005). Advanced spy satellites could provide intelligence about what has been called 'information battlespace', while unmanned electronic warfare planes could jam enemy radar or feed it false images, as well as block or intercept telephone or television transmission. Enemy computer systems, especially those running a country's financial networks, can be disabled with 'email bombs' and viruses. The US Army has developed a 'Land Warrior' equipped with computer radio – a PC-based system with a Pentium processor, protective clothing and a helmet with high-tech optics. During the 1999 NATO bombing of Yugoslavia – termed the first war on the Internet – hackers from both sides disrupted Serb and NATO websites, while American 'Information Operations' disabled the Yugoslav Government's email system (Dinnick, 1999).

In keeping with the times, the satellite imagery industry has also been gradually privatized as a sign of greater civilian–defence co-operation. The US Government permits its defence forces to use satellite intelligence from commercial companies. Now the general public in the USA can buy computer simulation developed for the army or download satellite imaging from the Internet. Space Imaging, a US-based company, formed in 1994 by Lockheed Martin and Raytheon, is moving into the commercial satellite-imaging market. Others, such as Google Earth, have also entered this lucrative market.

The USA already has an extensive international surveillance operation, Echelon, run by the US National Security Agency. Through a combination of spy satellites (such as Orion/Vortex for telecom surveillance and Trumpet to intercept cell phone calls) and sensitive listening stations, it eavesdrops on international electronic communication – phones, faxes, telexes, email and all radio signals, airline and maritime frequencies. Established in 1948, after a secret pact between major Anglo-Saxon countries – the USA, Australia, Britain, Canada and New Zealand – the Echelon system had main bases in Menwith Hill and Morwenstow in Britain, Yakima on the Pacific coast and Sugar Grove on the east coast of the USA, Leitrim in Canada, Shoal Bay and Geraldton in Australia and Waihopai in New Zealand. In the post-cold war era, spying was designed primarily for non-military targets, with business intelligence becoming important in the world of electronic commerce. The US/UK domination of this area of international activity – for example, NASA's biggest base for electronic spying is at Menwith Hill, jointly operated with the UK's Government Communications Headquarters (GCHQ) – can give a competitive advantage to Anglo-American corporations, which has generated some resentment among other industrial countries, especially France. Monitoring Islamist militants was another major preoccupation of global surveillance agencies.

US satellite operators have a pre-eminent position in reconnaissance, surveillance and imaging systems, and in a integrated space, air and terrestrial information and communications systems should ensure that US control over international communications – both soft entertainment and hard espionage – is likely to grow. Boeing, NASA's leading contractor, is developing the next generation of global positioning system satellites, known as GPS IIF. Industry projections indicate that the space and communications market will grow to $120 billion annually by 2010, primarily driven by growth in commercial and government information and communications systems and services. Partly to lessen their dependence on the American Global Positioning System, the European Union launched the first of its 30 Galileo navigation satellites into space in December 2005. China and India are also partners in this $4.3 billion satellite system, due to go into service in 2008. The Indian Space Research Organization (ISRO) signed an agreement in 2006, with Russia's Federal Space Agency (ROSCOSMOS), to participate in Russia's own Global Satellite Navigation System (GLONASS), an alternative to the Pentagon-controlled GPS.

The global digital divide

Despite its unprecedented expansion, the Internet has arguably accentuated the rich–poor divide. As Mattelart points out: 'just as in the nineteenth century, when London was the undisputed hub of the transcontinental network of underwater cables, today the United States has become the nodal point through which Net users from less developed countries must go in order to connect with each other' (Mattelart, 2003: 148). The global imbalance in access to information must be viewed within the overall context of international inequality: according to the UN, in 2004, the annual income flow of the richest 500 people exceeded that of poorest 416 million (UNDP, 2005a).

Inequality between the information-rich North and information-poor South was central to the 1970s' demands for a NWICO (*see* Chapter 1) but with the globalization of new information and communication technologies, the issue of access to information has once again become significant. Conceding that the costs of building new information infrastructures are prohibitive for developing countries, a UN report suggested that the cost of not doing so would risk exclusion from the global electronic economy (Mansell and Wehn, 1998) (*see* Tables 7.10 and 7.11).

Table 7.10 The global telecom divide

Region	Population (millions)	GDP ($bn)	Telephone subscribers (millions)	per 100 inhabitants
Africa	859	562	98	12
Americas	875	13,028	671	77
Asia	3791	8670	1249	33
Europe	802	11,441	894	112
Oceania	32	599	34	105
World	6360	34,210	2946	46

Source: ITU, 2005a, figures for 2004. Reproduced with the kind permission of ITU

Table 7.11 The global IT divide

Region	Internet use		PCs use	
	Users (millions)	Users per 100 inhabitants	Users (millions)	Users per 100 inhabitants
Asia	305	8	224	6
Europe	250	31	224	28
Americas	246	28	70	13
Africa	22	3	13	2
Oceania	17	52	16	51
World	842	13.3	549	10

Source: ITU, 2005a, figures for 2004. Reproduced with the kind permission of ITU

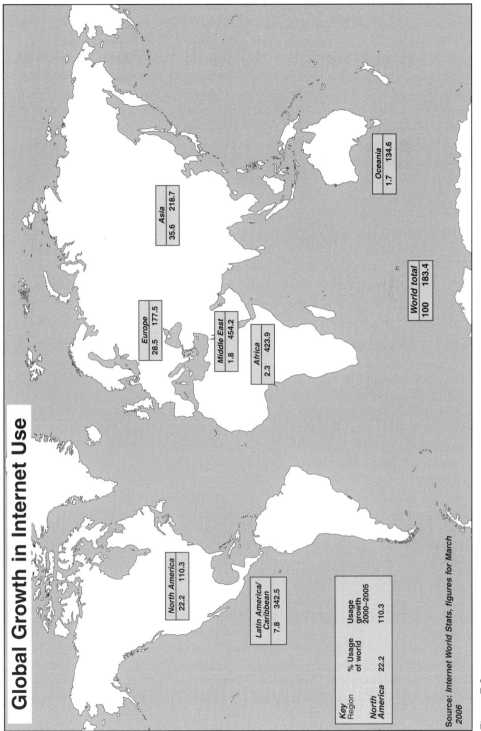

Global Growth in Internet Use

Asia	
35.6	218.7

Oceania	
1.7	134.6

Europe	
28.5	177.5

Middle East	
1.8	454.2

Africa	
2.3	423.9

World total	
100	183.4

North America	
22.2	110.3

Latin America/ Caribbean	
7.8	342.5

Key Region	% Usage of world	Usage growth 2000–2005
North America	22.2	110.3

Source: *Internet World Stats, figures for March 2006*

Figure 7.2

In 1957, the UN General Assembly endorsed the objective of universal access to basic communications for all, but the global information and communication disparity in terms of vast differences in access to telecommunications remains. Though 'the right to communicate' was promoted in 1996 by the ITU as a fundamental human right, the organization, which claims to be committed to redressing global inequity in telecommunication, admits the existence of an information poverty gap between the North and the South. The most common measure of telecommunication access, teledensity or the number of main telephone lines per 100 inhabitants, shows great disparities – in 2004, in Myanmar, with a population of 54 million, barely 1 out of 100 inhabitants had a telephone, while Luxembourg, with a population of only 460,000, had two telephones for each of its citizens. When the Maitland Commission published its report, 3 billion people, more than half the world's population, were living in countries with a teledensity of below one. The commission envisaged that by the first decade of the twenty-first century, everybody should be brought within easy reach of a telephone. However, by 2005, nearly 1 billion people worldwide had no access to telephones (ITU, 2005a). Sub-Saharan Africa was particularly deprived: in 2004, in Liberia, barely 0.3 per cent of the population had a telephone; in Sierra Leone 0.2 per cent of its citizens was using the Internet; while in Angola, PC use was as low as 0.2 per cent of the population; and mobile telephones in Guinea-Bissau were only used by 0.1 per cent (ITU, 2005a).

Table 7.12 Telephone subscribers: top 10

Country	Total subscribers (in millions)	per 100 inhabitants
China	647	50
United States	360	123
Japan	150	118
Germany	126	153
Brazil	108	60
Russia	114	9
India	91	8
Italy	89	153
France	78	130
South Korea	63	131

Source: ITU, 2005a, figures for 2004. Reproduced with the kind permission of ITU

Many developing countries lack affordable access to information resources and their telecommunication systems need technological upgrading. The biggest dilemma they face is that in order to widen access, telephone tariffs need to be reduced and the sector opened to international operators, thus undermining the often subsidized domestic telecoms operators. As the UN statement on Universal Access to Basic Communication and Information Services proclaims:

> We are profoundly concerned at the deepening maldistribution of access, resources and opportunities in the information and communication field. The information and technology gap and related inequities between industrialised and developing nations are widening: a new type of poverty – information poverty – looms.
>
> (ITU, 1998)

Supporters of communication technologies argue that such information poverty will be reduced with the deployment and distribution of new tools and technologies, yet this disparity is still in evidence. In recognition of this, in 2005 the ITU launched its 'Connect the World' initiative, with the aim to 'connect the unconnected' by 2015. Mobile telephony offers possibilities of improving telecommunication access in the South, as systems can be installed relatively cheaply and more rapidly than fixed-line networks. By 2004, an estimated 77 per cent of the world's population was able to access mobile networks, with more than 1.7 billion subscribers in the world (UNCTAD, 2005a).

However, mobile telephones are priced beyond the reach of the poor, and frequency constraints and the high level of initial investment in developing networks can be further barriers to telecoms in poorer countries. Internet connectivity is expensive in the South, as the cost of equipment and software makes it inaccessible for a vast majority of people who do not even have a telephone. In Africa, for example, though the Internet has opened up new forums of information access, the high telephone charges restrict its use. Where Internet cafés exist, they are relatively expensive and thus out of reach for a majority of people. In many countries state-run telephone monopolies act as Internet providers, thus controlling content. They can use the government-controlled gateway to ban access to certain sites and also to monitor email communication. In addition, many countries lack the infrastructure to allow wide-scale data transmission over their phone lines: the local phone lines and phone-switching networks are insufficient to permit a high level of traffic. In many others, there is not enough space on the lines connecting to the Internet.

In addition, English is the primary language of the Internet, being the language of a majority of web pages and also dominating global electronic mail traffic. Though digital technology has made it easier for non-European languages, such as Mandarin, Arabic and Hindi, to be made available on the Internet, online communication continues to be based on using a Roman alphabet. Those who are not familiar with English are therefore at a disadvantage. New software enables non-Roman alphabets to be displayed, but they are still difficult to locate on the WWW, as most search engines are generally optimized to run in English. For non-English users, being nearly invisible to most search engines is a major liability. However, this is changing as more and more non-Roman search engines start operating on the web.

Communication for development

Though the Internet has the potential of evolving into a new and relatively cheaper medium for alternative communication, the tradition of providing an alternative viewpoint to the mainstream media has a long history – from radical pamphleteers in Europe and the USA, to anticolonial newspapers and magazines in Asia, to alternative media organizations using video, fax, satellite and now the Internet.

In the USA, such organizations as PeaceNet, established in 1985 to co-ordinate peace activists internationally through computer networks, and the New York-based Deep Dish TV Satellite Network, which has been providing programming since 1986 to public access channels, have contributed to an alternative media discourse (Lucas and Wallner, 1993). In Britain, OneWorld, launched in 1995, has emerged as a site dedicated to providing alternative voices on issues of global importance.

In the context of the South, alternative communication has taken the form of development journalism, partly as a result of the NWICO debates (Aggarwala, 1979). Initially developed in Asia, this journalism claimed to pursue a news agenda different from the mainstream media, steeped in the so-called 'coups and earthquakes' syndrome (Rosenblum, 1979 and 1993), and investigate the process behind a story rather than merely reporting the news event itself. In a market-driven news environment there is a discrimination against news that cannot be 'sold', resulting in a distorted presentation of events to make them more marketable (Galtung and Ruge, 1965; Somavia, 1976; Masmoudi, 1979). The conflict in the Democratic Republic of Congo (DRC) (formerly Zaire) is a case in point. Whenever it is covered in the international media, the focus seem to be on 'traditional' tribal rivalry and ethnic nationalism. Rarely, if ever, are economic factors adequately covered, in the case of DRC control over the country's rich natural resources, including coltan, the mineral that is used as a conductor for electronic components in mobile phones and military aircraft: DRC is home to 64 per cent of the world's coltan reserves (Thussu, 2004).

An analysis of British television's coverage of the 1994 genocide in Rwanda, which claimed 1 million lives in a country of only 7 million, within just three months, found that it became a television story only after it was framed as a humanitarian crisis, with an emphasis on Western support for refugee camps. The study from Britain's Glasgow Media Group reported that most of the coverage was devoid of historical or political context. 'Through this distortion,' it found, 'the media unwittingly helped Western governments hide their lack of policy on genocide behind a mask of humanitarian zeal' (Philo *et al.*, 1999: 226). Such coverage may be rooted in racism in reporting – it is worth reflecting on how British television would have reacted if the dead were not black Rwandans but white South Africans.

Distortions in the media's coverage of crises in developing countries can affect the understanding of the South in the North and among the countries of the South, since most of the news flow continues to be from North to South and limited South–South news exchange takes place. Worse, in most of the developing world, the media generally caters to the requirements of the urban readership, with little contact with the villages where the majority of the population live. The acceptance of Western definitions of what constitutes news by most journalists in the South can affect the coverage of development issues directly and adversely.

One reason why a Southern-oriented news agenda has not emerged is that in much of the developing world governments have sought to use the media to promote their viewpoints, in the name of providing 'positive news'. Historically, the media in the Third

World formed part of the anticolonial nationalist movements. After independence the anticolonial press assumed, by and large, a supportive attitude towards the new states. In many African countries, for example, journalists were part of information bureaucracies as newspapers and the electronic media were wholly or partly controlled by the state or the ruling parties (Bourgault, 1995). Not surprisingly then, the news Third World agencies put out, often referred to as 'protocol news' – coverage of official functions and state visits – was perceived as government propaganda. Where independent journalism existed, the media's freedom to critically examine state policies was severely restricted by the governments' indirect editorial control by introducing draconian censorship laws or threatening to stop newsprint supply.

To improve South–South news and information traffic, regional exchange mechanisms, supported by the IPDC, were established in the late 1970s. Though regional news agencies, such as the Pan African News Agency (PANA), Caribbean News Agency (CANA) and Organisation of Asia-Pacific News Agencies (OANA), encouraged journalists in developing countries to think in terms of regional issues, they failed to make a major difference to the global or even regional news flow, as a UNESCO study found (Boyd-Barrett and Thussu, 1992).

The Non-aligned News Agencies Pool, an international exchange designed to promote news among Non-aligned countries, was another international contributor to promoting alternative communication, though as a collection of government-sponsored news agencies it was seen as lacking journalistic credibility. Media impact of other smaller organizations, such as the Third World Network – known for advocacy rather than conventional journalism – has been extremely modest. An equally small, but more effective, alternative voice was that of the London-based Gemini News Service, an international news features agency with an explicit development agenda. Established in 1967, Gemini was a non-profit agency, supplying topical news features to more than 100 subscribers in 80 countries around the world. Gemini's ideology, as characterized by its founder editor, Derek Ingram, was to promote the 'decolonization of news'. One factor which distinguished it from other Western-based news organizations was its emphasis on using local journalists to reflect local perspectives rather than the outsider's view provided by most of the transnational news agencies. During the NWICO debates, Gemini was almost alone in the West in recognizing the need to balance press freedom with an understanding of the role of the media for nation-building (Bourne, 1995; Thussu, 2000b). However, it ceased operations in 2001 for lack of funding.

One remaining alternative news agency is the Rome-based Inter Press Service (IPS). With its motto of 'Another communication is possible', this agency, set up by Roberto Savio, an Italian freelance journalist who served as Director General of IPS until 1999, and Pablo Piacentini, an Argentinian political scientist, as a journalists' co-operative in 1964, defined itself as 'civil society's leading news agency, an independent voice from the South and for development, delving into globalisation for the stories underneath' (www.ipsnews.net).

With its focus on covering the issues affecting developing countries, it was a major news initiative in the 1970s and 1980s, especially in Latin America, where its Spanish-language service received a good response (Giffard, 1984). However, by the 1990s it had ceased to be a global presence in the spot news category – with its relatively modest output and limited resources it could not compete with transnational news agencies such as AP and Reuters. It is now known more for its features and commentary pieces than on-the-spot reports. By 2006, it was producing 112,000 words daily and providing services in English and Spanish, with selected stories translated into other languages, including French, German, Portuguese, Mandarin, Japanese and Kiswahili.

In addition, IPS's services were accessed by other INGOs through the Association for Progressive Communications, OneWorld, Third World Network websites and Yahoo!, among many others. IPS also produces *Terra Viva/IPS Daily Journal*, a selection of its wire stories for UN officials and INGOs, especially at the World Social Forums. With regional desks in Johannesburg, Manila, Berlin, Montevideo and New York and 400 journalists covering more than 150 countries, IPS is a major source of information and analysis of the global South. Yet its financial situation has remained precarious. Dependent on funds from Western aid agencies and the UN organizations, IPS has failed to make itself economically and commercially viable and is recognized as an international non-governmental organization by the UN. Consequently, it has become more of a pressure group, putting Southern concerns on the UN agenda, rather than a news organization, and the NGO approach to journalism is evident in its coverage of global issues. The training programmes and projects that IPS undertakes have helped many Southern journalists to develop an alternative news agenda. 'IPS treats all news events as part of a process rather than as isolated phenomena. Reporting events without seeking to understand cause and effect means that readers will not have enough information to fully understand the world around them' (www.ipsnews.net).

Such an approach is crucial for the democratization of international communication. An alternative to corporatized global communication is a moral imperative and a necessary democratic requirement. There is a need for a news agenda which covers issues of relevance to the majority world and examines the impact of globalization on the world's poor, as a result of the policies of such multilateral organizations as the World Bank, the IMF and the WTO. However, given the encroachment of market-led media in the South, such an alternative seems difficult to evolve. Media agendas in most developing countries are set by an elitist, urban-based professional class, with an emphasis on entertainment. These are defined by the growing commercialization and privatization of state-controlled media, increasingly being bought by global conglomerates as a result of deregulation in broadcasting. Although the original mandate of many broadcasting systems in the South stressed education and information, there is an unmistakable trend towards commercialization.

Reflecting the ideology of privatization, official development assistance from the world's rich countries to the global South has been reduced. Instead, private companies are financing communication infrastructure and services in selected developing countries. In 1999, the US Government launched its Internet for Economic Development initiative to spread electronic commerce to developing countries. Creation of 'a pro-competitive policy and regulatory environment where the Internet and e-commerce can flourish' was one of its key goals (US Government, 1999). The World Bank has been the main international multilateral organization to push the privatization agenda. A review of its World

Development Reports (WDR) in the last 10 years (1995–2005) shows that a neo-liberal agenda is central for its policies, and has been particularly promoted in recent reports, such as in WDR 2002 – *Building Institutions for Markets*, WDR 2004 – *Making Services Work for Poor People* and WDR 2005 – *A Better Investment Climate for Everyone*. The decline in foreign aid can be contrasted with the unprecedented growth in foreign direct investment (FDI), which has become increasingly relevant as a source of external finance for many developing countries. As the UN's *World Investment Report* shows, it now overshadows inflows from official aid and exceeds lending by international banks (UNCTAD, 2005c).

There is little doubt that in the Internet Age international communication has become much wider in its scope, going beyond information flows between and among nations. Newspapers, non-governmental organizations, charities, political organizations all have a strong Internet presence, relying on both email and web pages to exchange information. Many governments are creating web pages, while multilateral organizations like UNDP have dedicated websites to collect funds for development activities, such as netaid.org. The Internet also provides fora such as bulletin boards, newsgroups and electronic journals. It has been argued that the Internet can strengthen cultural identities of diasporic populations. Such developments provide ammunition to those who see information as a strategic resource which can be deployed to create a global village. As one enthusiast comments:

> To communicate may not be enough to keep the nationals of the earth at peace with one another, but it is a start. Free to explore different points of view, on the Internet or on the thousands of television and radio channels that will eventually be available, people will become less susceptible to propaganda from politicians who seek to stir up conflicts. Bonded together by the invisible strands of global communications, humanity may find that peace and prosperity are fostered by the death of distance.

> (Cairncross, 1997: 279)

Since 9/11 and the 'war on terrorism', such early optimism about the potential of the Internet to create global harmony seems somewhat naive (Atton, 2004). In reality, digital connectivity has become largely a medium for commerce rather than a social tool to eradicate mass illiteracy and promote health care for the world's underprivileged. Developing countries are also at a disadvantage for not having access to the latest financial data, essential in a globalized electronic economy. Despite the establishment, in 1996, of Special Data Dissemination Standards by the International Monetary Fund, to improve the data collection and publication practice for countries seeking to maintain access to global financial markets, TNCs continue to dominate global data flow, whose speed and volume have increased significantly in an era of digital connectivity. Unbiased information about foreign-exchange trading and commodity prices are crucial for developing countries, though they are heavily dependent on Western information sources. The dependence is in most spheres of international information – technical, scientific and financial information. The international information technology media and research sector, for example, is dominated by the US-based International Data Group (2005 revenue, $2.7 billion), which has more than 400 targeted websites, as well as 300 newspapers and magazines reaching 120 million buyers in 80 countries (www.idg.com).

In an age when the refrain is 'globalize or perish', the South has to follow the global agenda, which privileges privatization and progressively undermines the idea of distributive justice associated with erstwhile socialist and welfare-oriented government policies. Countries in the South have little representation and influence within highly centralized global institutions – the UN Security Council, the G-8, and the World Bank, IMF and WTO troika – despite constant talk of 'global governance'. In a world where information has become a major tradeable commodity, there is also increasing concern about the capacity of the new technology to dictate the social and political agenda (Postman, 1992; Preston, 2001; Mattelart, 2003). This is another 'revolution' in which the South is lagging behind and letting the West reinvent its hegemony via the 'global knowledge economy'. As a UNESCO report observes:

> An excessive appropriation or commoditization of knowledge in the global information society would be a serious threat to the diversity of cognitive cultures. In an economy where the focus is scientific and technological knowledge, what role might certain forms of local indigenous know-how and knowledge play? They are already often deemed less valuable than technological and scientific knowledge. Is there a chance they might simply vanish, even though they are a priceless heritage and a precious tool for sustainable development?
>
> (UNESCO, 2005b: 22–3)

International communication – continuity and change

One recurring theme in this study of international communication has been the continued domination of the global information and entertainment industries (both hardware and software), by a few, mainly Western, nations and the transnational corporations based in these countries. From Marconi to Microsoft, a continuity can be detected in how a mainly Western technology has set the agenda of international communication, whether it was cabling the world, broadcasting to an international audience or creating a virtual globe through the Internet. The rest of the world, by and large, has followed the dominant ideology promoted by major powers through their control of international channels of communication – telegraph, radio, television and the Internet.

The expansion of European capitalism in the nineteenth and twentieth centuries could not have been possible without the creation of a global communication infrastructure. The post-Second World War US hegemony was built on the use of its 'soft power' to supplement its military supremacy. Much of the cold war was fought over the airwaves, though in the South the conflict was more often hot, claiming over 20 million lives in conflicts related to superpower rivalry for global domination. In the post-cold war era, the international media, especially television, have become a conduit for legitimizing free-market ideology, dominated by corporate capitalism. What distinguishes the new form of capitalism from its colonial predecessor is its emphasis on the almost mythical powers of the market and its use of mediated entertainment rather than coercion to propagate this message. It would appear that a 'global feel-good factor' is being promoted through myriad television channels, in partnership with the international entertainment industry, which, though a fast-growing business, is still in an 'entrepreneurial stage of development' as large population countries such as China and India are yet to fully integrate into free-market capitalism. However, the changes in media and communication industries in these two countries have been remarkable, making them the second and fourth largest users of the Internet (*see* Table 7.13).

Such demographic shifts may lead to the decline of English dominance on the Internet as other languages, including non-European ones, proliferate (UNESCO, 2005c). India and China, a British Council report notes, 'probably now hold the key to the long-term future of English as a global language' (Graddol, 2006). The so-called Tunis Agenda for the Information Society is also committed to 'multilingualization of the Internet' (WSIS, 2005).

It has been argued that an ethical dimension should be added to international communication to make it more equitable (Hamelink, 2000; Mowlana, 1997; Vincent *et al.*, 1999). Idealists feel that improved communication between and among nations will not only help make the world smaller, but also enable a more just and equitable global society (Cairncross, 1997; World Bank, 1999; UNDP, 2001). However, given the global disparity in access to information and communication technologies, how is this to be achieved?

There have been some worthwhile suggestions. UNESCO's World Commission on Culture and Development regards the airwaves and space as part of 'the global commons', a collective asset that belongs to all humankind. Commercial regional or international satellite interests, which use the global commons free of charge, it counsels, should pay 'property

Table 7.13 Internet users – the top 10 countries

Country	Internet users (millions)	Population (millions)	Internet penetration %	% of world users
USA	205	299	68	20
China	111	1,307	9	10.9
Japan	86	128	67	8.5
India	51	1,112	5	5
Germany	49	83	59	4.8
Britain	38	60	63	3.7
South Korea	34	51	67	3.3
Italy	29	59	49	2.8
France	26	61	43	2.6
Brazil	26	184	14	2.5
World	1,018	6,499	16	100

Source: Internet World Stats (www.internetworldstats.com), figures for March 2006

Table 7.14 Surfing in tongues: top 10 languages used on the Internet

Language	Users (million)	% of internet users	World speakers (million)	Internet penetration for language %	Internet growth % for language 2000–05
English	311	31	1126	28	127
Chinese	132	13	1340	10	310
Japanese	86	9	128	67	83
Spanish	64	6.3	392	16	164
German	57	5.6	96	59	106
French	41	4	381	11	236
Korean	34	3.3	74	46	78
Portuguese	32	3.2	231	14	327
Italian	29	2.8	59	49	119
Russian	24	2.3	144	17	665

Source: Internet World Stats (www.internetworldstats.com), figures for March 2006

rights' and thus 'contribute to the financing of a more plural media system. New revenue could be invested in alternative programming for international distribution' (UNESCO, 1995: 278). To ensure that the communications revolution is truly global, the UNDP has also suggested a 'bit tax' on data sent through the Internet. A tax of 1 US cent on every 100 lengthy emails, according to its estimates, would generate more than $70 billion a year (UNDP, 1999). Global civil society groups have proposed the introduction of the so-called Tobin Tax, named after the economist James Tobin, which would tax short-term speculation on currencies and would be administered by the UN. It has been argued that if proper policies are adopted, globalized liberalism can strengthen protection of 'global public goods' – environment, health, knowledge or peace (Kaul et al., 1999). Article 18 of UNESCO's 'Convention on the protection and promotion of the diversity of cultural expressions', approved by the world body in October 2005, has recommended the establishment of an International Fund for Cultural Diversity, although contributions to the Fund are voluntary. Others have campaigned for the creation of a global 'creative commons', where access to knowledge is guaranteed free of cost (Lessig, 2004). Yet such promises co-exist with a trend towards the monopolization of media and communication power, reflected in the rise of global media tycoons, the unelected power centres which can set the parameters of public debate in the media.

Despite exaggerated claims about the capacity of the free market and new technologies to empower and liberate individuals and create a 'global civil society', capitalism's contradictions are sharper at the beginning of the third millennium than ever before. As corporations strengthen their control over the portals of global power, while a majority of the world's population is excluded from the benefits of the emerging electronic economy, the potential for social unrest is enormous. According to UNDP's *Human Development Report* in

2005, 2.5 billion people lived on less than $2 a day; more than 1 billion had no access to safe drinking water and 2.6 billion to sanitation; in sub-Saharan Africa, 100 million more people lived on $1 a day in 2001 than in 1990 – per head income actually declined in the 1990s (UNDP, 2005a).

Even the World Bank seems to have recognized this problem, as its 2006 *World Development Report* notes:

> We live in an integrated world in which people, goods, ideas, and capital flow across countries. Indeed, most policy advice given to poor countries over the last several decades – including that by the World Bank – has emphasized the advantages of participating in the global economy. But global markets are far from equitable, and the rules governing their functioning have a disproportionately negative effect on developing countries. These rules are the outcome of complex negotiating processes in which developing countries have less voice. Moreover, even if markets worked equitably, unequal endowments would limit the ability of poor countries to benefit from global opportunities. Leveling the global economic and political playing fields thus requires more equitable rules for the functioning of global markets, more effective participation of poor countries in global rule-setting processes, and more actions to help build and maintain the endowments of poor countries and poor people.
>
> (World Bank, 2006a: 28)

Changing contours of global communication

Though the rich-poor dichotomy continues to define international communication, there are important new configurations emerging, reflecting the patterns of economic activity in the world (UNCTAD, 2005c; World Bank, 2006b). What has changed in recent years is the increased South–South trade, indicating a trend towards a 'new geography of trade', with East Asia and China in particular taking the lead and having 'a significant impact on international trade flows' (UNCTAD, 2005b: 153). By 2005 South Korea was leading the world in broadband penetration, with nearly a quarter of its population having access to broadband, while China had emerged as the world's largest television market, overtaking the United States. China also had the world's largest number of mobile phone users and had become the largest exporter of IT products (OECD, 2005). The growth in the use of personal computers and in Internet use has been extraordinary in China: the annual percentage growth rate between 1995–2003 was over 34 per cent for PCs and a massive 90 per cent for the Internet. In the other Asian giant, India, the growth rate was an impressive 25 per cent for PCs and nearly 54 per cent for Internet use. The global expansion of India's IT industry has created the phenomenon of 'offshore outsourcing', which may broaden to include offshoring of 'impersonal services', delivered electronically over long distances with little or no degradation in quality (Blinder, 2006). Yet Internet penetration rates were very low in these two countries: China, the second largest Internet market in the world (after the USA), had a penetration rate of only 6.3 per 100 inhabitants and computer penetration of only 2.7 per cent; while in India this figure was 3.2 per cent, and computer penetration was as low as 0.7 per cent (UNCTAD, 2005a).

In communication hardware too, China's presence is becoming increasingly visible globally. The country has made tremendous progress since 1984, when its Long March 3 carrier rocket successfully launched the first domestically built communications satellite into geosynchronous orbit. The China Great Wall Industry Corporation, a major satellite manufacturer and launcher, has launched 30 satellites since 1990, including commercial launches for overseas customers. It was involved in supplying satellite technology to various countries – including Venezuela for its Telesur satellite network. In 2004, state media announced that China planned to launch more than 100 satellites before 2020.

Over all, and in absolute numbers, developing countries have overtaken the developed world in Internet usage: in 2000, these accounted for only 25 per cent of Internet users in the world; by 2005 the figure was 40 per cent. In that year a majority of the world's Internet users lived in Asia (nearly 330 million), followed by Europe (243 million) and the USA (185 million) (UNCTAD, 2005a). As a report from UNESCO observes: 'The simultaneous growth of the Internet, mobile telephone and digital technologies with the Third Industrial Revolution – which, at first in the developed countries, has seen much of the working population migrate to the service sector – has revolutionized the role of knowledge in our societies' (UNESCO, 2005b: 18). A 'new ecosystem' is being constructed by the new information and communication technologies, with the Internet at its heart. As ITU professes:

> The Internet as we know it is transforming radically. From an academic network for the chosen few, it became a mass-market, consumer-oriented network. Now, it is set to become fully pervasive, interactive and intelligent. Real-time communications will be possible not only by humans but also by things at anytime and from anywhere. The advent of the Internet of Things will create a plethora of innovative applications and services, which will enhance quality of life and reduce inequalities whilst providing new revenue opportunities for a host of enterprising businesses.
>
> (ITU, 2005b: 13)

The trillion-dollar global entertainment and media market is predicted to show maximum growth, averaging about 12 per cent annually, in the Asia-Pacific region. New media segments – including online and wireless video games, online film rental subscriptions, licensed digital distribution of music, music downloaded to mobile phones, video on demand, satellite, radio and electronic books – generated only $160 million globally in 2000. In 2004, this figure had climbed to $11.4 billion. By 2009, according to a PricewaterhouseCoopers report, it is estimated to touch $73 billion worldwide (PricewaterhouseCoopers, 2005: 15).

Corporations are already speaking about a 'pervasive media' environment. As an IBM report envisioned:

> Between now and 2010, the increasing affordability, saturation, transmission speed and massive data storage capacity of emerging digital technologies will enable new formats and functionalities, multiplying and deepening the

connectivity of users around the globe. Digital networks and devices will continue to load more megabytes per year at more affordable prices. Businesses will be able to offer new tools to customers and consumers, and will realize greater efficiencies by managing content, inventory, production and marketing on an 'on demand' basis. Consumers will be able to compile, edit, produce, create and broadcast complex content and manipulate huge files from the comfort of their homes and personal budgets.

(IBM, 2004)

New digital delivery mechanisms offer unprecedented levels of new content from around the globe. In the new broadcasting ecology, there will be little need for schedules and specific channels as content would be available anytime in myriad forms and shapes. One implication of this would be on quality, as almost anyone with basic technology could put across their self-generated content. As search engines become increasingly sophisticated, as well as simple to navigate, it will become easier for consumers to find what they are looking for 24/7 – a sports result, an adult website, a reality TV show, a music channel or unfolding news being streamed on to their tiny screens. The phenomenon has been called 'social computing' by industry analysts. In this brave new world of interactive, individualized and innovative communication, of citizen journalists, net-activists and entrepreneurs – where facts and fiction will increasingly blur under the pressure of speed and hypertext, and hysteria and 'Googlization' will meet Wikipedia and the blogosphere – the people who are on the wrong side of the digital divide are likely to be further marginalized. Perhaps more importantly, is the type of individualized lifestyle that this neo-liberal media and communication ecosystem seems to promote sustainable in the long run? If every citizen in China and India started mimicking the Western way of life, driving their own cars and celebrating a consumerist existence, what will be the future of the planet and its non-renewable energy resources? As Arthur C. Clarke, the man credited with championing the cause of global satellite communication, wrote:

The information age has been driven and dominated by technopreneurs – a small army of 'geeks' who have reshaped our world faster that any political leader has ever done. *And that was the easy part...* We now have to apply these technologies for saving lives, improving livelihoods and lifting millions of people out of squalor, misery and suffering.

(quoted in UNDP, 2005b: vi, italics in the original)

It is important to remind ourselves that the word 'communication' is derived from the Latin word *communis* and has the same roots as 'community' and 'communion'. Thus a sense of sharing is central to the idea of communication. The new global communication infrastructure, which has the potential to deliver digital democracy, could be harnessed to develop and sustain a people-centric capitalism, which would privilege public goods and creativity rather than commodified information and communication, colonized by a few multimedia mega-corporations and their localized clones.

Glossary

Advanced Mobile Phone System (AMPS) The original North American cellular system. Now used in North America, Latin America, Australia and parts of Russia and Asia.

Affiliate A broadcast station that airs a network's programmes and commercials, but is not owned by that network.

American Standard Code for Information (ASCII) A binary digital code used in computer and data communications systems.

Analogue A method of storing, processing or transmitting information through a continuous varied signal.

Antenna Device which picks up and delivers satellite signals to a receiver, usually a dish.

ASTRA The trademark and commercial name of Société Européenne des Satellites, which owns and operates the ASTRA Satellite System.

Asymmetric Digital Subscriber Line (ADSL) A broadband communications technology enabling normal telephone line for connecting to the Internet at high speed.

Asynchronous Transfer Mode (ATM) Very high-speed data transmission technology, based on a high bandwidth, low-delay, connection-oriented, packet-like switching and multiplexing technique.

Bandwidth The width (i.e. range of frequencies) of a channel or signal carried between a transmitter and a receiver: the wider the bandwidth, the more information can be transmitted.

Baud rate A measure of the speed at which data is transmitted, as the number of units of information per second; the speed in which computers can transfer data through a modem using communications software.

Beam The directed electromagnetic rays transmitted from a satellite.

Bluetooth A radio technology built around a new chip that makes it possible to transmit signals over short distances between computers and handheld devices without the use of wires. A global initiative by Ericsson, IBM, Intel, Nokia and Toshiba to set a standard for cable-free connectivity between mobile phones, mobile PCs, handheld computers and other peripherals.

Booster A television or FM broadcast station, that receives, amplifies and retransmits signals on the same channel.

Broadband A channel using a wide bandwidth capable of carrying complex systems. Used to describe the potential of digital technologies to offer consumers integrated access to high-speed voice, data, video and interactive services. Broadband is also used to refer to analogue transmission technologies that provide multiple channels.

Broadcast To transmit a signal from a single point to multiple receivers.

Browser A software programme used to query, search and view information on the Internet.

Byte A group of binary digits that operate as a unit. Usually there are eight bits in a byte.

Cable television A television broadcasting system in which signals are transmitted by cable to subscribers' sets (see also **CATV**).

Carrier The basic radio signal that transfers the information signal, occupying a single radio frequency (see also **common carrier**).

CATV, Community Antennae Television Television broadcast system in which signals are received on one satellite receiver and retransmitted via cable to subscribers' sets.

C-band The range of frequencies from 4 to 6 gigahertz (billion cycles per second) used by most communications satellites.

Cellular mobile radio telephone system A system of mobile radio-telephone transmission using a number of short-wave radio transmitters covering a defined service area (or cell) that retransmit signals from one area to another as the user travels about.

Common carrier A provider of communication transmission services to the public, such as telephone and telegraph, on a non-discriminatory basis.

Communications Satellite Corporation (COMSAT) A corporation, chartered by US Congress, as an exclusive provider of international telecommunications satellite channels to the United States. COMSAT also represents the USA in INTELSAT.

Compact disc (CD) A five-inch disc on which a digital audio signal is inscribed so that it can be read, especially by a laser beam device in a computer or CD player.

Compression A technique to reduce the amount of data to be transmitted and thus the bandwidth needed to transmit video or audio, increasing the capacity of a satellite transponder. The main way that compression works is by eliminating some of the redundant data in the signal.

Coverage The 'coverage' of a satellite is defined as the number of households receiving at least one channel transmitted by it.

Cyberspace A term introduced by science fiction author William Gibson in 1984. 'Cyberspace' is where human interaction occurs over computer networks, through email, games or simulations.

Cyberwar Information warfare conducted in **cyberspace**.

DBS band A range of frequencies (11.70–12.40 GHz) intended for direct TV broadcast by satellite.

Decoder Unit that unscrambles a signal protected by encryption, used normally in conjunction with a **smart card**, to allow access to the service.

Digital A system in which information or data from any medium or source is coded in binary form (ones or zeros, corresponding to on/off switches). Digital data has less redundancy (error) in transmission and so can be compressed into a narrower bandwidth than analogue signals (see **compression**).

Digital audio broadcasting (DAB) Radio broadcasting using digital modulation and digital source coding techniques.

Direct broadcast satellite (DBS) Transmits TV signals directly to dishes in viewers' homes. Usually a high-powered satellite that requires only small dishes.

Domain name Name that identifies one or more Internet addresses. The suffix indicates which top-level domain it belongs to. There are only a limited number of such domains, e.g. .com, .org.

Downlink Transmissions from a satellite to a ground station; also, the dish used for reception.

Download (receive) To receive data from another computer. The opposite is **upload**.

DTH (direct to home) The reception of satellite programmes by a satellite dish at the viewer's home (see also **direct broadcast satellite**).

Earth station The dishes, receivers, transmitters and other equipment needed on the ground to transmit and receive satellite communication signals.

Electronic commerce (e-commerce) The production, advertising, sale and distribution of products via electronic networks, specifically the Internet.

Electronic data interchange (EDI) The exchange of routine business transactions in a computer-processable format.

Electronic funds transfer (EFT) An electronic system that transfers money and records financial transactions, replacing the use of paper.

Electronic mail (email) Messages sent via a computer instantly to one or many persons around the world.

Electronic programme guide (EPG) An interactive on-screen guide to programmes and other services, which can help the viewer to select their choice of programmes.

Facsimile (fax) The electronic transmission of printed material by electronic means over a telephone system. An image is scanned at a transmitting point and reconstructed at a receiving station, where a printed copy can be produced.

Fibre optics Transmission of signals via light pulses travelling down ultra-thin flexible silicon or glass fibres, with very little degradation and providing very high capacity, much greater than that of copper wire.

Footprint The geographic area covered by a satellite, the limit of which is determined by the quality of communication received due to the spacecraft antenna pattern, power of the signal or curvature of the Earth.

Frequency The number of oscillations of electromagnetic waves that pass a given point in a given time period. It is equal to the speed of light divided by wavelengths, and is expressed in hertz (cycles per second).

G7 Group of seven leading industrial countries: Canada, France, Germany, Italy, Japan, the United Kingdom, the United States.

G77 Group of developing countries set up in 1964 at the end of the first United Nations Conference on Trade and Development (UNCTAD) (originally 77, but now more than 130 countries).

Gateway Single source through which users can locate and gain access to a wide variety of computer services. Gateways typically offer a directory of services available through them and provide billing for these services.

Geostationary satellite A satellite that orbits around the Earth at the equator at 36,000 km, thus travelling at the same orbital speed as the Earth's rotation, so that it appears stationary in the sky (see also **geosynchronous orbit**). This allows satellite dishes to be trained at the same satellite at all times and so can provide 24-hour services.

Geosynchronous orbit The orbit of satellites at a distance of 36,000 km from the Earth so that it is synchronous with the Earth's rotation. Satellite receivers can be trained on the same satellite for 24 hours a day and do not have to move to track its orbit.

Global Positioning System (GPS) A network of radio transmitting satellites developed by the US Department of Defense to provide accurate geographical tracking of entities, e.g. individuals, vehicles, etc.

Global System for Mobile Communications Service (GSM) Most widely adopted, digital cellular technology which uses time and frequency division techniques to optimize the call-carrying capacity of a wireless network.

High-band The band used for satellite transmission from 11.70 to 12.75 GHz. The **ASTRA** satellite system uses this band to transmit digital services only.

High-definition television (HDTV) An improved television system with around twice the resolution of the existing television standards. It also provides video quality approaching that of 35 mm film, and audio quality equal to that of compact discs.

Home page The main page of a website. Typically, the home page serves as an index or table of contents to other documents stored at the site.

Hybrid satellite A satellite which carries two or more different communications payloads (i.e. **C-band** and **Ku-band**).

Hypermedia 'Hypermedia' implies the facility to navigate across multimedia and hypermedia objects using links.

Hypertext Electronic text links from one document to another on the Internet.

Hypertext Markup Language (HTML) The programming language used to design and present sites on the **World Wide Web (WWW)**, that enables hypertext links to other documents.

Hypertext Transfer Protocol (HTTP) The method for moving 'hypertext' files across the Internet, requiring an HTTP programme at one end and a server at the other.

Information superhighway A term describing a network of integrated telecommunications systems connecting people around the world to information, businesses, governments and each other.

Integrated services digital network (ISDN) Switched network providing end-to-end digital connection for simultaneous transmission of voice and/or data over multiple communication channels using internationally defined standards.

Intellectual property Ownership of ideas, including literary and artistic works (protected by copyright), inventions (protected by patents), signs for distinguishing goods of an enterprise (protected by trademarks) and other elements of industrial property.

Internet Protocol (IP) addresses An identifier for a computer or device on a network, such as the Internet. Within an isolated network, one can assign IP addresses at random as long as each one is unique. However, connecting a private network to the Internet requires using registered IP addresses (called Internet addresses) to avoid duplicates.

Internet service provider (ISP) Provides Internet access to people or corporations, serving as an entry point to the worldwide network. ISPs normally provide several means of access to their customers, including dial-up modem, **ADSL** and **ISDN**.

Ka-band The frequency range between 17.7–20.2 and 27.5–30.0 GHz, also known as the 20/30 GHz band, used for HDTV.

Ku-band The frequency range between 10.7–13.25 and 14.0–14.5 GHz, also known as the 11/14 and 12/14 GHz band, used for **DBS** TV.

L-band The frequency range between 0.39 and 1.55 GHz, also known as the 1.5 GHz band, used for **digital audio broadcasting (DAB)**.

LEO Low-Earth orbit of up to 800 km above the Earth. This orbit is used by a constellation of satellites to provide a worldwide mobile phone service.

Local area network (LAN) A group of interconnected computer terminals or nodes, often co-located and managed from a single point as a single network.

Mobile IP An Internet protocol designed to support host mobility, the goal being to provide the ability of a host to stay connected to the Internet regardless of location.

Mobile satellite service (MSS) Services transmitted via satellites to provide mobile telephone, paging, messaging, facsimile, data and position location services directly to users.

Modem An abbreviated term for 'modulator-de-modulator'. A modem converts digital signals into analogue signals (and vice versa), enabling computers to send and receive data over the telephone networks.

Modulation The alteration of a carrier wave in relation to the value of the data being transferred. Analogue satellite transmissions use FM modulation.

Multimedia Messaging Service (MMS) A type of messaging comprising a combination of text, sounds, images and video.

Multipoint distribution services (MDS) Service with two-way capability to transmit voice, data and other video information. MDS can offer two-way interactive video, advanced teleconferencing, telemedicine, telecommuting and high-speed data services.

Multicast To transmit a message to a select group of recipients. An example of multicasting is sending an email message to a mailing list; multicasting refers to sending a message to a select group whereas broadcasting refers to sending a message to everyone connected to a network.

Multimedia The combination of various forms of media (texts, graphics, animation, audio, etc.) to communicate information. The term also refers to information products that include text, audio and visual content.

Multiplex To combine two or more independent signals into one transmission channel; the combined digital signals transmitted on one satellite **transponder**.

Narrowband A term applied to telecommunications facilities capable of carrying only voice, facsimile images, slow-scan video images and data transmissions. The term is applied to voice-grade analogue facilities and to digital facilities operating at low speeds.

Narrowcasting Network or programming aimed at a specialized audience; the opposite of a broadcast.

NTSC (National Television Standard Committee) TV transmission standard used in the United States and parts of Asia.

Online Electronic availability on demand from a computer-based system.

PAL (Phase Alternate Line) Analogue standard for television transmission, mainly used in Europe.

Pay-per-view Programming (usually movies or special events) that a subscriber specially requests to receive for a single fee, not available for the subscription fee.

Personal digital assistant (PDA) A handheld computer that can be used for viewing and editing documents.

PIN Personal Identification Number.

Piracy Unauthorized copying of copyright materials for commercial purposes and unauthorized commercial dealing in copied materials.

Pixel A contraction of picture element.

Protocol A set of rules or conventions that governs a data communications system and enables devices to intercommunicate.

Public switched telephone network (PSTN) Any **common carrier** network that provides circuit switching among public users.

Radio frequency A frequency that is higher than the audio frequency but below the infrared frequencies, usually below 20 KHz.

Radiotelegraphy Wireless telegraphy using radiowaves to transmit messages over a distance.

Real time Usually used to describe situations when two or more people are interacting via their keyboards on the computer in real time, versus asynchronous communication, such as email.

Receiver Satellite receiver, part of reception equipment used to tune in to a single channel broadcast from a satellite.

Resolution The amount of detail that can be seen in a broadcast image. The resolution of a TV screen is defined by the number of horizontal lines of picture elements that the screen displays and the number of pixels per line.

Satellite A radio relay station that orbits the Earth used to communicate between Earth stations. The satellite receives a signal transmitted by an originating Earth station and retransmits that signal to the destination Earth station(s). Satellites are used to transmit telephone, television and data signals originated by **common carriers**, broadcasters and distributors of **CATV** programme material.

Satellite carrier An entity that owns or leases the facilities of a satellite or satellite service to establish and operate a channel of communications for point-to-multipoint distribution of television station signals.

Satellite dish A kind of antenna used to pick up transmissions broadcast from a satellite.

Scrambler A device that electronically alters a programme signal so that it can be seen only by persons, typically paid subscribers, with appropriate decoding devices.

Search engine A programme that searches documents on the **WWW** for specified keywords and returns a list of the documents where the keywords were found.

Secam *Séquentiel couleur à mémoire*; French broadcasting standard.

Signal A physical, time-dependent energy value used for the purpose of conveying information through a transmission line.

Short Message Service (SMS) 'Text messaging' is a mechanism that allows brief text messages (up to 160 characters) to be sent to the mobile phone.

Smart card Card used to enable descrambling of encrypted broadcasts when placed in a decoder or receiver with a built-in decoder.

Streaming A technique for transferring data so that it can be processed as a steady and continuous stream. Streaming technologies are becoming increasingly important with the growth of the Internet because most users do not have fast enough access to download large multimedia files quickly. With streaming, the client browser or plug-in can start displaying the data before the entire file has been transmitted.

Subscriber identity module (SIM card) A subscriber removable printed circuit and chip set card that must be present in GSM phones before they are recognized by a GSM network. The SIM holds information identifying the subscriber to the network.

Surfing Switching a television from channel to channel with a remote control. Also used to describe the process of scanning sites on the Internet.

Telecommunications Any transmission, emission or reception of signs, signals, writing, images, sounds or intelligence of any nature by wire, radio, optical or other electromagnetic systems.

Teleconferencing The use of audio, video or computer equipment brought together through a communications system to permit geographically separated individuals to participate in a meeting or discussion.

Telephony The word used to describe the science of transmitting voice over a telecommunications network.

Teletext Textual and graphic information broadcast in the vertical blanking interval between conventional video frames in television signals.

Telex service A public switched service in which teletypewriter stations are provided with lines to a central office for access to other stations.

Terrestrial broadcasters Broadcasters who transmit through the airwaves from one Earth-bound aerial to another.

Terrestrial transmission Transmission which uses transmitters located on the ground, as opposed to satellite and cable. Analogue TV programmes were first transmitted via terrestrial transmission.

Transcoder Device which translates signals from one broadcasting standard to another, e.g. **PAL** to **Secam**.

Transmission control protocol (TCP) The suite of communications protocols used to connect hosts on the Internet.

Transponder Equipment in a satellite which receives a signal via a single uplinked channel from an **Earth station**; amplifies it, converts the frequency and changes the polarization, then rebroadcasts it to Earth.

Ultra-high frequency (UHF) The part of the radio spectrum from 300 to 3000 megahertz that includes TV channels, as well as many land mobile and satellite services.

Uniform resource locator (URL) The standard way to give the address of any resource that is on the Internet and is part of the **World Wide Web (WWW)**.

Universal Mobile Telecommunications System (UMTS) Almost universally subscribed to standard for the third generation mobile phones.

Uplink The signal from an **Earth station** to a satellite.

Upload To send a text file or software programme via telecommunications to another computer.

Usenet groups Usenet groups are also known as newsgroups or discussion groups. Users exchange information generally provided in a chat room.

User name A unique name assigned to a user on an Internet service provider's system.

Value-added network (VAN) An enhanced network that is designed expressly to carry data communications. VANs provide special services to their customers, such as access to databases.

Very high frequency (VHF) The part of the radio spectrum from 30 to 300 megahertz which includes TV channels, the FM broadcast band, and some marine, aviation and land mobile services.

Very small aperture terminal (VSAT) A type of satellite receiving dish, usually 60 cm or less, used for high-speed data communication.

Video compression Data reduction and compression of analogue television signals into a digital stream, to allow several channels to be broadcast through a single transponder.

Video-on-demand Films provided to subscribers from a menu of titles. The film starts at the subscriber's request.

Virtual reality A computer simulation usually experienced through headgear, goggles and sensory gloves that allows the user to experience being present in a computer-generated environment, and to interact with the images being displayed there.

Webcasting Using the Internet, and the **World Wide Web (WWW)** in particular, to broadcast information.

Wide area network (WAN) A general term referring to a large network spanning a country or around the world. The Internet is a WAN, as is a public mobile communication system.

Widescreen TV or TV signal with a wider aspect ratio than the traditional television standard. Widescreen TVs are 16:9 as opposed to the conventional 4:3.

Wireless Application Protocol (WAP) A family of protocols allowing mobile devices to access wireless services, including access to the Internet.

World Wide Web (WWW) Created in Switzerland, WWW is a client/server software that enables computers connected to the Internet to access and exchange documents and images using the **HTTP (Hypertext Transfer Protocol)**.

X-band The frequency range between 7.25–7.75 and 7.9–8.4 GHz, also known as the 7/8 GHz band. Typically used for telecommunications.

The definitions in this glossary were adapted from various web-based sources, including International Telecommunication Union, Federal Communication Commission, Hughes, ASTRA, Ericsson, Asiasat, as well as Fortner (1993) and Pavlik (1996).

Appendix I

A chronology of international communication

BC

4000 Sumerian writing on clay tablets.

3000 Early Egyptian hieroglyphics.

2500 Papyrus replaces clay tablets in Egypt.

1500 Phonetic alphabet in use in West Asia.

300 Phoenicians bring Phonetic alphabet to Greece.

100 Roman alphabet developed from Greek model.

AD

100 Papermaking invented in China.

150 Parchment in use, books begin to replace scrolls.

600 Book printing invented in China.

618 China's T'ang Dynasty (618–907) creates a formal handwritten publication, the *ti pao* or 'official newspaper' to disseminate information to the elite.

676 Paper and ink used by Arabs and Persians.

1000 Movable type made of clay in China.

1150 Moors bring paper from China to Europe.

1170 Arabic numerals introduced in Europe.

1453 Gutenberg Bible printed.

1465 First printed music produced.

1476 First print shop in England.

1511 First printing press in the Ottoman Empire.

1535 First press in the Americas set up in Mexico.

1578 First printing press set up in India.

1644 Private bureaux which compose and circulate official news in the printed form known as the *Ch'ing pao*, start in China.

1650 *Einkommende Zeitung* ('incoming news'), the world's first daily publication starts in Leipzig.

1665 Newspapers first published in England.

1704 First newspaper advertisement published in the *Boston News Letter*.

1742 *General Magazine* prints first American magazine advertisement.

1777 First regular newspapers in France.

1780 *Bengal Gazette* founded in India.

1783 *Pennsylvania Evening Post* is America's first daily newspaper.

1785 First issue of *The Times* newspaper in London.

1789 Article XIX of Rights of Man declares 'free communication of thought and opinion'. First Arabic newspaper *Al-Hawadith al-Yawmiyah* (The Daily Events) in Egypt.

1791 First Amendment of the US Constitution provides model for freedom of press. The *Observer*, Britain's oldest surviving Sunday newspaper, established.

1793 Inauguration of the optical telegraph in France.

1821 *Manchester Guardian* founded.

1822 The beginnings of the modern Catholic missionary press in France.

1826 *Le Figaro* founded in France.

1827 Photography invented. *El Mercurio*, Chile's national newspaper, founded.

1828 *Freedom's Journal*, first African American newspaper in the USA, launched.

1831 *The Sydney Morning Herald* founded. First Turkish newspaper in the Ottoman Empire, the 'Almanac of Events', published.

1833 The first issue of the *New York Sun* – the beginning of the penny press.

1835 Creation of the Havas news agency, the world's first wire service.

1837 Invention of electric telegraph by Samuel Morse.

1838 *The Times of India* founded. First commercial telegraph link in England.

1840 Invention of the adhesive postage stamp and reform of the postal service in England.

1843 Creation of the first modern US advertising agency. *The Economist* founded.

1844 First commercial telegraph – between Washington and Baltimore.

1845 First issue of *Scientific American*.

1848 Creation of *Associated Press*.

1849 Creation of the German news agency Wolff.

1851 France–England underwater cable link. Creation of Reuters.

1852 Havas launches into advertising, then in its infancy.

1854 Telegraph used by military in Crimean War. First overseas Chinese newspaper founded in San Francisco.

1856 British decree regulating the relations between the press and military during the Crimean War.

1858 *The Straits Times* starts as a daily in Singapore.

1860 Telegraph is widely used to distribute news accounts of US Civil War. England and India linked by telegraph.

1861 *New York Times* founded.

1865 Founding of the International Telegraph Union – first telegraph regulations. Creation of the US advertising agency J. Walter Thompson. International Morse code adopted.

1866 First transatlantic cable becomes operational. Typewriter invented.

1869 Creation of the US news agency APA, later UPI.

1870 News agency cartel (Havas/Reuters/Wolff) divides up world market. More than 140 newspaper titles published in Indian languages.

1871   Underwater cables laid down in China and Japanese seas.

1874   Cable network laid down in the South Atlantic.

1875   Creation of the International Bureau of Weights and Measures. Universal Postal Union founded. *Al-Ahram* established in Cairo.

1876   Alexander Graham Bell patents telephone. *Buenos Aires Herald* founded in Argentina. *Corriere della Sera* founded in Italy.

1878   Invention of the phonograph. First telephone lines in the USA.

1880   *New York Graphic* prints first halftone photographs.

1881   French law passed establishing freedom of the press.

1884   Adoption of Greenwich Mean Time as world standard time.

1885   Berlin Telegraph Conference: first provisions for international telephone service.

1886   Invention of the linotype. Berne International Convention on Copyright.

1888   Founding of the *Financial Times*.

1889   Founding of the *Wall Street Journal*. Launch of Coca-Cola in the USA.

1890   French popular daily *Le Petit Journal* reaches a circulation of a million copies. *Asahi Shimbun* (morning sun) founded in Japan.

1891   *Jornal do Brasil* founded.

1893   United International Bureaux for the Protection of Intellectual Property (best known by its French acronym BIRPI) created in Berne. First international press congress in Chicago.

1894   *Rossiiskoe Telegrafnoe Agentstvo* (RTA), first Russian news agency, founded. First comics appear in US newspapers.

1896   Colour printing for comics. Lumière Brothers develop motion picture camera. Britain's first popular newspaper, *Daily Mail*, founded. Adolph Ochs adopts an 'information' style of journalism at the *New York Times*.

1897   The Gramophone Company, predecessor of EMI, founded in London. Marconi patents wireless telegraph.

1898   The Dreyfus Affair in France and the Spanish-American war in Cuba – widely covered by the press.

1899   J. Walter Thompson establishes 'sales bureau' in London. Sun Yat Sen founds *Chung-kuo Jih-pao* (Chinese daily paper).

1901   First wireless transatlantic telegraph transmission – from England to Canada.

1902   First radio transmissions of the human voice.

1905   Radio telegraphy used in Russo-Japanese war. First US public cinema – The Electric Theatre – opens in Pittsburgh.

1906   Berlin Conference on Wireless Telegraphy: creation of the International Radiotelegraph Union. Electromagnetic spectrum divided into bands for different services. Opening of first public cinema in France.

1907   Founding of the French newsreel, *Pathé*.

1909   Creation of the first syndicate for the distribution of comic strips, crossword puzzles and other features.

1911   First marketing firms in the USA. Woodbury Soap launches its 'The skin you love to touch' campaign in the *Ladies' Home Journal*, marking the first time sex appeal is used in advertising. First film studio built in Hollywood.

1912 First editions of *Pravda* (Truth). US film companies – Fox and Universal – founded.

1913 First Indian feature-length film, *Raja Harishchandra*, released.

1914 Audit Bureau of Circulation formed in the USA, standardizing auditing procedures and tightening up definitions of paid circulation.

1915 First foreign advertising agency established in Shanghai. Creation of the King Feature Syndicate and beginning of the internationalization of comics.

1917 Founding of the American Association of Advertising Agencies. Petrograd Telegraph Agency declared central information organ of Soviet government. Radio used to announce victory of communist revolution.

1918 Kodak develops portable camera. Establishment in France of a special committee for 'aesthetic propaganda abroad'.

1919 Soviet Russia begins international broadcasting. USA links with Japan via wireless. General Electric creates Radio Corporation of America to take over monopoly of American Marconi Company and create first transnational US communications conglomerate.

1920 First illustrated news magazines published in Germany. KDKA of Pittsburgh is first commercial radio station in the USA. IBM produces first electric typewriter. International Telephone and Telegraph founded. First radio station in Africa set up in Johannesburg. Turkish newsagency Anadolu Ajaansi founded.

1921 The Komintern becomes an instrument of international communication. KDKA transmits the world's first religious broadcast.

1922 First regular radio broadcasts and first radio commercial in New York. First issue of *Reader's Digest*.

1923 *Time*, first 'news magazine', founded.

1924 Creation of CCIF (International Telephone Consultative Committee) in Paris. Columbia Pictures founded. Disney creates first filmed cartoon.

1925 The Telegraph Agency of the Soviet Union (TASS) founded. Creation of CCIT (International Telegraph Consultative Committee) in Paris. Brazil's *O Globo* newspaper founded.

1926 Beginning of sound cinema. NBC begins network broadcasting, linking 25 stations in 21 US cities. First commercial telephone service between the USA and the UK by long-wave radio.

1927 Radiotelegraph Conference in Washington: creation of the CCIR (International Radio Consultative Committee). BBC founded. *One Man's Family*, popular radio soap opera, begins in the USA, lasts until 1959. Establishment of the first two international advertising networks (J. Walter Thompson and McCann Erickson). First radio broadcasts in China. AP begins newsphoto distribution. CBS formed.

1928 First 'all-talking picture' – *Lights of N.Y.* First public display of Disney's *Mickey Mouse* cartoon, with sound.

1929 First regular Soviet radio broadcasts destined for abroad, in German, French and later in English. *Business Week* launched. Cable & Wireless founded, merging all British international communications interests.

1930 First modern supermarket opens in New York.

1931 International religious radio starts with creation of Radio Vatican. India's first talkie motion picture, *Alam Ara*, released. Chinese news agency, Xinhua, founded.

1932 Empire Service of the BBC set up. Telegraph Union changes name to International Telecommunication Union (ITU). Gallup poll established.

1933 Hitler creates the Ministry of Propaganda and Enlightenment of the People under Goebbels. First 'Fireside Chats' by US President Roosevelt, utilizes radio medium. Radio Luxembourg, Europe's first major commercial broadcaster, goes on air. *Newsweek* starts publication.

1934 Creation of the Federal Communications Commission in the USA. Regular TV transmission in Soviet Union. First news agency in Iran, Pars Agency, founded. The documentary *Triumph of the Will* celebrates Nazi power.

1935 Italy begins Arabic broadcasting to the Middle East. France starts short-wave radio transmission for overseas listeners.

1936 First issue of *Life*. First Gallup polls in a political campaign. Inauguration of BBC television studio.

1937 *West African Pilot*, first nationalist newspaper, founded in Nigeria. *Guiding Light*, first radio soap opera, aired in the USA. Disney's first feature-length film, *Snow White and the Seven Dwarfs*, premièred.

1938 The International Convention Concerning the Use of Broadcasting in the Cause of Peace comes into force. The International Advertising Association founded in New York. Radio surpasses magazines as source of advertising revenue in the USA. Arabic Service becomes the first foreign-language section of the BBC Empire Service. First international edition of *Reader's Digest* published in London.

1939 First TV broadcasts in the USA. Paperback books start publishing revolution.

1941 First TV advertisement broadcast – in the USA. China Radio International founded.

1942 Creation of Voice of America. The USA organizes the War Advertising Council to help voluntary advertising for war effort. *Why We Fight* series of effective documentary propaganda.

1944 Agence France Presse founded. First issue of *Le Monde*.

1945 UNESCO established. France creates commercial international station Radio Monte Carlo.

1946 First large-scale electronic digital computer – Electronic Numerical Integrator And Calculator (ENIAC) founded in the USA. First TV sponsorship for a sporting event in the USA.

1947 Transistor developed. International photo agency, Magnum, founded in the USA. International Organization for Standardization founded.

1948 UN Conference on Freedom of Information. *People's Daily* (*Renmin Ribao*) launched in China. First drive-through McDonald's restaurant – the term 'fast food' coined.

1949 Network TV begins in the USA. *Stop the Music*, first TV quiz show in the USA.

1950 First broadcast by Radio Free Europe. First international credit card, Diner's Club, launched.

1951 NBC's *Today* programme begins, mixing news and features. International Press Institute founded.

1952 Universal Copyright Convention adopted. Sony develops stereo broadcasting in Japan. International Federation of Journalists, the world's largest organization of journalists, founded.

1953 United States Information Agency (USIA) created. Deutsche Welle starts broadcasting. First broadcast by Radio Liberty.

1954 First transistor radio produced in the USA. McCarthy hearings on television. CBS becomes the largest advertising medium in the world. Trans World Radio, US-based global evangelical radio, starts broadcasts from Morocco. Colour TV broadcasting begins in the USA.

1955 'The Marlboro Man' advertisement for Marlboro, the world's best-selling cigarette, launched – it becomes top advertising icon of twentieth century. First Disneyland opens. Independent Television (ITV) starts transmission in Britain.

1956 First transatlantic underwater telephone cable.

1957 The Soviet Union launches the first space satellite – sputnik ('travelling companion'), sending first radio signals from space.

1958 UN establishes Committee on the Peaceful Uses of Outer Space.

1959 ITU Geneva conference makes first radio-frequency allocations for space communications.

1960 Nixon–Kennedy debates televised. NASA launches ECHO-1, first telecommunications satellite. In-flight movies introduced on airlines.

1962 AT&T launches Telstar-1, first privately owned active communications satellite, linking the USA with Europe. First telephone communication and TV broadcast via satellite – ECHO-1.

1963 ITU organizes First World Space Radiocommunication Conference in Geneva. Hughes designs and launches the world's first geosynchronous communications satellite, SYNCOM-II.

1964 Creation of Intelsat (International Telecommunications Satellite Organization). The USSR launches its first communication satellite (Molnya). Inter Press Service founded. First electronic mail – in the USA.

1965 Launching of the first geostationary communications satellite, Early Bird, of the Intelsat system.

1966 Xerox introduces facsimile machines.

1967 The USA and the Soviet Union sign Treaty on Peaceful Uses of Outer Space.

1968 Portable video recorders introduced. Reuters starts the world's first computerized news distribution service.

1969 The Internet born as a US Defense-backed experimental network called APRANET (Advanced Research Projects Agency Network). Brazilian television company Globo established. Intelsat provides global TV coverage of Apollo lunar landing to 500 million people.

1970 International direct dialling between London and New York first introduced.

1971 ITU conference on space communications adopts Regulation 428A to prevent spillover of satellite broadcast signals into countries without their prior consent. Soviet Union organizes Intersputnik, a satellite telecommunications network linking socialist countries. Intel introduces first microprocessor – 'the computer chip'.

1972 Debate in UNESCO and UN General Assembly on an agreement to regulate direct-broadcast satellites. UNESCO adopts declaration of principles for satellite broadcasting, including requirement that for direct satellite broadcasting there be prior agreement between the sending country and the receiving countries.

1973 First steps towards New World Information and Communication Order (NWICO) debate.

1974 First direct broadcasting satellite, ATS 6, launched. Opinion polls show that TV overtakes newspapers as prime source of news for most Americans.

1975 Non-aligned news agencies pool created. European Space Agency formed. Fibre-optic transmission developed. Cable brings multichannel TV to the USA. Radio France Internationale created. Microsoft founded.

1976 India launches SITE project satellites for education. UNESCO conference in Nairobi endorses call for NWICO. Apple computer launched.

1977 Creation of the International Commission for the study of communications problems (UNESCO) under Sean McBride. Eutelsat (European Telecommunications Satellite Organization) founded.

1978 Videotext developed. Japan launches first Yuri satellite. Intelsat provides coverage of World Cup Football matches to 1 billion people in 42 countries.

1979 World Administrative Radio Conference (WARC) in Geneva (ITU) revises radio regulations. Inmarsat formed. First consumer advertisements on Chinese television. Sony invents Walkman.

1980 Publication of the McBride Commission report. Ted Turner launches CNN, world's first all-news network.

1981 IBM brings out its first personal computer. The all-music channel MTV goes on air.

1982 The Falklands War: first appearance of the practice of organizing pools of journalists. INSAT (Indian National Satellite) communication satellite launched. Compact disc (CD) player launched in Japan.

1983 World Communication Year. First Eutelsat satellite launched. Embargo on information by the Pentagon during the US intervention in Grenada. Worldnet, USA's global public affairs, information and cultural TV network, launched. USA starts anti-Cuban Radio Martí. Cellular (mobile) telephones available in the USA.

1984 Green Paper by the EC on 'Television Without Frontiers'. US giant Hughes launches Leasat to create a global military communications network. Indonesia launches its first satellite Palapa. Federal Communications Commission grants PanAmSat (Pan American Satellite) rights to launch and exploit a private satellite system. China develops first Chinese-language computer operation system. Canal Plus, first pay TV channel in France, launched. Michael Jackson's *Thriller* album sells more copies than any other to date.

1985 The USA withdraws from UNESCO. PeaceNet – the first alternative national computer network in the USA – established. Arabsat launches its first communication satellite. Brazil becomes first South American country to launch its own satellite – Brazilsat. CNN International launched. Reuters starts a news picture service and takes control of TV news agency Visnews. Capital Cities buys American Broadcasting Corporation (ABC), creating the world's largest entertainment company. Reporters Sans Frontières founded in Paris. America Online (AOL) founded.

1986 Uruguay Round of GATT negotiations begin. The UK withdraws from UNESCO. First alternative satellite network Deep Dish TV Satellite Network established in the USA. China's national satellite telecommunications network operational.

1987 EC Green Paper on telecommunications. USSR ends jamming of VOA.

1988 First ASTRA satellite launched by a private European organization. Pan-Arabic newspaper, *Al-Hayat*, launched in London. USSR ends jamming Russian service of Deutsche Welle.

1989 Merger of Time and Warner Bros. Sony buys Columbia Pictures. First private satellite launched in the USA. Sky, first satellite TV, launched in Britain. Interfax agency started in Soviet Union to supply news, mainly to foreigners. UNESCO publishes first *World Communication Report*. British researcher Tim Berners-Lee creates World Wide Web.

1990 ASIASAT, first commercial Asian satellite, launched. The USA starts TV Martí. CNN becomes a global news network with Gulf crisis. Microsoft launches Microsoft Windows 3.0.

1991 BBC World television launched as a commercial venture. STAR TV, the first pan-Asian television network, launched. France launches Telecom 2A satellite. Russian edition of *Reader's Digest*.

1992 Turkey's TRT Avrasya channel beams programmes via satellite to Turkic republics in Central Asia. Operation Restore Hope in Somalia backed by media logistics. The browser Mosaic brings the Internet to non-technical computer users. ITU organizes WARC-92 on frequency allocations. Intelsat and NASA in joint space mission. Spain launches Hispasat satellite.

1993 World Radio Network launched on ASTRA in Europe. OIRT, the former union of eastern European broadcasters merges with European Broadcasting Union. First World Telecommunication Standardization Conference in Helsinki (ITU). China's first international optical cable system, linking it with Japan, becomes operational.

1994 CD-ROM becomes a standard feature on personal computers. Turkish-owned satellite Turksat launched. World Trade Organization (WTO) created. APTV, a global video news-gathering agency, launched. Clinton signs International Broadcasting Act, establishing International Broadcasting Bureau. BBC Worldwide, commercial arm of BBC, created. DirecTV launches first digital DBS service in the USA. Yahoo! launched.

1995 PanAmSat becomes the world's first private company to provide global satellite services with the launch of its third satellite – PAS-4. Trade-Related Aspects of Intellectual Property Rights (TRIPS) agreement, comes into force. Bloomberg television launched. First computer-animated feature film, *Toy Story*, released.

1996 CNN becomes part of Time Warner, making it the world's biggest media corporation. The USA passes Telecommunications Act. Radio France Internationale takes over Radio Monte Carlo. WIPO enters into a co-operation agreement with WTO to implement TRIPS Agreement. The USA launches Radio Free Asia. Information Technology Agreement signed within WTO to liberalize global trade in IT. The French Canal Satellite becomes Europe's first digital platform. MSNBC, a cable and online news service, launched by Microsoft and NBC. Cybermag *Slate* launched. Japan launches digital versatile disc (DVD) video players.

1997 EU revises its directive on 'Television without Frontiers'. European Commission Green Paper on *Convergence of Telecommunications, Media and Information Technology Sectors*. Lockheed Martin Intersputnik, a joint venture of Lockheed Martin and Intersputnik, comes into force. WTO's telecommunication accord. PanAmSat and Hughes Galaxy combine operations.

1998 ITU's World Telecommunication Development Conference launches project on e-commerce for developing countries. RFE/RL launches Radio Free Iraq. AP takes over Worldwide Television News. Monica Lewinsky story breaks on the Internet. British consortium On-Digital launches world's first terrestrial digital TV service. Google founded.

1999 World Wide Web used for propaganda during NATO's war in Kosovo. Internet advertising heads toward $3 billion. Global mobile satellite communications provider, Inmarsat, becomes first intergovernmental organization to be transformed into a commercial company. Viacom merges with CBS.

2000 Billions watch the millennium celebrations on global TV. AOL merges with Time Warner. CCTV-9, the English-language channel launched from Beijing. EMI and Time Warner Music merge to form the world's second largest music company. Internet becomes accessible over mobile phones. Britain's Vodafone merges with Germany's Mannesmann to create world's biggest telecommunications company. GATS negotiations begin.

2001 Terrorist attacks in New York and Washington. Intelsat privatized. *Al-Jazeera* becomes internationally known for its coverage from Afghanistan. Videophones used for reporting. Shanghai Media Group, China's first media conglomerate formed.

2002 Fox News in USA redefines broadcast journalism. *Fahrenheit 9/11* becomes most successful documentary film.

2003 Texting makes the SARS epidemic internationally known. USA launches *Al-Hurra*, a propaganda channel in the wake of Iraq invasion.

2004 Weblogs become important during US presidential election. China emerges as the world's largest exporter of information technology products. South Korea has highest broadband penetration in the world.

2005 Mobile phones exceed fixed lines in the world. Pod-casting introduced. Television companies start providing content for mobile telephones. *Telesur*, first public news network reaching across Latin America, launched. Intelsat takes over PanAmSat. Internet governance dominates UN World Summit on Information Society. Russia TV, a global English-language channel, launched from Moscow. UNESCO adopts the Convention on the Protection and Promotion of the Diversity of Cultural Expressions. EU launches first satellite of its Galileo global navigation project. Mobile telephone subscribers cross 2 billion mark, 31 per cent mobile penetration worldwide.

2006 *Al-Jazeera* starts international service in English. BBC plans an Arabic-language TV channel. Inmarsat launches Broadband Global Area Network.

Appendix II

Useful websites

International organizations

ILO	www.ilo.org
IMF	www.imf.org
ITU	www.itu.int
OECD	www.oecd.org
UN	www.UN.org
UNCTAD	www.unctad.org
UNDP	www.undp.org
UNESCO	www.UNESCO.org
WIPO	www.wipo.org
World Bank	www.worldbank.org
WTO	www.WTO.org

Governmental and intergovernmental organizations

Asia-Pacific Broadcasting Union	www.abu.org.my
Department of Commerce (USA)	www.doc.gov
European Audiovisual Observatory	www.obs.coe.int
European Broadcasting Union	www.ebu.ch
European Union	www.europa.eu.int
Federal Communications Commission	www.fcc.gov
Indian Space Research Organisation	www.isro.org
Institut National de l'Audiovisuel	www.ina.fr
NASA	www.nasa.gov

Non-governmental and commercial organizations

AC Nielsen	http://acnielsen.com
Adbusters	www.adbusters.org
AIDCOM	www.aidcom.com
AMIC	www.amic.org.sg

BBC Monitoring Service	www.monitor.bbc.co.uk
British Film Institute	www.bfi.org.uk
Fairness and Accuracy in Reporting	www.fair.org
Free Speech	www.freespeech.org
Indymedia	www.indymedia.org
Inktomi	www.inktomi.com
International Intellectual Property Alliance	www.iipa.com
Internet Society	www.isoc.org
Internet Software Consortium	www.isc.org
Motion Picture Association of America	www.mpaa.org
NASSCOM (India)	www.nasscom.org
One World.Net	www.oneworld.net
Open Democracy	www.opendemocracy.net
Paper Tiger	www.papertiger.org
Project Censored	www.sonoma.edu/projectcensored
Third World Network	www.twnside.org.sg
TV France International	www.tvfi.com/english
Undercurrent	www.undercurrent.org
World Wide Web Consortium	www.w3.org
Zenith Media	www.zenithmedia.com

Satellite organizations/companies

Arabsat	www.arabsat.org
Asiasat	www.asiasat.com.hk
Eutelsat	www.eutelsat.org
Hispasat	www.hispasat.es
Hughes	www.hughes.com
Inmarsat	www.inmarsat.telia.com
Intelsat	www.intelsat.com
Intersputnik	www.intersputnik.com
Lockheed Martin	www.lmgt.com
Loral Space and Communication	www.loral.com
PanAmSat	www.panamsat.com
SES-Global	www.ses-global.com

Multimedia corporations

Bertelsmann	www.bertelsmann.com
Disney	http://disney.go.com
News Corporation	www.newscorp.com
Sony Corporation	www.world.sony.com
Telecommunication Inc.	www.tci.com
Time Warner	www.timewarner.com
Viacom	www.viacom.com

Computer and telecommunication companies

AT&T	www.att.com
Cisco Systems	www.cisco.com
Dell Computer	www.dell.com
Ericsson	www.ericsson.com
IBM	www.ibm.com
Intel	www.intel.com
Microsoft Corporation	www.microsoft.com
Motorola	www.motorola.com
Network Associates	www.networkassociates.com
Network Solutions	www.netsol.com
Nokia	www.nokia.co.uk
Oracle	www.oracle.com
Sun Microsystems	www.sun.com

News agencies

Agence France Presse	www.afp.com
APTN	www.aptn.com
Associated Press	www.ap.org
Bloomberg	www.bloomberg.com
Inter Press Service	www.ips.org
Itar-Tass	www.itar-tass.com
Reuters	www.reuters.com
United Press International	www.upi.com
Xinhua	www.xinhuanet.com/english

Radio stations

All India Radio	http://allindiaradio.org/
BBC World Service	www.bbc.co.uk/worldservice
China Radio International	http://en.chinabroadcast.cn/
Deutsche Welle	www.dwelle.de
Radio France International	www.rfi.fr
Radio Free Europe/Radio Liberty	www.rferl.org
Voice of America	www.voa.gov
Voice of Russia	www.vor.ru
World Radio Network	www.wrn.org

Television channels

Al-Jazeera	http://english.aljazeera.net
American Broadcasting Corporation	http://abc.go.com
ARD (Germany)	www.ard.de
Asahi Broadcasting Corporation (Japan)	www.tv-asahi.co.jp

Australian Broadcasting Corporation	www.abc.net.au
B4U (Bollywood for You)	www.b4utv.com
BBC World	www.bbcworld.com
Black Entertainment Television	www.betnetworks.com
Canadian Broadcasting Corporation	www.cbc.ca
Canal Plus	http://www.canalplus.fr/
Cartoon Network	www.CartoonNetwork.com
Channel 4 Television (UK)	www.channel4.com
China Central Television	www.cctv.com.cn/english
CNBC	www.cnbc.com
CNN	www.cnn.com
Columbia Broadcasting System (CBS)	www.cbs.com
DirecTV	www.directv.com
Discovery	www.discovery.com
Doordarshan (India)	www.ddindia.net
ESPN	http://espn.go.com
Euronews	www.euronews.net
Fox Network	www.fox.com
Foxtel (Australia)	www.foxtel.com.au
France 2	www.france2.fr
Globo (Brazil)	www.redeglobo.com.br
Independent Television News (UK)	www.itn.co.uk
Korean Broadcasting System	www.kbs.co.kr
Middle East Broadcasting Centre (MBC)	www.mbc1.tv
MNet (South Africa)	www.mnet.co.za
MSNBC	www.msnbc.msn.com
Music Television (MTV)	www.mtv.com
National Broadcasting Company (NBC)	www.nbc.com
NDTV (New Delhi Television)	www.ndtv.com
Nickelodeon	www.nick.com
Nippon Hoso Kyokai (NHK)	www.nhk.or.jp/english
Orbit	www.orbit.net
Phoenix Chinese channel	www.phoenixtv.com
Public Broadcasting Services	www.pbs.com
Russia Today	www.russiatoday.ru/
Showtime	www.showtimearabia.com
Sky News	www.sky.com/skynews
Sony Entertainment Television	www.setindia.com
South African Broadcasting Corporation	www.sabc.co.za
South Asia World	www.southasiaworld.tv
STAR TV	www.star-tv.com
Televisa (Mexico)	www.televisa.com.mx
ZDF (Germany)	www.zdf.de

Zee TV (India)   www.zeetelevision.com

Newspapers and magazines

Al-Ahram (Egypt)   http://weekly.ahram.org.eg
al Hayat (Saudi Arabia)   www.alhayat.com
Buenos Aires Herald (Argentina)   www.buenosairesherald.com
Business Week   www.businessweek.com
China Daily   www.chinadaily.com.cn/english
Editor & Publisher   www.mediainfo.com
Filmfare (India)   http://filmfare.indiatimes.com
Fortune   www.pathfinder.com/fortune
Frontline (India)   www.frontlineonline.com
India Today   www.india-today.com
International Herald Tribune   www.iht.com
Le monde-diplomatique   www.monde-diplomatique.fr/en
Newsweek   www.newsweek.com
People's Daily (China)   http://english.people.com.cn/
Reader's Digest   www.readersdigest.com
SatNews magazine   www.satnews.com
Slate   www.slate.com
The Economist   www.economist.com
The Financial Times   www.ft.com
The Guardian   www.guardian.co.uk
The Hindu (India)   www.the-hindu.com
The New Straits Times (Singapore)   http://straitstimes.asia1.com.sg
The New York Times   www.nyt.com
The Times   www.the-times.co.uk
The Times of India   www.timesofindia.com
The Washington Post   www.wp.com
Time   www.pathfinder.com/time
Variety   www.variety.com
Via Satellite magazine   www.viasatellite.com/
Wall Street Journal   www.wsj.com

Publishers

Amazon.com   www.amazon.com
Barnes and Noble   www.barnesandnoble.com
International Data Group   www.idg.net
International Thomson   http://thomson.com/
McGraw-Hill   www.mcgraw-hill.com
Pearson Group   www.pearson-plc.com
Random House   www.randomhouse.com

Reed-Elsevier	www.reed-elsevier.com
Wolters-Kluwer	www.wolters-kluwer.com

Journals

Asian Journal of Communication	www.tandf.co.uk/journals/titles/01292986
Canadian Journal of Communication	www.cjc-online.ca
Columbia Journalism Review	www.cjr.org
European Journal of Communication	http://ejc.sagepub.com
Foreign Affairs	www.foreignaffairs.org
Foreign Policy	www.foreignpolicy.com
Ecquid Novi	http://academic.sun.ac.za/ecquidnovi
Global Media and Communication	http://gmc.sagepub.com
Global Media Journal	http://lass.calumet.purdue.edu/cca/gmj
Harvard International Journal of Press/Politics	http://hij.sagepub.com
International Communication Gazette	http://gaz.sagepub.com
International Journal of Cultural Studies	http://ics.sagepub.com
Javnost (The Public)	www.euricom.si/javnosg
Journal of Communication	www.joc.oupjournals.org
Journalism	http://jou.sagepub.com
Media, Culture & Society	http://mcs.sagepub.com
New Media & Society	http://nms.sagepub.com
Nordicom Review	www.nordicom.gu.se
Public Culture	www.newschool.edu/gf/publicculture
Television & New Media	http://tvn.sagepub.com
Theory, Culture & Society	http://tcs.sagepub.com
Transnational Broadcasting Studies	www.tbsjournal.com

Internet search engines

Alta Vista	www.altavista.com
Baidu	www.baidu.com
Excite	www.excite.com
Google	www.google.com
Infoseek	www2.infoseek.com
Lycos	www.lycos.com
Webcrawler	www.webcrawler.com
Yahoo!	www.yahoo.com

Please note: Web addresses current at the time of publication.

Appendix III

Discussion questions

Chapter 1

- What was the impetus for the development of a global telegraph network and what impact did it have?
- What does it mean to say that the news agency Reuters was an 'empire within the British Empire'?
- What was the role of covert radio stations during the cold war and were they effective?
- How relevant are the 1970s NWICO debates in the twenty-first century?
- Assess the impact of the development of global communications systems on processes of democratization in authoritarian regimes.
- To what extent have the broadcasters 'news values' in post-communist countries been shaped by increasingly commercial imperatives?

Chapter 2

- How relevant is the concept of media imperialism in understanding information inequality in the world?
- Is globalization an inevitable consequence of the diffusion of communications technologies?
- How far is globalization a special feature of postmodern times? What are the media that embody its main aspects?
- Colonialism may have ended, but is it fair to say that cultural colonialism lives on?
- How relevant is dependency theory in understanding the globalization of Western media organizations?
- Evaluate the relevance of the concept of 'public sphere' for debates on contemporary political communications.

Chapter 3

- Has the privatization of broadcasting widened or reduced choice for audiences worldwide.
- What role has the World Trade Organization played in the globalization of telecommunication?
- To what extent have global media companies engaged in corporate marriages? Is this healthy for the democratic flow of communications or should they be regulated?
- Why was Intelsat privatized? Who benefited from this and who might lose out?
- What are the implications of transnational electronic media for space, place and time?
- What strategies have the media conglomerates, such as News Corporation, adopted to enter media markets in Asia?

Chapter 4

- What are the political and economic implications of the trend towards the concentration of media power among so few transnational conglomerates?
- Are there significant differences between the processes of globalization of news and that of entertainment? What might this mean for audiences?
- Do American media corporations have a competitive advantage in the international television programme market?
- Is it fair to say that the US-dominated, Western news media shape the global news agenda?
- How useful is the concept of 'public service' in the era of global broadcasting?
- Which brands and products lend themselves best to global advertising campaigns? What problems have to be overcome in order to be successful?
- Are 'global' media helping to create a global public sphere?
- Is the concept of 'cultural imperialism' relevant in understanding globalization of Anglo-American media?

Chapter 5

- What global newspapers and magazines are there? How do they differ from 'local' newspapers and magazines?
- Is it fair to speak of a Hollywood hegemony? What might be the reasons for the US domination of global film production and distribution?
- How far, and in what ways, has the 'Television Without Frontiers' process affected television production and transmission in the European Union?
- What is the 'local' and what is its relationship to the 'global' in the context of globalization processes?

- Why is English the dominant language for global commerce and communication?
- Is there evidence to suggest hybridization of media and cultural products?
- Are transnational television and the Internet creating a unified 'global' culture?

Chapter 6

- Why are telenovelas popular around the world?
- How has digital and mobile technology affected international broadcasting?
- Are television networks such as Phoenix only aimed at a geo-linguistic market? How might they reach a wider audience?
- To what extent have non-Western news networks such as al-Jazeera challenged the US/UK version of the 'global war on terrorism'?
- Why was the English-language CCTV-9 launched? Who might be its intended audience?
- Do non-Indians watch Indian films? If yes, why? If no, why not?
- To what extent are countries like Brazil, Egypt and India independent actors in the international media market?

Chapter 7

- What is meant by a global civil society? How has the Internet contributed to creating such a society?
- What do you understand by 'global digital divide'? What are the main obstacles to Internet diffusion in developing countries and what might facilitate its diffusion?
- Is it fair to say that the 'coups and earthquake syndrome' continues to dominate coverage of Africa in the international media?
- How does the nature of the state affect the development of the media? Think in terms of a contrast between India and China.
- Should an international statutory body be created to regulate global media?
- Is the rise of market-led infotainment leading to disengagement with the political process?
- Who should govern the Internet? Should it be regulated and how?
- Is there a need to internationalize media and communication studies? How might this be done?

References

ABBAS, A. and ERNI, J. N. (eds) (2005) *Internationalising cultural studies: an anthology.* Oxford: Blackwell.

ADAY, S., LIVINGSTON, S. and HEBERT, M. (2005) Embedding the truth: a cross-cultural analysis of objectivity and television coverage of the Iraq War. *Harvard International Journal of Press/Politics*, **10**, 1: 3–21.

ADORNO, T. (1991) *The cultural industry: selected essays on mass culture.* London: Routledge.

ADORNO, T. and HORKHEIMER, M. (1979) *Dialectic of enlightenment.* London: Verso. (originally published in German in 1947).

AGGARWALA, N. (1979) What is development news? *Journal of Communication,* **29**: 180–1.

AGRAWAL, B. (ed.) (1977) *Satellite Instructional Television Experiment, social evaluation: impact on adults.* Two volumes, Bangalore: Indian Space Research Organisation.

AGRAWAL, B. (1978) *Satellite Instructional Television Experiment: television comes to villages.* Bangalore: Indian Space Research Organisation. [On SITE, see also articles in *Journal of Communication*, **29**, 4 in 1979.]

AHLERS, D. (2006) News consumption and the new electronic media. *Harvard International Journal of Press/Politics*, **11**, 1: 29–52.

AHMAD, A. (1992) *In theory: classes, nations, literatures.* London: Verso.

AKSOY, A. and ROBINS, K. (1992) Hollywood for the 21st century – global competition for critical mass in image markets. *Cambridge Journal of Economics*, **16**, 1: 1–22.

ALEXANDRE, L. (1993) Television Marti: 'open skies' over the South. In Nordenstreng, K. and Schiller, H. (eds), *Beyond national sovereignty.* Norwood, NJ: Ablex Publishing.

ALI, T. (2001) *The clash of fundamentalisms: crusades, jihads and modernity.* London: Verso.

ALI, T. (2003) *Bush in Babylon: The recolonization of Iraq.* London: Verso.

ALLAN, S. and ZELIZER, B. (eds) (2004) *Reporting war.* London: Routledge.

ALLEN, R. (ed.) (1995) *To be continued ... soap opera around the world.* New York: Routledge.

ALTERMAN, J. (2005) The challenge for Al-Jazeera International, *Transnational Broadcasting Studies*, **14**, Spring. http://www.tbsjournal.com/schleifermbc.html

ALTHUSSER, L. (1971) *Lenin and philosophy and other essays*. London: New Left Books.

AMIN, S. (1976) *Accumulation on a world scale: a critique of the theory of underdevelopment*. New York: Monthly Review Press.

AMIN, S. (1988) *Eurocentrism*. Translated by R. Moore, New York: Monthly Review Press. First published in French as *L'eurocentrisme: critique d'un idéologie*. Paris: Anthropos.

AMIN, S. (1997) *Capitalism in the age of globalization*. London: Zed Books.

ANDERSON, B. (1991) *Imagined communities: reflections on the origin and spread of nationalism*. Second edition, London: Verso.

APPADURAI, A. (1990) Disjuncture and difference in the global cultural economy. *Public Culture*, **2,** 2: 1–24.

APPADURAI, A. (1996) *Modernity at large: cultural dimensions of globalization*. Minneapolis: University of Minnesota Press.

APPADURAI, A. (ed.) (2001) *Globalization*. Durham, NC: Duke University Press.

ARCHIBUGI, D. and HELD, D. (eds) (1995) *Cosmopolitan democracy*. Cambridge: Polity.

ATKINSON, D. and RABOY, M. (eds) (1997) *Public service broadcasting: the challenges of the 21st century*. Paris: UNESCO.

ATTON, C. (2004) *An alternative Internet: radical media, politics and creativity*. Edinburgh: Edinburgh University Press.

BAGDIKIAN, B. (1997) *The media monopoly*. Fifth edition, Boston: Beacon.

BAGDIKIAN, B. (2004) *The new media monopoly*. Seventh edition, Boston: Beacon.

BANKS, J. (1996) *Monopoly television – MTV's quest to control the music*. Boulder, CO: Westview Press.

BARAN, P. (1957) *The political economy of growth*. New York: Monthly Review Press.

BARBER, B. (1995) *Jihad vs. McWorld*. New York: Times Books.

BARDHAN, P., BOWLES, S. and WALLERSTEIN, M. (eds) (2006) *Globalization and egalitarian redistribution*. New Jersey: Princeton University Press.

BARKER, C. (1997) *Global television*. Oxford: Blackwell.

BARNETT, S. and DOVER, C. (2004) *The world on the box: International issues in news and factual programmes on UK television 1975–2003*. London: Third World and Environment Broadcasting Project (3WE).

BARNOUW, E. and KRISHNASWAMY, S. (1980) *Indian film*. Second edition, New York: Oxford University Press.

BAROOAH-PISHAROTY, S. (2006) Time now for Birbal and company, *The Hindu*, 20 January.

BARRIER, M. (1999) *Hollywood cartoons: American animation in its golden age*. Oxford: Oxford University Press.

BATTELLE, J. (2005) *The Search: how Google and its rivals rewrote the rules of business and transformed our culture*. London: Nicholas Brealey.

BAUDRILLARD, J. (1994) *The illusion of the end*. Translated by C. Turner, Cambridge: Polity. First published in 1992 as *L'illusion de la fin,* Paris: Editions Galilee.

BBC (2004) 'The power of nightmares', BBC 2, October 20, 27 and November 3.

BBC (2005a) *BBC World Service annual report, 2005*, London: British Broadcasting Corporation.

BBC (2005b) *BBC Worldwide annual report, 2005*, London: British Broadcasting Corporation.

BECK, U. (2006) *Cosmopolitan vision*. Cambridge: Polity.

BECKER, J. (2004) Lessons from Russia: a neo-authoritarian media system. *European Journal of Communication*. **19**, 2: 139–63.

BELL, D. (1973) *The coming of post industrial society: a venture in social forecasting*. New York: Basic Books.

BELLAMY, R. (1998) The evolving television sports marketplace. In L. Wenner (ed.), *MediaSport*. New York: Routledge.

BENIGER, J. (1986) *The control revolution*. Cambridge, MA: Harvard University Press.

BENNETT, W. L. (2003) *News: the politics of illusion*. Fifth edition, New York: Addison Wesley Longman.

BERFIELD, S. (1996) Satellite TV: Asia's no pushover. *Asiaweek*, 8 November.

BERNERS-LEE, T. and FISCHETTI, M. (1999) *Weaving the web*. London: Orion Business.

BETTIG, R. (1996) *Copyrighting culture: the political economy of intellectual property*. Boulder, CO: Westview Press.

BHABHA, H. (1994) *The location of culture*. London: Routledge.

BIELBY, D. D. and HARRINGTON, C. L. (2005) Opening America? The telenovelaization of US soap operas. *Television & New Media*, **6**, 4: 383–99.

BLINDER, A. S. (2006) Offshoring: the next industrial revolution? *Foreign Affairs*, March/April.

BLIX, H. (2004) *Disarming Iraq*. London: Pantheon.

BLUMENTHAL, H. and GOODENOUGH, O. (1998) *This business of television*. Second edition, New York: Billboard Books.

BLUMENTHAL, M. (2005) Toward an open-source methodology: What we can learn from the blogosphere, *Public Opinion Quarterly,* **69**, 5: 655–69.

BOK, D. (2003) *Universities in the marketplace: The commercialization of higher education.* New Jersey: Princeton University Press.

BONNELL, V. and FREIDIN, G. (1995) *Televorot* – the role of television coverage in Russia's August 1991 coup. In N. Condee (ed.), *Soviet hieroglyphics: visual culture in late-twentieth century Russia*. Bloomington: Indiana University Press, and London: British Film Institute.

BOURGAULT, L. (1995) *Mass media in sub-Saharan Africa.* Bloomington: Indiana University Press.

BOURDIEU, P. (1998) *On television and journalism.* London: Pluto. Translated from the French by Priscilla Parkhurst Ferguson. Originally published in 1996, Liber – Raison de'agir.

BOURNE, R. (1995) *News on a knife-edge: Gemini journalism and a global agenda.* London: John Libbey.

BOYD-BARRETT, O. (1977) Media imperialism: towards an international framework for the analysis of media systems. In J. Curran, M. Gurevitch and J. Woollacott (eds), *Mass communication and society*. London: Edward Arnold.

BOYD-BARRETT, O. (1980) *The international news agencies.* London: Constable.

BOYD-BARRETT, O. (1998) Media imperialism reformulated. In D. Thussu (ed.), *Electronic empires.* London: Arnold.

BOYD-BARRETT, O. and RANTANEN, T. (eds) (1998) *The globalization of news.* London: Sage.

BOYD-BARRETT, O. and THUSSU, D. (1992) *Contraflow in global news: international and regional news exchange mechanisms.* London: John Libbey, in association with UNESCO.

BRADER, T. (2005) *Campaigning for hearts and minds: how emotional appeals in political ads work.* Chicago: University of Chicago Press.

BRAMAN, S. (ed.) (2004) *The emergent global information policy regime.* Basingstoke: Palgrave.

Brandt Commission (1981) *North-South: a programme for survival.* The Report of the Independent Commission on International Development Issues under the Chairmanship of Willy Brandt, London: Pan Books.

BRECKENRIDGE, C., POLLOCK, S., BHABHA, H. and CHAKRABARTY, D. (2002) *Cosmopolitanism.* Durham, NC: Duke University Press.

BRIGGS, A. (1970) *A history of broadcasting in the United Kingdom, vol. 3, The war of words.* Oxford: Oxford University Press.

BRUNER, R. (2005) *A decade of on-line advertising: 1994–2004*. Double Click (www.doubleclick.com).

BURKE, J. (2004) *Al-Qaeda – The true story of radical Islam*. London: I. B. Tauris.

Business Week (1999) The Internet age, special section. 4 October, 40–113.

CAIRNCROSS, F. (1997) *The death of distance: how the communications revolution will change our lives*. London: Orion Business Books.

CALDER, B. J. and MALTHOUSE, E. C. (2005) Managing media and advertising change with integrated marketing. *Journal of Advertising Research*, **45**: 356–61.

CALHOUN, C. (ed.) (1992) *Habermas and the public sphere*. Cambridge, MA: MIT Press.

CAMMAERTS, B. and AUDENHOVE, L. (2005) Online political debate, unbounded citizenship, and the problematic nature of a transnational Public Sphere. *Political Communication*, **22**, 2: 179–96.

CAREY, J. (1988) *Communication as culture*. Boston: Unwin Hyman.

CASTELLS, M. (2000a) *The information age: economy, society and culture*, vol. 1: *The rise of the network society*. Second edition, Oxford: Blackwell.

CASTELLS, M. (2000b) *The information age: economy, society and culture*, vol. 3: *End of millennium*. Second edition, Oxford: Blackwell.

CASTELLS, M. (2004) *The information age: economy, society and culture*, vol. 2: *The power of identity*. Second edition, Oxford: Blackwell.

CATALBAS, D. (2000) Broadcasting deregulation in Turkey: uniformity within diversity. In J. Curran (ed.), *Media organisations in society*. London: Arnold.

CHALABY, J. (1996) Journalism as an Anglo-American invention. *European Journal of Communication*, **11,** 2: 303–26.

CHALABY, J. (ed.) (2005) *Transnational television worldwide – towards a new media order*. London: I. B. Tauris.

CHAMORRO, E. (1987) *Packaging the Contras: a case of CIA disinformation*. New York: Institute for Media Analysis.

CHANAN, M. (1985) The Reuters Factor: myth and realities of communicology: a scenario. In Radical Science Collective (eds), *Making waves: the politics of communications*. London: Free Association Books.

CHANDLER, R. (1981) *War of ideas: the US propaganda campaign in Vietnam*, Boulder, CO: Westview Press.

CHEAH, P. and ROBBINS, B. (eds) (1998) *Cosmopolitcs: thinking and feeling beyond the nation*. Minneapolis: University of Minnesota Press.

CHERRY, C. (1978) *World communication: threat or promise?* New York: John Wiley.

CLARK, I. (1997) *Globalization and fragmentation: international relations in the twentieth century.* Oxford: Oxford University Press.

CLARKE, S. (2005) UK leader in global format sales, *Television Business International*, April.

COHEN, B. (1963) *The press and foreign policy.* New Jersey: Princeton University Press.

COLINO, R. (1985) Intelsat: facing the challenge of tomorrow. *Journal of International Affairs*, **39**, 1: 129–46.

COLLINS, R. (1998) *From satellite to single market: new communication technology and European public service television.* London: Routledge.

COOK, T. E. (2005) *Governing with the news: the news media as a political institution.* Chicago: Second edition, University of Chicago Press.

CORNER, J. and PELS, D. (eds) (2003) *Media and the restyling of politics: consumerism, celebrity and cynicism.* London: Sage.

CRITCHLOW, J. (1995) *Radio Hole-in-the-Head: Radio Liberty: an insider's story of Cold War broadcasting.* Washington, DC: American University Press.

CROTEAU, D. and HYNES, W. (2005) *The business of media: corporate media and the public interest.* Second edition, London: Sage.

CRYSTAL, D. (1997) *English as a global language.* Cambridge: Cambridge University Press.

CURRAN, J. and SEATON, J. (1997) *Power without responsibility: the press and broadcasting in Britain.* Fifth edition, London: Routledge.

CURRAN, J. and PARK, J. (2000) *De-Westernizing media studies.* London, Routledge.

CURRAN, J. and COULDRY, N. (eds) (2003) *Contesting media power.* Lanham, MD: Rowman & Littlefield.

CURTIN, M. (2003) Media capital: towards the study of spatial flows. *International Journal of Cultural Studies*, **6**, 2: 202–28.

CURWEN, P. (1997) *Restructuring telecommunications: a study of Europe in a global context.* London: Macmillan.

DAHLGREN, P. (2003) *Media and civic engagement.* Cambridge: Cambridge University Press.

DAHLGREN, P. (2005) The Internet, public spheres, and political communication: dispersion and deliberation. *Political Communication,* **22**: 147–62.

DAYAN, D. and KATZ, E. (1992) *Media events: the live broadcasting of history.* Cambridge, MA: Harvard University Press.

DCMS (2005) *Creative industries economic estimates: Statistical bulletin,* October 2005. London: Department of Culture, Media and Sport.

DE BENS, E. and DE SMAELE, H. (2001) The inflow of American television fiction on European broadcasting channels revisited. *European Journal of Communication*, **16**, 1: 51–76.

DE JONG, W., SHAW, M. and STAMMERS, N. (eds) (2005) *Global activism, global media.* London: Pluto.

DESAI, J. (2004) *Beyond Bollywood – the cultural politics of South Asian diasporic film.* London: Routledge.

DESHPANDE, S. (2000) Dear reader, *The Hindu*, 2 January.

DESMOND, R. (1978) *The information process: world news reporting to the twentieth century.* Iowa City: University of Iowa Press.

DICKEN, P. (1998) *Global shift: transforming the world economy.* Third edition, London: Paul Chapman Publishing (Sage).

DINNICK, R. (1999) Caught in the web of war. *Internet Magazine*, June, 38–41.

DORFMAN, A. and MATTELART, A. (1975) *How to read Donald Duck: imperialist ideology in the Disney comic.* New York: International General Editions.

DOWNING, J. (2001) *Radical media: rebellious communication and social movements.* Thousand Oaks, CA: Sage.

DRAKE, W. (1993) Territoriality and intangibility: transborder data flows and national sovereignty. In K. Nordenstreng and H. Schiller (eds), *Beyond national sovereignty.* Norwood, NJ: Ablex Publishing.

DRAKE, W. and NICOLAIDIS, K. (1992) Ideas, interests and institutionalization: 'trade in services' and the Uruguay Round. *International Organization*, **46**: 37–100.

DUNNETT, P. (1990) *The world television industry: an economic analysis.* London: Routledge.

DURHAM, M. G. and KELLNER, D. (eds) (2006) *Media and cultural studies: key works.* Second edition, Oxford: Blackwell.

DYSON, K. and HUMPHREYS, P. (eds) (1990) *The political economy of communications: international and European dimensions.* London: Routledge.

EISENSTEIN, E. (1979) *The printing press as an agent of change.* 2 vols, Cambridge: Cambridge University Press.

EL-NAWAWY, M. and ISKANDAR, A. (2002) *Al-Jazeera: how the free Arab news network scooped the world and changed the Middle East.* Cambridge MA: Westview.

ELLINGHAUS, W. and FORRESTER, L. (1985) A U.S. effort to provide a global balance: The Maitland Commission Report. *Journal of Communication*, Spring, 14–21.

ELLIOT, I. (1988) How open is 'openness'? *Survey*, **30**, 3: 1–24.

ELSTER, J. (ed.) (1997) *Democratic deliberation*. Cambridge: Cambridge University Press.

ERNI, J. N. and CHAU, S. K. (eds) (2005) *Asian media studies – politics of subjectivities*. Oxford: Blackwell.

European Audiovisual Observatory (2005) *Focus 2005: world film market trends*. Strasbourg: European Audiovisual Observatory.

European Commission (1998) *Telecommunications: liberalised services*. The Single Market Review, Subseries III – Impact on Services, vol. 6, Luxembourg: Office for Official Publications of the European Communities.

European Commission (1999) *Principles and guidelines for the Community's audio-visual policy in the digital age*. Document (99) 657, 14 December, Brussels: European Commission.

EWEN, S. (1976) *The captains of consciousness*. New York: McGraw-Hill.

FANON, F. (1970) *A dying colonialism*. Harmondsworth: Pelican. Originally published in the UK in 1965 under the title *A study in dying colonialism*. London: Monthly Review Press.

FEBVRE, L. and MARTIN, H. (1990) *The coming of the book: the impact of printing 1450–1800*. Translated by D. Gerard. London: Verso. Originally published in 1958 as *L'Apparition du livre*. Paris: Editions Albin Michel.

Federal Communications Commission (1999) *A new FCC for the 21st century* (http://www.fcc.gov/21stcentury/).

FICCI (2004) *The Indian entertainment industry: an unfolding opportunity*. Mumbai: Federation of Indian Chambers of Commerce and Industry.

FISCHER, H. and MERRILL, J. (eds) (1976) *International and intercultural communication*. Second edition, New York: Hastings House Publishers.

FISKE, J. (1987) *Television culture*. London: Routledge.

FLOURNOY, D. and STEWART, R. (1997) *CNN: making news in the global market*. Luton: University of Luton Press.

FORTNER, R. (1993) *International communication: history, conflict and control of the global metropolis*. Belmont: Wadsworth Publishing.

Fortune (2005) Fortune Global 500. *Fortune*, August.

FOX, E. (1997) *Latin American broadcasting: from tango to telenovela*. Luton: University of Luton Press.

FRANKLIN, B. (1997) *Newszak and news media*. London: Arnold.

FRANKLIN, B. (2004) *Packaging politics: political communication in Britain's media democracy*. Second edition, London: Arnold.

FREDERICK, H. (1992) *Global communication and international relations*. Belmont: Wadsworth Publishing.

FREIRE, P. (1974) *Pedagogy of the oppressed.* Translated by M. Ramos, New York: Seabury Press. Originally published in 1970.

FRIEDEN, R. (1996) *International telecommunications handbook.* Boston: Artch House Publishing.

FUKUYAMA, F. (1992) *The end of history and the last man.* London: Hamish Hamilton.

FÜRSICH, E. (2003) Between credibility and commodification: nonfiction entertainment as a global media genre. *International Journal of Cultural Studies,* **6**, 2: 131–53.

GALPERIN, H. (1999) Cultural industries in the age of free-trade agreements. *Canadian Journal of Communication,* **24**: 49–77.

GALTUNG, J. (1971) A structural theory of imperialism. *Journal of Peace Research,* **8**, 2: 81–117.

GALTUNG, J. and RUGE, M. (1965) The structure of foreign news. *Journal of Peace Research,* **2**, 1: 64–91.

GANDY, O. (1993) *The panoptic sort: a political economy of personal information.* Boulder, CO: Westview Press.

GARCIA CANCLINI, N. (1995) *Hybrid cultures: strategies for entering and leaving modernity.* Minneapolis: University of Minnesota Press. Original Spanish edition published in 1989 as *Culturas híbridas: estrategias para entrar y salir de la modernidad.* Mexico City: Grijalbo.

GARNHAM, N. (1990) *Capitalism and communication: global culture and the economics of information.* London: Sage.

GATT (1993) *Final Act embodying the results of the Uruguay Round (General Agreement on Trade in Services – Annex on Telecommunications).* Geneva: General Agreement on Tariff and Trade Secretariat.

GERADIN, D. and LUFF, D. (eds) (2004) *The WTO and global convergence in telecommunications and audio-visual services.* Cambridge: Cambridge University Press.

GERSHON, R. A. (1990) Global cooperation in an era of deregulation. *Telecommunication Policy,* **14**, 3: 249–59.

GIDDENS, A. (1990) *The consequences of modernity.* Cambridge: Polity.

GIFFARD, C. A. (1998) Alternative news agencies. In O. Boyd-Barrett and T. Rantanen (eds), *The globalization of news.* London: Sage.

GITLIN, T. (2002) *Media unlimited: how the torrent of images and sounds overwhelms our lives.* New York: Metropolitan Books.

Global Media and Communication (2005) From NWICO to WSIS. Special issue of *Global Media and Communication,* **1**, 3: 264–373.

Globo website: http://www.redeglobo.com.br

GOLDING, P. and HARRIS, P. (eds) (1997) *Beyond cultural imperialism: globalisation, communication and the new international order.* London: Sage.

GOLDING, P. and MURDOCH, G. (eds) (1997) *The political economy of the media.* 2 vols, Cheltenham: Edward Elgar.

GOONASEKERA, A. (1997) Cultural markets in the age of globalisation: Asian values and Western content: *Inter Media*, Special Report, 25, **6**: 4–43.

GOONASEKERA, A., HAMELINK, C. and IYER, V. (eds) (2003) *Cultural rights in a global world.* Singapore: Asian Media Information and Communication Centre.

GOULDNER, A. (1976) *The dialectic of ideology and technology.* London: Macmillan.

GRADDOL, D. (2006) *English next: Why global English may mean the end of 'English as a foreign language'.* London: British Council.

GRAMSCI, A. (1971) *Selections from the prison notebooks.* Edited and translated by Q. Hoare and G. Nowell-Smith. London: Lawrence and Wishart.

GUBACK, T. (1969) *The international film industry: Western Europe and America since 1945.* Bloomington: Indiana University Press.

GUNDER FRANK, A. (1969) *Capitalism and underdevelopment in Latin America.* New York: Monthly Review Press.

GUNDER FRANK, A. (1998) *Reorient: Global economy in the Asian age.* California: University of California Press.

HAASS, R. (1999) What to do with American primacy. *Foreign Affairs*, **78**, 5: 37–49.

HABERMAS, J. (1989) *The structural transformation of the public sphere: an inquiry into a category of bourgeois society.* Cambridge: Polity. Original German edition published in 1962.

HABERMAS, J. (2001) *The postnational constellation.* Cambridge: MIT Press.

HACHTEN, W. (1999) *The world news prism: changing media of international communication.* Fifth edition, Ames: Iowa State University Press.

HACKETT, R. A. and ZHAO, Y. (eds) (2005) *Democratizing global media: one world, many struggles.* Lanham, MD: Rowman & Littlefield.

HAFNER, K. and LYONS, M. (1996) *Where wizards stay up late: the origins of the Internet.* New York: Simon & Schuster.

HALE, J. (1975) *Radio power: propaganda and international broadcasting.* London: Paul Elek.

HALL, S. (1980) Encoding and decoding in the television discourse. In S. Hall, D. Hobson, A. Lowe and P Willis (eds), *Culture, media, language.* London: Hutchinson.

HALL, S. (1991) The local and the global: globalization and ethnicity: In A. King (ed.), *Culture, globalization and the world-system: contemporary conditions for the representation of identity*. London: Macmillan.

HALLIN, D. (1986) *The uncensored war: the media and Vietnam*. Oxford: Oxford University Press.

HALLIN, D. (1994) *We keep America on top of the world: television journalism and the public sphere*. New York: Routledge.

HALLORAN, J. (1997) International communication research: opportunities and obstacles. In A. Mohammadi (ed.), *International communication and globalization*. London: Sage.

HAMELINK, C. (1979) Informatics: Third World call for new order. *Journal of Communication*, **29**, 4: 144.

HAMELINK, C. (1983) *Cultural autonomy in global communications*. New York: Longman.

HAMELINK, C. (1994) *The politics of world communication: a human rights perspective*. London: Sage.

HAMELINK, C. (2000) *The ethics of cyberspace*. London: Sage.

HAMM, B. and SMANDYCH, R. (eds) (2005) *Cultural imperialism: essays on the political economy of cultural domination*. Peterborough: Broadview Press.

HANNERZ, U. (1997) *Transnational connection*. London: Sage.

HARASIM, L. (ed.) (1994) *Global networks: computers and international communication*. Cambridge, MA: MIT Press.

HARDT, M. and NEGRI, A. (2000) *Empire*. Cambridge, MA: Harvard University Press.

HARDT, M. and NEGRI, A. (2004) *Multitude: war and democracy in the age of empire*. London: Penguin.

HARGREAVES, I. and THOMAS, J. (2002) *New News, Old News*. London: Independent Television Commission and Broadcasting Standards Commission.

HARLEY, W. (1984) Memorandum presented by Harley, William G., Communication consultant, United States Department of State, 9 February 1984, reflecting the views of the state department on what the US government is thinking and doing about UNESCO. *Journal of Communication*, **34**, 4: 89.

HARRIS, P. (1981) News dependence and structural changes. In J. Richstad and M. Anderson (eds), *Crisis in international news: policies and prospects*. New York: Columbia University Press.

HARTLEY, J. (ed.) (2005) *Creative industries*. Oxford: Blackwell.

HARVEY, D. (1989) *The condition of postmodernity*. Oxford: Blackwell.

HARVEY, D. (2003) *The new imperialism*. Oxford: Oxford University Press.

HEADRICK, D. (1981) *The tools of empire: technology and European imperialism in the nineteenth century.* New York: Oxford University Press.

HEADRICK, D. (1991) *The invisible weapon: telecommunications and international politics, 1851–1945.* New York: Oxford University Press.

HELD, D., McGREW, A., GOLDBLATT, D. and PERRATON, J. (1999) *Global transformations: politics, economics and culture.* Cambridge: Polity.

HELD, D. and McGREW, A. (eds) (2003) *The global transformations reader – An introduction to the globalization debate.* Second edition, Oxford: Polity.

HEMEL, VAN A. (ed.) (1996) *Trading culture: GATT, European cultural policies and the transatlantic market.* Amsterdam: Boekman Foundation.

HERMAN, E. (1999) *The myth of the liberal media: an Edward Herman reader.* New York: Peter Lang Publisher.

HERMAN, E. and CHOMSKY, N. (1994) *Manufacturing consent: the political economy of the mass media.* London: Vintage. Originally published in 1988, New York: Pantheon.

HERMAN, E. and McCHESNEY, R. (1997) *The global media: the new missionaries of corporate capitalism.* London: Cassell.

HESMONDHALGH, D. (2002) *The cultural industries.* London: Sage.

HESS, S. (1996) *International news and foreign correspondents.* Washington, DC: Brookings Institution.

HICKMAN, T. (1995) *What did you do in the war, Auntie?: The BBC at war 1939–45.* London: BBC Books.

HILL, A. (2005) *Reality TV – audience and popular factual television.* London: Routledge.

HILL, A. (2006) The Bin Laden tapes, *Journal for Cultural Research*, **10**, 1: 35–46.

HILLS, J. (2002) *The struggle for control of global communication: the formative century.* Champaign, IL: University of Illinois Press.

HIRST, P. and THOMPSON, G. (1999) *Globalisation in question: the international economy and the possibilities of governance.* Second edition, Cambridge: Polity.

HOBSON, J. M. (2004) *The Eastern origins of Western civilisation.* Cambridge: Cambridge University Press.

HOCKX, M. and STRAUSS, J. (eds) (2006) *Culture in the contemporary PRC.* Cambridge: Cambridge University Press.

HOEKMAN, E. and KOSTECKI, G. (1995) *The political economy of the world trading system: from GATT to WTO.* Oxford: Oxford University Press.

HOFFMANN, S. (2002) Clash of globalizations, *Foreign Affairs.* **81**, 4: 104–15.

HOGE, J. (1994) Media pervasiveness. *Foreign Affairs*, **73**, 4: 136–44.

HOGE, J. and ROSE, G. (eds) (2005) *Understanding the war on terror*. New York: Council on Foreign Relations.

HOLLIS, N. (2005) Ten years of learning on how online advertising builds brands, *Journal of Advertising Research*, **45**, 2: 255–68.

HOLUB, R. (1991) *Jürgen Habermas: critic in the public sphere*. London: Routledge.

HORSMAN, M. (1997) *Sky high: the inside story of BSkyB*. London: Orion Business Books.

HOSKINS, G. and MIRUS, R. (1988) Reasons for US dominance of the international trade in television programmes. *Media, Culture and Society*, **10**: 499–515.

HOSKINS, C., MCFYDEN, S. and FINN, A. (2004) *Media economics: applying economics to new and traditional media*. London: Sage.

HUGHILL, P. (1999) *Global communications since 1844: geopolitics & technology*. Baltimore: Johns Hopkins University Press.

HUNTINGTON, S. (1993) The clash of civilizations. *Foreign Affairs*, **72**, 3: 22–49.

IBM (2004) *Media and entertainment 2010*. IBM Business Consulting Services (ibm.com/bcs).

IFPI (2005) *IFPI online music report 2005*. London: International Federation of the Phonograms Industry.

IGNATIUS, A. (2006) In search of the real Google, *Time*, February 20, 32–42.

IIPA (2004) *Copyright industries in the U.S. economy: the 2004 report*. International Intellectual Property Alliance (www.iipa.com).

ILO (2005) *Key indicators of the labour market*. Geneva: International Labour Organization.

INGLIS, A. (1990) *Behind the tube: a history of broadcasting technology and business*. London: Focal Press.

INNIS, H. (1972) *Empire and communications*. Revised edition, Toronto: University of Toronto Press. Originally published in 1950 by Oxford University Press.

Intelsat (1999) Annual report 1998. International Telecommunications Satellite Organisation.

Intelsat (2005) Annual report 2005. International Telecommunications Satellite Organisation.

ITO, Y. (1981) The *Johoka Shakai* approach to the study of communication in Japan. In G. Wilhoit and H. de Bock (eds), *Mass communication review yearbook*. Vol. 2, London and Beverley Hills: Sage.

ITU (1985) *The missing link*. Report of the Independent Commission for Worldwide Telecommunications Development (Maitland Commission). Geneva: International Telecommunication Union.

ITU (1998) *World telecommunication development report 1998*. Geneva: International Telecommunication Union.

ITU (1999) *Trends in telecommunication reform*. Geneva: International Telecommunication Union.

ITU (2005a) *World telecommunication development report 2005*. Geneva: International Telecommunication Union.

ITU (2005b) *The Internet of things, The ITU Internet report 2005*. Geneva: International Telecommunication Union.

IWABUCHI, K. (2002) *Recentering globalization: popular culture and Japanese transnationalism*. Durham, NC: Duke University Press.

JAIN, M. (1997) The God factory. *India Today*, 31 May, 70–3.

JAMESON, F. (1991) *Postmodernism, or, the cultural logic of late capitalism*. London: Verso.

JARVIE, I. (1992) *Hollywood's overseas campaign: the North Atlantic movie trade, 1920–1950*. Cambridge: Cambridge University Press.

JEFFREY, J. (1978) The Third World and the Free Enterprise Press. *Policy Review*, **5**: 59–70.

JENKINS, H. and THORBURN, D. (eds) (2003) *Democracy and new media*. New Haven, CT: Yale University Press.

JENSEN, K. (ed.) (1998) *News of the world: world cultures look at television news*. London: Routledge.

JETRO. (2005) Japan animation industry trends. *Japan Economic Monthly*, June.

JOHNSON. D. W. (2004) *Congress online: bridging the gap between citizens and their representatives*. London: Routledge.

JONES, J. (ed.) (1999) *The advertising business: operations, creativity, media planning, integrated communications*. Thousand Oaks, CA: Sage.

JORDAN, T. and TAYLOR, P. (2004) *Hacktivism and cyberwars – rebels with a cause*. London: Routledge.

JOSEPH, A. and SHARMA, K. (eds) (1994) *Whose news? the media and women's issues*. New Delhi: Sage.

KABBANI, R. (1986) *Europe's myths of orient*. London: Pandora Press.

KAHIN, B. and NESSON, C. (eds) (1997) *Borders in cyberspace: information policy and the global information infrastructure*. Cambridge, MA: MIT Press.

KALDOR, M. (2003) *Global civil society: an answer to war*. Cambridge: Polity.

KAPUR, G. (1997) Globalisation and culture. *Third Text*, **39**: 21–38.

KARIM, K. A. (ed.) (2003) *The media of diaspora: mapping the global*. London: Routledge.

KASHLEV, Y. (1984) *Information imperialism*. Moscow: Novosti Press.

KATZ, E. and LIEBES, T. (1990) *The export of meaning: cross-cultural readings of Dallas*. New York: Oxford University Press.

KAUL, G. (1998) *Cinema and the Indian freedom struggle*. New Delhi: Sterling.

KAUL, I., GRUNBERG, I. and STERN, M. (eds) (1999) *Global public goods: international cooperation in the 21st century*. New York: Oxford University Press.

KAUR, R. and SINHA, A. (eds) (2005) *Bollyworld: popular Indian cinema through a transnational lens*. New Delhi: Sage.

KEANE, J. (2003) *Global civil society?* Cambridge: Cambrige University Press.

KENNEDY, P. (1971) Imperial cable communications and strategy, 1879–1914. *English Historical Review*, **86**: 728–52.

KERBEL, M. R. and BLOOM, J. D. (2005) Blog for America and civic involvement. *Harvard International Journal of Press/Politics*, **10**, 4: 3–27.

KESSLER, K. M. (1998) The Latin American satellite market: a prophecy fulfilled. *Via Satellite*, March.

KHALIDI, R. (2004) *Resurrecting Empire: Western footprints and America's perilous path in the Middle East*. New York: Beacon.

KHARE, H. (2000) President cautions against social, economic disparities. *The Hindu*, 26 January.

KOBRIN, S. (1998) The MAI and the clash of globalizations. *Foreign Policy*, Fall, 97–109.

KRAIDY, M. (2005) *Hybridity, or, the cultural logic of globalization*. Philadelphia: Temple University Press.

LANCHESTER, J. (2006) The global id: is Google a good thing? *London Review of Books*, **28**, 2, 26 January.

LARGE, K. and KENNY, J. (2004) Latino soaps go global, *Television Business International*, January.

LASSWELL, H. (1927) *Propaganda techniques in the world war*. New York: Alfred Knopf.

LATOUCHE, S. (1996) *The Westernization of the world: the significance, scope and limits of the drive toward global uniformity*. Translated by R. Morris, Cambridge: Polity. Originally published in French in 1989 as *L'occidentalisation du monde: Essai sur la signification, la portée et les limites de l'uniformisation planétaire*, Paris: Editions la Découverte.

LAURIA, J. and NELSON, F. (2006) Annan prepares for privatisation of UN. *The Business*, 12/13 February, 1.

LAWRENSON, J. and BARBER, L. (1985) *The price of truth, the story of the Reuters £££ millions.* London: Mainstream Publishing.

LAZARSFELD, P. (1941) Remarks on administrative and critical communications Research. *Studies in Philosophy and Social Sciences,* **9**: 2–16.

LEE, C. C. (ed.) (2003) *Chinese media, global contexts.* London: RoutledgeCurzon.

LEITE, J. C. (2005) *The world social forum: strategies of resistance.* New York: Haymarket Books.

LENNON, A. (ed.) (2003) *The battle for hearts and minds: using soft power to undermine terrorist networks.* New Haven, CT: MIT Press.

LERNER, D. (1958) *The passing of traditional society: modernizing the Middle East.* New York: Free Press.

LESSIG, L. (2004) *Free culture: how big media uses technology and the law to lock down culture and control creativity.* London: Penguin.

LEWIS, J. (2005) *Language wars: The role of media and culture in global terror and political violence.* London: Pluto.

LEWIS, S. (1996) *News and society in the Greek polis.* London: Duckworth.

LID, D. (2003) Indymedia.org – A new communications commons. In M. McCaughey and D. Machael (eds), *Cyberactivism – online activism in theory and practice.* London: Routledge.

LIPPMANN, W. (1922) *Public opinion.* New York: Free Press.

LISANN, M. (1975) *Broadcasting to the Soviet Union: international politics and radio.* New York: Praeger Publishers.

LIVINGSTON, S. and VAN BELLE, D. A. *(*2005) The effects of satellite technology on newsgathering from remote locations. *Political Communication,* **22**: 45–62.

LOPEZ, A. (1995) Our welcome guests: *telenovelas* in Latin America. In R. Allen (ed.), *To be continued ...* New York: Routledge.

LORD, C. (1998) The past and future of public diplomacy. *Orbis,* Winter. 49–72.

LOWE, G. F. and PER, J. (eds) (2005) *Cultural dilemmas in public service broadcasting.* Goteborg: Nordicom.

LUCAS, M. and WALLNER, M. (1993) Resistance by satellite: the Gulf Crisis project and the deep dish satellite TV network. In T. Dowmunt (ed.), *Channels of resistance.* London: BFI in association with Channel 4 Television.

LULL, J. (ed.) (1988) *World families watch television.* Beverley Hills, CA: Sage.

LULL, J. (1995) *Media, communication, culture: a global approach.* Cambridge: Polity.

LUTHER, S. (1988) *The United States and the direct broadcast satellite: the politics of international broadcasting in space.* New York: Oxford University Press.

LYNCH, M. (2006) *Voices of the new Arab public: Iraq, al-Jazeera, and Middle East politics today.* New York: Columbia University Press.

LYON, D. (1994) *The electronic eye: the rise of surveillance society.* Minneapolis: University of Minnesota Press.

LYOTARD, J. (1984) *The postmodern condition: a report on knowledge.* Translated by G. Bennington and B. Massumi, Manchester: Manchester University Press. Originally published in French in 1979.

MacBride Report (1980) *Many voices, one world: communication and society today and tomorrow.* International Commission for the Study of Communication Problems. Paris: UNESCO.

MACGREGOR, B. (1997) *Live, direct and biased? Making television news in the satellite age.* London: Arnold.

MACHET, E. (1999) *A decade of EU broadcasting regulation.* Dusseldorf: The European Institute for the Media.

MACHLUP, F. (1962) *The production and distribution of knowledge in the United States.* New Jersey: Princeton University Press.

MACLEAN, D. (1999) Open doors and open questions: interpreting the results of the 1998 ITU Minneapolis Plenipotentiary Conference. *Telecommunications Policy,* **23**: 147–58.

MADER, R. (1993) Globo village: television in Brazil. In T. Dowmunt (ed.), *Channels of resistance.* London: BFI in association with Channel 4 Television.

MAMDANI, M. (2004) *Good Muslim, Bad Muslim: America, the Cold War, and the roots of terror.* New York: Pantheon.

MANHEIM, J. (1994) *Strategic public diplomacy and American foreign policy: the evolution of influence.* New York: Oxford University Press.

MANSELL, R. and WEHN, U. (eds) (1998) *Knowledge societies: information technology for sustainable development.* Report of the UN Commission on Science and Technology for Development. Oxford: Oxford University Press.

MARCUSE, H. (1964) *One dimensional man.* Boston: Beacon Press.

MARLING, W. H. (2006) *How 'American' is globalization?* Maryland: Johns Hopkins University Press.

MARTIN, J. (1976) Effectiveness of international propaganda. In H. Fischer and J. Merrill (eds), *International and intercultural communication.* New York: Hastings House Publishers.

MARTIN-BARBERO, J. (1993) *Communication, culture and hegemony: from media to mediations.* Translated by E. Fox. London: Sage.

MARTINEZ, I. (2005) Romancing the globe. *Foreign Policy,* November.

MASMOUDI, M. (1979) The new world information order. *Journal of Communication*, **29**, 2: 172–85.

MASTERS, C. (2006) The new *Maxim*: go east. *Time*, January 30.

MATHJIS, E., JONES, J., HESSELLS, W. and VERRIEST, L. (eds) (2004) *Big Brother international: critics, format and publics*. London: Wallflower Press.

MATO, D. (2005) The transnationalization of the telenovela industry, territorial references, and the production of markets and representations of transnational identities. *Television & New Media*, **6**, 4: 423–44.

MATTELART, A. (1979) *Multinational corporations and the control of culture*. Atlantic Highlands, NJ: Humanities Press.

MATTELART, A. (1991) *Advertising international: the privatisation of public space*. Translated by M. Chanan, London: Routledge. Originally published in 1989 as *L'Internationale publicitaire*, Paris: Editions La Découverte.

MATTELART, A. (1994) *Mapping world communication: war, progress, culture*. Translated by S. Emanuel and J. Cohen, Minneapolis: University of Minnesota Press. Originally published in 1991 as *La Communication-monde, Histoire des idées et des stratégies*, Paris: Editions La Découverte.

MATTELART, A. (1996) *The invention of communication*. Minneapolis: University of Minnesota Press.

MATTELART, A. (2003) *The information society*. London: Sage.

MATTELART, A. and MATTELART, M. (1990) *A carnival of images: Brazilian Television fiction*. New York: Bergin and Garvey.

MATTELART, A. and MATTELART, M. (1998) *Theories of communication: a short introduction*. London: Sage.

McANANY, E. and WILKINSON, K. (eds) (1996) *Mass media and free trade*. Austin, TX. University of Texas Press.

McCANN Worldgroup (2006) Advertising growth http://www.mccann.com/news/pdfs/insiders05.pdf

McCHESNEY, R. (1993) *Telecommunications, mass media and democracy: the battle for the control of US broadcasting, 1928–1935*. New York: Oxford University Press.

McCHESNEY, R. (1999) *Rich media, poor democracy: communication politics in dubious times*. Champaign, IL: University of Illinois Press.

McCHESNEY, R. (2004) *The problem of the media: U.S. communication politics in the 21st century*. New York: Monthly Review Press.

McLUHAN, M. (1964) *Understanding media*. London: Methuen.

McNAMARA, K. (1992) Reaching captive minds with radio. *Orbis*, Winter, 23–40.

McNARY, D. (2005) H'w'd finds world isn't flat: unlikely markets yield big returns. *Variety*, 27 November.

McNEAL, J. (1992) *Kids as customers*. New York: Lexington Books.

McPHAIL, T. (1987) *Electronic colonialism: the future of international broadcasting and communication*. London: Sage.

McPHAIL, T. (2006) *Global communication: theories, stakeholders, and trends*. Second edition, Oxford: Blackwell.

McQUAIL, D. (2005) *McQuail's mass communication theory: an introduction*. Fifth edition, London: Sage.

McQUAIL, D. and SIUNE, K. (eds) (1998) *Media policy: convergence, concentration and commerce*. Euromedia Research Group. London: Sage.

MERMIN, J. (1999) *Debating war and peace: media coverage of US intervention in the post-Vietnam era*. New Jersey: Princeton University Press.

MICKELSON, S. (1983) *America's other voice: the story of Radio Free Europe and Radio Liberty*. New York: Praeger.

MICKIEWICZ, E. (1997) *Changing channels: television and the struggle for power in Russia*. New York: Oxford University Press.

MILLER, T., GOVIL, N., MAXWELL, R. and MCMURRIE, J. (2005) *Global Hollywood*. Second edition, London: BFI.

MILES, H. (2005) *Al-Jazeera: How Arab TV news challenged the world*. London: Abacus.

MISHRA, V. (2002) *Bollywood cinema – temples of desires*. London: Routledge.

MITRA, A. (1993) *Television and popular culture in India: a study of the Mahabharat*. New Delhi: Sage.

MITSIS, N. (2005) Industry trends and developments: Via Satellite's measuring the state of the industry, *Via Satellite*, July.

MITSUI, T. and HOSOKAWA, S. (eds) (1998) *Karaoke around the world: global technology, local singing*. London: Routledge.

MOHAMMADI, A. and SREBERNY-MOHAMMADI, A. (1994) *Small media, big revolution: communication, culture and the Iranian revolution*. Minneapolis: University of Minnesota Press.

MOOIJ, M. (1998) *Global marketing and advertising: understanding cultural paradoxes*. Second edition, London: Sage.

MORAN, A. (1998) *Copycat TV: globalisation, program formats and cultural identity*. Luton: University of Luton Press.

MORRIS, M., LI, S. and CHAN CHING-KIU, S. (2006) *Hong Kong connections: transnational imagination in action cinema*. Durham, NC: Duke University Press.

MORROW, R. W. (2005) *Sesame Street and the reform of children's television*. Maryland: Johns Hopkins University Press.

MOSCO, V. (1996) *The political economy of communication: rethinking and renewal*. London: Sage.

MOWLANA, H. (1996) *Global communication in transition*. London: Sage.

MOWLANA, H. (1997) *Global information and world communication: new frontiers in international relations*. Second edition, London: Sage.

MOWLANA, H., GERBNER, G. and SCHILLER, H. (eds) (1992) *Triumph of the image: the media's war in the Persian Gulf*. Boulder, CO: Westview Press.

MURDOCH, G. and GOLDING, P. (1977) Capitalism, communication and class relations. In J. Curran *et al.* (eds), *Mass communication and society*. London: Edward Arnold.

MYTTON, G, TEER-TOMASELLI, R and TUDESQ, A. (2005) Transnational television in sub-Saharan Africa, in J. Chalaby (ed.) *Transnational Television Worldwide*. London: I.B. Tauris.

NAFICY, H. (1993) *The making of exile cultures: Iranian television in the United States*. Minneapolis: University of Minnesota Press.

NASSCOM (2006) *NASSCOM Strategic Review 2006*. Mumbai: National Association of Software Service Companies.

NAUGHTON, J. (1999) *A brief history of the future*. London: Weidenfeld and Nicolson.

NEDERVEEN PIETERSE, J. (1995) Globalisation as hybridization. In M. Featherstone, S. Lash and R. Robertson (eds), *Global modernities*. London: Sage.

NEDERVEEN PIETERSE, J. (2004) *Globalization or empire?* London: Routledge.

NEGROPONTE, N. (1995) *Being digital*. New York: Alfred A. Knopf.

NELSON, M. (1997) *War of the black heavens: the battle of western broadcasting in the Cold War*. Syracuse: Syracuse University Press.

NEUMAN, W. (1991) *The future of the mass audience*. Cambridge: Cambridge University Press.

News Corporation (1999) *Annual report 1999*. New York: News Corporation.

News Corporation (2005) *Annual report 2005*. New York: News Corporation.

NINCOVICH, F. (1981) *The diplomacy of ideas: US foreign policy and cultural relations, 1938–1950*. Cambridge: Cambridge University Press.

NOAM, E. (1993) Media Americanization, national culture, and forces of integration. In E. Noam and J. Milonzi (eds), *The international market in films and television programmes*. Norwood, NJ: Ablex Publishing.

NORDENSTRENG, K. (ed.) (1986) *New international information and communication order source book*. Prague: International Organisation of Journalists.

NORDENSTRENG, K. and VARIS, T. (1974) *Television traffic – a one-way street? A survey and analysis of the international flow of television programme material*. Reports and Papers on Mass Communication, No. 70. Paris: UNESCO.

NORDENSTRENG, K. and SCHILLER, H. (eds) (1993) *Beyond national sovereignty: international communications in the 1990s*. Norwood, NJ: Ablex Publishing.

NOWELL-SMITH, G. and RICCI, S. (eds) (1998) *Hollywood and Europe: economics, culture, national identity, 1946–95*. London: British Film Institute.

NYE, J. (1990) Soft power. *Foreign Policy*, **80**: 153–71.

NYE, J. (2004) *Power in the global information age: from realism to globalization*. London: Routledge.

NYE, J. and OWENS, W. (1996) America's information edge. *Foreign Affairs*, March/April, 20–36.

OBERST, G. (1999) Regulatory review: European spectrum policy. *Via Satellite*, February.

OECD (1985) *Declaration on transborder data flows*. (Press/A(85) 30), 11 April. Paris: Organization for Economic Cooperation and Development.

OECD (1993) *Services: statistics on international transactions, 1970–1991*. Statistics Directorate. Paris: Organization for Economic Cooperation and Development.

OECD (2004) *OECD Information Technology Outlook, 2004*. Paris: Organization for Economic Cooperation and Development.

OECD (2005) *Science, Technology and Industry Scoreboard*. Paris: Organization for Economic Cooperation and Development.

OHMAE, K. (1995) *The end of the nation state: the rise and fall of regional economies*. London: HarperCollins.

OKRENT, D. (2000) Happily ever after. *Time*, 24 January, 43–7.

OLIVEIRA, O. (1993) Brazilian soaps outshine Hollywood: is cultural imperialism fading out? In K. Nordenstreng and H. Schiller (eds), *Beyond national sovereignty*. Norwood, NJ: Ablex Publishing.

OSLIN, G. (1992) *The story of telecommunications*. Macon, GA: Mercer University Press.

PAGE, B. (2003) *The Murdoch archipelago*. London: Simon & Schuster.

PAGE, D. and CRAWLEY, W. (2001) *Satellites over South Asia: broadcasting, culture and the public interest*. New Delhi: Sage.

PANDIT, S. (1996) *From making to music: the history of Thorn EMI*. London: Hodder & Stoughton.

PAPATHANASSOPOULOS, S. (1999) The political economy of international news channels: more supply than demand. *Intermedia*, **27**, 1: 17–23.

PARKS, L. (2004) *Cultures in orbit: satellites and the televisual*. Durham, NC: Duke University Press.

PARTOS, G. (1993) *The world that came in from the cold*. London: BBC World Service/Royal Institute of International Affairs.

PATERSON, C. (1998) Global battlefields. In O. Boyd-Barrett and T. Rantanen (eds), *The globalization of news*. London: Sage.

PAVLIK, J. (1996) *New media technology – cultural and commercial perspectives*. Boston: Allyn and Bacon.

PECORA, N. (1998) *The business of children's entertainment*. New York: Guilford Press.

PENDAKUR, M. (2003) *Indian popular cinema: industry, ideology, and consciousness*. Cresskill, NJ: Hampton Press.

Pew Center (2002) *Public's News Habits Little Changed by September 11 – Americans Lack Background to Follow International News*. Pew Research Center for the People and the Press (people-press.org/reports).

Pew Center (2005) *Trends 2005*, Pew Research Center for the People and the Press, Washington (people-press.org/commentary/display.php3?AnalysisID=104).

PHILLIPSON, R. (1992) *Linguistic imperialism*. Oxford: Oxford University Press.

PHILO, G. (ed.) (1995) *The Glasgow media group reader*. Vol. 2, London: Routledge.

PHILO, G., HILSUM, L., BEATTIE, L. and HOLLIMAN, R. (1999) The media and the Rwanda crisis: effects on audiences and public policy. In G. Philo (ed.), *Message received: Glasgow media group research 1993–1998*. London: Longman.

Phoenix website: http://www.phoenixtv.com

POSTER, M. (1995) *The second media age*. Cambridge: Polity.

POSTMAN, N. (1985) *Amusing ourselves to death: public discourse in the age of show business*. London: Methuen.

POSTMAN, N. (1992) *Technopoly: the surrender of culture to technology*. New York: Alfred A. Knopf.

PRESTON, P. (2001) *Reshaping communications: technology, information and social change*. London: Sage.

PRESTON, W., HERMAN, E. and SCHILLER, H. (1989) *Hope and folly: the United States and UNESCO, 1945–1985*. Minneapolis: University of Minnesota Press.

PRICE, M. (1999) Satellite broadcasting as trade routes in the sky. *Public Culture*, **11**, 2: 69–85.

PRICE, M. (2002) *Media and sovereignty: the global information revolution and its challenges to state power*. New Haven, CT: MIT Press.

PricewaterhouseCoopers (2005) *Global entertainment and media outlook: 2005–2009*, New York and London: PricewaterhouseCoopers.

Project for Excellence in Journalism (2006) *2006 annual report on the state of the news media* (www.journalism.org/resources/research/reports).

PYE, L. (ed.) (1963) *Communications and political development*. New Jersey: Princeton University Press.

RAJADHYAKSHA, A. and WILLEMEN, P. (1999) *Encyclopaedia of Indian cinema*. Second edition, New Delhi: Oxford University Press and London: British Film Institute.

RAJAGOPAL, A. (2001) *Politics after television: Hindu nationalism and the reshaping of the public in India*. Cambridge: Cambridge University Press.

RANTANEN, T. (2005) *The media and globalization*. London: Sage.

RAWNSLEY, G. (1996) *Radio diplomacy and propaganda: the BBC and VOA in international politics, 1956–64*. Basingstoke: Macmillan.

READ, D. (1992) *The power of news: the history of Reuters, 1849–1989*. Oxford: Oxford University Press.

REEVES, B. and NASS, C. (1996) *The media equation: how people treat computers, television, and new media like real people and places*. Cambridge: Cambridge University Press.

RENAUD, J. (1986) A conceptual framework for the examination of transborder data flows. *The Information Society*, **4**, 3: 146–9.

Reuters (2005) *Annual report*. London: Reuters Holdings PLC.

RICHARDSON, K. and MEINHOF, U. (1999) *Worlds in common: television discourse and a changing Europe*. London: Routledge.

RIGHTER, R. (1978) *Whose News? Politics, the Press and the Third World*. London: Burnett Books.

RITZER, G. (1993) *The McDonaldization of society*. Thousand Oaks, CA: Sage.

RITZER, G. (1999) *Enchanting a disenchanted world: Revolutionising the means of consumption*. Thousands Oaks, CA: Pine Forge Press.

RITZER, G. (2002) *McDonaldization – the reader*. London: Sage.

ROACH, C. (1987) The US position on the new world information and communication order. *Journal of Communication*, **37**, 4: 36–51.

ROBERTSON, R. (1992) *Globalization: social theory and global culture*. London: Sage.

ROBINS, K. (1995) The new spaces of global media. In R. Johnston, P. Taylor. and M. Watts (eds), *Geographies of global change*. Oxford: Blackwell.

ROBINS, K. and AKSOY, A. (2005) Whoever looks always finds: Transnational viewing and knowledge-experience. In J. Chalaby (ed), *Transnational television worldwide – towards a new media order*. London: I. B. Tauris.

ROBINSON, A. (1989) *Satyajit Ray: the inner eye*. London: André Deutsch.

ROBINSON, P. (2002) *The CNN effect – the myth of news, foreign policy and intervention*. London: Routledge.

RODRIGUEZ, C. (2001) *Fissures in the mediascape: an international study of citizen's media*. Creskill, NJ: Hampton Press.

ROGERS, E. (1962) *The diffusion of innovations*. Glencoe, IL: Free Press.

ROGERS, E. (1976) Communication and development: the passing of a dominant paradigm. *Communication Research,* **3**, 2: 213–40.

ROGERS, E. and ANTOLA, L. (1985) *Telenovelas*: a Latin American success story. *Journal of Communication,* **35**, 4: 24–35.

RONCAGLIOLO, R. (1995) Trade integration and communication networks in Latin America. *Canadian Journal of Communication,* **20**, 3: 335–42.

ROSENBLUM, M. (1979) *Coups and earthquakes: reporting the world for America*. New York: Harper and Row.

ROSENBLUM, M. (1993) *Who stole the news? Why we can't keep up with what happens in the world and what we can do about it*. New York: John Wiley.

ROSSER, M. (2005) Telenovelas, the next instalment. *Television Business International,* December.

ROTHKOPF, D. (1997) In praise of cultural imperialism? *Foreign Policy*, Summer, 38–53.

ROTHKOPF, D. (1999) The disinformation age. *Foreign Policy*, Spring, 82–96.

ROXBURGH, A. (1987) *Pravda: inside the Soviet news machine*. London: Victor Gollancz.

SAID, E. (1978) *Orientalism,* London: Routledge and Kegan Paul.

SAID, E. (1993) *Culture and imperialism*. London: Chatto and Windus.

SAID, E. (1997) *Covering Islam: how the media and the experts determine how we see the rest of the world*. Second edition, New York: Vintage. First edition published in 1981, London: Routledge and Kegan Paul.

SAKR, N. (2001) *Satellite realms: transnational television, globalization and the Middle East*. London: I. B. Tauris.

SAMARAJIVA, R. (1985) Tainted origins of development communication. *Communicator*, April–July, 5–9.

SANDIN, J. (2005) Moving pictures. *Television Business International*. April.

SASSEN, S. (1996) *Losing control? Sovereignty in an age of globalization*. New York: Columbia University Press.

SATCHIDANANDAN, K. (1999) Globalisation and culture. *Indian Literature*, **190**, XLIII: 2, March–April, 8–11.

SatNews (1999) Satellite market growing at 15% annually according to new study. 2 November.

SCHILLER, D. (1999) *Digital capitalism: networking the global market system*. Cambridge, MA: MIT Press.

SCHILLER, D. and MOSCO, V. (2001) *Continental order? Integrating North America for cybercapitalism*. Lanham, MD: Rowman & Littlefield.

SCHILLER, H. (1969) *Mass communications and American empire*. New York: Augustus M. Kelley. Second revised and updated edition published by Westview Press in 1992.

SCHILLER. H. (1976) *Communication and cultural domination*. New York: International Arts and Sciences Press.

SCHILLER, H. (1996) *Information inequality: the deepening social crisis in America*. New York: Routledge.

SCHILLER, H. (1998) Striving for communication dominance: a half-century review. In D. Thussu (ed.), *Electronic empires*. London: Arnold.

SCHNEIDER, C. and WALLIS, B. (eds) (1988) *Global television*. Cambridge, MA: MIT Press.

SCHRAMM, W. (1964) *Mass media and national development: the role of information in the developing countries*. Stanford, CA: Stanford University Press.

SCHRAMM, W. (1988) *The story of human communication: cave painting to microchip*. New York: Harper and Row.

SCHUDSON, M. (1995) *The power of news*. Cambridge, MA: Harvard University Press.

SCOTT, K. (2005) Surveying the kids scene. *Television Business International*, August.

Screen Digest (1995) African television leaps to satellite age. December, 273–6.

Screen Digest (1999) Children's television: a globalised market. May, 105–7.

SEGRAVE, K. (1998) *American television abroad: Hollywood's attempt to dominate world television*. Jefferson, NC: McFarland.

SEIB, P. (1997) *Headline diplomacy: how news coverage affects foreign policy*. Westport, CT: Praeger.

SHAPIRO, A. (1999) The Internet. *Foreign Policy*, Summer, 11–27.

SHAW, M. (1996) *Civil society and media in global crises*. London: Pinter.

SHIM, D. (2006) Hybridity and the rise of Korean popular culture in Asia. *Media, Culture & Society*, **28**, 1: 25–44.

SHOHAT, E. and STAM, R. (1994) *Unthinking Eurocentrism: multiculturalism and the media*. New York: Routledge.

SINCLAIR, J. (1996) Mexico, Brazil, and the Latin world. In E. Jacka *et al.* (eds), *New patterns in global television*. Oxford: Oxford University Press.

SINCLAIR, J. (1999) *Latin American television: A global view*. Oxford: Oxford University Press.

SINCLAIR, J., JACKA, E. and CUNNINGHAM, S. (eds) (1996) *New patterns in global television: peripheral vision*. Oxford: Oxford University Press.

SINGH, K. and GROSS, B. (1981) 'MacBride': The report and the response. *Journal of Communication*, **31**, 4: 104–17.

SINGHAL, A. and ROGERS, E. (2004) The status of Entertainment-Education worldwide. In A. Singhal, M. Cody, E. Rogers and M. Sabido (eds), *Entertainment-education and social change*. Mahwah, NJ: Lawrence Erlbaum.

SIWEK, S. (2005) *Engines of growth: Economic contributions of the US intellectual property industries*, produced by Economists Incorporated and Commissioned by NBC Universal (http://www.nbcumv.com/corporate/Engines_of_Growth.pdf).

SLACK, T. (ed.) (2004) *The commercialisation of sport*. London: Routledge.

SMITH, A. (1979) *The newspaper: an international history*. London: Thames and Hudson.

SMITH, A. (1980) *The geopolitics of information: how Western culture dominates the world*. London: Faber and Faber.

SMITH, A. (ed.) (1998) *Television: an international history*. Second edition, Oxford: Oxford University Press.

SOMAVIA, J. (1976) The transnational power structure and international information. *Development Dialogue*, 2: 15–28.

Sony (2005) *Annual report, 2004*. Tokyo: Sony Corporation.

SORENSEN, T. (1968) *The word war – the story of American propaganda*. New York: Harper and Row.

SOSIN, G. (1999) *Sparks of liberty – an insider's memoir of Radio Liberty*. University Park, PA: Penn State University Press.

South Commission (1990) *The challenge to South: the report of the South Commission*. Geneva: The South Centre.

SPARKS, C. (1998) Is there a global public sphere? In D. Thussu (ed.), *Electronic empires*. London: Arnold.

SPARKS, C. and TULLOCH, J. (eds) (2000) *Tabloid tales – global debates over media standards*. Lanham, MD: Rowman & Littlefield.

SPIGEL, L. and OLSSON, J. (eds) (2004) *Television after TV: essays on a medium in transition*. Durham, NC: Duke University Press.

SPLICHAL, S. (1994) *Media beyond socialism: theory and practice of East-Central Europe*. Boulder, CO: Westview Press.

SREBERNY-MOHAMMADI, A. (1991) The global and the local in international communication. In J. Curran and M. Gurevitch (eds), *Mass media and society*. London: Edward Arnold.

SREBERNY-MOHAMMADI, A. (1994) *Women, media and development in a global context*. Paris: UNESCO.

SREBERNY-MOHAMMADI, A. (1997) The many cultural faces of imperialism. In P. Golding and P. Harris (eds), *Beyond cultural imperialism*. London: Sage.

STEEMERS, J. (2004) *Selling television: British television in the global marketplace*. London: BFI.

STEVENSON, R. (1988) *Communication, development and the Third World: the global politics of information*. London: Longman. Reprinted by the University Press of America in 1993.

STEVENSON, R. (1992) Defining international communication as a field. *Journalism Quarterly*, **69**: 543–53.

STIGLITZ, J. (2002) *Globalization and its discontents*. New York: W. W. Norton.

STROBEL, W. (1997) *Late-breaking foreign policy: the news media's influence on peace operations*. Washington, DC: United States Institute of Peace Press.

SUNG, L. (1992) WARC-92: Setting the agenda for the future. *Telecommunications Policy*, **16**, 8: 624–34.

SUSSMAN, G. and GALIZIO, L. (2003) The global reproduction of American politics. *Political Communication*, **20**: 309–28.

TARJANNE, P. (1999) Preparing for the next revolution in telecommunications: implementing the WTO Agreement. *Telecommunication Policy*, **23**: 51–63.

TARROW, S. (2005) *The new transnational activism*. Cambridge: Cambridge University Press.

TAWNEY, R. (1937) *Religion and the rise of capitalism*. London: Penguin Books. First edition published in 1926.

TAYLOR, P. (1997) *Global communications, international affairs and the media since 1945.* London: Routledge.

TAYLOR, P. (2003) *Munitions of the mind: a history of propaganda from the ancient world to the present era.* Third edition, Manchester: Manchester University Press.

TAYLOR, P. A. (2005) From hackers to hacktivists: speed bumps on the global superhighway? *New Media & Society,* **7,** 5: 625–46.

TEHRANIAN, M. (1999) *Global communication and world politics: domination, development and discourse.* London: Lynne Reiner.

The Economist (1998) Wheel of fortune: a survey of technology and entertainment. 21 November, 22 pages.

The Economist (2005) Arab satellite television: the world through their eyes. Special Report, February 24.

THOMAS, A. W. (2005) *Imagi-nations and borderless television: media, culture and politics across Asia.* New Delhi: Sage.

THOMPSON, J. (1995) *The media and modernity: a social theory of the media.* Cambridge: Polity.

THUSSU, D. K. (ed.) (1998a) *Electronic empires: global media and local resistance.* London: Arnold.

THUSSU, D. K. (1998b) Localising the global – Zee TV in India. In D. Thussu (ed.), *Electronic empires.* London: Arnold.

THUSSU, D. K. (2000a) Legitimizing 'humanitarian intervention'? CNN, NATO and the Kosovo crisis. *European Journal of Communication,* **15,** 3: 345–61.

THUSSU, D. K. (2000b) Development news versus globalised infotainment. In A. Kavoori and A. Malek (eds), *The global dynamics of news: studies in international news coverage and news agenda.* Stamford, CT: Ablex Publishing.

THUSSU, D. K. (2002a) Privatizing Intelsat: implications for the global South. In M. Raboy (ed.), *Global media policy in the new millennium.* Luton: University of Luton Press.

THUSSU, D. K. (2002b) Managing the Media in an era of round-the-clock news: notes from India's first tele-war. *Journalism Studies,* **3,** 2: 203–12.

THUSSU, D. K. (2004) Media plenty and the poverty of news. In A. Sreberny *et al.* (eds), *International news in the twenty-first century.* Luton: University of Luton Press.

THUSSU, D. K. (2005) Selling neo-imperialism, television and US public diplomacy. In J. Curran and M. Gurevitch (eds), *Mass Media and Society.* Fourth edition, London: Arnold.

THUSSU, D. K. (2006) Mapping global media flow and contra-flow. In D. K. Thussu (ed.), *Media on the move – global flow and contra-flow.* London: Routledge.

THUSSU, D. K. and FREEDMAN, D. (eds) (2003) *War and the media: reporting conflict 24/7*. London: Sage.

Time (1988) New silence, new disquiet with glasnost and no jamming, what about those radios? 19 December, 19.

TOBIN, J. (ed.) (2004) *Pikachu's global adventure: The rise and fall of Pokemon*. Durham, NC: Duke University Press.

TOFFLER, A. (1980) *The third wave*. London: Collins.

TOMLINSON, J. (1991) *Cultural imperialism: a critical introduction*. London: Pinter.

TOMLINSON, J. (1999) *Globalization and culture*. Cambridge: Polity.

TRACEY, M. (1998) *The decline and fall of public service broadcasting*. Oxford: Oxford University Press.

TUCH, H. (1990) *Communicating with the world: US public diplomacy overseas*. New York: St Martin's Press.

TUFTE, T. (2000) *Living with the rubbish queen:* telenovelas, *culture and modernity in Brazil*. Luton: University of Luton Press.

TUNGATE, M. (2004) *Media monoliths: how great media brands thrive and survive*. London: Kogan Page.

TUNSTALL, J. (1977) *The media are American: Anglo-American media in the world*. London: Constable.

TUNSTALL, J. (1992) Europe as world news leader. *Journal of Communication*, **42**: 84–99.

TUNSTALL, J. and PALMER, M. (1991) *Media moguls*. London: Routledge.

TUNSTALL, J. and MACHIN, D. (1999) *The Anglo-American media connection*. Oxford: Oxford University Press.

UN (1995) *Our global neighbourhood: the report of the commission on global governance*. Oxford: Oxford University Press.

UN (2005) *Migration in an interconnected world: New directions for action*. Report of the Global Commission on International Migration. Geneva: United Nations Publications.

UNCTAD (2005a) *Information economy report 2005: E-commerce and development*. Geneva: United Nations Conference on Trade and Development.

UNCTAD (2005b) *Trade and Development Report 2005*. Geneva: United Nations Conference on Trade and Development.

UNCTAD (2005c) *World investment report 2005: transnational corporations and the internationalization of R & D*. Geneva: United Nations Conference on Trade and Development.

UNDP (1999) *Globalization with a human face. The 1999 Human development report.* United Nations Development Programme. Oxford: Oxford University Press.

UNDP (2001) *Making new technologies work for human development. The 2001 Human Development Report.* United Nations Development Programme. Oxford: Oxford University Press.

UNDP (2003) *Human Development Report 2003: Millennium Development Goals: A compact among nations to end human poverty.* United Nations Development Programme. Oxford: Oxford University Press.

UNDP (2004) *Cultural liberty in today's diverse world: Human Development Report 2004.* United Nations Development Programme. Oxford: Oxford University Press.

UNDP (2005a) *The world at a crossroads, Human Development Report 2005.* United Nations Development Programme. Oxford: Oxford University Press.

UNDP (2005b) *Promoting ICT for human development in Asia.* Regional Human Development Report: New York: United Nations Development Programme.

UNESCO (1980) The new world information and communication order. Resolutions 4/19 in Records of the General Conference Twenty-First Session, Belgrade, 23 September to 28 October. Paris: United Nations Educational, Scientific and Cultural Organization.

UNESCO (1982) *Culture industries: a challenge for the future of culture.* Paris: United Nations Educational, Scientific and Cultural Organization.

UNESCO (1995) *Our creative diversity: report of the World Commission on Culture and Development.* Paris: United Nations Educational, Scientific and Cultural Organization.

UNESCO (1997) *World communication report: the media and the challenge of the new technologies.* Paris: United Nations Educational, Scientific and Cultural Organization.

UNESCO (1998) *World culture report 1998: culture, creativity and markets.* Paris: United Nations Educational, Scientific and Cultural Organization.

UNESCO (2000) *International Flows of Selected Cultural Goods 1980–1998.* UNESCO Institute for Statistics. Paris: United Nations Educational, Scientific and Cultural Organization.

UNESCO (2005a) *International Flows of Selected Cultural Goods and Services 1994–2003.* UNESCO Institute for Statistics. Paris: United Nations Educational, Scientific and Cultural Organization.

UNESCO (2005b) *Towards knowledge societies: UNESCO world report.* Paris: United Nations Educational, Scientific and Cultural Organization.

UNESCO (2005c) *Measuring linguistic diversity on the Internet.* Paris: United Nations Educational, Scientific and Cultural Organization.

UNESCO (2006a) *What is public service broadcasting?* Paris: United Nations Educational, Scientific and Cultural Organization (http://portal.unesco.org/ci/en/ev.php).

UNESCO (2006b) *Education for all – global monitoring report 2006.* Paris: United Nations Educational, Scientific and Cultural Organization.

URBAN, G. (1997) *My war within the Cold War.* New Haven, CT: Yale University Press.

US Government (1993) *Globalization of the mass media.* Washington, DC: US Department of Commerce.

US Government (1995) *Global information infrastructure: agenda for cooperation.* Information Task Force, February. Washington, DC: US Government Printing Office.

US Government (1997) *A framework for global electronic commerce.* Washington, DC: The White House, 1 July.

US Government (1999) *Towards digital equality, U.S. Government Working Group on electronic commerce.* 2nd Annual Report. Washington, DC (www.ecommerce.gov).

US Government (2003) *United States delegation report World Radiocommunication Conference 2003 Geneva, Switzerland June 9–July 4, 2003.* Submitted to the Secretary of State by Ambassador Janice Obuchowski, United States Head of Delegation, United States Department of State, 8 December 2003. Washington, DC (http://www.fcc.gov/wrc-07/docs/WRC03DelReport_final.doc).

US Government (2005) *US international services: cross-border trade in 2004.* Washington, DC: US Bureau of Economic Analysis, October.

US Government (2006) *Quadrennial Defense Review Report.* Washington, DC: Department of Defense (www.defenselink.mil/qdr/report/Report20060203.pdf).

UTLEY, G. (1997) The shrinking of foreign news: from broadcast to narrowcast. *Foreign Affairs*, **76**, 2: 2–10.

VARIS, T. (1985) *International flow of television programmes.* Reports and Papers on Mass Communication, no. 100. Paris: UNESCO.

VASEY, R. (1997) *The world according to Hollywood.* Madison, WI: University of Wisconsin Press.

VENTURELLI, S. (1998) *Liberalizing the European media: politics, regulation and the public sphere.* Oxford: Oxford University Press.

VINCENT, R., NORDENSTRENG, K. and TRABER, M. (eds) (1999) *Towards equity in global communication: MacBride Update.* Cresskill, NJ: Hampton Press.

VISE, D. and MALSEED, M. (2005) *The Google story.* London: Macmillan.

VOGEL, H. (2004) *Entertainment industry economics: a guide for financial analysis.* Sixth edition, Cambridge: Cambridge University Press.

VOLKMER, I. (1999) *News in the global sphere: a study of CNN and its impact on global communications.* Luton: University of Luton Press.

WAISBORD, S. (2004) McTV: undertanding the global popularity of television formats. *Television & New Media*, **5**, 4: 359–83.

WALKER, A. (1992) *A skyful of freedom: 60 years of the BBC World Service.* London: Broadside Books.

WALLERSTEIN, I. (1974, 1980) *The modern world-system.* 2 vols, New York: Academic Press.

WALLERSTEIN, I. (2004) *World-Systems analysis: an introduction.* Durham, NC: Duke University Press.

WANG, J. (2005) Youth culture, music, and cell phone branding in China, *Global Media and Communication*, **1**, 2: 185–201.

WASKO, J. (2003) *How Hollywood works.* London: Sage.

WATERMAN, D. (2005) *Hollywood's road to riches.* Cambridge, MA: Harvard University Press.

WATERS, M. (1995) *Globalization.* London: Routledge.

WEBER, C. (2005) Imagining America at war: morality, politics and film. London: Routledge.

WEBBER, I. (2003) *Localising the global: successful strategies for selling programmes to China.* London: Sage.

WEBSTER, F. (1995) *Theories of the information society.* London: Routledge.

WEBSTER, F. (ed.) (2004) *The information society reader.* London: Routledge.

WELLS, A. (1972) *Picture tube imperialism? The impact of US television on Latin America.* New York: Orbis.

WELLS, A. (ed.) (1996) *World broadcasting: a comparative view.* Norwood, NJ: Ablex Publishing.

WELLS, C. (1987) *The UN, UNESCO and the politics of knowledge.* London: Macmillan.

WESTAD, O. A. (2005) *The global cold war: Third World interventions and the making of our times.* Cambridge: Cambridge University Press.

WESTERN, J. (2005) *Selling intervention and war: The presidency, the media, and the American public.* Maryland: Johns Hopkins University Press.

WHITTELL, G. (2000) Hollywood targets Russia's Mir. *The Times*, 18 February, 19.

WINDRICH, E. (1992) *The Cold War guerrilla: Jonas Savimbi, the US media and the Angolan war.* New York: Greenwood Press.

WINSECK, D. (1997) The shifting contexts of international communication: possibilities for a New World Information and Communication Order. In M. Bailie and D. Winseck (eds), *Democratizing communication?* Cresskill, NJ: Hampton Press.

WOLL, J. (1989) Fruits of glasnost: a sampling from the Soviet press. *Dissent*, Winter, 25–38.

WOOD, J. (1992) *History of international broadcasting*. London: Peter Peregrinus.

World Bank (1998) *Knowledge for development, world development report 1998–1999*. Washington, DC: World Bank Publications.

World Bank (2006a) *Equity and development: 2006 World Development Report*. Washington, DC: World Bank Publication.

World Bank (2006b) *Global Economic Prospects 2006: Economic Implications of Remittances and Migration*. Washington, DC: World Bank Publication.

WSIS (2005) *Tunis agenda for the information society* WSIS-05/TUNIS/DOC/7-E, 18 November. Geneva: World Summit on the Information Society.

WTO (1997) *Fourth Protocol to the General Agreement on Trade in services* (Global Telecoms Agreement) S/L/20. Geneva: World Trade Organization.

WTO (1998) *Annual report 1998*. Geneva: World Trade Organization.

WTO (2005a) *Annual report 2005*. Geneva: World Trade Organization.

WTO (2005b) *International trade statistics 2005*. Geneva: World Trade Organization.

YUDICE, G. (2004) *The expediency of culture: uses of culture in the global era*. Durham, NC: Duke University Press.

ZAYANI, M. (ed.) (2005) *The al-Jazeera phenomenon: critical perspectives on new Arab media*. London: Pluto.

Zee TV (2005) Zee Annual Report 2005 (www.zeetelevision.com).

ZHAO, B. (1999) Mouthpiece or money-spinner? The double life of Chinese television in the late 1990s. *International Journal of Cultural Studies*, **2**, 3: 291–305.

ZHAO, Y. (1998) *Media, market and democracy in China: between the party line and the bottom line*. Urbana: University of Illinois Press.

Author Index

Subject Index